Martin Weitz is an investigative journalist specialising in health and the environment. He has worked for foreign and British television and radio as well as writing for numerous newspapers and magazines. He is now Features Editor of *The Times Health Supplement*.

'Startling information . . . vital reading'
Liverpool Daily Post

'What a shocker!'
Manchester Evening News

'Should be read by everyone in the country'
Simon Martin, Editor of *Here's Health*

'Very competent inquiry . . . deserves wide distribution'
Journal of the Institute of Health Education

'I can only welcome the publication of this book'
Dr Vernon Coleman, syndicated medical columnist

'Easy to read . . . backed up with extensive evidence'
Dr David Ryde, Thames TV's *Afternoon Plus*

'A brave book . . . factually accurate . . . all doctors should read it'
Professor Gordon Stewart, Border Television

'Explodes many popular ideas about the efficacy of modern medicine'
Sun Herald (Australia)

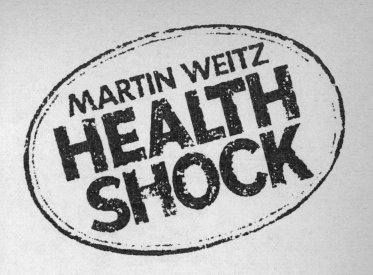

MARTIN WEITZ
HEALTH SHOCK

Hamlyn Paperbacks

HEALTH SHOCK
ISBN 0 600 20441 3
First published in Great Britain 1980
by David and Charles (Publishers) Ltd
Hamlyn Paperbacks revised edition 1982

Copyright © 1980, 1982 by Martin Weitz

Cartoons by ffolkes

Hamlyn Paperbacks are published by
The Hamlyn Publishing Group Ltd,
Astronaut House,
Feltham, Middlesex, England

For Lynnie

This book is dedicated to all the members of the medical
profession who have carried out research into the effectiveness and safety
of medical treatment.

Printed and bound in Great Britain by
Cox & Wyman Ltd, Reading

Contents

I would like to dedicate Part Four (Birth) of this book to the midwives and doctor who safely delivered Sam Weitz at home on October 5, 1981.

Introduction to Revised Edition

There are two sides to every story, and this is the side of the medical story you probably haven't heard before. *Health Shock*, 'an unashamedly one-sided book', concentrates on reasons *not* to have medical treatment because of its ineffectiveness, because it is unnecessary or because of its risks.

OK. Valium *may* reduce anxiety; Distalgesic *may* kill pain; X-rays *may* help doctors see inside your body and glasses *may* help you see outside it. But in the words of the great song: 'It ain't necessarily so'.

Your doctor, dentist and optician will be the first to tell you about the benefits of what they are doing, but probably the last to tell you about the lack of need for and possible harm of their treatment. We can always rely on the drug firms to keep everyone well informed of the 'benefits' of their products, but unfortunately their opinions and advertising messages do not always coincide with the views of independent medical experts.

The aim of *Health Shock* is to restore the balance of medical information in favour of people. The evidence gathered in this volume dramatically shows that we cannot rely on doctors and professionals to always act in *our* best interests. *Health Shock* is designed to be a counter-balance to the one-sided information provided by many doctors and an antidote to the promotional half-truths provided by many drug companies.

The most surprising discovery I made whilst writing and assembling the information in this book is that the most devastating critics of modern Western medicine are doctors themselves. All the information collected here is derived from the medical profession itself—and you have the right to know about it.

What's Your Personal Risk?

Living is risky. Crossing the road, driving a car, flying, swallowing an aspirin tablet or eating a chicken sandwich – they can all be fatal! Clearly some risks are worth taking, especially when the stakes are high: a man engulfed in flames and smoke generally considers that jumping out of a second-floor window is a risk worth taking to save his life. But in medicine few procedures, drugs, operations or tests are really a matter of life and death. There may be sound medical reasons for taking every item of treatment investigated in *Health Shock,* but such reasons are totally dependent on the balance of risks and benefits to the patient.

Surgery for cancer may save or prolong a life, but the removal of tonsils and adenoids cannot (in anything but extremely rare circumstances) save anything other than a sore throat. Blood pressure drugs definitely help some people live after a heart attack, but these same drugs may be both unnecessary and harmful for those with only mild blood pressure problems (see page 212 onwards). Unless we know about the effectiveness, risks and hazards of treatment, we are unable to make the vital risk-benefit decisions affecting our health.

Deciding how much discomfort and risk we are prepared to put up with in the name of better health is a highly personal matter, not a decision we should leave to doctors alone. I hope the information gathered here enables more people to make better informed decisions about their health treatment. Knowledge is health.

Introduction to First Edition

Every day thousands of people suffer from the effects of unnecessary, ineffective and hazardous medical treatment. Here are just a few of the facts and figures demonstrating the epidemic of doctor-induced disease.

* At least 2 out of every 5 patients receiving drugs from their doctors suffer from side effects.[1]

* Identical drugs sold in Britain and the USA contain totally contradictory information on side effects. Many over-the-counter medicines on sale today cannot pass current safety regulations[2] yet they remain on sale outside the arm of the law. Thousands of prescription-only drugs have never been shown to be effective.

* In 1981 the British Medical Association and the Pharmaceutical Society jointly produced a drug guide for doctors advising them NOT to prescribe over 600 drugs, many of them top-selling brands such as Distalgesic, Benylin, Veganin, Codis, Strepsils and others.[3]

* X-rays given to pregnant mothers during the 1950s and 1960s caused between 5 and 10 per cent of all childhood cancers in Western Europe and North America.[4]

* 12,000 people are killed each year from unnecessary surgery in the USA, more than the total number of Americans who died in the Korean and Vietnamese wars.[5]

* One in every twelve admissions to hospital is caused by the side effects of treatment,[6] life expectancy has not improved since 1950 for men aged over 45 and there are 10 per cent more admissions to psychiatric hospitals.[7]

* 5 per cent of people consider that going to their doctor makes them feel worse.[8]

* One out of every six visits to the doctor is made by people with illnesses that the doctor can do nothing about (colds, coughs, 'flu). Yet the great majority of these patients receive drug treatment.[8]

* Sir Ronald Bodley Scott, Chairman of the British Medicines Commissions, has said: 'Doctors of my generation, particularly in general practice, have no idea how to use 90

per cent of modern drugs.'
* At least 1 in every 10 patients admitted to hospital suffers from the side effects of the treatment received there. [9]
* No amount of animal experimentation can ensure the safety of drugs for human beings. The only way to establish drug safety is to get doctors to prescribe a new drug to many thousands of patients; only then do side effects surface. [10]

What is *Health Shock*?

Health Shock is a guide to useless, unnecessary and hazardous treatment. It tells the reader of medical reasons not to take drugs, not to have surgery, X-rays, dental or other kinds of treatment. But *Health Shock* is *not* a guide to medical treatment per se. Nor is it a guide to drugs used for different illnesses, or a dictionary of symptoms. There are plenty of books already available on these subjects.

All the information contained in *Health Shock* is derived from respected medical and scientific journals or books and a complete list of references is provided. Fortunately, the medical profession is slowly becoming open and diverse enough to have within it a growing number of critics, a few of whom are concerned that their treatment may be doing patients more harm than good. *Health Shock* has pooled together the latest views and findings of these members of the medical profession: *they* constitute the critics of wasteful, useless, unnecessary and harmful medical treatment. It is to these people that *Health Shock* is dedicated.

This book started its life six years ago as a series of newspaper articles entitled 'Health versus Medicine' which I wrote for the popular but none-the-less distinguished Scottish campaigning newspaper, the *Sunday Mail.*

In the course of researching these articles and this book, I made what was for me at least an alarming discovery: I found that little of accepted medical practice has been shown to be effective. Health care is the only business which spends billions on treatments and methods which have never actually been tested to make sure they work. [11]
'Most industrial organisations the size of the National Health Services would have had a large research section checking on the effectiveness of the service it was provid-

ing. There was none for 15 years'—reveals Professor Archie Cochrane in his classic work on useless medical treatment, *Effectiveness and Efficiency*. For example there is no requirement for the drug companies to prove the effectiveness of 18,000 drugs now on the market but introduced before 1971 – prior to the Medicines Act. Although the British Committee for the Review of Medicines has recently started to plough through all these dubious products, they remain on sale and are paid for out of public funds. A surgeon can introduce a new operation which will be copied all over the country by other surgeons without any requirement that the new operation be shown to prolong life or reduce suffering. New medical tests and expensive equipment can be used without first producing any proof they are of any benefit to patients.

The popular media are justifiably obsessed with the question of drug dangers and damage, which is important but surely not as important as the fundamental question of effectiveness. If a drug does not work in the first place it does not matter if it has harmful side effects because no one needs to take ineffective drugs in the first place. Unfortunately the present British law does not stop unscrupulous drug firms from continuing to sell many useless products.

Health Shock frequently refers to American action taken by the US Food and Drug Administration (FDA) against ineffective and hazardous drugs and other medical treatments. Whilst the FDA's record is by no means perfect they have spared the American public the horrors of Thalidomide babies and Eraldin deaths plus many other smaller drug disasters suffered in Britain. FDA policy is to *openly confront* the drug industry in public, whereas in Britain the Department of Health's policy is to *negotiate in secret,* out of the public eye. The Department of Health refuses to release information about drugs which its own expert panels consider to be ineffective and hazardous, on the dubious grounds that it is protecting commercial secrets. By contrast the FDA regularly publishes its drug evaluations for all to see. Much of the information contained in *Health Shock* is not easily available in Britain and had to be obtained from sources in the United States. Many American drugs which are identical to products

5

available in Britain have completely different lists of warnings and side effects to those accompanying their British counterparts.

It is customary in Britain to express shock and horror at the inequalities of the American health care system and at the same time to congratulate ourselves on the equalities afforded by the National Health Service. Whilst the NHS is certainly a great advance over private medical treatment it has done little to promote equality in health. A bricklayer from Glasgow or Newcastle still has a much shorter life expectancy than a civil servant from Surrey or Oxford. If all men were as healthy as those professionally qualified men in Social Class I there would be 22,000 fewer deaths each year! If every part of Britain had as few stillbirths and infant deaths as North-east Scotland there would be 5,000 fewer baby deaths each year.[7] Every year health expenditure rises without any increase in the benefits to the population. In the last thirty years life expectancy has not risen for anybody over the age of 45 at all. A person aged 65 today can expect to live only two years longer than a person aged 65 in 1870![7]

In any book of this kind there are bound to be omissions and some errors, for which I apologise. I hope that readers will write to me c/o Hamlyn Paperbacks to suggest any alterations, corrections and additions for possible future editions of *Health Shock*.

How to approach your doctor after reading *Health Shock*
It is the author's sincere hope that the information contained in this book will not drive a wedge in the doctor-patient relationship. However it cannot be denied that some doctors are very sensitive to criticism or to any questioning of their treatment. The reader is, therefore, advised to be diplomatic when raising any doubts about treatments.

Dr Andrew Herxheimer writes in *The Lancet,* 'Some doctors easily take offence when the patient appears to "question" his treatment, so it is important for the patient not to seem to cast doubt on the treatment, but to make it clear that he would merely like to understand certain aspects of it.'[12] If patients make efforts to take some responsibility for their illness, then recovery or successful adjustment is hastened, according to Dr Herxheimer. He has devised a valuable set of patient-doctor questions which are reproduced at the beginning of Part 8 on page 158.

Above all, it should be remembered that everyone has the right to a second opinion or ultimately to change their GP.

1

Doctors — General

The secret of useless doctors

One of the great mysteries in medicine is why so few people take notice of anything doctors say. It has been shown, for example, that many patients are unable to remember most of what their doctor tells them within minutes of seeing him. Not only do many people instantly forget their doctor's advice but around half of all patients ignore it. Nearly every survey that has been performed on patients who have been given drugs by their doctor shows that as many as 50 per cent do not actually swallow the pills prescribed.

Why is there this epidemic of disobedience amongst patients? Why do patients put so little value on the advice given to them by their doctor? A fascinating experiment conducted in Los Angeles has shed some light on these questions. The Los Angeles researchers studied a group of mothers who had brought their children for emergency treatment at a local children's hospital. By measuring the amount of time that the doctor spent talking about social and other non-medical matters it was discovered that there was a definite relationship between the amount of social chitchat and the patient's satisfaction with the meeting. Generally speaking the mothers would carry out the doctor's instructions when they felt the doctor had been friendly. Any lack of understanding and interest shown by the doctors was particularly annoying to mothers who felt that concern for them as human beings was far more important than the actual amount of time the doctor spent with them.

The most disturbing result of all, perhaps, to emerge

from the Los Angeles experiment was that the majority of doctors *thought* they had acted in a friendly manner, whilst fewer than half of the mothers went away with this impression.[1]

Does it matter if patients ignore the advice of their doctors by not taking the drugs which they are prescribed? Probably not, according to an editorial in the *British Medical Journal*. Over 90 per cent of patients fail to complete a ten-day course of penicillin, states the editorial, adding that 'we have no evidence that this matters, it probably does not'. Another example given is that half the people taking the powerful heart drug digitalis (or Digoxin, as it is called) do not take it properly. 'But if the drug can be withdrawn from them without difficulty what is the real problem: compliance or unnecessary prescribing?' asks the editorial.[2]

A startling confession then follows in this editorial article, for it states quite clearly that the medical profession has no idea what it is doing when it prescribes many popular drugs: 'In the case of much treatment with antibiotics and psychotropic drugs (tranquillisers such as Valium and other drugs that affect the mind) *we know virtually nothing* (my italics) . . . not the optimum dose, nor the frequency, nor the duration of treatment.' The editorial ends by advising doctors to consider the following question before doling out drugs: Is it established that treatment would do more good than harm to those who do not comply?

Why we use useless medicines: the mystery of placebo power

'Doctors who show little personal interest in their patients are seldom liked by them and their placebo power is diminished'—so says S. Rachman, Professor of Psychiatry in *Psychology and Medicine*.[3]

Much of *Health Shock* identifies medical treatments which do not work or are unnecessary in the first place. The reader may be puzzled as to why so many ineffective 'useless' treatments still remain in use.

Until about fifty years ago virtually all medicines used by doctors were ineffective placebos, yet they *did* work in the hands of a good doctor. Crocodile dung, teeth of swine, asses' hooves, frog sperm, eunuch fat, fly specks, lozenges of dried vipers, human sweat, oil of ants, earthworms, spiders, animal and human excrement, all these wonderful substances and more have been successfully used by doctors through the ages.[4] Patients have been purged, puked, poisoned, punctured, bled, blistered, leached, heated, frozen, sweated and shocked! Despite this horrific list of now mainly abandoned treatments doctors have always managed to maintain their powerful position in society because they have often achieved successful cures with useless treatments.[4] But why?

'The history of medicine is the history of the placebo effect.'[4] The placebo is the magical pill or potion that only works because the doctor *says* it will work and because the patient believes the doctor. The psychological or placebo effect of medical treatment was recognised by Hippocrates and it is considered that between 50 and 80 per cent of all symptoms are of emotional rather than physical origin, say Drs Arthur Shapiro and Louis Morro in their discussion of the placebo effect in the *Handbook of Psychotherapy and Behaviour Change.*[4] They quote the famous advice until recently given to pupil doctors: 'Treat as many patients as possible with the new remedies – whilst they still have the power to heal'!

'Treatments recommended by medical authorities in a confident way that is designed to arouse hope and expectations will frequently have a beneficial outcome,' writes Professor S. Rachman.[3] He also says that a doctor's expectations or belief in a treatment can be crucial in determining effects. One researcher has shown that drugs tested by doctors themselves are found to be effective five times more frequently than independently assessed investigations. Many drugs still on the market today have *at first* been shown to be effective in uncontrolled case studies where the same doctor has *both* given the treatment *and* evaluated its success. But when 'double-blind' controlled investigations have been conducted it has often been discovered that the drug itself was really useless and that the cure relied on the personality and enthusiasm of that one particular doctor. 'Medical history is full of prestigious doctors attached to their own therapies. They were often dangerous, elaborate and expensive and the majority of these treatments disappeared when they later were judged to be useless' (for example, see Useless Surgery, page 20).[4]

Professor Rachman also describes how our reaction to intense pain is modified by our expectations of the pain we 'should' feel. For example, wounded soldiers require far fewer painkilling drugs than voluntary patients in hospital, because of their different expectations. A soldier is so glad to be alive away from the battle he feels no pain. A remarkable demonstration of how people obtain the results they want or expect was made by Dr R. Rosenthal:[5] 'A group of animal experimenters were told that their rats had been specially bred for brightness or dullness' – although in reality they were all from the *same* pure strain! Amazingly the experimenters found that the 'bright' rats obtained significantly better scores on learning than the 'dull' rats. This is *not* an isolated finding and Dr Rosenthal believes it happens because 'humans engage in highly effective and influential, unintended communication with one another – so subtle that casual observation does not reveal it'. But how can Dr Rosenthal be certain he himself did not affect the outcome of this piece of research in some unintended way?

Consultants or witchdoctors?

'The effect of placebos has been shown by controlled trials to be very large,' says Professor Archibald Cochrane.[6] He adds: 'Their use in the correct place is to be encouraged. What is inefficient is the use of relatively expensive drugs as placebos. It is a pity some enterprising drug company does not produce a wide range of cheap, brightly coloured non-toxic placebos.'

But it has been shown that placebo drugs can produce side effects and that they are more likely to work in outgoing sociable and anxious patients. The colour of a medicine or a pill can also affect the outcome of treatment. If the patient and the doctor like each other too there is more likely to be a successful outcome. The prestige of the doctor is important, hence the awe with which the witch-doctor has been traditionally viewed in primitive societies. A 'consultant' should obtain greater success than an equally qualified GP, merely because of his greater status in society.

Clearly there is nothing wrong with using placebos, although they can produce side effects. Many of the treatments described in this book have been shown to be no better than a placebo, and also to produce side effects. Unfortunately few doctors are blessed with sufficient personality and enthusiasm not only to make all these ineffective drugs work, but also to make them work without producing side effects.

Who has the power over illness – patients or doctors?

Not only does the personality and attitude of the doctor affect the success of a treatment, so also does the attitude and personality of the patient alter the course of disease. A positive mental attitude has been shown to improve the chances of survival for women with breast cancer. Research completed at the Cold Research Laboratory in 1979 shows that colds are most likely to strike individuals who are introverted and who have allowed the stresses of life to interfere with their social life and their work.[7]

People decide when to be ill; it has found that 90 per cent of the population experience some symptoms of illness in any two-week period – an average of four symptoms each.[8] 'Further studies have shown that the decision on whether or not to seek medical advice for these symptoms is strongly influenced by social and psychological factors.'[9]

Ulcers, asthma, high blood pressure, backache, angina are all nowadays acknowledged to have a strong psychological component and there is increasing evidence of a mental factor in the development of some cancers as the breast cancer results (see page 39) indicate.

It is not difficult to see how illness can be created by mood and feelings. The hormonal system controlled by the pituitary organ in the brain is very responsive to changes in mood. The adrenal–pituitary system is sensitive to any external stressful events. The mental control over involuntary organs and the control of the nervous system with the aid of biofeedback equipment also demonstrates the great abilities of the 'mind' to control disease in the body. Blood pressure can be lowered and a whole host of conditions from migraine to muscle paralysis and asthma can be improved by mental willpower and a biofeedback machine.

What is the meaning of your illness?

Doctors and patients ignore the meaning of their illnesses; illness serves a purpose, according to Dr Thomas Holmes, Professor of Psychiatry at Washington University, who has shown that a change of lifestyle can trigger off serious disease. Moving house, death of a spouse or close relative, divorce, loss of a job and other stressful events have been shown to be significantly related to the onset of TB, skin diseases, asthma, heart disease and even cancer. His investigations covered all social classes and professions in many countries including USA, Spain, France, Sweden and Denmark.[10]

For some people illness could be one way out of an emotional problem or a period of tension and anxiety. But doctors rarely ask *why* we feel unwell; instead we are asked to describe isolated symptoms. Most doctors are trained to work on people as if they were mechanics repairing parts of a motor car that has broken down, a method that is highly effective when treating accident victims but somewhat lacking when it comes to acute and chronic disease.

Lack of information in hospital

'For many people admission to hospital is an event of considerable emotional significance . . . fear, increased irritability, loss of interest in the outside world, unhappiness, preoccupation with one's bodily processes are commonly encountered.'[11]

Professor Rachman makes this disturbing observation on the plight of the patient, and points out that hospital staff are only concerned with the physical state of patients admitted to their care. Yet there is evidence from a number of experiments which all show that fear can only be reduced by telling patients what is happening to them in hospital, and that this reduction in their stress or fear improves their recovery significantly.

Two investigations carried out by an American, Dr I. Janis,[12] found that when patients were told about the possible nasty effects of the operation they were going to have, they suffered far less emotional distress than patients who were not told about their operation. It seems that if you are moderately frightened *before* you have an operation it inoculates you against emotional disturbances afterwards. But if you show no fear beforehand, you are more likely to feel severe pain, and complain a lot because you had no realistic impression of the effects of the operation. Too much fear before the operation however is also associated with bad experiences post-operatively.

Professor Rachman describes further research carried out by Dr R. Lazarus[13] at the University of California which shows that stress can be reduced by mentally rehearsing what is about to take place. 'It seems that rehearsals achieve their effects by reducing at least two of the major determinants of fear and anxiety – novelty and suddenness.'

How your recovery in hospital is delayed by doctors and nurses

Patients who are informed by doctors about their treatment/operation require less sedation and painkillers and recover more quickly from their illness than patients who are kept in the dark. This dramatic and important discovery was made over sixteen years ago, in 1964, yet little notice seems to have been taken of its great significance. I am indebted to Professor S. J. Rachman of the Institute of Psychiatry in London and Clare Philips for bringing it to my attention in their important book *Psychology and Medicine.*[14]

The original experiment was carried out in the United States by Dr L. Egbert in a hospital where 94 patients were undergoing abdominal surgery. They were split into two groups, equal in all respects. But the first group were paid a visit by a member of the surgical team who gave them detailed information about the operation they were about to undergo: they were told its length, when and where they would regain consciousness, the location and intensity of post-operative pain and they were given assurances about drugs. The other group were treated as most people are today: they were given none of this preparatory information. The experiment was rigorously controlled, neither the surgical nor the nursing staff knew which patients had received this pre-operation chat, in other words it was a 'double blind' experiment.[15]

The results of this clever experiment were quite startling. After their operations, the informed group of patients needed less painkilling morphine and fewer tranquillisers than the non-informed patients. They were also a lot less anxious and emotionally disturbed and, most important of all perhaps, they were discharged on average three days *earlier* than the patients who were kept in ignorance of what was going to happen to them.

Psychological damage to children from being in hospital

Hospitals are particularly upsetting places for young children, not only because of the lack of information they receive but also because of the separation from the mother and father.

'Children should not be admitted to hospital if there is a reasonable alternative,' the Platt Committee recommended in 1959 when they investigated the welfare of children in hospital. They made this conclusion on the basis of evidence that mother – child separation could lead to a damaged personality and even anti-social behaviour. Professor S. Rachman comments that these adverse effects were exaggerated in the 1950s by some psychologists such as Spitz and Bowlby; nevertheless he still accepts that admission to hospital can cause distress in the short term and enduring damage if the separation is for a long time.[16]

'It appears that the unfamiliarity of the hospital, the staff and the routine is a major cause of psychological upset,' says Rachman. Psychiatrist Michael Rutter found that the most hazardous age for a child to enter hospital was between 7 months and 4 years,[17] when children are most upset by the break from the parents. The general finding is that if the children have a good relationship with their parents then they are less likely to be psychologically damaged by going to hospital. In children, as in adults, the damage caused can be reduced and the speed of recovery enhanced by rehearsing beforehand.

By showing children a film which showed admission to the hospital, blood tests and meeting the surgeon and anaesthetist, Dr Barbara Melamed of Cape Western

Reserve University in Cleveland, found that anxiety was considerably reduced and cooperation was greatly increased in young children having their tonsils out.[18] As Professor Rachman says 'this is common sense', but unfortunately it is a rare commodity in many hospitals.

2

Hospital Hazards

Heart attack: intensive care: the fear creator

A heart attack victim lies pale and motionless in the intensive care ward as all around him electronic equipment monitors the smallest changes in his heart rhythm and blood pressure. At the speed of light cardiograms, oscilloscopes and miniature computers analyse his every breath whilst a team of specially trained nurses maintain a non-stop vigil at his bedside. Consultants are a radio bleep away, every known clinical measure has been taken to extend the patient's life. BUT does this orgy of medical razzmatazz actually prolong life?

When an experiment was conducted at a Bristol hospital in 1971 to test the effectiveness of such coronary care units. Dr H. Mather and his colleagues found that intensive care was no better than simply sending the patient home![1] It is believed that a heart patient recuperating at home can relax much more than in a tense hospital ward. Stress is a key factor in heart disease, so whilst doctors apply all the techniques of modern medicine they may frighten the poor patient to death.

Cardiologists (ie heart specialists) have been most unwilling to have their expensive procedures evaluated, according to arch-critic of medical inefficiency Professor Archibald Cochrane.[2] He says there is a great deal of bias within the speciality. In his classic book *Effectiveness and Efficiency* he writes: 'The bias is beautifully illustrated by a story of the early days of Mather's trial. The first report after a few months of the trial showed a slightly greater death rate in those treated in hospital than in those treated

17

at home. Someone reversed the figures and showed them to a Coronary Care Unit enthusiast who immediately declared that the trial was unethical and must be stopped at once. When however he was shown the table the correct way round he could not be persuaded to declare the coronary care units unethical!'[3]

Dr Mather's trial has been criticised by cardiologists but Professor Cochrane defends it. He writes: 'Mather's trial is not perfect. Very few are. But if the cardiologists were dissatisfied why didn't they do a better one? They had, and have a clearly defined duty to do so. The rest of the profession and the public still want to know who should with advantage be admitted to a coronary care unit.'

Private health care hazards

Unnecessary surgery is probably the greatest hazard arising out of private medical care. Britain's private health care industry is booming; there are over 2 million subscribers to BUPA alone (the largest private treatment organisation in Britain) and now that trade union organisations have somehow convinced themselves that it is not a contradiction to belong to private medical schemes the industry is set for even greater expansion.

Ignoring the political and moral arguments against private health care, the hazards of unnecessary surgery make a compelling argument for remaining in the NHS, where proportionately fewer surgeons operate than in the private sector.

Surgery increases with the availability of surgeons. In the United States where there are double the number of surgeons compared to Britain twice the number of operations are performed per capita of the population.[4]

When Dr Sidney Wolfe of the US Public Citizens' Health Research Group gave evidence before the US Senate investigation on unnecessary surgery, he quoted the 40-year-old words of Dr Richard Cabot, former Harvard Professor of Medicine who said: 'We would never put a judge on the bench under conditions such that he might be influenced by pecuniary considerations. Suppose that if the judge were to hand down one decision he got $5,000, and if he decided the other way he got nothing. But we allow the private practitioner to face this sort of temptation.

'The greatest single curse in medicine is the curse of unnecessary operations, and there would be fewer of them, if the doctor got the same salary whether he operated or not.'

'I am not accusing the medical profession of dishonesty, but I am saying that we should be defended from unfair temptation.'[5]

Cowboy surgery is still mainly an American problem, but what is to stop British surgeons cashing in on the private health care boom?

In 1974 the US Senate investigation into unnecessary surgery reported that US doctors performed 2.4 million unnecessary operations causing 11,900 deaths and costing about $3.9 billion.[6] It has been calculated by Professor John McKinlay, a noted critic of medical waste, that more deaths are caused by surgery each year in the US than the annual number of deaths during the wars in Korea and Vietnam, which were considered national tragedies, comments McKinlay.[6]

The Cowboy Surgeon.

The situation has reached such crisis proportions in the US that consumer organisations have begun to publish 'best buy' guides to surgeons. *Cutting Prices: A Guide to Washington Area Surgeons' Fees* published in 1979 by the US Public Citizens' Health Research Group lists fees by named surgeons for twelve common surgical procedures in the Washington area. The non-secretive open government that Americans are so fortunate to have has enabled consumers to find out, under the Freedom of Information Act, whether a particular surgeon's fees are above or below those of his or her local colleagues. It was discovered in 1976, for example, that fees were sometimes four times more expensive with certain surgeons. Some private doctors were charging over 2,000 dollars for a hysterectomy, whilst others were charging only 500 dollars. In Britain, the same operation in 1979 cost anything from £800 to £1,500 according to figures compiled by Private Patients' Plan published in the November 1979 edition of *Accountancy*. No matter how much the British private surgeon charges, most medical insurance schemes will reimburse his fee so there is little pressure for patients to worry about how much their surgeon charges. What they need to be concerned about is the possibility of having *unneeded* surgery in the first place.

Critics of the American health system, such as US surgeon Dr George Crile,[7] want to have surgeons paid by salary because, in his judgement, fee for service provides an incentive for excessive surgery. See Dental Section, page 122, to see how 'fee for service' encourages unnecessary dental treatment in Britain. It is ironic that Britain, the home and birthplace of free and equal health care from the NHS, is now turning the clock backwards and inviting unnecessary surgery (and other unnecessary medical treatment as well) with its newly found luxury of private medicine.

Surgery: more an art than a science

Until very recently operations have largely been performed because of a fashion or out of habit and with little *hard* evidence that they improve health. Even as recently as 1978 a group of unhappy surgeons felt compelled to complain to *The Lancet* that this distinguished medical journal lowered its editorial standards of scientific rigour when it published reports on surgery. 'Relatively few controlled trials of surgical therapy have been done and these have followed rather than preceded the widespread introduction of new operations,' wrote surgeon David Spodick and twelve of his colleagues. They continued: 'Uncertainty about the effectiveness of operations for common diseases like peptic ulcer, breast cancer and coronary artery obstruction will continue unless this is recognised.'[8]

In the thirties between one-half and three-quarters of all British children had their tonsils removed, and at the beginning of this century Sir Arbuthnot Lane, distinguished surgeon to royalty, was convinced that the best cure for constipation was the surgical removal of the large bowel (colon). This replaced the miseries of constipation with the joys of continuous diarrhoea. Sir Arbuthnot Lane performed over a thousand of these operations before the fashion faded.[9] Perhaps the great turning point in fanciful and useless surgery came when it was conclusively shown that a sham operation or a placebo operation was just as effective at preventing angina pain as the 'genuine' operation. During the late 1950s a fashion arose of cutting the mammary artery to treat angina. Its popularity was boosted by an enthusiastic report in the *Reader's Digest* in 1957, writes Dr Ernest Barsamian in his fascinating report entitled 'The Rise and Fall of Internal Mammary Artery Ligation in Treatment of Angina Pectoris.'[10] The *Reader's Digest* article made many patients aware of the operation and it sent many to surgeons requesting it.

But in 1958 and 1959 an extraordinary thing happened. Two surgeons decided to carry out a controlled trial to see if this treatment really had any effect.[11, 12] Patients (all suffering from angina) were randomly split into two groups. In both groups incisions were made in the chest, but in one group the incisions were simply sewn up again without any further treatment. In the second group the entire procedure of cutting off the artery was completed. When both groups were measured for their improvement in pain, no difference was found and both groups were equally satisfied with their operations. Nowadays, perhaps, it would be considered unethical to perform fake operations on people without their consent. But is it unethical? Isn't it more unethical for surgeons to continue to perform risky operations that have never been proved to actually work? The coronary bypass operation for severe angina was used for many years before any attempt was made to test its effectiveness (see page 50).

The Tragic Reluctance of Doctors to Test their Treatment

'I need permission to give a drug to half of my patients, but not to give it to them all.' (Professor Richard Smithells)[13] Many doctors cling to untested, risky and expensive treatments because they are frightened to test them scientifically.

'To maim or kill with well-intentioned guesswork is acceptable because it is not perceived as "human experimentation": it is the experimental trial that draws the pejorative headlines' – this is how a stinging editorial published in *World Medicine* described the absurd situation in Western medicine when doctors are under pressure NOT to find out if the treatments they use actually work.[14] The editorial notes that over 10,000 premature babies were blinded by being given oxygen in the first few days of life because doctors were reluctant to test the safety of this procedure. They thought it would be unethical to deny any of these babies what they believed to be life-saving treatment, so they *all* suffered.

Avoiding unnecessary surgery: a simple solution

In the United States a second-opinion programme has cut down dramatically the number of operations performed each year. Two unions in New York, for example, started a scheme in which it was necessary for all recommendations for surgery to be reviewed by independent certified specialists. This has two benefits, argues Dr Sidney Wolfe, of the US Public Citizens' Health Research Group.[15] Firstly, the patient is exposed to a doctor who stands in no way to profit if surgery is performed and in no way to lose if alternative treatment is advised. Secondly, it gives the patient a chance to hear a second impression of the medical problem. In Britain the 3 million people who currently subscribe to public health care schemes may well find this useful advice, as their operations are being performed on a fee-paying basis. The New York scheme found that 18 out of every 100 operations were not actually needed. The cost of the scheme comes out of the vast savings made by not performing unnecessary operations. In the United States Dr John McCarthy has shown that it saves eight dollars for every dollar spent.[16] The NHS perhaps could save millions of pounds too by enforcing a second-opinion scheme before every operation was performed. Such a scheme would save money and lives. At present every NHS patient has the right to obtain free of charge a second opinion on his or her treatment, but few patients ever exercise this right. Recently the *Drug and Therapeutics Bulletin* claimed that 20,000 appendix operations alone are performed unnecessarily each year in Britain.[17]

The crazy world of consultants

Following an operation or the birth of a child there is no agreed length of time that an otherwise healthy person should remain in hospital. It has been repeatedly shown that it makes no difference to the rate of recovery if patients are discharged from hospital quite soon after an operation.

The Department of Community Medicine at St Thomas's Hospital in London investigated the length of stay for patients having operations for hernias and for varicose veins. Leaving aside patients who had to stay in hospital because there was no one at home to look after them they found that it made no difference to the number of post-operative complications if patients were discharged after 48 hours instead of after the normal period in hospital of 6 to 7 days.[18] Economics apart, infection rates are so high in hospital it is probably safer for patients to go home as soon as possible.

The researchers also found that there was no difference in the convalescence time either. Patients when interviewed did not mind these shorter stays in hospital, but predictably their families who had to look after them when they got out of hospital were less keen.

Other surveys have shown the following wide range of recommended hospital stays:

> Birth in maternity hospital in Wales – 5 days
> in London – $8\frac{1}{2}$ days
> Peptic ulcer operation – 6 to 26 days
> Hernia operation – 2 to 12 days
> Appendicectomy – 3 to 10 days
> Tonsillectomy – 1 to 5 days
> Hysterectomy – 3 to 18 days[19]

A recent survey of 177 hospitals found that the number of admissions and the length of time they stayed in hospital increased according to the number of available beds in the hospital. The *Sunday Times* comments: 'A new Parkinson's Law operates: sickness expands to fill the beds available'.[19]

In the United States consultants are vetted to see how long they need their patients to be kept in hospital. As American consumers are paying for their hospital treatment they have initiated schemes to ensure that doctors do not abuse their clinical powers.[19] Fines up to 5,000 dollars are imposed on US doctors who keep their patients in hospital longer than necessary.[19]

Infections after surgery

'3,000 die needlessly in hospitals,' declared a headline in the *Sunday Times* in March 1978. 'Poor operating theatres and inadequate techniques mean that about 3,000 people in Britain die unnecessarily each year from infected surgical wounds. Many more suffer from agonising illnesses which can drag on for years.' The estimate comes from an orthopaedic surgeon, Charles Bingold, who say that 'the seriousness of the problem has gone unrecognised in British hospitals.' In December 1979 Mr Bingold told me that he stood by these figures and explained that he preferred to publish his survey of operating-theatre infections in a newspaper instead of a medical journal because he was annoyed and 'wanted to get something done'.

Mr Bingold's survey found that as many as 1 in 20 patients who underwent orthopaedic surgery at Lewisham Hospital suffered from wound infections afterwards. The survey showed that Lewisham then had a rate of serious deep-wound surgical infection which was four times higher than that of the National Orthopaedic Hospital and six times higher than that of the Wrightington Hospital in Wigan. The age of hospital buildings seems not to influence the risk of infection as the modern research hospital of Northwick Park had an infection rate which was triple that of the much older Royal National Orthopaedic Hospital. But a survey of 3,215 hip replacement operations[20] performed at the Mayo Clinic found that infected wounds were twice as common in patients who had been operated on in an older theatre compared to a more modern one. This older theatre was fitted with an air-exchange system providing only thirteen air exchanges per hour. A much lower rate of infection was found in a theatre which had thirty air exchanges per hour (see Hip Replacement Surgery, page 56). Clearly unless air is changed frequently in operating theatres bacteria can cause infections.

Few doctors could get away with such accusations of the type made by Mr Bingold. It is not permitted in the medical profession to openly criticise poor medical facilities. The only way Mr Bingold was able to publish these facts was in a newspaper just after his retirement.

The risks of anaesthetics

'Anaesthesia is 99 per cent boredom and 1 per cent panic' – anonymous doctor. 'Perhaps anaesthetists, like lorries, should be equipped with a tachograph,' says *The Lancet.*[21]

No one has figures for the number of deaths caused by anaesthetics in Britain. Official records held by the OPCS (Office of Population Census Studies) disguise the true occurrence of such accidents. For example, doctors will write on a certificate 'death due to appendicitis' if a patient dies in the operating theatre from an anaesthetist's error whilst undergoing the operation to remove his 'abnormal' appendix. Even the officials at the Office of Population and Census Studies admitted this was the case.[22]

Each year more than 4 million operations are performed so the risks of having an accident are in broad terms pretty unlikely. But some people are much greater risks under anaesthetic. The greatest risk factor is where a patient has had a heart attack in the six months prior to an operation.[23] When surgery with anaesthetics is undertaken three months after a heart attack more than one-third of patients have another heart attack after the operation. After six months this risk is reduced to 5 per cent or one in twenty. Hypertension, ie high blood pressure, also significantly increases the risk of heart attack (myocardial infarction). The longer the patient is under the anaesthetic the greater the risk; every additional hour of anaesthesia increases the risk of a heart attack by 22 per cent.[23] Anaesthetists are just as good in America as in Britain, a British anaesthetist told me, so these American figures equally apply to Britain. Even if patients are put into an intensive care unit after an operation there is no reduction in the risk of having another heart attack (yet a further argument by the way against the use of these expensive, labour-intensive coronary care units which have been shown to be no better than simple care at home!). No particular type of anaesthetic was found to be associated with any greater risk of heart attack, but a spinal anaesthetic protected against post-operative heart failure. The obvious conclusion is that anaesthesia is very risky within six months of a heart attack, according to *The Lancet*.[23]

The other rare hazard associated with anaesthetics is brain damage; this can occur when insufficient oxygen reaches the brain whilst the patient is unconscious and the heart has stopped beating. This is mostly caused by human error, or occasionally by faulty machinery.

An investigation in the US revealed that when 359 'near-misses' were looked into, 4 out of 5 were found to be due to human error.[21] The most common error was described as 'breathing circuit disconnection', ie the oxygen supply was switched off by mistake (or the connecting tubes came apart) – an error that can result in irreversible brain damage that can transform a healthy patient into a human vegetable. *The Lancet* comments that where similar tasks in other occupations require constant vigilance, work cycles are required by law, but this is not the case for anaesthetists. Is *The Lancet* hinting at something? For then it drops a disturbing bombshell by asking: 'How many anaesthetists can remember near-misses due to pilot error during periods of personal fatigue? And how many types of anaesthetic machine would be grounded by order, if they were flying machines?'[21] The question is put, but unfortunately it is not answered.

It is likely that the greatest risks of anaesthetics occur whilst having dental treatment, as dentists are not required to employ fully trained anaesthetists and have only a limited amount of training themselves.

One way of reducing the patient's risk from anaesthetics is for doctors to ask if there is any family history of allergic reactions to anaesthetics. Drs P. Singh and K. Hancock describe in a letter to *The Lancet*[24] a case of a woman who had problems with an anaesthetic given to her during a Caesarian. On questioning her mother it was discovered that the patient's sister had previously had an abnormal reaction to a dental anaesthetic. It appears that the commmon blood type of these two women affected their response to the anaesthetic.

Another hazard of anaesthetics

Women who work in operating theatres have a higher incidence of miscarriage and foetal abnormalities because the anaesthetics used can damage the unborn child. Dental assistants – generally female – also suffer from these problems. The hazard also affects men, so the fertility of male anaesthetists, etc. is at risk as well.

'On the present evidence a theatre nurse or female anaesthetist becoming pregnant or wishing to become pregnant should be advised to avoid working in an environment contaminated with anaesthetic gases' say Professor Martin Vessey of Oxford University and Dr J. F. Nunn in a recent review of the hazard in the *British Medical Journal.*[25] They add, however, that 'there is no certainty that some other occupations in the hospital service, or elsewhere for that matter, are any more favourable'.

Anaesthetics given to mothers before delivery of their child can cause severe side effects in the foetus. These powerful drugs cross the placenta as soon as they are in the mother's bloodstream (see page 82).

The risks of surgery

The most common cause of accidental death from surgery is uncontrollable haemorrhage or bleeding. But what seems most important is the age of the patient. The very young and the very old are most vulnerable. The old may have conditions such as high blood pressure which can increase the risks from anaesthesia and the very young are more likely to have difficult surgery for congenital deformities. A child less than a year old has the same risk of death from surgery as a person aged 60 to 70 years old, according to figures published by John N. Lunn.[26]

Another major determinant of high risk is whether or not the operation is an emergency one or an elective operation (ie one the patient chooses to have). Emergency operations on average have a 6 per cent risk of death, whereas elective operations carry just under a 1 per cent risk. Men have a slightly higher risk than women, probably because they have fewer operations performed altogether.

Why hospitals are above the law
No one would suggest that doctors and nursing staff should be superhuman and never make an error or have an accident. But every skill can be performed either competently or incompetently. Insufficient care, sloppiness and negligence are quite different from occasional accidents. It is strange that in many other professions where human lives are at stake rigorous tests are performed on staff and equipment, yet in medicine neither doctors nor much of their high technology and risky equipment is required to be tested by law. Most disturbing of all, hospitals cannot be prosecuted if their hygiene standards become so bad that they break the law. The food hygiene regulations, for example, do not apply in hospitals, because they are theoretically the property of the Crown, and as the Crown cannot prosecute itself they are outside the arm of the law.

When the MP Michael Thomas tried to introduce a Private Member's Bill requiring GPs to have compulsory refresher courses in drug prescribing he was attacked by the medical profession. Is it really unreasonable to expect doctors to undergo such courses and even exams – considering that they deal with human lives as do airline pilots? Nevertheless, despite the need and sense of such a bill Mike Thomas's attempt was described as 'an impertinence' by the Chairman of the General Medical Services Committee, Dr Keable Elliot. As Donald Gould, of the *New Scientist*, pointed out at the time, some doctors believe themselves only answerable to God, and not even to God when there is a difference of opinion!

'Obvious blunders continue to occur in operating theatres,' said the *Nursing Standard*, journal of the Royal College of Nursing, when reporting figures for mistakes during surgery.[27] One of the commonest errors is operating on the wrong patient, according to the Medical Defence Union. Patients are not always labelled when they go in for an operation and, as a result, between 15 and 30 people each year have the wrong operations. There are occasionally cases of first-time mothers going to the theatre for a Caesarian delivery, and coming out sterilised; arms and legs *do* get wrongly amputated; objects such as surgical instruments and swabs (cotton wool and gauze) are sometimes, but rarely, left inside patients after they have been sewn up. There were 48 cases of foreign bodies abandoned inside patients reported to the Medical Defence Union 1976 (this excludes cases which went unreported or reported to other medical defence organisations, like the Medical Defence Protection Society).

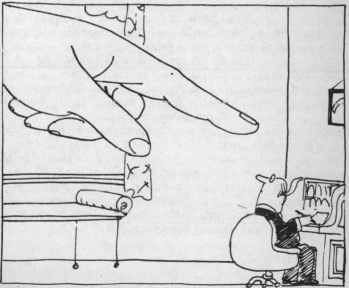

The Doctor–God relationship – let the finger of God and the nose of the doctor always point in the same direction.

In 1976 twenty cases of wrong operations were reported to the Medical Defence Union. The main cause of having a wrong operation was found to be the failure to label patients on admission to hospital. It was also revealed that when beds were moved around in hospital at a time before surgery there was also greater chance of a slip-up occurring. Mistakes also occur when there are changes in the order of patients to be operated upon. The new guidelines issued by the Medical Defence Union in 1976 stress that there must be reliable and routine measures for identifying patients, preferably by sending for them by name and number. A spokesman at the time admitted that 'the most we can claim is that we have stopped the number of cases climbing'.

'Safeguards against wrong operations', the title of the Medical Defence Union's guidelines and another booklet entitled 'Safeguards against failure to remove swabs and instruments from patients' were described in the weekly paper Doctor in the following manner: 'It is not sufficient to say these two booklets should be looked on as among the most important pieces of equipment in every operating theatre. They should be made compulsory reading at least once a year for every member of the theatre team – from the consultant surgeon to the theatre porter.'[28]

Ultimately it is the surgeon who is responsible for checking that all instruments, swabs, needles etc are removed from patients undergoing surgery, but in practice they are jobs often performed by nursing staff. A swab count is meant to be performed before the surgeon sews the patient up, but it has been reported that nurses may not be able to check completely if the surgeon is anxious to sew up quickly. The possibility of leaving a swab inside a patient after surgery cannot be completely dismissed since swabs are now designed with a metal strip which will show up on an X-ray. These measures do not exactly inspire 100 per cent confidence, yet on the other hand they make sense and can lower the risks of human error.

3

Surgery Guide

Abortion

A woman can avoid risks to herself and any future offspring by making sure she obtains the safest kind of abortion. Many researchers have investigated the safety of abortion and found that the earlier the abortion is performed the safer it is. The type of operation used depends on the size of the foetus, ie the number of weeks that a woman has been pregnant. The importance of seeking and obtaining an abortion *without delay* is underlined by all research studies.

Which type of abortion?

1. Under 12 weeks: the suction method, or vacuum aspiration, can be performed with just a local anaesthetic in a day centre, ie without the need to stay overnight. In this method the foetus is sucked out of the uterus through a tube. Vacuum aspiration in the first 12 weeks is the method of choice in most countries for abortion; in a quarter of a million operations in Britain from 1968–73, there were only 6 deaths using this method or just over 2 deaths per 100,000 abortions. In the USA this type of abortion was even four times safer still if performed in the first 8 weeks, assuming that British surgeons are as good as their American colleagues.[47] After 12 weeks, abortions are 'surgically and emotionally' a more complex matter and many more times dangerous, although they are still safer than childbirth until the 16th week.

2. D & C type of abortion: requires general anaesthetic, the lining of the uterus is scraped off with a curette (up

31

to 16 weeks). The cervix can be dilated gently and more safely with special water-absorbing stalks of kelp (seaweed) called laminaria, which provide a slow and gentle effect on the woman. D & C has a death rate of 8.3 per 100,000 abortions.

3. After 16 weeks, prostaglandin: administration of the substances that normally produce contractions of labour force the foetus to be expelled through the cervix. Death rate is 21 per 100,000 abortions.

4. Later still, hysterotomy: an incision is made in the abdomen and the foetus is removed as in a Caesarian.

5. Hysterectomy: removal of the entire womb – the most dangerous type of abortion operation. The Lane Committee Report on the Working of the Abortion Act reported that in pregnancies less than 13 weeks the death rate was five times higher than for any other group, especially in women over 30.[48]

What is the risk of abortion to the woman?

Abortions performed before the 16th week of pregnancy are safer than childbirth. This is the conclusion of a study over four years of deaths associated with legal abortion which occurred between 1972 and 1975 in the USA. Even when it is taken into account that abortions are mainly performed on young healthy women and that deaths from pregnancy occur in older high-risk women, this conclusion still remains valid.[47] Up to 8 weeks of pregnancy, the risk of death from abortion is less than one in 100,000. From 9–10 weeks the risk is less than one in 50,000. Up to 16 weeks the risk is still only 7 deaths in 100,000 abortions, and remains twice as safe as having a baby. Only after 16 weeks does the risk rise to over 20 deaths for every 100,000 abortions and then it becomes slightly more risky than childbirth.

What is the risk of having a miscarriage after having an abortion?

It all depends on which type of abortion is performed. A massive study involving thirteen clinics in California has followed the medical histories of over 31,000 women who became pregnant. Published in 1979 in the *New England Journal of Medicine*, it showed that an abortion does indeed lead to a small increase in the risk of miscarriage (between 3 and 6 months into pregnancy) when the dilatation and curettage (D & C) method was employed for the abortion. But this risk only applies to women who have never had children before and it seems that such women are more likely to suffer damage to their cervix than women who have had their cervix stretched in the course of childbirth. But, since 1973, this risk has been virtually eliminated in the USA and Britain when the D & C method of abortion was replaced by a more gentle technique of suction with the aid of what are called laminaria. These are water-absorbing stalks of kelp (seaweed) which are inserted into the cervix. They swell up in contact with water, thus gently dilating the cervix over a period of several hours.

Another study by Jennie Kline,[49] of Columbia University, School of Public Health in New York, looked at women attending three Manhattan hospitals for abortions from 1974 to 1976. In a group of 700 women who had miscarriages no relationship was found between having had an abortion and a later miscarriage. The vacuum method and the D & C method were found to be equally safe. However, a study carried out in Singapore obtained a different result when it compared two groups of 1,200 women. The Singapore research team showed that the D & C method was followed by a slight increase in the incidence of miscarriage. In the Singapore survey, it was found that 1 in 10 of the poor Chinese women who had a D & C type of abortion, suffered a miscarriage, whereas only 1 in 13 had a miscarriage when the vacuum method of abortion was employed. A report in *Family Planning Perspectives* magazine commented: 'Whilst these figures are not statistically significant they agree with the preliminary findings of the WHO* study of the effect of a previous abortion on pregnancy.'[50] The WHO looked at figures from eight countries where abortion is legal, and found the same factor cropping up again and again: D & C abortion is followed by a greater number of miscarriages as well as a possible increase in the number of premature, low-birth-weight babies.

Is there a connection between abortion and later birth defects?

Three huge studies, from Boston, Hawaii and Seattle, have

*World Health Organisation

found no evidence that an abortion makes a woman any more likely to have a subsequent stillborn child, an ectopic pregnancy (a pregnancy occurring in the Fallopian tubes), a complication of delivery, low birthweight, ill-health, congenital malformations, or an increased likelihood of a baby's death shortly after birth (neonatal death). When added together, these three surveys combined looked at over 26,000 women.[50]

One surprising and interesting discovery, made by the Seattle team of researchers (and also confirmed by Dr Michael Bracken at Yale School of Medicine), was that white women who had *previously* had an abortion were found to be significantly *less* likely to deliver a congenitally malformed child. The authors in trying to explain this finding suggest that women who have aborted are probably more careful during later pregnancies which they really desire to maintain.[51] But there are many factors affecting the foetus which are outside the mother's control.

Sir Cyril Clarke, of Liverpool University, has also noted that if a woman has a miscarriage then the chances of her having a malformed baby afterwards are greatly reduced if she waits several months before conceiving again. There is a quadrupled risk of spina bifida/major deformation if she becomes pregnant immediately following a miscarriage.[52] But the major determinants of those abnormalities are low social class and a previous abnormal child.

Other hazards of abortion

Some women are offered sterilisation at the same time as having an abortion; sometimes an authoritarian doctor puts pressure on a woman to have this operation at the same time.

One survey of over 100 women who requested reversal of sterilisation found that many of them had been sterilised at a young age, often immediately or shortly after giving birth and in a situation of marital unhappiness.[53]

If sterilisation *is* wanted by a woman, it should be done by tubal ligation (ie tying the Fallopian tube) or with a laparascope (see page 64 for details) and not the removal of the womb (hysterectomy) which is a more hazardous operation and completely irreversible. The chances anyway of getting sterilisation reversed are slim and generally it is restricted to those women whose children have died.

Appendix operation

'In West Germany three times more appendices are removed than elsewhere and three-quarters of them are quite normal. But deaths from appendicitis are three times more common because of this unnecessary surgery' (editorial in *New England Journal of Medicine*).[40]

Is your operation necessary? Do you need psychiatry instead?

Appendicitis is a serious cause for surgery; delaying an appendix operation when it is needed could be fatal. Unfortunately the hazardous consequences of leaving an inflamed appendix alone have sometimes made doctors a little too keen to remove perfectly healthy organs. Surveys in Germany have shown that more people die from the complications of unnecessary appendix operations than from appendicitis itself. Six people in every thousand have their appendices removed every year in Germany, but more than three-quarters of all those appendices removed are normal![41]

It has been discovered that men who have had normal appendices removed have higher than average levels of anxiety, says Dr B. M. Barraclough, writing in the *Journal of Psychosomatic Medicine.*[42] The most likely age at which perfectly healthy appendices are surgically removed is the 21–30 age group. Men of this age group were found to be psychologically abnormal on a test of anxiety. They were also more likely to have lost a parent before the age of 16 when compared to the men whose appendices were really inflamed. Dr Barraclough suggests that their abdominal pains could be a leading sign of depressive illness and suggests that such patients may need psychiatric help. The so-called 'grumbling appendix' may also have its origins in the mind and nowadays few specialists believe that such a condition really exists. An editorial in the *British Medical Journal* in August 1979 doubts the existence of the 'grumbling appendix'. 'The existence of chronic appendicitis is still a subject of controversy but now there are many more sceptics than believers. Few surgical units actually plan in advance to perform appendix operations. It is emergencies only nowadays,' adds the *British Medical Journal,* and it maintains that surgeons were quite right to react against the wide use of these operations when they were planned in advance for a whole range of abdominal complaints. It suggests that one-fifth of the operations done in Britain, a not inconsiderable 20,000, are probably unnecessary. Surgeons should 'cast a more critical eye on many patients whom they are advising to have this operation', warns the editorial. It has also been found that women are twice as likely to be wrongly diagnosed as having appendicitis.[43]

Occasionally surgery can be avoided when antibiotics are given for an abscess of the appendix. *The Lancet* asks in a 1978 editorial: 'Is it surgical heresy to propose that an initial attack of presumptive appendicitis which has persisted for several days and in which an abscess, ie an infection, is found should be treated with a full course of the appropriate therapeutic agent (drugs)?'[44] It concludes that the operation could be reserved for only high-risk patients or those with recurrent symptoms. One investigation, reported by Dr E. L. Bradley in the *Archives of Surgery*,[45] of 13 patients all with an abscess of the appendix who either refused to have the operation or were bad risks for surgery, found that 12 of these patients had no problems afterwards. Only one of these patients had a reinfection of the abscess after six months.

The number of appendix operations was reduced by over 17 per cent in one experiment with a 'second-opinion' programme used in the United States, without damage to anyone's health. Dr John White, of Johns Hopkins Medical School in New York, found that when rigorous guidelines for the operation were imposed on doctors, there was keener examination of appendicitis cases. The number of operations was reduced by one-sixth, yet the number of deaths from appendicitis remained stable. There were no additional ruptures of the appendix or recurrences of symptoms amongst all the patients sent home without surgery. Dr Sydney Wolfe of America's Public Citizens' Health Group calculates that such a second-opinion policy carried out across the entire USA would save 300 lives which are currently lost by annually performing 60,000 unnecessary operations.[46]

Breast cancer surgery
The horror of losing a breast under surgery may be

36

foremost in the mind of a woman who has been told she has cancer of the breast. But there is increasing evidence that the old-style radical mastectomy – removal of the entire breast and surrounding tissue – or the ordinary mastectomy are no more effective than a much simpler and less disfiguring operation.

'Extensive surgery or radiotherapy (X-ray treatment) might even accelerate the course of the disease rather than lead to cure,' comments American cancer expert, Dr B. A. Stoll.[7] It has been very difficult for surgeons to test whether the traditional treatment for breast cancer actually works because of the fear that in denying a woman a radical mastectomy in a clinical trial, they would be condemning her to die. This is not the case, as studies now show with women who have refused or been unable to have their breast removed.[8]

But with or without treatment 40 per cent of women with cancer of the breast do die from the disease at present and there is little evidence that surgery offers any benefit to most sufferers.[9] Dr Klim McPherson, statistician of Oxford University, points out that survival has not improved since the thirties; new therapies and surgical techniques have made no difference to survival rates up to 1975.[10]

'Surgery is performed,' says McPherson, 'in the unproven belief that if all cancer cells are obliterated the disease will disappear, but whilst this may be correct there is little evidence to support this idea.' For example, it may be that secondary cancers retain a memory of their origins in the breast and unless they receive chemical 'orders' to stop growing from their original locations in the breast they will continue to grow through the body. (There are cells in the body, in the liver for example, that stop growing in this way.) If this were true, then surgery might actually be harmful to a woman with breast cancer that has spread through the body, speculates Dr McPherson.

Another possibility with evidence to support it, is that the lymph nodes, which are often removed as part of surgery for breast cancer, might in fact provide a defence or an 'immune' response, as it is called, against the cancer and secondary cancers. This could mean that X-ray treatment of the lymph nodes may well have the opposite of the desired effect, thereby reducing the body's vital immune responses.[11]

There is growing evidence too that breast cancer is not one single disease but consists of four or more chronological stages, each of which are quite different in the way they respond to treatment.[12] There is also some evidence that certain women with breast cancer have high-risk cells in their breasts compared to other women with the disease. Dr Robert Peyster and others[13] at Massachusetts General Hospital found that in women aged between 30 and 49 (ie pre-menopausal women) those with a P2 pattern of breast cells (identified by their 'parenchymal cell pattern') had a four-times greater risk of developing breast cancer. These patterns of breast cells begin in young adulthood; they are not themselves cancerous but merely are associated with women who are at high risk of getting cancer. This might mean that some women can be cured and others cannot, or that treatment should differ according to the type of cancer that is present.

Many studies have shown that simple mastectomy is just as effective as the much more mutilating operation known as radical mastectomy which not only removes the breast but chest muscles and lymph nodes as well. This latter operation is much more popular in America than in Britain, possibly because surgeons make more money performing it, says Dr George Crile.[11] A Swedish researcher has found that there are even *more* deaths when the operation is followed by X-ray therapy.[14]

Simple removal of the tumour without removing the breast itself is a procedure known as tylectomy. It can be as effective as the more extensive surgery. A study by Atkins[15] found that patients with a tylectomy who had only early stages of the disease (where it had not spread beyond the breast), survived after ten years as often as those who had undergone radical surgery, although there was a high degree of local recurrence of cancer. But these women survived and were spared the unpleasantness of having one of their breasts removed. However the local recurrence of cancer is not acceptable or pleasant for many patients either.

Dr Vera Peters, of the Princess Margaret Hospital in Toronto, studied and compared these two types of treatments in over 8,000 women suffering from breast cancer between 1938 and 1963 and concluded that they were equally effective. Survival rates up to twenty years were not affected by the type of surgery used; instead, the most important factors affecting survival were age and the clinical stage of the disease.[16] This has been confirmed in a study over ten years at Guy's Hospital, which found that early stage-one cancer responded as well to this partial mastectomy compared to the more major surgery normally used.[8]

New research with chemotherapy, ie drug therapy for breast cancer, may well reduce the amount of surgery even further. However, there is still little agreement on its value, as letters published in the correspondence columns of medical journals illustrate. Clinical trials are continuing.

Breast cancer and the mind: latest developments

Another idea now being explored is that surgery may not be as important as the mental state of the patient. Women who have a 'fighting spirit' are more likely to survive than those who think their chances of survival are low. This was discovered by Dr S. Greer who investigated, over a five-year period, the attitudes of 69 women who had been diagnosed as having early breast cancer, at King's College Hospital Medical School.[17]

Dr Greer assessed the patients' psychological feelings towards their disease three months after surgery and found there were four typical responses to the disease. (1) Denial: patients who would deny that their breast was removed for cancer, and would say things like 'it wasn't serious, they just took off my breast as a precaution'. They neither showed nor reported any emotional distress. Another group, (2), showed fighting spirit, were optimistic, very interested in the disease and planned to do everything to conquer it. 'I can fight it and defeat it' was a typical comment. These two groups of women were twice as likely to survive then those (3) who accepted the diagnosis and just carried on with life as normal, or those (4) who felt their lives were finished, and were very emotionally distressed.

This is not the first time that the will to live has been identified as a potent weapon against illness. In a thought-provoking book and an article in the *New England Journal of Medicine,* US journalist Norman Cousins has described how he harnessed his 'will to live' to conquer ankylosing spondilitis. He was given just a 1-in-500 chance of recovery but, as he says, 'If I was to be that one case in 500 I decided that I'd better be more than a passive observer.'[18] Cousins nursed himself back to health with the aid of funny stories and classic 'Candid Camera' television shows. 'Since I didn't accept the verdict, I wasn't trapped in the cycle of fear, depression and panic that frequently accompanies a supposedly incurable illness', wrote Cousins.

In the USA the husband-and-wife team of Drs Carl and Stephanie Mathews Simonton have pioneered the use of *visualisation* techniques alongside conventional therapies for cancer. Patients become active participants in visualising their cancers getting smaller and smaller. Meditation and relaxation also help to reduce stress and build up the body's immune response to cancerous cells.

Dr Basil Stoll has found that women who had been taking tranquillisers before diagnosis of breast cancer have more rapidly spreading cancers than those not taking tranquillisers. Why? Tranquillisers stifle the emotional expression of anger and frustration, but Dr David Horrobin believes it may be due to the cancer-promoting chemical properties of such drugs as Valium (see pp. 164-6).

Eight things a woman can do to prevent breast cancer
No single cause of breast cancer has been clearly identified, but the way the disease affects different races and groups of people provides several clues.

Whilst none of these measures can *guarantee* protection, just as giving up smoking cannot guarantee immunity from lung cancer, the risks can clearly be reduced if action is taken to change lifestyle. Most women will not be able to put all eight measures into action for practical reasons – but personal risk will be reduced even if they succeed with only some of them.

1. *Get married and have children early on*
Married people generally suffer from fewer diseases than single persons,[19] they also tend to live longer. Research carried out at the American National Cancer Institute by Dr Haitung King shows also that there is a definite relationship between breast cancer and a late first preg-

nancy, after the age of 30.[20]

Countries with a low birth rate have a much higher incidence of breast cancer than those where it is common to have large families, as in African communities. As a group, nuns have an above-average risk because they are childless, but their puritanical lifestyle protects them from other ills, such as cervical cancer which is related to sexual activity. A woman who waits until she is 35 to have her first child increases her risk four times compared to an 18-year-old.[21]

2. *Breast-feed, don't bottle-feed your baby*

'Breast cancer rarely seems to arise in women who have been successful breast feeders,' wrote Dr Marjorie Reid in the *British Medical Journal* in 1977.[22] Her views were confirmed over twenty years ago by studies carried out in the city of Los Angeles, where many races were compared. Dr P. Steiner found that mother who had breast-fed their babies were less likely to get breast cancer.[23] But a recent study by Oxford University researchers Dr A. Kalache, Professor Martin Vessey and Dr Klim McPherson failed to find any relationship between breast-feeding and protection from breast cancer after interviewing 707 women with breast cancer.[24] However, their results are questioned by Dr Herbert Ratner, who claims that if breast-feeding reduces the risk it will most likely be found in women whose babies are totally breast-fed for the first six months, with mixed feeding thereafter, and with more than one baby.[25] The Oxford study did not investigate such long-term breast feeding. Dr Ratner suggests that the prolonged amenorrhoea (absence of periods) caused by breast-feeding could be the factor associated with the hormonal state that protects against cancer.

3. *Avoid drugs containing oestrogen*

Breast cancer occurs during the years that a woman is fertile, but reaches a peak shortly after the menopause, at around ages 45–49. This pattern strongly suggests it is connected with the ovaries' hormonal secretions of oestrogen, other facts support this idea:

* women who have had their ovaries surgically removed have a reduced risk of breast cancer.[27]
* dozens of animal experiments show that rats and mice fed on oestrogens suffer from tumours of the breast.[28]

* other female cancers have been linked with oestrogen drugs. Endometrial, or uterine, cancer has been linked with oestrogen given to post-menopausal women. Hormone Replacement Therapy as it is known, 'accounts for much of the recent increase in the incidence of endometrial cancer in the USA', says Sir Richard Doll.[29] One study reports, that there is 1.3 times increased risk of breast cancer with hormone therapy. Also it is known that the oestrogen-receptor cells are very similar in the breast and the womb.[30]

* Professor of Oncology at Glasgow University, Dr Kenneth Calman, says that hormone replacement therapy is the best evidence that oestrogen can cause cancer. He says 'hormones alter the way cells divide and grow, they switch cells on and off; if you give a woman hormones, cancerous cells could be switched on'.[31]

* See page 152 for details of disturbing new evidence of increased risk of breast cancer to young women who have taken the Pill.

* Latest reports on the contraceptive pill show it has been responsible for what is described as 'a sudden increase in liver cancers amongst young women', according to Drs Christophersen and Mays, of the US National Cancer Institute.[32] They point out, though, that the lower-dosed mini-pill appears to produce fewer cases of liver cancer.

4. *Eat whole, unrefined food*

Sir Richard Doll, Oxford University Professor of Medicine, believes that the differences in the incidence of breast cancer from one country to another cannot be explained only by fertility patterns, or the size of families, in Africa, for example. Western diets, he says, 'can create the bowel conditions favourable for the formation of extra oestrogen', which can switch on cancer cells elsewhere.[33]

Western diets contain mainly *refined* carbohydrates, like *white* flour and *white* sugar, so that there is little fibre or roughage to speed waste products through the gut. British nutritionist Dr Denis Burkitt has shown a clear link between bowel diseases and the consumption of refined food.[34]

5. *Avoid fat in the diet*

The amount of fat in the diet has been directly linked with

cancer of the breast, the uterus and the colon, by Drs E. L. Wynder and B. S. Reddy[35] of the US National Cancer Institute.

Oestrogen can be formed in the fatty tissues of the body from a substance called *oestrone*, it is itself derived from secretions made by the adrenal glands. Sir Richard Doll says that this is how post-menopausal women can manufacture oestrogen in their bodies.[29]

Groups such as Mormons and Seventh Day Adventists who do not eat meat suffer from a much *lower* incidence of cancers as a whole, compared to other religious groups who permit meat in the diet.[36]

6. *Don't smoke*

Several surveys show that some cancers (in addition to lung cancer) occur more frequently when people smoke. A Japanese study carried out by Hirayama in 1975 found that stomach cancer could be reduced by drinking milk, but the greatest reduction in this cancer was amongst *non-smoking* milk drinkers.[37]

7. *Avoid non-essential X-rays*

One reason the British Department of Health gives for its decision not to screen all women for breast cancer is the danger of raising the overall levels of cancer in the population by exposing millions of women to X-rays.[38]

X-rays change the basic structure of living cells; they can alter DNA, the genetic material in cells. Too much radiation and cells will not reproduce properly, their self-regulating mechanisms go haywire – this is cancer.

The human body stores X-ray radiation, so several *'safe'* doses can add up to make one *unsafe* dose.

X-rays can cause cancer in all parts of the body.[29]

8. *Regularly look for the early signs of breast cancer*

'Early diagnosis is of prime importance in obtaining high survival rates and minimising risk of death from breast cancer,' concluded a recent report in the *British Medical Journal*.[39] Most reports claim that if it is treated at a stage where it has not spread to other parts of the body, the prospects of recovery are very good.

Women who carry a high risk:
(a) women with relatives who have had breast cancer;
(b) women with a late menopause, after the age of 51;
(c) childless women;

(d) women who had their first child after the age of 30;
(e) overweight women.

What to look for:
(a) any unusual lump or thickening in the breast;
(b) alteration in shape of the breast;
(c) swelling in the armpit.

The breasts should be examined by gently feeling them; visual examination should be done in front of a mirror with the arms raised.

Caesarian delivery

'Once a Caesarian always a Caesarian.' Most women who have a Caesarian delivery usually have to have all their later children by Caesarian as well. The risks attached to this operation are quite substantial as it increases the risk of death by between three and thirty times in an otherwise healthy woman. As a result of the operation, subsequent children are likely to be born underweight – a condition that is associated with mental and physical handicaps.

Like any operation, there are *genuine* reasons for having a Caesarian delivery such as when the baby's head is too large to get past the pelvis or a complicated breech presentation when the baby is facing the wrong way (and a number of other reasons). But with the increased use of what is called electronic foetal monitoring of the unborn child (EFM for short) a large number of perfectly normal babies are being unnecessarily delivered by Caesarian section.[59] The problem with EFM is that 4 out of 10 babies who are perfectly normal are wrongly identified as being in distress. This means many women will unnecessarily undergo all the risks of a Caesarian.

One of the major hazards to the baby from a Caesarian is severe breathing difficulties, leading to death, caused by the 'respiratory distress syndrome', as doctors call it. This is more likely to occur when the baby is delivered prematurely at a time when its lungs are not completely formed. In the US and UK this is the greatest cause of death of babies around the time of birth. When Dr Robert Goldenberg[60] looked at 100 babies at Yale New Haven Hospital which were suffering from this breathing problem he discovered that 15 were definitely caused by the doctors' 'untimely or unwarranted intervention'. Another 18 cases were probably caused by such action, making a total of 33 out of 100 babies which were probably put at risk by the unnecessary action of the doctors in charge.

Dr Goldenberg recommends that before a Caesarian operation is performed or before induction, the maturity of the baby should be checked and double checked (with ultrasound scan and a lung maturity study for example). He says if any question of the baby's maturity remains then doctors should wait for the natural start of labour: 'If any doubt whatsoever exists as to the maturity of the infant the spontaneous onset of labour presents little hazard to the mother and should be awaited prior to the Caesarian section.' He concludes by saying that his research has shown that prematurity and breathing distress continue to be a problem in Caesarian births 'despite the fact that modern techniques of surveillance are available'.

Caesarians also result in much higher rates of infection in the mother, damage to other organs, bowel obstruction, haemorrhage and fever. For further details of these and other hazards see page 89), which covers the risks of Electronic Birth.

Cataract surgery

'Many patients are sorely disillusioned after a perfect cataract operation has made them functionally disabled' – *New England Journal of Medicine*, 1978.[61]

Contrary to popular opinion an operation to remove cataracts is not a passport to-restored vision. 'It may not be fully appreciated how disabled a person can be after a perfectly executed uniocular cataract operation (removal of lens from one eye only),' says American eye expert Dr Norman Jaffe in the *New England Journal of Medicine*.[61] He adds: 'There are countless patients who have corrected vision in one eye after an operation but cannot use it because the other eye has still got useful vision.'

The greatest problem of cataract surgery is that it leaves the patient without any lens to see through. Most patients are given special glasses to wear but these magnify everything by 30 per cent. Vision around the edges of the visual field (peripheral vision as it is called) is reduced so what the post-cataract-surgery patient sees is more like the view out of a tunnel than, say, looking at a wide panorama.

'Spectacles can only provide a magnified topsy turvy and confusing world which takes weeks or months to become accepted by the patient.'[62]

These two consequences of cataract surgery lead to great difficulties for elderly people who form the majority of patients undergoing this type of surgery. As a result they suffer from spatial disorientation and have to learn to see all over again. Pouring a cup of coffee or walking downstairs are very difficult procedures if everything suddenly appears 30 per cent larger. 'It is still widely believed that a cataract is a skin that grows across the eye and that the surgeon can just remove it and life is back to normal,' a consultant at Moorfields Eye Hospital told me.

'It is not unusual for patients to prefer to perform most manual and physical activities with the help of the eye not operated on. Sometimes surgeons will do both eyes but in the end the patient may be little better off after two cataract operations than before.'[61]

Some hospitals operate only when vision is very bad, a lot less than 6/12 (good vision is 6/6). 'Many patients cry

'Now, where did I put the cat?'

with joy when they have their sight restored,' one ophthalmologist told me. 'Only a few feel unhappy with them.'

Some of the problems can be eased with the aid of contact lenses which magnify by only 5 to 10 per cent. However, many old people find these tiny lenses difficult to use. Another option open to such people is the much newer intraocular lenses, plastic lenses which are surgically placed inside the eye. Though they do provide good vision, few places in Britain will provide them and only the most highly trained ophthalmic surgeons are capable of fitting them. A final possibility for the cataract sufferer is the extended-wear lenses which can be worn over the eye for three to six months but again these may produce problems of infection.

In the United States cataract surgery has become a growth industry; more cataract operations are performed there than in any other country in the West, over 400,000 annually. Intraocular lenses are very popular because they produce only 1 to 3 per cent magnification and never need attention in theory, but this all depends on the skills of the surgeon who has fitted them. American eye expert Dr Jaffe recommends them for elderly people, ie those who will not wear them for thirty years or so. For younger people hard contact lenses in contrast to the newer softer ones are recommended. Soft lenses are associated with a greater risk of damage to the eye from infections which they can produce (see Contact Lens Hazards, page 294). Also hard lenses are known to be safe for long-term use but this remains an unknown quantity for the implants.

Generally speaking any form of surgery carries increased risks with advanced age of the patient, however cataract surgery is, I am assured, an easier operation to perform on an older patient than a younger one. The older cataract is more likely to be rigid whereas the younger one will be soft and squishy and so slightly more difficult to remove.

It is important to realise that there are no universally accepted criteria amongst eye experts for cataract surgery, warned American ophthalmologist Dr Wayne Wong in 1978.[63] He makes the crucial point that a cataract is not a distinct physical entity that can be definitely identified like a case of measles or VD. The cataract condition is a continuum that includes, at one end of the spectrum, any opacity (darkening or clouding) in the lens without any effect on vision and, at the other end of the spectrum, a completely opaque lens which does not permit any vision at all. Everyone has some type of opacity in the lens as they get older, so we all tend to get 'tiny cataracts' but they do not affect vision. 'The needs of the patient are most important,' says Wong. When deciding about surgery, the question of whether the patient wants to drive, his job, age and so on will affect his visual needs. Older people, he says, tend to appreciate good near vision (for reading/TV etc) rather than good distance vision. An article in the *British Medical Journal* by Sussex eye specialist M. J. Gilkes reminds doctors that many eyesight problems can often be resolved by providing people with better lighting.[64] 'Moving a light nearer can help many a person suffering from eyesight problems,' says Gilkes. He also points out that dramatic improvements in vision can be obtained by wearing hats or other types of sun visors to eliminate glare. 'The persistence of "old ladies hats" is almost certainly due to their wearers' unconscious understanding that they can see better with their hats on,' claims Gilkes.

Circumcision

Circumcision has been described as ritual surgery, which is certainly true for Jews and Muslims who perform this operation on males at the age of seven days in Jews and at puberty or before amongst Muslims. But for those people not compelled by their religious beliefs to perform this operation, the question remains open as to whether such operation is really necessary. In Scandinavia the operation is unknown[54] and in Britain it is disappearing. During the thirties about one-third of British boys were circumcised; now the figure is only 6 per cent, 20,000 of these operations being performed each year in the UK. The original rationale was that it should be performed on newborns whose foreskins did not retract properly. But studies have shown that by the age of 3 most foreskins nearly always retract fully. Additionally, the arguments supporting circumcision say that some uncircumcised men fail to wash underneath their foreskin, leading to an increased risk of penile cancer and also a subsequent higher risk of cervical cancer in their spouses. There have been only six recorded cases of penile cancer amongst Jews, who are virtually immune from the disease. Correspondingly 'the South African Hottentots[55] who do not practise circumcision and among whom a tight and elongated prepuce (foreskin) appears to be a racial characteristic', writes R. J. C. Harris in his classic book on cancer, 'have cancer of the penis as their most common malignant tumour'. He points out that Muslim males have a penile cancer rate somewhere between those who are circumcised at birth and those who are not circumcised at all, which tends to support the theory that cancer of the penis can be prevented by circumcision.

However an editorial in the *British Medical Journal* argues that in Sweden where hardly any males are circumcised, penile cancer rates are very low anyway (15 deaths per year amongst a male population of 3.7 million). In Britain this type of cancer accounts for over 100 deaths per year. This risk, argues the editorial, is very small compared to the risks of surgery in the average hospital – Jewish ritual circumcision is generally carried out away from the germs of a hospital in the home of the child. 'There is a big difference between these rites and routine circumcision of newborn boys. Too often this is seen as an uninteresting chore to be passed to inadequately trained junior staff which evidently is not without risk . . .' 'The present day hospital surgery often colonised by antibiotic resistant organisms is a dangerous place for a newborn baby with a raw penile wound,' says the *British Medical Journal*. The *BMJ* adds that all male babies who lose their foreskin lose the natural protection of the glans penis which can prevent burning from ammoniacal urine on the wet nappy.[54] On the other hand, whilst this is a possible side effect of circumcision, we are told that 'surgeons and urologists in Britain know that many men conceal a dirty mess beneath the foreskin'. This may result from a condition known as phimosis (a tightness of the foreskin so it cannot be retracted over the glans penis). This problem can be kept in check by penis examination at schools' medical inspections, together with parental exhortations 'to maintain personal hygiene', suggests the *British Medical Journal.*[54] Circumcision at birth prevents this situation arising and also prevents the need for adult circumcision, an uncomfortable and embarrassing procedure.

Clearly the risks of penile disease can be ruled out with circumcision but with adequate hygiene precautions the need for this operation is put into question. The *British Medical Journal* argument against this surgery seems to rest partially on the decreased risk of getting cancer of the penis in non-circumcised males and on the medical profession's general inability to perform the operation with proper care and under suitably antiseptic conditions.

Coronary bypass operation

This is surgery to treat severe angina and blocked coronary arteries. A healthy vein is taken out of the leg and grafted into position to take the place of the blocked heart artery. It is called a bypass operation because the blood flow can avoid the blockage and blood pressure is consequently reduced.

'An increasing number of patients are being operated upon . . . because of the hope, largely *without objective supporting evidence at present*, that coronary artery bypass graft prolongs life or diminishes the frequency of subsequent myocardial infarction (ie heart attack).' This is how an editorial in the *New England Journal of Medicine* in September 1977, by Dr Eugene Braunwald of Harvard Medical School, described the mania for this operation in the seventies.[4] The editorial asks the embarrassing question whether people who have the operation survive any longer than those who do not. A large-scale study conducted by the US Veterans' Administration Hospitals reported in the same edition of the *New England Journal* that the operation made no difference to the survival of almost 600 patients with 'chronic stable angina', though the operation did reduce the severity and incidence of angina. A previous study conducted by Dr R. A. Rosati and his colleagues[5] in 1976 also found that this operation did not prolong life except in patients with severe obstruction of the left main heart artery.

Most recently the European Coronary Surgery group reported that two years after surgery there was no difference in death rates between those who had been operated upon and those who received drugs. The patients studied were 768 men aged under 65 with angina, with 50 per cent blockage in two or more blood vessels. Half of these patients were given drugs and half were given surgery. But in patients with three blocked vessels survival *was* improved with surgery. The death rate from surgery was 3.6 per cent, though as surgeons improved their skills the death rate went down – the last third of the patients who received surgery suffered only a 1.5 per cent death rate due to surgery. The report did find also that symptoms were greatly improved and deterioration was less in the surgical group.[6]

Although the operation will control the pain of angina not normally reduced by drugs, according to the *Drug and Therapeutics Bulletin* the beneficial effect is only temporary.[26] The angina returns, in about 50 per cent of cases, seven years after the operation.

Dilatation and curettage

The D & C is the most common operation that is performed in women. Over 120,000 such operations are performed each year. But is this type of operation, which puts the woman into hospital overnight and necessitates having a general anaesthetic, really needed? Many D & Cs are performed unnecessarily; for example young women with heavy, irregular or painful periods are traditionally given a D & C but it may often be possible to treat them simply with drugs, usually the Pill. There is also an alternative (to the D & C) called the *Vabra* or aspiration type of curettage which can be done on the spot without an anaesthetic. It works by negative pressure, sucking up tissues. It saves the woman a long wait for a hospital bed and means that she can go back to work the same day. An editorial in *The Lancet* points out that most women prefer an outpatient procedure such as this.[65]

D & C means dilatation (ie stretching of the canal leading to the cervix) and then curettage (ie scraping some tissue from inside the uterus (the womb)). With the *Vabra* method there is no need to stretch or dilate the canal as a thin metal tube only 3mm in diameter is carefully passed into the uterus through the cervix by the gynaecologist. This tube connects to a pump which creates a vacuum that sucks up the sample of uterine tissue needed for the performance of a biopsy.

This method dates back to 1935 and it seems strange that such a useful and economic measure has failed to become the main technique used for D & C operations. It has been compared in safety and effectiveness to ordinary D & C procedure many times over. *The Lancet* says that only women with a very large uterus or suspected pregnancy are unsuitable for this type of biopsy.

The Lancet also states that this method readily detects malignant disease, and because *Vabra* relies on a negative pressure to suck up tissue samples there is no possibility of accidentally pushing malignant cells up the Fallopian tubes into the peritoneal cavity. This is theoretically possible with the ordinary D & C technique because the pressure increases inside the womb with the dilatation process.

Research has found too that women accept this method in 71 to 97 per cent[66] of cases, and indicates that full explanation of the procedure makes it less unpleasant for patients. The manual dexterity of the gynaecologist also plays a part, but by most standards it is described in medical journals as an easy technique.

About two-thirds of D & Cs are performed on women suffering from irregular or heavy periods, another third are tests for fertility and a small percentage are carried out as annual screening tests for women on Hormone Replacement Therapy (for whom there is an increased risk of uterine cancer). All these could be performed instead with aspiration curettage. Only if a woman is unusually tense or plump is it necessary to perform the ordinary D & C. However, when there is suspicion of cancer in the uterus, it is vital for a gynaecologist to perform the conventional D & C, with an examination under anaesthesia.

Gallstone operation

Around 10 per cent of the general population between the ages of 45 and 69 have gallstones. Most of these people are unaware of their presence because they cause no problems. These 'silent' gallstones as they are called are often removed surgically for the spurious reason that they might cause 'trouble later on', ie cancer or inflammation of the pancreas and some other conditions. They are generally spotted during routine X-ray examinations or during surgery on the abdomen for some other complaint. But removal of the gall-bladder is the most risky operation that a patient can choose to have; and the risk increases with the age of the patient.

It is by no means agreed that gallstones should be automatically removed, as the surgery may do more harm than good. In Britain a survey in Wales found that almost 1 person in 10 over the age of 45 carried gallstones, and if everyone with a gallstone were operated on it would mean that hundreds of thousands of healthy people would undergo surgery. Until gallstones cause problems it appears to be quite unnecessary to remove them.[69]

American and Canadian hospital studios have found that there is a dramatic rise in the number of deaths from surgery at this operation as the patient's age increases.[70] A person over 60 years of age has a one-in-thirty chance of dying from the operation, whereas for a person under the age of 50, the risk is reduced to 1 in 500.

Autopsy reports have shown that there is a high incidence of gallstones present in patients who die from other diseases, so that the mere presence of the gallstone is clearly not itself a danger.[71] Gallstones may cause problems later on, including cancer, but as a person gets older the risks of surgery may not be worth the alleged advantages of having the gallstone removed. Until there are some symptoms, the operation is probably unnecessary, according to a study of the operation's effectiveness by Dr Garry Fitzpatrick.[72] The worst that could happen if a gallstone was left after being discovered accidentally, is that it could develop into gall-bladder cancer, but calculations by Dr Gary Fitzpatrick and his colleagues show that this is in fact extremely unlikely to happen. 'We calculate that the risk to people with gallstones of developing gall-bladder cancer over a 20-year period is only 4.3 per 1000.' They maintain. 'This is a very small risk and does not appear to justify the removal of gall-bladders solely as cancer prevention.' They point out that it is not even agreed that gall-bladder cancer is caused by the presence of gallstones; it is possible, they say, that the malignancy itself might cause the gallstones. But there may be reasons for removing the gall-bladder such as septicaemia, perforations and because of the pain they can cause.

Haemorrhoids ('piles')

'Once it is accepted,' states a *British Medical Journal* editorial of 1975, 'that haemorrhoids should not be treated unless they produce symptoms and that it is unnecessary to remove them completely in order to relieve symptoms, then it becomes clear that many patients are undergoing needless operations.'[76]

One expert, Dr J. Ferguson, writing in *Advances in Surgery* states that 'in general haemorrhoids need no treatment at all'.[77] *The Lancet* says that the aim should be 'to avoid hospital admission and operation if possible'.[78] Clearly nowadays surgery is being abandoned for the treatment of haemorrhoids. Instead, if anything at all, a non-surgical technique called 'rubber band ligation' is gaining in popularity. This consists of tying the vein responsible for discomfort with a tight rubber band, specially made for the purpose. Dr D. Steinberg and others looked at a group of patients who had been treated in this way. After more than three years 89 per cent of these patients were still cured though a complete lack of symptoms was found in only 44 per cent.[79]

The *British Medical Journal* maintains that rubber-band treatment is a quick and simple procedure requiring no anaesthetic and that it can be undertaken by an experienced GP. It says that there is 'mild discomfort, but complications are rare and the patient usually returns to work the next day'. The band works by cutting off the blood supply to the irritating veins and results in the haemorrhoids just falling away from the skin.

Patients with early piles are advised to take up a diet which ensures that they do not strain their bowels, ie a high-fibre diet, with plenty of bran and wholemeal bread for example. *The Lancet* adds that the operation for piles or haemorrhoids should be reserved for those who have severe third-degree piles, or for those in whom all other methods have failed.

Heart transplants

Whether you think this is 'a medical Concorde', as *The Lancet* suggests,[87] 'technologically magnificent but socially erroneous' *or* your last chance, the crucial question for everyone is whether or not it works.

In 1977 figures issued in the US[88] showed that of a total of 346 hearts that had been inserted into 338 patients (some needed more than one heart transplant), only 77 were still alive at the time of the survey; the longest-living survivor held on for over eight years. This means that less than 23 per cent of the heart-transplant patients survived, or in other words there is a one-in-four chance of survival with a new heart. Dr Norman Shumway, though less publicity-seeking than Dr Christiaan Barnard, is, in fact, the most prolific and determined heart transplanter in the world and is based in Stanford, California. He found that two-thirds of his heart-transplant patients survived their first year after the operation, but this was reduced to 58 per cent by the third year. But this is as good (or as bad) as the survival figures following a kidney transplant from an unrelated donor, ie where the tissues do not match and there is therefore a greater chance of rejection of the graft.

British transplants carried out in 1980-81 are achieving the same type of survival rate as the Americans, now that the techniques have been refined. A leader in *The Lancet* in 1980 explains that the earlier 'largely disastrous results' of heart transplantation were caused by the misuse of immunosuppressive drugs (drugs that stop the body rejecting the heart) in already very sick patients.[56]

Hernia

It is four times more dangerous for a person aged 65 or over to have an operation for hernia than to go without an operation (and thereby risk having an emergency operation at some later stage) – so says a leading article in the *New England Journal of Medicine.*[73]

The risk of dying under surgery for a hernia is slightly greater than the risk of death associated with having an emergency operation for an untreated hernia. Hernias can be harmlessly carried around for many years without causing any discomfort or any medical problems. They can, however, sometimes become strangulated and require an emergency operation to prevent gangrene, but this is rare.[74]

American hernia specialist, Dr Duncan Neuhauser,[74]

has made a study of the benefits to elderly people from hernia surgery and concludes that the operation does not extend life, though it may improve the quality of life. Much will depend on whether the hernia sufferer is willing to wear a truss to support his rupture. Dr Neuhauser describes the two different attitudes of a pair of surgeons both suffering from hernia; one, who once used a truss, described it as 'dirty, tight, uncomfortable, hot and smelly'; the other surgeon, aged 69, had a painless hernia and decided to wear a truss instead of risking surgery.

A recent study in Jerusalem[75] has shown that many men can go about with hernias without even knowing that they have them, and clearly they do not bother many people. 459 males in Jerusalem were found to have clinical signs of a hernia yet only half of these men reported any discomfort; for the remainder it was of no significance. Two-thirds of these Jerusalem hernias had not been operated on and the author of the investigation Dr J. Abramson of the Hadassah Hospital, Jerusalem, comments: 'In spite of the risk of acute complications the large number of unrepaired hernias does not necessarily imply a need for intensive efforts to find and repair them. Even at age 75 or over national figures for deaths from hernia are only 2 per 1,000.' He concludes, 'It is clear that increased hernia surgery could not save many lives.'

Hip replacement surgery

'Let us hope that orthopaedic surgeons will soon master the problem of the infected prosthesis (ie artificial hip)' (editorial in *The Lancet*, 4 March 1978).

This is the concluding sentence of an editorial in *The Lancet* which states that infection after total hip replacement is highly likely to jeopardise the result of the operation. It reports that infection rates after surgery can vary from less than 1 per cent to as high as 11 per cent. Nevertheless, it does point out that this new technique has been the greatest technical advance in orthopaedic surgery in the last twenty-five years. Your doctor will no doubt tell you how marvellous it is, that is his job, but what about the possible hazards of this 'great technical advance'? What he is unlikely to tell you about is the serious problem of infection after an otherwise perfect operation. At worst, the hip may have to be removed and the patient will be left with a shortened limb and an unstable hip: 'a far cry from the hoped-for pain-free hip and normal gait' declares *The Lancet*.[67]

The patient may not become aware of any deep infection for as long as two or three years after the operation. The cause of such infection seems to be inadequate filtering of contaminated air in operating theatres. A survey done at the Mayo Clinic in New York[68] found that infected hips were twice as common after surgery performed in older operating theatres which had slower and more antiquated air-exchange systems than in new theatres (see Infections, page 24) equipped with faster air-changing devices. Infections were found to be nearly three times more common amongst patients who were having a second or further hip operation, also it was found that the longer the surgery took to perform the greater was the risk of infection.

Hysterectomy

'If she is convinced that the uterus is essential for orgasm there will be sex problems if it is removed.'

'If she expects horrendous menopause problems she will get them' (editorial in *The British Medical Journal*, 17 September 1977).

The surgical removal of the womb or uterus is without doubt necessary in cases of cancer, or precancerous conditions, but in the great majority of cases, this operation is not performed for that reason. Instead, it is often performed unnecessarily: as a way of sterilising women; at the request of patients who think it may solve their problem of depression; as a way of stopping irregular menstrual bleeding and menstrual pain; and, finally, merely to prevent, 'trouble' later on, 'trouble' being the doctors' euphemism for cancer.

However, the risks and consequences of this operation make it a highly questionable procedure. Hysterectomy rates are double in America and Canada compared to those in Britain,[80, 81] and the operation is much more common in America amongst the wives of doctors and surgeons,[82] which suggests that as informed consumers they know what is good for them or, alternatively, that the wives of surgeons trust their husbands infallibly. Sixty per cent of the wives of American surgeons, but only 30 per cent of the American population and only 15 per cent of women in England have had a hysterectomy. This huge variation in the incidence of the operation strongly suggests it is performed unnecessarily on many occasions. As Dr John Bunker points out, in his survey of this operation,[82] 'It seems unlikely that the prevalence of gynaecological disease varies to any such large degree and therefore, we assume that they are being performed for markedly varying reasons, or that access to gynaecological care varies widely, or both.'

Whether a woman gets the operation or not depends more where she lives and on the attitude of the doctors than on the existence of any symptoms. It has been found that in Vermont, USA, the amount of womb surgery performed depends strictly on the number of surgeons working in the various areas of the state, so that the incidence of surgery has little to do with the incidence of disease.[83]

'There are a good many potential unpleasant side effects associated with the operation and the recovery is prolonged compared to other abdominal operational procedures. It may be several months before the patient feels that she can return to her pre-operative level of activity. Complications of surgery are common and troublesome, most notably urinary-tract infections, which are reported in a high percentage of women following hysterectomies.'[80] One survey found that recovery was 11.9 months for hysterectomy compared to 3 months for appendix operation.[80] But the major drawback of the operation (apart from the risks of surgery, which increase with age) is the depression experienced afterwards. It is like an exaggerated form of the menopause according to one researcher. 'The fact that psychiatric illness is more common in women who have had hysterectomies than amongst the female population as a whole is common knowledge in the medical profession,' says Jean Robinson in the *New Women's Health Handbook*.[84] She dismisses the popular view held by gynaecologists that women with gynaecological complaints are prone to be psychologically unstable anyway. Instead she urges that women should be spared the operation and given psychotherapy. Unfortunately women will need even more psychotherapy after the operation than before it.

Women with psychiatric illness have been found to be more than ten times more likely to have further mental problems *after* a hysterectomy, according to a study by Dr Montagu Barker on over 700 women who had hysterectomies. He also found that women who had never been to a psychiatrist were five times more likely to do so after having the operation.[85]

Another, earlier, study by Katharina Dalton, author of *The Menstrual Cycle,* found that dissatisfaction with the operation increased with time, and that after five years most women were not satisfied with the results of the operation.

In 1974 another study found that it was particularly younger women, under the age of 40, who were more likely to suffer depression after having a hysterectomy. Most important of all was the discovery that the majority of the women who became depressed following the operation need not have had it in the first place, as no abnormality was found in the uterus of these patients. It had been removed for trivial symptoms such as bleeding,[86] according to researcher Dr D. Richards. He had also discovered with surprise that menopausal symptoms such as hot flushes were present even in women who had kept their ovaries, the organs which secrete the female hormone oestrogen.[86] The uterus itself then may have a hormonal secretion of its own, suggests Dr Richards in trying to explain this unexpected finding.

Other side effects that researchers have discovered amongst women who had the operation are: loss of sexual interest, increase in accident proneness, petty crime such as shoplifting, shortened vagina. As the number of hysterectomies increases so will mental illness among the female population, says Jean Robinson.[84]

If a woman has also had her ovaries removed most gynaecologists will offer a hormone implant or tablets to replace the lost oestrogen hormone (see Hormone Replacement Therapy, page 247), but although this may reduce the symptoms of the artificial menopause created by the surgery, replacement therapy has its hazards. There is a slightly increased risk of breast cancer associated with

HRT, and then, when HRT is stopped, the menopausal symptoms return. HRT merely delays the incidence of hot flushes, it does not cure them. There is also the danger of becoming psychologically addicted to these oestrogen supplements. Of course the main danger – cancer of the uterus, known to be caused by HRT – is no longer a threat to a hysterectomised woman.

Balancing the risks of a hysterectomy operation

The risks associated with this operation have been evaluated in a remarkable book – *Costs, Risks and Benefits of Surgery* by John Bunker and colleagues – which calculates the possible losses and gains of surgery in terms of the number of days a woman would expect to live with or without surgery.[80] A healthy woman might improve her life expectancy by about one month if she has the operation. This is calculated by balancing the increased risk of death under surgery against the lowered risk of cancer which the operation secures for a woman. It is noted that for a 40-year-old woman 'death as a consequence of elective hysterectomy comes at an age when a woman is apt to have many responsibilities as a mother, homemaker or worker and when her enjoyment of life may be large. Even if she chooses not to undergo hysterectomy she may never develop cancer, or it may occur only many years in the future, at a time when responsibilities and enjoyment of life are apt to be less and when our ability to detect and treat cancer might be improved. *On the other hand* death from cancer is widely feared and many might gladly undergo a small risk of death today to lessen the risk of cancer in the future.'

A 50-year-old woman, it is stated, would have ten times greater risk under surgery if she suffered from moderately severe hypertension, and her life expectancy would be reduced by 81 days if she had the operation. But they point out that women have the operation in order to reduce symptoms and not to increase life expectancy.

Note a special hazard: Hysterectomy if used as such, is the most dangerous kind of abortion.

There is a much safer alternative to hysterectomy if a woman wishes to be sterilised: she can have her Fallopian tubes tied in a simpler and less risky operation (see Sterilisation, page 64).

Kidney transplants

Young people with kidney transplants have a 70 to 80 per cent chance of surviving at least five years, but older recipients have an even 50–50 chance of survival for that length of time. If the donor is related then the chances of a successful operation are some 20 per cent higher than normal. The major problem with kidney transplants is that of rejection; 'the surgical questions have been answered, the problem remains the need to find a way round the body's highly effective immune defence system which will destroy or reject any graft from another individual'.[89] A promising drug called Cyclosporin A which seemed an effective suppressant of the body's rejection mechanism has a fatal side effect: it can cause cancer. In a trial of this drug, at Addenbrooke's Hospital, Cambridge, reported in 1979, 3 out of 34 patients developed cancer of the lymph systems. In fact, the majority of deaths in kidney transplant patients are caused by drug side-effects.[90]

A massive survey of the drugs used to suppress the body's natural rejection of transplanted organs has been in progress since 1970 and has found that one type of cancer (of the lymphatic system) was sixty times more frequent in those taking the immuno-suppressive drugs; skin cancer incidence was also found to be significantly higher amongst transplant patients. These results are not totally negative however, for it was feared that these drugs might increase the incidence for *all* cancers, which they do not. These skin and lymph cancers only resulted in 16 deaths and account for only 3 out of every 100 deaths amongst transplant patients.[91]

Another problem of transplants is that as many as 18 per cent of patients develop ulcers after a kidney transplant. 'It is a serious disease in such patients, often complicated by perforation or haemorrhage and carries an overall mortality of 43 per cent,' says *The Lancet*.[92] Steroid drugs given to prevent rejection of the graft are known to increase the incidence of ulcers, but it is also known that people suffering from diseased kidneys also have a higher rate of ulcers anyway. Most ulcers arise in transplant patients who have had no previous symptoms, says the report. The majority of patients seem to require further surgery on their ulcers but drug treatment with the anti-ulcer drug

Cimetidine may be able to prevent this in future; only clinical trials will tell.

Lung cancer surgery: an alternative

Only one-fifth of lung cancer cases are suitable for surgery and two-thirds of those operated on will die within three years.[93] Put another way, less than 10 per cent of people with lung cancer who have surgery survive for more than five years.[94] Some investigations, however, show that the average survival rate is as high as 24 per cent, or even 33 per cent, if it is detected early enough and secondary cancers have not spread through the body, according to Dr Barbara McNeil.[95] She has studied the attitudes of patients who have been diagnosed as having lung cancer. She discovered that the vast majority of patients with lung cancer prefer to avoid surgery, which has not only high risks attached to it but a poor record of success. Instead, most patients when given a choice and an explanation of the risks, opt for the less risky alternative of X-ray treatment even though its long-term success rate is lower. She found that most patients felt it was more important to enjoy the next few months of their lives and avoid the high risks of surgery rather than worry about some future time years ahead.

'Clearly, however, most patients today are treated with the operation because of the overwhelming belief of most physicians that the operation is better,' comments Dr McNeil, adding that this is probably why few proper surveys have been made of the usefulness of radiation therapy. She has produced evidence to show that radiation therapy without surgery gives a survival rate of 21 per cent after five years, which is only slightly less than the survival rate with surgery. Surgery carries very high risks anyway: between one-twentieth and one-fifth of all patients undergoing surgery die from the operation itself. It is not surprising that patients prefer radiation treatment, when they hear the statistics. Survival after treatment for cancer is always measured by counting the number of patients who are still alive five years later, but Barbara McNeil points out that this is totally misleading for it can mean that if one patient dies two weeks after surgery and another carries on living for four years, they are *both* counted as having failed to survive for five years. 'This is a misleading statement and it ignores the patients' own attitude to risk-taking,' she argues. An early death can be caused by the operation whereas death after four years may be caused by the spread of the disease itself.

Dr McNeil found the patients showed a wide spectrum of attitudes towards the risk of treatment. Above all, her investigation shows the importance of explaining to patients all the benefits and risks of surgery and where possible leaving the final decision to them.

Prostate operation

This is the second most risky operation on average that a patient can undergo; it only trails behind the gall-bladder operation in its hazards. But some types of operations for a prostate condition are safer than others.

Although the rate for this operation is fairly static in Britain, around 25,000 per year, it more than doubled in the USA between 1965 and 1975 and it is now eight times more frequent in parts of America than in some parts of Britain. In Britain incidence of this operation varies by over 100 per cent according to where one lives. These marked variations in the incidence of the operation, depending on geography, strongly suggest that in America *and* Britain, unnecessary operations are being performed.

'Why, then, has there been no concern expressed? The principal reason,' asserts Dr A. Wennberg,[96] 'seems to be that the urologist (ie a specialist in conditions of the urinary system) has not broken rank to question.' 'This is in marked contrast to the sharp professional disagreements surrounding hysterectomy, gall-bladder operations and tonsillectomy,' comments Dr Wennberg, trying to stir things up a little!

Nevertheless, there are two distinct camps, says Dr Wennberg. The first group believes in early intervention – as soon as there is any sign of a urinary obstruction, operation is advised, whilst the patient is still relatively young. The second group believes that the risks of surgery should be delayed as long as possible, so that an operation may never become necessary. The issue then rests with the patient and his consideration of the effect of the operation on his quality of life: if he decides that he can happily get by with a mild prostate condition then he may feel a lot happier and less worried, having avoided a risky operation.

The first signs that an operation may be necessary are an increased urgency and frequency in peeing. The flow of urine can become blocked by the pressure of the prostate gland which compresses the urethra. The main reason why the death rate is so high for prostate operation is that it is mainly performed on elderly patients who are much greater risks in surgery generally (see page 27).

Another reason for the high death rate associated with the operation is the resulting bleeding and infection that follow from one particularly dangerous form of operation, in which the prostate is cut out from above through the abdomen. However there is another much safer operation called the transurethral resection – but unfortunately this demands a high degree of skill to do well. In this operation a fine surgical instrument is inserted up the penis and the prostate is literally chipped away piece-meal. This type of operation is not only safer but requires a hospital stay only half as long as that required for the other types of surgery.[97] One in every ten men who pass the age of 40 will sooner or later need a prostate operation, according to an editorial in the *British Medical Journal*[116] But only 20 per cent of these operations are being performed using this safer method, which is virtually painless and has a death rate half that of the traditional 'open' technique. But the operation is difficult to perform without special training, and there simply are not enough surgeons trained in urology to bring it into wider use.

Sterilisation

'One third of the women in my clinic are complaining of after effects from sterilisation. At least one in ten who are sterilised regret their decision' – Professor Peter Huntingford, Professor of Obstetrics and Gynaecology.[117]

'A high percentage of women who have had tubal sterilisation complain later of menorrhagia (heavy periods) and dysmenorrhoea (painful periods)' – editorial in *The Lancet*.[1]

There are two main types of operation used to sterilise

women: the first and probably the safest is the simple tubal ligation (but see below). In this operation the Fallopian tubes are simply cut in two, by making an incision in the abdomen. The second type is called a *laparascopic sterilisation* because it is performed with the aid of a thin periscopic tube called a laparascope which is inserted into the abdomen and allows the surgeon to see the position of the Fallopian tubes. He then inserts another thin instrument carrying a heating element which cauterises the Fallopian tubes and blocks them off.

Both operations sound simple enough yet the laparascopic sterilisation is often followed by heavy, painful and irregular periods. Also published reports suggest the operative risks of laparascopic sterilisation may be of the same order as those of hysterectomy, according to an editorial in *The Lancet.*[1] (See page 57 for the risks associated with hysterectomy.)

As many as 1 in 5 of all women who are sterilised have a hysterectomy sometime during the following ten years, according to a study made by Dr M. J. Muldoon,[2] because of problems with their periods. *The Lancet* also points out that symptoms such as increased bleeding following a sterilisation 'become more common with the passage of time'.[1] It raises the possibility that women who are used to the light periods associated with being on the Pill 'may dislike their normal periods when these return after sterilisation'. There have been no large-scale controlled studies of the effects of sterilisation on women, but a case study by Dr J. Neil and colleagues[3] of women who had been sterilised by tubal ligation or by laparascopic diathermy (cauterisation) found that increased menstrual loss and pain were significantly higher amongst sterilised women compared to the wives of men who had been vasectomised.

What is the safest operation: latest findings
There is now increasing pressure against using any method of sterilisation which involves heating the Fallopian tubes by diathermy or electrocoagulation. Plastic or metal clips are much safer, as they do less damage to surrounding tissues and make reversal of sterilisation possible.

An editorial published in the *British Medical Journal* says that, despite reports of burns of the abdominal wall and high pregnancy rates, electrocoagulation is still being used even in some British teaching hospitals.[118] 'Requests by patients for reversal of sterilisation are now focusing attention on the extraordinarily destructive effect of this procedure'.

According to the *BMJ*, it is essential to perform the least destructive form of sterilisation possible because an increasing number of women (and vasectomised men) are asking for reversal operations. It should only be done at the patient's own request and not immediately following an abortion or delivery of a baby. Not only may a woman be unable to make sound decisions at these times, but sterilisation is less successful when performed at these times and results in above average rates of pregnancy.[119]

Tonsils and adenoids

The removal of the tonsils and adenoids is the most commonly performed useless operation in the western world. Studies have repeatedly shown that this operation fails to improve health yet in Britain it still remains the second most popular operation, where the latest figures available show that 93,000 children have the operation annually. It is still the main reason for admitting children to hospital. In America over a million of these operations are performed each year. Rates are falling but are still ridiculously high on both sides of the Atlantic. Not only is the operation of no benefit to health but investigations have shown that children without tonsils are four times more likely to suffer from polio,[98] and three times more likely to have childhood cancer (Hodgkin's disease).[99]

'The tonsils have been subjected to a widespread uncontrolled experiment over the past half century. At times and in certain segments of society less than half the children have reached adulthood with intact organs.'[100]

An indication of the uselessness of this surgery is given by the waiting lists for this operation in British hospitals. On average a child must wait twenty-seven weeks before having the operation, longer than for any other common type of surgery.[101] There is some sense in having such a long waiting list since children might recover spontaneously in this time and never suffer the operation.

An interesting event in Australia lends support to this view. When a polio epidemic struck Australia in the early fifties a batch of 681 children were forced to postpone their tonsil operations. When they were re-examined eighteen months later more than one-third were found not to need the operation.[102] Also, at Birmingham's Children's Hospital, a study in 1972 found that half the children on the waiting list improved spontaneously, ie without any treatment at all.[103] Another study in America followed 5,000 children for ten years, half of whom had their tonsils removed and the other half did not. No difference was found between the two groups in their incidence of colds, sore throats and upper respiratory infections.[104] Other studies in New York City, Cleveland, Ohio and England have obtained similar results.

Another clue showing that the operation is largely useless comes from the extraordinary variations in its popularity even within England (the rate of surgery generally is double in America compared to England so American statistics perhaps are not appropriate). The Registrar General found that the operation was twenty-seven times more common in Boxhill, Surrey, than in Northern Birkenhead, for example,[105] without any adverse effect on those in Birkenhead who did not get the operation. Clearly it is, or was, more popular amongst the middle-classes to have a tonsil operation.

Swollen tonsils confuse parents and doctors alike because it is perfectly normal for the adenoids and the tonsils to become swollen in most children as a result of doing their natural job: filtering the air that the child breathes and trapping harmful bacteria. Both organs act as a net, a protective mechanism, and when they work hard they can become swollen and infected. It is perhaps not surprising that polio and cancer rates are lower in children who still have their tonsils as these organs act as barriers to infection.

A possible reason for performing the operation in the 1940s and 1950s might have been the lack of antibiotics in those days, but nowadays most authorities recommend that any such throat infections will clear up on their own or with the use of antibiotics. It is only necessary to operate in the case of an obstruction, says Professor Archibald Cochrane, the man who has destroyed more sacred cows in medicine than any other in his classic work on useless medical treatment called *Effectiveness and Efficiency.*[106]

The most popular reason cited for performing the operation is that the young child, aged between 4 and 6, has got tonsils that are too big ('hypertrophy' in medical jargon). But by the time the child has reached the age of 7 the tonsils that were considered too big are now of normal size.[107] 'Four year olds with abnormally large tonsils become 7 year olds with ordinary tonsils because of their relatively quicker growth,' says one expert.[108]

The symptoms of infected tonsils and adenoids may be caused by an allergy to environmental substances or to certain foods[104] and this is another avenue that parents and doctors should explore if drugs fail.

Enlarged tonsils naturally shrink as children get older. Before surgery is contemplated, one American surgeon[104] recommends that for adenoid infections 'decongestants, allergy therapy, antibiotics and drainage through ear drum puncture' should be considered. Finally, he advises that parents should wait a year even when the operation is indicated by symptoms, as often the symptoms will disappear spontaneously before the operation is performed.

It has been found that the smoking habits of parents can also give rise to even more of these operations being performed unnecessarily. A remarkable survey recently carried out in France has shown that the operation is far more common amongst the children of parents who smoke cigarettes.[109] Dr G. Said discovered this fact by giving questionnaires to nearly 4,000 pupils at nine different secondary schools in Paris. Their answers showed that as the number of cigarettes smoked by mothers and fathers increased so did the likelihood of the operation increase in their children. Intermediate rates of surgery were found for children whose fathers smoked a pipe or cigars.

The link between smoking by parents and respiratory disease in their children has been shown on a number of occasions before. The incidence of pneumonia and bronchitis was found to double if a parent smoked and another study found that the occurrence of a cough in school children was directly related to smoking in parents.

Two further problems bedevil the parent who still (after all this?) thinks that his/her child should have the operation. The first is the real hazard of surgery: death rates for

'Mon petit, only 300 more tins of tobacco for me to smoke and we'll have enough coupons to pay for the tonsils operation, and that'll get rid of your sore throat!'

tonsillectomy (the technical name for this operation) have been estimated at between 1 in 1,000 to 1 in 5,000. Under the very best conditions this operation is eight times more hazardous than the Pill.[110] Taking the most conservative estimate of a death of 1 in 5,000 it means that in Britain 19 children each year will die from having the operation.

A further problem is the psychological damage to a young child through putting him/her in hospital. This alien environment full of odd strangers and the separation from parents is said by some psychologists to do lasting psychological damage[111] (see Children in Hospital, page 15). Tonsils are a first line of defence – they should not be taken out. One surgeon says: 'This is the operation I least like doing. I would prefer to operate for cancer on an old man than a young child for the removal of tonsils.'[112]

Final word: the one symptom for which the operation is required

There is only one relatively rare condition that does require the tonsils and adenoids to be surgically removed. When they become obstructed they can interfere with breathing and result in a shortened supply of oxygen getting into the brain and heart. This is a serious condition which can be diagnosed by a doctor; there are various symptoms such as high blood pressure. This genuine indication for the operation will not necessarily be accompanied by enlarged tonsils or adenoids; an unusually large epiglottis (the flap of tissue behind the tongue) may be an important sign, though.

Ulcer surgery

The surgical treatment of duodenal ulcers has been virtually abandoned in the last two or three years with the advent of a new drug called Cimetidine (ie Tagamet). Millions of people around the world are now taking this drug which works quite well to control the pain caused by ulcers, but does not actually cure them. It should always be tried first, according to Dr M. Dronfield of Nottingham General Hospital, as it avoids surgery which has definite risks. Dr Dronfield explains that if one chose not to operate on all bleeding ulcer patients then some would die, but on the other hand, if one operated on *all* ulcer patients then *too many* would die. The problem is to find the best level at which surgery saves lives. 'The surgical treatment of patients admitted to hospital with bleeding peptic ulcer has never been subjected to controlled clinical trial, despite the fact that a substantial proportion of the deaths in these patients are post-operative,' says Dr Dronfield.[113]

Most routine and non-emergency surgery is performed on non-bleeding but painful ulcers. There are a whole variety of operations possible. Parts of the stomach can be removed, or the vagus nerve can be cut (vagotomy) to prevent the stomach secreting acid. All these different kinds of ulcer surgery have their own pros and cons. The larger operations involving the removal of the stomach often result in very severe symptoms after meals: 'the dumping syndrome'. But before surgery is attempted nowadays drug treatment is generally tried first, as surgery carries a much greater risk.

No one has compared the drug Cimetidine with surgery so far, but trials show that it makes no difference to bleeding ulcers. The main question that remains is the long-term effect of the drug and it is clearly linked with a number of problems. Some ulcer patients will have to remain on it for years and until the drug has been in use for a good many years its long-term safety remains in doubt. Fears have been raised in the correspondence columns of *The Lancet* and the *British Medical Journal* that Cimetidine may be associated with an increased risk of gastric cancer or that it may mask cancer. But since so many ulcer patients are now taking this drug, it is argued that some people who already have cancer will anyway be taking it (see page 234 for information on the hazards of Cimetidine).

Vasectomy

Unless you live in India under Mrs Gandhi's government you may still choose *not* to have a vasectomy. It has been reported that between 1975 and 1976, she enforced compulsory sterilisation on 10 million Indian males under threats of physical violence to any who refused the operation. To we more fortunate people in the West, the main questions of the procedure arise from its long-term safety. Its effectiveness in preventing conception is pretty good, though it may take as long as six months after the operation for sperm to be completely blocked off by the cutting of the vas deferens.[114] During this time alternative methods of contraception must be used.

One study demonstrates that vasectomy is not always completely effective first time around. In 1972, 1,000 vasectomies were performed by the Family Planning Association's clinic in London: and six men still remained fertile. When a second operation was performed on these patients it was discovered in one that the cut ends of the vas deferens had spontaneously re-united. In another patient an additional vas deferens was found to exist. Until sperm tests show the operation to be a complete success other forms of contraception must be used.[115]

The most worrying factor is the production of sperm antibodies in the blood. Following the operation sperm are still made in the testicles and as their passage is blocked they may enter the bloodstream. (Only castration – the removal of the testicles themselves – actually stops the body from manufacturing sperm; it also stops production

71

of testosterone, resulting in high voice, loss of beard and other undesirable side effects.) A 1979 report in *The Lancet*[114] found that 2 out of 3 men sterilised by vasectomy produced antibodies to their own sperm which persisted for about five years after the operation. Although there is no information yet available of the long-term effects of these antibodies, animal experiments on vasectomised rabbits and guinea pigs showed that inflamed testicles and changes in the cell structure of the kidney could occur after the operation.

Another possible hazard from vasectomy is heart disease. A study of vasectomised monkeys[114] found that the operation increased the incidence of atherosclerosis (hardening of the arteries). Food high in fat content was fed to ten monkeys; five of them were vasectomised following which all the monkeys remained on this high-fat diet for a further ten months. When the monkeys were killed and examined under a microscope, the vasectomised ones had a significantly greater degree of blocked arteries. All of these monkeys produced antibodies to their own sperm. Studies of humans vasectomised have only been short term so far but an American study of 400 vasectomised men has found no increase in heart disease or hormone diseases after three years. Another initial study of 4800 American vasectomised men has not found any increased signs of heart disease after five years when compared to 24,000 non-sterilised men.[57]

Another consideration that must be looked at is the possibility of reversing the operation. Fertility can often be restored after a vasectomy because sperm is still produced. Its passage is simply blocked by the operation.

In a recent review of over 2,500 cases of attempted vasectomy reversal, 49 per cent of men produced normal sperm again and 21 per cent of their wives became pregnant. Some figures show as many as 70 per cent of wives becoming pregnant after a reversal, according to *The Lancet*.[58] The best results are achieved when the operation is reversed using micro-surgery, ie performed under a special microscope, a technique commonly used in some centres to reverse female sterilisations. 'With good surgical technique vasectomy reversal should restore fertility in over 50 per cent of cases.' But 'if the operation is unsuccessful, the scrotum should be re-explored', says *The Lancet*.

The final factor that may put off men from having the operation, is the fear that the operation may affect their libido, or make them impotent. But there is *no* evidence that a sexually contented and non-neurotic male will have any sexual difficulties following the operation. It has been reported by the Simon Population Trust who carried out a study of over 1,000 vasectomised males that frequency of sexual intercourse is sometimes higher after the operation. This is considered by experts[120] to be a neurotic response to feelings of sexual emasculation and not a healthy reaction to the operation.

4

Birth

Introduction

Hospital birth with all its advanced technology and electronic and chemical extras has much in common with sliced white bread. We know that it does you no good, that it has been shown to be harmful, dehumanising and unnatural, but it remains the most commonly used because it is convenient, it suits modern living very well, it can be tailored around the 'needs' of modern society and most of all it benefits the industry but not the consumer.

The medical treatment of childbirth

In many ways the manner in which doctors treat childbirth encapsulates all the problems of medicine which this book is trying to warn the reader about and trying to identify. The majority (over 70 per cent) of births in Britain are normal and straightforward and do not require any medical treatment. But, of course, there is a minority of pregnant women who do need special medical attention to ensure that they have a safe birth and a healthy baby. But the techniques and technology which have been developed to help these high-risk women have over the years been extended and they are now put to use in perfectly healthy women, who do not actually need this medical razzmatazz. Electronic monitoring of the foetus, artificial induction, episiotomy, powerful addictive painkillers and so on, have become standard procedures of childbirth which are generally applied to pregnant women even though there is scant evidence that they need these medical aids.

Why should anyone suffer from the risks of a treatment that is unnecessary in the first place?
Whether it is a drug that does not work, or an operation that someone does not really need, the principle is the same: useless or unnecessary treatment exposes the public to hazards to which they need not subject themselves in the first place. Junk medicine will not disappear; according to medical sociologists there is now an epidemic of medically induced or doctor-induced illness in Western society.[1] Only the well-informed consumer/patient can protect him/herself from the hazards of this new epidemic.

The hazards of a hospital birth
Nearly every routine intervention that is made in hospitals in the course of delivering babies has been shown by serious investigations to damage either the mother or the baby or both. On the other hand, natural childbirth, without the use of drugs and anaesthetics, out of hospital, has been repeatedly found to produce healthier babies.

'Well Mrs Van Eyck, either you're 8 ½
months pregnant, or you're not telling me something.'

Only a small minority of high-risk mothers actually need hospitalisation to have their babies, yet in Britain 97 per cent of babies are born in hospital. In countries such as Holland and Finland, 70 per cent of babies are delivered at home, yet they have a much lower rate of stillborn babies.[2]

'Dutch obstetricians point out that when a normal woman's labour is unhurried and allowed to progress normally, unexpected emergencies rarely occur . . . The small risk involved in a Dutch home delivery is more than offset by the increased hazards resulting from the use of obstetrical medication and tampering which are more likely to occur in a hospital environment.'[2]

A large number of books could be written documenting the great volume of research studies that have now demonstrated the hazards of a hospital birth, but for the sake of clarity and brevity, it is useful to list them under the following fourteen headings. Each of these routine hazards is discussed in the ensuing sections.

1 the damage caused by anaesthetics given during labour;
2 damage caused by hormone drugs used to induce birth;
3 the unnecessary induction of labour causing premature birth;
4 harm produced by separating the mother from the child after the birth;
5 unnecessary and harmful Caesarian deliveries;
6 unnecessary and harmful X-rays of the unborn child;
7 hazards of electronic foetal monitoring;
8 hazards of lying down to give birth;
9 unnecessary shaving of the pubic hair;
10 unnecessary cutting of the vagina (episiotomy);
11 hazards of artificially rupturing the membranes;
12 anxieties caused by hospital environment;
13 negative effects of staying in bed during labour;
14 hazards of forceps delivery.

Could you have your baby at home?

More than 70 per cent of women could have their babies at home because they are at low risk. This score chart originally appeared in the *Sunday Times* Lifespan series on

The Art of Body Maintenance. It claims that if you score 2, or less than 2, points then you are of low risk.

Unmarried	1
More than 30 years old	1
Non-European	1
Previous baby died	2
3 or more abortions	2
Previous Caesarian	1
Previous malformed child	1
First baby	1
Fourth or later baby	1
Kidney or heart disease	4
High blood pressure	2
Diabetes	4
Anaemia	1
Rhesus blood complication	3
Height less than 5′ 2″	1

NB The score of 1 recommended for a 'previous Caesarian' seems surprisingly low according to some doctors.
(Adapted by Oliver Gillie from A. D. Haeri et al, *J. of Obst. and Gyn. Brit. Com.*, July 1974.)

There are only four requirements for a home birth, says Professor of Obstetrics and Gynaecology Norman Morris: a telephone; efficient transport to a hospital (in case of an emergency a flying squad ambulance should be standing by); a midwife and a doctor capable of carrying out resuscitation; and a home that is not off the beaten track or hours away from a hospital. These conditions were described by Prof Morris at a symposium held at the Royal Society of Medicine in February 1981, organised by the National Childbirth Trust.[3]

What is the safest place for birth?

'Most members of the medical profession are convinced that all births are safer if they take place in hospital under the care of a consultant obstetrician,' writes Dr Marjorie Tew in *The Lancet*.[4] She then proceeds to show that the incidence of stillbirths and newly-born babies dying is actually *higher* in hospitals, when compared to the figures for deliveries at home. She writes, 'Doctors have to accept that for as long as there have been reliable records, rates of stillbirth and neonatal (newly born) death have been higher, usually much higher in consultant hospitals than at home or in general practitioner maternity units.' The figures support her arguments, for there were over 27 deaths per 1,000 births in consultant hospitals, but only 4.3 deaths in homes and 5.4 in general practice maternity units (see page 80). Dr Tew skilfully tackles the usual objection that 'of course home deliveries are safer, because only the non-risk mothers are allowed to have their babies delivered at home'.

In fact, Dr Tew's analysis of statistics obtained from the Registrar General and the Office of Population and Census Statistics shows that it is not true that all high-risk births actually take place in hospital. Only a 'small part' of the increased risks of a hospital birth can be explained away on this basis. Dr Tew cites evidence from a report called *The British Births Survey* 1970 which collected together the risk factors that mothers face when having a baby. It was put together in order to try and explain the great geographical differences in the numbers of babies that are stillborn. It considers factors such as: the mother's age, her social class, the number of children she has already had, her previous medical experiences in child-birth, any abortions or Caesarian deliveries and any other medical risk factor such as high blood pressure or diabetes. Dr Tew accepts that this research does explain away a great deal of the number of baby deaths that occur in hospitals, but she claims that there still remains a large number of baby deaths in hospitals which cannot be explained away in those terms. Most important of all perhaps is her argument that hospitals, if their procedures are benefiting the patients, should really have *lower* numbers of baby deaths, yet they consistently have *higher* numbers of babies dying at birth. If the risks of stillbirth were as small in hospital as they are at home then there would be 26,000 fewer baby deaths each year, according to Dr Tew.

She concludes that knowledge of the risks of childbirth have been immensely advanced by the impartial analysis of successive birth surveys, but then adds plaintively that that 'knowledge would be advanced even further if the place of delivery were recognised as a risk factor and the relevant data analysed with equal impartiality'.

In case the impression is given that Dr Tew is a lone doctor bent on undermining hospital care of the newborn with the aid of elegant statistical arguments, it is worth looking at how another objective expert considers the issue. Professor Archibald Cochrane, until recently the head of the Medical Research Council's Epidemiology Unit in Cardiff and one of the most internationally distinguished epidemiologists, writes about hospital births policy in his influential book *Effectiveness and Efficiency*. He says that without any evidence to support their conclusion 'the Peel Committee (1970) suggest that provision be made for all deliveries to take place in hospital'. He points out that if one looks at different areas of England 'there is little to show that a high rate of hospital admissions is linked to low rates of baby deaths. This seems very thin evidence on which to demand hospital beds for all mothers.' In Holland, says Professor Cochrane, only 29 per cent of mothers have their babies in hospital, yet it has one of the lowest baby death rates in the world.

Dr Tew's and Professor Cochrane's views are supported by the evidence of dozens of researchers who have uncovered the serious hazards associated with medical intervention in normal births in hospital.

Home Births: Are mothers irrelevant? (the latest view)

'Many obstetricians regard the home deliveries issue as unimportant. To them the challenge of obstetrics is to reduce the perinatal mortality rate further, particularly in the lower social classes. The worry of a few – mostly middle class – women about where they have their baby is seen as almost an irrelevance' (report of a conference on pregnancy care in the 1980s at The Royal Society of Medicine).[5]

'For obstetric services to oppose home deliveries when they could produce no evidence that they were dangerous is an act of professional bullying' – Dr Luke Zander at the Royal Society of Medicine conference.[5]

A report of this meeting in the *British Medical Journal*

stated that most delegates were convinced that, when selection was careful, home births were safe. A Dutch obstetrician, Professor G. J. Kloosterman, supported free choice and stated that women with low-risk pregnancies should be able to choose where they wanted their baby delivered. The report admits that, in many parts of Britain, women who want to give birth at home are faced with the difficult (if not impossible) task of finding someone to deliver them. A Scottish man was fined in 1981 for delivering his wife's baby at home (they were unable to find a doctor willing to provide a home birth). The high rate of home births in Holland encouraged cooperation between home and hospital obstetric services. As a result *both* were safer and used less medical intervention, said Professor Kloosterman.

Delegates thought the British system could be revitalised to handle more home births and combine them with a *humanised* hospital service, with more women enjoying the experience of childbirth.

A safer place to be born

'The GP does not overreact with drips, machines and other interventions . . . thus he avoids exposing large numbers of normal mothers and children to the risks of unnecessary medical interference' (Dr G. N. Marsh, GP, writing about his general practice maternity unit).[6]

If a woman feels unhappy about having her baby at home, perhaps because she has been alarmed by stories she has heard, and is equally horrified by the procedures of the average maternity hospital, she may be lucky enough to live in an area where GPs – not hospital specialists – look after antenatal care and deliver babies. Such a unit, in Stockton-on-Tees, has managed to dramatically reduce the number of stillbirths by more than half the national and local averages. The secret of their success, claims Dr Marsh, writing in the *British Medical Journal*, is the continuing personal care and encouragement by a doctor who has known his patients for a long time, and also by the GP's reluctance to unnecessarily mechanise labour. Dr Marsh bemoans the fact that GPs as a whole have been made to feel less confident in dealing with pregnancy, because of the high proportion of artificially induced

80

labours and mechanised births in hospitals.

As the health of pregnant women steadily improves year by year and the age of having the first child gets lower, there is clearly *less* need for intervening in the pregnancies and births than ever before, argues Dr Marsh. His GP maternity unit consists of a team of receptionists and nurses to run antenatal clinics, midwives, health visitors to supervise the overall care of the pregnant women and to run relaxation classes and motherhood classes, a family planning nurse, social workers, marriage counsellors and local GPs of course! The GPs stay with their patients right through pregnancy and birth and are responsible for the birth itself. Only high-risk patients are referred to specialists. The general practioner unit in Stockton-on-Tees is used by almost every medical practice in the town and they have not only achieved a superior safety record compared to ordinary maternity hospitals, but also the practice shows a significantly higher percentage of spontaneous (non-induced) deliveries, fewer Caesarian sections and significantly fewer 'forceps' deliveries than hospitals in the neighbouring area of Newcastle. The reader will appreciate from the following sections that all of these procedures can be performed unnecessarily in a hospital at great risk to the mother and her baby. Caesarian deliveries, it is said, are performed sometimes just to give junior doctors a bit of practice![7]

The GP unit described also encourages breast feeding and the gentle delivery of the baby by the Leboyer technique of birth. Mothers are not kept in overnight but are returned home within a few hours of the birth. Ironically, the only drawback about this unit is that since it moved in 1968 from a maternity home (its original premises) to the first floor of a district hospital the number of patients receiving specialist care has risen dramatically. Since then more babies have been delivered by hospital specialists with the unfortunate result that since 1968 the number of induced deliveries and forceps deliveries has doubled. Nevertheless even with these increases their record is far superior to the maternity hospitals elsewhere in Britain. Their medical intervention rate is still half the national average and their stillbirth rates are also half the national rate.

The hazards of narcotics given to unborn babies

'Many of the discomforts of labour are in practice the result of pethidine' (a painkiller given to mothers in childbirth) – Professor Kieran O'Driscoll.

Painkilling drugs and anaesthetics given to mothers during their labour stage of pregnancy pass rapidly through the placenta into the baby's bloodstream, in fact virtually every drug given to mothers is quickly absorbed into the bloodstream of the unborn child. 'The placenta is not a barrier but a "bloody sieve" ' (as one expert has put it).[8] The harmful effects on the unborn child of these adult doses of powerful narcotic drugs that block the nervous system, have been studied by many investigators.

Dr Martin Richards of Cambridge University Medical Psychology Unit discovered that babies exposed in the womb to painkillers, were more sleepy and unresponsive, had shorter feeds and difficulty in staying awake whilst their mothers tried to feed them.[9] They were also slower to breathe and cry at birth compared to non-drugged babies. Their mothers had to work hard to get them to suck and as late as thirty to sixty weeks after their birth Dr Richards noticed that the drugged infants were less closely involved in social play with their mother. These infants also showed an increase in self-stimulation activities such as thumb-sucking. The babies under study had been exposed to a popular drug called Pethilorfan, which is made from the narcotic pethidine, a morphine-type drug that is addictive. It used to be commonly given to mothers in labour, not only by doctors but also by midwives who are permitted to give injections of this drug. Some sedatives such as Valium given to mothers in labour can also badly affect the baby's sucking reflexes for up to four or five days after birth, according to one study (see page 166 for details). 'One of the problems of pethidine is that if it is given too early before about two-thirds dilatation of the cervix, for example, it tends to slow down labour,' comments Sheila Kitzinger.[10] As evidence, she quotes Professor Kieran O'Driscoll[11] on the side effects of this drug. 'Nausea, vomiting, disorientation and mental confusion lead to the failure to cooperate especially in the 2nd stage of labour. Many of the discomforts attributed to labour are in practice the result of pethidine . . . labour can be transformed easily into a nightmare experience by pethidine after which the mother may remain unaware that her baby is born and may suffer a profound sense of depression which continues into the next day.' When Sheila Kitzinger did a survey on attitudes towards childbirth she found that 'many described the effects of pethidine as unpleasant', women reported that the rest of labour was a 'complete haze', or they were 'nearly asleep' during delivery, especially when they had no choice about taking the drug. But if they had a close relationship with their midwife then a small dose of pethidine was enough to ease the pain. Sheila Kitzinger comments that 'it looked as if, in fact, analgesic drugs were sometimes used in place of good emotional support in labour. When there was understanding support from midwives, this took the place of – and was much more effective than – pharmacological pain relief.'

The epidural problem

The other kind of anaesthetic given to mothers in labour is the epidural, which is an injection around the spine anaesthetising the nerves which supply the lower part of the body. With an epidural the mother can remain awake and mentally alert and conscious of her birth experience, without feeling pain. Unfortunately, as a result it also blocks the spontaneous delivery of the child. A number of hazards are linked with the use of 'epidural blocks' as they are called. The major risk is the increased need for a delivery using forceps, because the mother is no longer able to push the baby out. The use of forceps is five times more common with epidurals, according to a survey by Dr I. Hoult and his colleagues.[12] His team found that a forceps delivery was especially common in first-time mothers having an epidural, where 7 out of 10 mothers were found to need a forceps delivery. The position of the baby's head was also pushed the wrong way round three times more often in mothers having epidurals. Only when the drug has worn off was it easier for mothers to push the baby out without the aid of forceps, but even then the chances of the baby's head being the wrong way round were still as great in 1 out of 5 mothers having epidurals. The use of forceps to deliver the child can increase the risk of haemorrhage inside the baby's skull, and cause damage to the facial nerve or the nerves in the neck.[8]

The other hazard of the epidural block is the effect on the heart of the baby. 'It is difficult to give spinal anaesthesia (epidural block) without any change in the maternal blood pressure and even if pressure is restored by the use of drugs there is no assurance that circulation remains normal through the womb,' according to Dr L. Stanley James, the Chairman of the Committee on Fetus and Newborn at the American Academy of Pediatrics.

Epidural may cause brain damage

After the epidural is given to the mother there is a temporary drop in the heart rate of the unborn baby which means that a shortage of oxygen is occurring which may result in brain damage. 'Any neurological damage may not be recognised for several years,' comments Doris Haire in her excellent review of modern childbirth practices, *The Cultural Warping of Childbirth.*[2] She adds that it is ironic that 'this transient drop in oxygen reaching the fetus is taken so lightly as no one would purposely inject a drug or apply a device to a newborn child which would possibly decrease the oxygen supply for even a few minutes without grave cause'. Tests on the physical and mental abilities of the newly born show that abnormally low scores were three times more common amongst mothers who had received epidural blocks.[13] The tests used are the classical 'Apgar' tests which score the baby's heart rate, breathing effort, muscle tone, reflexes and the tone of its skin on marks out of 10. These test scores obtained at the time of birth have been found to be an accurate indicator of the baby's attentiveness and intelligence up to one year or more afterwards. One researcher found the babies with scores of 7 to 9 were significantly less attentive after twelve months than babies who scored all possible 10 marks.[14]

Anaesthetics given to mothers in childbirth can also decrease the affection and attachment displayed by the mother towards her baby. One study (described on page 97) has found that mothers who are less aware of their childbirth as a result of the painkillers/anaesthetics given to them, show less interest in their babies afterwards.[15]

Mothers should not necessarily assume that they will only be given painkillers if they ask for them or show signs of pain during childbirth. An investigation[16] has shown that it is the doctor's opinion of the mother's condition and attitude (which the doctor has formed *weeks beforehand*) which determines the kind and the amount of drug given to mothers in childbirth.

US childbirth expert Doris Haire has identified eight medical problems[8] associated with the use of local and general anaesthetics:

The eight hazards of epidurals

1   mother cannot eat or drink from the onset of labour;
2   mother's contractions must frequently be started with drugs, eg an oxytocin intravenous drug: 'the drip' as it is commonly known;
3   mother must be moved into a delivery room equipped for emergencies – as the anaesthetics increase the probability of needing to resuscitate the baby;
4   mother must be placed in the *lithotomy position* (lying down flat on her back, with her legs apart and feet strapped into stirrups) for delivery – she will not be in control of her legs, making it difficult for her to push the baby out of the womb;
5   the use of forceps delivery and an episiotomy (cutting of the vagina) will probably be needed to deliver the baby;
6   the infant's umbilical cord will be clamped very early on to allow immediate resuscitative measures and to reduce the baby's intake of drugs given to the mother;
7   the placenta (afterbirth) will be forced out of the mother with drugs, manipulation, or manually to prevent a haemorrhage in the mother;
8   it is always necessary to have a 'sugar drip' because of the risk of low blood pressure in the mother. Some mothers had died after a precipitous fall in blood pressure after the epidural is given.

adapted from Doris Haire[8]

Are mothers' natural painkillers increased during pregnancy?

One of the best reasons to avoid epidurals and other painkillers during pregnancy is that there is now evidence from animal experiments that the state of pregnancy itself reduces a woman's sensitivity to pain. Particularly during the latter stages of pregnancy, it is considered very likely that women automatically produce large quantities of the body's own natural painkilling substances, called endorphins. They are the body's own version of morphine – but because of their different chemical structure we do not get addicted to our own endorphins.

Experiments carried out on pregnant rats by Dr Alan Ginzler of Columbia University (USA) have shown that during the last 18 days of pregnancy they became increasingly tolerant of electric shock pains, especially in the last three days. But afterwards the rats' normal sensitivity to pain returns. Dr Ginzler believes that pregnancy activates the human endorphin system and probably protects women from the pain of childbirth.[17] If he is correct, artificial epidural anaesthetics or other synthetic painkillers may not only be unnecessary, but may also prevent the body's own painkilling agents from working, as they occupy the same chemical sites in the body.

The extra hazards of giving birth whilst lying flat on the back

Lying flat on the back with the legs up and wide apart, strapped into stirrups, otherwise tactfully referred to as 'the lithotomy position', has been shown to be an unnatural and harmful way to deliver a baby. Just as women who walk about during labour have healthier babies (see page 94), much the same type of benefits apply to women who adopt what is called the 'semi-sitting' position during delivery of their baby. Several researchers have shown that the lithotomy position (with the mother flat on her back) reduces the mother's blood pressure and consequently adversely affects the oxygen supply to the baby.[18] It also reduces the strength of the contractions and inhibits the mother's own efforts to push the baby out through her cervix. This in itself increases the probability of a forceps delivery, or having pressure applied to the 'fundus' (the top of the womb). The natural and spontaneous expulsion of the placenta (afterbirth) is also inhibited when lying on the back, and it may have to be removed manually or with the aid of drugs. There is an increased likelihood of having the vagina cut (episiotomy) because of the increased tension on the floor of the pelvis and the stretching of skin tissue around the vagina.

The healthy alternative to lying on the back in the lithotomy position is the 'semi-sitting position', with the back at a 45° angle and the legs lower down in a sort of armchair position. With this position many researchers in Australia, Russia and the USA have found that all of the aforementioned problems are eliminated or reduced.[19] In Holland, a country which has one of the finest records for survival at birth and a very high rate of non-hospital home deliveries (70 per cent), the semi-sitting position results in a much reduced use of forceps deliveries and the employment of fewer drugs in pregnancy and labour. Figures quoted by Doris Haire in her review *The Cultural Warping of Childbirth* show that forceps or vacuum extraction is used in only 4 to 5 per cent of births in Holland compared to a staggering 65 per cent in 'many American hospitals'. She points out that there are no physical differences in the size of Dutch women that make this practice any more easy to perform in Holland.

The dangers of drug-induced birth

'Jaundice is now a serious problem at this hospital,' wrote Dr Neil Campbell in the *British Medical Journal*[20] about Queen Charlotte's Hospital in 1975. He continued: 'It involves not only a hazard to infants but also much valuable time of laboratory and medical staff.'

This is a remarkable admission – that the rate of jaundice amongst babies born at Queen Charlotte's almost doubled (from 8.1 per cent to 15.4 per cent) after the hospital changed its methods of delivering babies. These changes included an increased use of oxytocin drugs (the drugs which are used to artificially induce birth), epidural anaesthetics (painkilling anaesthetics) and a change in the artificial feed given to normal infants. Several investigations have quite conclusively shown that the use of oxytocin to induce birth is linked with higher rates of the liver disease, jaundice, in the newborn. Jaundice in severe forms can become a cause of permanent brain damage, says Dr Campbell, because of the build-up of toxic substances in the body. Dr Campbell speculates that the anaesthetics given to mothers might also be contributing to the increase. The only factor which he rules out totally is the new baby feed that was introduced. It has been shown, though, that breast feeding results in healthier babies.

When Dr Ian Chalmers examined over 10,000 babies born in Cardiff between 1970 and 1972, he found that the incidence of jaundice was higher amongst artificially induced babies. The seriousness of their jaundice was directly related to the quantity of oxytocin that the mother received during labour. A secondary effect on these mothers and their babies was that they were almost twice as likely to have to delay their discharge from the hospital as a result of the jaundice in their babies.[21]

More recently, in 1979, Dr S. D'Souza[22] and a team at St Mary's Hospital, Manchester, found a similar pattern of oxytocin side effects amongst a group of 180 mothers that they studied. Again they found that the degree of jaundice was related to the dose of drug used on the mother. They report also that at St Mary's the rate of jaundice doubled (from 11 per cent to 23 per cent) amongst babies after commencement of the use of induction methods in 1971. So we have the same disturbing picture as at Queen Charlotte's in London. Dr D'Souza's survey found that when induction was performed by first piercing or breaking the membrane that holds the baby in the womb (amniotomy) and then giving the drug oxytocin to the mother, the baby suffered from an increased loss of red blood cells. He suggests that the baby's blood cells are damaged by the drug-induced contractions of the womb, whereas normally in nature there is a buffer of fluid in the womb to protect the baby from these violent movements. Every contraction reduces the amount of oxygen reaching the baby's brain. There are important implications arising from the finding, says Dr D'Souza: it means there are special risks associated with oxytocin use for premature babies and babies suffering from blood disorders. 'Clearly this is not an area for complacency since oxytocin is widely used in present-day obstetric management.'

The least-appreciated problem connected with the use of oxytocin is that the contractions it produces can be more violent than those produced by nature; they can be very sudden and their abruptness makes it extremely difficult for even the well-prepared mother to tolerate without the aid of painkilling drugs or anaesthetics, comments American childbirth expert Doris Haire.[23] In childbirth it would seem that one drug begets another drug. In natural child-birth the baby can tolerate the contractions of labour because the intensity of the contractions builds up only gradually.

The routine use of induction clearly poses many threats to the unborn child, and it has been shown that even when a baby remains inside the womb beyond the 41st week there is still no medical necessity to induce the infant. There is apparently no increase in risk to the baby nor any subsequent impairment in learning ability to the age of 7, according to the findings of *The British Births Survey*. [24]

The American government bans oxytocin for routine use
In October 1978 the US drug authority, the FDA, announced a ban on the use of oxytocin for inducing babies as a routine measure when there was no medical necessity to use it[25] (this is called an *elective* induction). The FDA listed the following side effects of an oxytocin-induced birth: uterine hypertonicity which means violent contractions of the womb; rupture of the womb; a slow pulse in the baby; and the premature delivery of the baby resulting in respiratory distress syndrome, damage to the central nervous system and possibly death.

The FDA does of course permit the use of oxytocin for certain medical problems such as diabetes, ruptured membrane, or rhesus negative blood group complications. For those women who must have an induced birth, the FDA insists that the oxytocin should be administered to them with the aid of an intravenous drip. The drip method allows the dose of this drug to be gradually increased until the patient experiences contractions.

Foetal monitoring – the electronic birth hazard
During the labour stages of birth, the unborn baby can be monitored electronically to make sure that it is getting enough oxygen. The natural contractions of labour can cause a reduced supply of oxygen to reach the baby across the placenta and this can result in the unborn baby suffocating before birth. To prevent such a stillbirth the heart rate of the baby is checked and electrodes are placed on the scalp which can indicate 'in theory' whether or not the foetus is receiving sufficient oxygen. The electrode is

passed through the cervix and clipped to the scalp of the foetus. The problem is that, wonderful as this technology may sound, it does not appear to have any good effect on the number of babies saved from brain damage or death during labour. Three studies from the USA show no increase in the number of babies saved although one Australian study has found some improvement.[26] In the United States it has been shown that electronic monitoring of the foetus has resulted in a distinct and unnecessary increase in the number of babies delivered by Caesarian section. More than 4 out of every 10 warnings that the foetus is in danger are false alarms, while nearly 1 in 5 babies who do really have oxygen problems go undetected.

Use of the more primitive monitoring techniques such as listening to the baby's heart with a stethoscope are less likely to result in an unnecessary Caesarian operation, according to American government researchers Dr H. Banta and S. B. Thacker.[27]

Electronic foetal monitoring includes the use of ultrasound: a sound picture of the unborn baby is obtained on a TV screen by radiating the baby with high-frequency sound waves by means of a probe rubbed over the belly of the mother. Electrodes can also be attached direct to the foetus to monitor the foetal heart rate.

Another disturbing method employs a small scalpel which is passed through the cervix to make a small wound in the baby's scalp so that a sample of blood can be collected through a tube. In theory this can also tell doctors about the baby's oxygen needs but it is often inaccurate. In the US the vast majority of hospitals use this type of electronic monitoring, with the result that over half the children born are monitored electronically.[27] It is also a widespread practice in Britain.

The US government report by Dr Banta and his colleages also found that monitoring of the heart rate can give false reports of distress in over one-third of babies. In one study, foetal distress was four and a half times less common in reality than the equipment indicated.

Hazards to baby from electronic monitoring

'The most immediate risk to the infant is laceration (wounding) by the electrode or by the knife that punctures the scalp. Infections of the scalp are common, occurring in up to 4 out of every 100 babies,' says Dr Banta.[27]

Babies born by Caesarian section are more likely to suffer from severe breathing difficulties and possible collapse (called in medical jargon the 'respiratory distress syndrome') as are all premature babies who have immature lungs. RDS is the major cause of death at the time of birth.

Mothers undergoing this electronic mechanised birth, and the subsequent surgery, will find themselves separated from their baby after birth. They will not be able to sit up and hold their babies. This may increase the risk of later child abuse, says Dr Banta. The maternal bond may be critically damaged by early separation and later maternal behaviour such as playing and fondling with the child may be adversely affected.

Is ultrasound safe?

'We need more information on both safety and efficacy before we can endorse the unrestrained use of ultrasound during pregnancy. Where there are clinical indications to use ultrasound then one hopes it will be used prudently while we await definite answers as to biological effects.' – Dr M. E. Stratmeyer of the Bureau of Radiological Health at the American Food and Drug Administration.[28]

The American public health watchdog body, the Food and Drug Administration, questioned the accepted safety of utrasound in 1979. They said, 'Increasing concern has arisen regarding the foetal safety of widely used diagnostic ultrasound in obstetrics. Animal studies report delayed neuromuscular development, altered emotional behaviour, EEG (brain wave) changes, anomalies and decreased survival.'[29]

Ultrasound radiation shows no signs yet of injuring the mother or baby and no chromosome damage is reported, but the American FDA is 'unwilling' to say it is safe in the long term until babies are followed up for many years after exposure to these rays. X-rays were commonly believed to be safe for the foetus until long-term studies showed they later caused leukaemia in childhood.

Hazards to mother from electronic monitoring and Caesarian operations

The uterus (womb) can be wounded by the electrodes or catheters (tubes) and so can the placenta. Compared to a normal delivery a woman having a Caesarian delivery is three to thirty times more likely to die in childbirth. The Caesarian operation is also linked with a greater incidence of anaesthesia psychosis, urinary-tract infections, trauma to other organs, infection, hernia, bowel obstruction, haemorrhage, respiratory infection and pneumonia, especially following the inhalation of stomach contents. If that was not enough, future children (who will probably also have to be delivered by Caesarian) will be born with a low birthweight, which is bad news. In one study, women who had Caesarians and electronic monitoring had a 40 per cent higher rate of uterine infection. Fever is one-third to one-half times more common in women who have Caesarians; more than half the women who have electronic monitoring before the Caesarian suffer from high fever afterwards. These enormously high rates of fever in mothers can be reduced with antibiotics, but as Dr Banta says: 'This places the mother at risk of side effects. Antibiotics also foster the growth of resistant organisms and complicate care of the newborn. Birth has to be a natural process in a healthy mother; now it has become an electronic experience.'

A negative emotional reaction to all the electronic technology by the mother could harm the baby; experiments with monkeys have shown that stress in the mother can cause stress hormones like adrenalin and noradrenaline to be released into her bloodstream. This release of hormones can reduce the pulse and blood pressure of the unborn baby and aggravate any breathing problems or may cause oxygen starvation.[30]

Shaving the pubic hair

A survey of 7,600 women who did not have their pubic hair shaved before giving birth has shown that this procedure is an unnecessary humiliation and that it does not reduce infection. In fact the rate of infection was *lower* in women who had been left unshaved. The procedure of shaving itself can result in cuts to the skin which can then become easily infected. The author of the survey suggests that the pubic hair can be more safely clipped with scissors instead of it being shaved.[31] Another investigation showed that unshaven mothers do not have any more bacteria in their pubic areas than mothers who shave.[32]

Another more recent study, by Dr Mona Romney and Dr Harold Gorden, has confirmed again that shaving is not beneficial to the mother.[33]

The Myth of the Enema

'It was clear that most of our patients disliked the enema and accepted it only because of the advantages claimed, especially a clean delivery. We found no evidence to support these claims.' – Dr Mona Romney and Dr Harold Gordon.[34]

The enema is given to women in labour because, according to the folklore, an empty bowel is thought to stimulate activity of the uterus and to reduce contamination and infection by faeces. But when Drs Romney and Gordon compared a group of mothers given enemas with those who had not received enemas they found that neither infection nor contamination of babies was reduced, nor was there any evidence of any effect on the duration of labour with the enema. Furthermore, the researchers reported that enemas caused 'distress to a few patients and discomfort to many'.

The only occasion on which an enema is justified is when a woman has not emptied her bowel in the past 24 hours and when there is 'an obviously loaded rectum', according to Romney and Gordon.

Episiotomy (cutting of the vagina)

The surgical widening of the vaginal opening is sometimes carried out if there are indications that the baby will be damaged if it is not delivered quickly. There is indeed the possibility sometimes that the baby will suffer oxygen shortage and consequent brain damage if it gets stuck too long in the womb. However, this procedure can be performed unnecessarily. Doris Haire (*The Cultural Warping of Childbirth*) points out that doctors will perform this type of surgery to shorten the second stage of labour, without the presence of any signs that the baby is distressed. *The British Birth Survey*[35] found that with a normal baby the second stage of labour can safely continue for as long as $2\frac{1}{2}$ hours without any risk of brain damage occurring. This important finding was based on the investigation of 17,000 babies who were studied up to the age of 7.[35] Also women who avoid this form of surgery are more likely to have a satisfactory sex life than are those who have had an episiotomy. Special exercises can be performed to strengthen the muscles of the vagina before and after childbirth, particularly to restore sexual enjoyment.

'Interviews with obstetricians, gynaecologists in many countries indicate that they tend to agree that a superficial first degree tear is less traumatic to the perineal tissue than an incision which requires several sutures for reconstruction,' says Doris Haire.[36]

Don't stay in bed during labour – your baby won't breathe properly

If pregnant women are encouraged to walk about during labour instead of staying in bed, they have labours which are more than 2 hours shorter than women kept in bed. They also have little or no need for painkillers or epidural anaesthesia; they have fewer and more efficient contractions, and five times less need for a forceps-assisted delivery of their baby. These remarkable differences were discovered when a study was recently made comparing two groups of women, who only differed in whether or not they were made to walk about during labour.[37] A total of 68 women were investigated with the aid of radio transmitters to measure the baby's reactions to the mother's movements. In this way it was found that the unborn baby also benefited from the mother's activity during labour. Compared to babies whose mothers stayed in bed, their heart beat was more regular and after birth they scored greater points on the Apgar test (see page 84). The explanation behind this finding is that when a mother lies on her back the unborn child receives less oxygen because there is increased pressure on the veins leading to the heart. As a result blood reaches the placenta, leading to a reduced oxygen supply for the foetus. Professor Mendex-Bauer, a Spanish obstetrician, has shown that a woman who lies flat on her back is not making the best use of the uterine contractions. The opening of the cervix is increased in size (dilated) more effectively in a standing position and consequently the mother does not feel as much pain, nor does the baby suffer from any breathing difficulties. (I am indebted to Sheila Kitzinger for drawing my attention to this research in her valuable book *The Experience of Childbirth*, Penguin 1978).[38] Sheila Kitzinger says, 'Almost any position is better than lying down on the back. Squatting, kneeling on all fours, walking around and lying on the side may all be comfortable. It is a good idea to change position frequently. So experiment to find how you are most comfortable.' Another champion of natural childbirth, American expert Doris Haire, comments that any 'activity that the woman does during labour distracts her attention from the discomfort of pains and encourages the more rapid engagement of the fetal head'.[39]

Do relaxation exercises really reduce the pain of childbirth?

A report published in the highly respected *Drug and Therapeutics Bulletin*[40] found that women interviewed after birth who had learnt relaxation techniques (which also aim to involve the *father* in the birth procedure) did feel some pain but they saw the pain as 'positive', 'functional', 'unimportant' or merely a 'side effect of contractions'. The *Bulletin* explains that according to the theory of psychoprophylaxis (as the technique is called) the pain sensations are the same as in an unprepared woman but the interpretation is different, making them seem less painful and threatening. The *Bulletin* refers to one study of two groups of 600 women which found that prepared women have shorter labours, used less drugs, had fewer episiotomies and their children had higher Apgar scores (see page 84).

Mothers left alone in hospital have more difficult deliveries

Labour has been found to last half as long for mothers who have a friend or supportive companion with them at the time of delivery of their child, according to the results of a study carried out by Dr Robert Sosa and his team at Guatemala City Hospital.[41] Mothers on their own during labour were also found to spend less time stroking, smiling and talking to their newborn babies and more time sleeping.

The *doula*, which is the name given by Guatemalans to these birth companions, clearly helps to reduce the mother's anxiety, and though modern hospitals may be particularly frightening and alien places to Latin American women, the researchers believe that the findings of the investigation have significance in the West too. The anxiety produced by a hospital environment may cause foetal distress and the researchers point out that these results are particularly relevant to the care of low-income, single or teenage mothers who may not receive positive support from their families during labour.

The sensitive period after birth

There is important scientific evidence that when babies are separated from their mother shortly after birth the mother/child relationship can be drastically damaged for some time afterwards, or possibly even permanently. But it is standard procedure in many maternity hospitals to restrict the amount of time mothers spend with their newly-born babies.

The psychological significance and importance of this critical (or sensitive) period after birth, as it is called, was originally demonstrated in several species of animals. Unless mother goats, for example, are allowed to lick and smell their kids within an hour of birth the offspring are later rejected; but just 5 minutes' contact during the 'sensitive period' following birth will prevent this rejection happening, even if the subsequent separation is extended to three hours.[42] Research has shown that if puppies are kept isolated during their first fourteen weeks of life they do not respond socially to other dogs and have very abnormal behaviour as adult dogs. But if puppies are allowed social contact in the first three to ten weeks of age then they are able to form proper relationshps with other dogs and humans.[43] Many ornithologists have also shown that birds and ducks will follow other birds, or models of birds, even if they are inanimate objects, if they are exposed to these stimuli in the first days of life. These creatures become 'imprinted', as animal researchers would say, on to these objects.

A fascinating experiment on the 'sensitive period' in babies was conducted by Dr M. H. Klaus, and colleagues.

They took 28 women who had just given birth and randomly divided them into two groups of 14. The first group were allowed to have the usual contact with their babies that the maternity hospital regimen permitted, ie 'a glimpse of the baby shortly after birth, brief contact and identification at 6–12 hours and then 20–30 minutes every 4 hours for feeding', reports Doris Haire. But the second group of 14 women were given their babies to fondle and play with for 16 hours *extra* during the first 3 days following the birth. Apart from this they were identical in every respect to the first group. One month later Dr Klaus's team tested both groups of women and their babies. They found that the mothers given the extra period of time with their babies were more reluctant to leave their babies with someone else. They usually stood and watched during the examination of their babies, they showed more soothing behaviour towards their babies, more eye-to-eye contact, and fondled their babies more than the other group of mothers. 'It is surprising,' comments Dr Klaus, 'that with the multitude of factors that influence maternal behaviour (genes, social background, relationship with husband and family, her own experiences as a child, personality and so on) that just 16 hours in the first three days had an affect that persisted for 30 days.'[44] One suggestion to explain this observation is that there is a chemical reaction that occurs between a mother and baby that is not yet understood. Dr Klaus also mentions that the intense interest that mothers showed in the eyes of their babies especially in the first hour of life suggests that the period immediately after birth may be 'uniquely important'. It has been found by other researchers that an increase in attentiveness by mothers contributes to the intellectual development in children. This factor is known to be linked with a high degree of exploration and activity in young babies. This exploratory behaviour at an early age is thought to be a vital element in the mental growth of children.

It may be interesting to mention here that the degree to which a mother shows affection and attachment to her baby is also connected to the quantity of painkilling and anaesthetic drugs that she has received during childbirth. It has been found by an American doctor[45] that when mothers are physically aware of the birth and emotionally involved, they subsequently show a more positive attitude towards their babies. The investigation found that the strongest affectional attachment occurred in mothers who were completely awake and physically aware of the sensations of childbirth. But mothers who had been given local or epidural anaesthetics (which left them alert but with reduced sensations of the birth) had significantly lower scores on their maternal attachment to their babies.

The continued hazardous use of unnecessary X-rays in pregnancy

'X-rays given to pregnant mothers during the 50s and 60s were the cause of between 5 and 10 per cent of all childhood cancers in Western Europe and North America' – Professor Richard Doll.[46]

X-rays are still the major known cause of leukaemia. It was in the late 1950s that Dr Alice Stewart and her colleagues at Oxford University discovered that X-rays given to mothers during their pregnancy could double the risk of their offspring developing leukaemia by the age of 10. Children under the age of 4, who have had asthma, have a twenty-five times greater risk of leukaemia if they have been X-rayed whilst in the womb.[47] Despite this horrific side effect of X-rays, research shows that it is still quite common for hospitals to X-ray pregnant mothers, according to a survey carried out by Dr J. Carmichael, a Liverpool radiologist.[48] He discovered in 1976 that major hospitals in Britain were still X-raying over one-third of all pregnant mothers, as well as one in ten of all newly born children. A subsequent survey by Dr E. Fletcher of Oxford University[49] found that in 1976 and 1977 10 per cent of foetuses at the Radcliffe Hospital in Oxford were still being X-rayed. 'They need not have been, they could have been examined by ultrasound techniques,' commented Dr Fletcher, pointing out, however, that ultrasound machines then cost £10,000 per year to run.

Mothers are scanned or X-rayed to check that the baby is growing, to show the position of the placenta, to confirm twins and to check maturity before the baby is artificially induced. The earlier an X-ray is taken the greater the damage done to the foetus. If a foetus is not fully grown then a premature child will be induced with all the consequent hazards and risks that such a child is associated with. If they are being used responsibly, X-rays or ultrasound checks should in the long run reduce the number of stillbirths which results from the delivery of premature babies. But do they in practice? After Alice Stewart published her findings about the increase in leukaemia amongst X-rayed babies there was thankfully a sudden drop in the number of pregnant mothers who were X-rayed. Beforehand 40 per cent of all mothers were X-rayed, but the figure dropped to just 11 per cent; in other words, the number of pregnant mothers X-rayed dropped by over one-third. But Dr Carmichael points out that in those years between 1957 and 1960 when there was a drop in the number of mothers being X-rayed, there was not the expected rise in the number of stillbirths. This is contrary to what one would expect if it were true that X-raying mothers really was helping to reduce the number of stillbirths. Despite the worrying findings by Dr Stewart on leukaemia, by 1974 the number of unborn babies exposed to X-rays had climbed again to 23 per cent of all babies born.

The general introduction of the apparently safer ultrasound scans should have reduced the number of mothers X-rayed, but Dr Carmichael found that although ultrasound *was* available at two hospitals in his survey, 25 per cent and 34 per cent of all pregnant mothers were still X-rayed! He comments: 'It seems that when a patient attends a hospital with readily-accessible X-ray facilities, the facilities will be used.' Despite these disturbingly high figures, all the senior consultants in the hospitals surveyed by Dr Carmichael were under the mistaken impression that only 5 to 10 per cent of mothers were being X-rayed!

The hazards do not only extend to the unborn child. Dr Carmichael maintains that the newborn baby up to the age of four weeks also suffers the same risk as the child who is X-rayed four weeks *before* birth. He found that up to 1 in 10 of all newborn babies were also being X-rayed.

More electronic medical nonsense
Intensive care units: how to produce more handicapped babies

If a baby is born prematurely and underweight he is nearly always put into a special care baby unit to help him to survive. So far so good, but do these intensive care units result in healthy babies? As *The Times* science report put it: 'one serious doubt has remained; resuscitation of extremely premature babies could lead to an increase in the numbers surviving with serious mental and physical handicaps.'[50]

A twelve-year-old study carried out at the Royal Women's Hospital in Melbourne, Australia, shows that these special units are turning out more handicapped babies than routine facilities. The researchers investigated all the births of babies born underweight (from 1000–1500 g, ie 2.216–3.316lb) between 1966 and 1970. Half were given intensive care and the other half were given 'simple routine care', says the report. Despite intensive care 35 babies died, and 45 deaths occurred amongst the babies given no special care. When the surviving babies of both groups were measured in later years (at ages 2, 6 and 8) for mental and physical ability, it was discovered that nearly three times as many children given intensive care had severe handicaps. This included IQ below 70 or serious deafness. Seventeen babies had serious handicaps and a further 31 had significant handicaps, such as IQ less than 84, epilepsy or visual problems. But with the non-treated babies, only 6 had serious handicaps and 28 significant handicaps.

The improvement in survival rates produced by intensive care has been brought about at the expense of a higher proportion of severely handicapped survivors, says *The Times* report, concluding that the answer lies in preventing low-birthweight babies being born and not in the Health Service setting up more of these expensive units.

Low-birthweight babies are most common amongst the low-social-class mothers and it is perhaps only by improving their standards of living, their nutrition and so on that any real improvement will be achieved. Since it costs half a million pounds to bring up a handicapped child no society can afford to use expensive technology that produces more handicapped babies.[51]

Baby incubator causes deafness

Although it might be thought from these findings that the incubators used for intensive care only help already handicapped babies to survive there is evidence that the incubators themselves might actually cause one handicap: deafness. Tests performed at Guy's Hospital Hearing Research Department have shown that prematurely born test animals (guinea pigs) have their hair cells of the ear permanently damaged by the internal noise produced by these incubators. Results show that mature animals do not have their hearing damaged because their hair cells have 'hardened up'. Such hearing damage can occur at levels of noise which were previously thought to be safe. Before this experiment was performed premature baby deafness had puzzled investigators because it is the type of deafness normally only found in industry caused by noisy machinery, eg road drills, and babies were of course not being exposed to high-level noise. The implications of this finding are disturbing for it means that there may be no 'safe' level of noise for a premature baby, or perhaps even for any young baby. Parents living in noisy environments such as in the vicinity of airports may inadvertently produce deaf babies.[52]

5

Tests

Are you having useless and hazardous tests?

'The concept of a "normal" human being which has been so firmly embodied in the teaching of medicine has done immeasurable harm. There is no such animal.' – Professor George Teeling Smith, Director of the Office of Health Economics.[1]

Don't worry if you have 'abnormal' test results on admission to hospital. Research shows that so-called *abnormal* results in a medical test are not an indication of illness or disease, but a sign of health! Dr A. R. Bradwell, of Birmingham's Queen Elizabeth Medical Centre, discovered this paradox when he looked into the cases of 2,000 patients who underwent tests there.[2] More than one-third of all these patients had abnormal readings when their levels of cholesterol, iron, glucose, sodium, potassium, calcium, urea and so on, were measured. Puzzled by this large number of odd results, Dr Bradwell decided to follow up 200 patients who had obtained these abnormal readings. When given the tests again, 72 (36 per cent) obtained perfectly normal results and after five years only 3 of these 200 patients developed a disease which could have been indicated by their abnormal results five years earlier!

Results from tests are meaningless when compared to so-called normal values unless age, sex and a detailed case history are also taken into account. The laws of statistics will always make 5 per cent of any population look as if they are medically abnormal.[3] This means that if as few as fifteen tests are performed on one patient it is almost impossible for that patient to obtain a normal result on all the tests.

The test was normal but the patient died

Further evidence of the unnecessary nature of screening tests comes from a massive ten-year study of over 7,000 patients conducted by Professor Walter Holland of the Department of Community Medicine at St Thomas's Hospital, London.[4] The patients under study were divided into two groups: the screened and the unscreened. Initially, in 1967, nearly 2,500 of the screened patients were given a physical examination by their GP and a whole batch of medical tests were performed on them including chest X-rays, heart and lung function tests, blood pressure, blood levels of sugar, cholesterol, urea, and so on. These patients also had to complete lengthy health question- naires. After two years the patients were all screened again. Every time a screening measure showed that something needed attention, patients were treated accordingly. But although the screening tests did discover a number of previously undiscovered diseases the group who were screened did not show *any* health benefits whatsoever from having been screened! After nine years there were just as many deaths, illnesses and stays in hospital amongst those people who had been screened compared to those who had never been tested in the first place.

Professor Holland points out that the only other con- trolled trial investigating the usefulness of screening tests has also produced negative results. The Kaiser Permanente Group of Hospitals in California found there there were no statistically significant differences in overall death rates when treatment and control groups were compared seven years after the screening took place.

At worst screening may actually be a cause of disease – stress is one of the primary causes of high blood pressure and related heart disease, the major cause of death in Western society.

'Screening in the middle-aged can no longer be advo- cated on scientific, ethical or economic grounds as a desirable public health measure' concludes Professor Holland and his colleagues at St Thomas's Hospital, London.[4]

The screening hazard

Despite the lack of evidence that screening does anything apart from induce anxiety, BUPA, the largest private health care organisation in Britain, are widely promoting their expensive screening facilities. They test 30,000 people per year and the trend is accelerating. They say, 'Over the past 15 years very few companies who use our medical centre for screening have stopped their schemes and demand seems to be growing all the time – particularly now from Unions!' (as if popularity amongst trade unions was evidence of effectiveness). What is most disturbing about their claims for screening is the way they attempt to justify their use. They refer to the Kaiser Permanente Hospital screening programme as evidence for the effectiveness and usefulness of screening yet, as Professor Holland has pointed out, these results do not demonstrate any significant reduction in deaths.

This organisation tells its customers about the deficiencies of Professor Holland's own investigation. Whilst they admit that he found no reduction in death rates amongst those screened they attempt to make his findings appear unimportant and insignificant. They also neglect to mention that Professor Holland's investigation was sponsored by the Department of Health, who would be screening people now within the NHS if it had been shown that screening was of some benefit to the general population.

Breast cancer screening hazards

According to the BUPA organisation's handouts 'screening detects cancer and helps to prolong life'. Neither of these statements is strictly true because often screening wrongly diagnoses cancers which are not there at all. Screening also exposes women to X-rays, a procedure in itself which can increase the likelihood of getting cancer. It seems strange that this company should proudly boast that 'in *seven* years' it 'has not lost a single person who had the disease (ie breast cancer) diagnosed by X-ray alone', but two pages later their leaflet to potential clients argues that an eight-year follow-up conducted by Professor Holland was 'too short to be conclusive'.[5]

Breast screening for cancer is by no means a useful or a safe procedure, according to the British Department of

Health's book entitled *Prevention and Health: Everybody's business.*[6] It points out that the disease can neither be prevented nor easily cured. However, one widely quoted study (the American Health Insurance Plan investigation) *has* indeed shown that there were one-third fewer deaths among the women who had been offered four annual breast screening tests. But that is not the *whole* story. In this large-scale American study which involved 60,000 patients the numbers of deaths from breast cancer in the two groups were relatively low anyway – 70 and 108 respectively (for screened and unscreened women). The reduction in the number of deaths was only found amongst screened women in their fifties; screening was of no benefit to younger women or women in their sixties who together constitute 75 per cent of the women who get breast cancer.

X-rays nowadays should involve smaller doses of radiation than ten years ago when the American study was performed and it was possible that the dosages used at the time might have caused as many breast cancers as were being detected by screening, says the British Department of Health.[6] But no one knows yet if the modern lower doses of X-rays might not also be responsible for an *increase* in the incidence of breast cancer.

The American Food and Drug Administration's expert panel on radiation recommended in 1975 against routine screening of women under the age of 35 for breast cancer[7] because of the increased risk of inducing cancer with X-rays.

The risks of false test results

Even when X-ray tests are combined with palpation tests (ie just feeling the breast for lumps), studies show that there will still be 'at least 5 wrongly diagnosed cases of cancer, for every real case of cancer which is detected by screening'.[6] This means in practice that some women will have to undergo totally *unnecessary*, anxiety-provoking surgery (a biopsy) which carries some risks of its own. Furthermore a number of women who really do have cancer will be told *incorrectly* by the screening test that they are healthly. The danger in such cases is that once women have been falsely reassured they may delay seeking advice even when the cancer becomes apparent at a later time, says the British Department of Health.

Thermography

This is a technique of detecting cancer growth using very sensitive heat sensors. Since cancer cells multiply more rapidly than normal cells they emit more heat, which can be photographed on heat-sensitive film. In theory the thermogram has one great advantage over X-rays: there is no risk of inducing cancer with X-ray radiation. Unfortunately the technique is so unreliable that it must be used in conjunction with X-rays and a physical examination. 'Women screened only by a thermograph should not be given the impression that a fully satisfactory breast examination has been made' according to one American study[8]

The American FDA state that 'thermography contributes no additional information to an evaluation derived from both a mammogram (ie X-ray screening) and a physical examination'.[8]

Cancer test: to smear or not to smear?

The so-called smear test for cancer of the cervix, like the breast-cancer screening test, is not necessarily a beneficial procedure, particularly in younger women below the age of 35. It is said by the Department of Health that the test was introduced in response to intense public pressure but before its effectiveness had been fully demonstrated.[9] Professor Archibald Cochrane, former director of the Medical Research Council's Epidemiology Unit, was pilloried and attacked by medical colleagues when he said in 1967 that 'I know of no hard evidence, at present, that cervical smears are effective.'[10]

More recently, an editorial article in *The Lancet* in November 1978[11] discussed the considerable disadvantages of screening young women. 'The first reason is economic, the number of lives potentially saved per smear taken is low, under the age of 35. The second reason relates to the danger of performing unnecessary uterine surgery and causing unnecessary anxiety to women, many of whom may not have completed their child-bearing. Screening aims to detect and treat precursors of malignant disease; but diagnostic errors are not uncommon and there is doubt also about the frequency with which the various premalignant conditions progress to invasive cancer.' *The Lancet* adds that present evidence suggests that these precancerous conditions often revert back to normal, whereas rapid progression to malignant cancer is extremely rare. Even when precancerous cells do progress to cancer it takes more than ten years to occur. *The Lancet* therefore asks 'Is it necessary to detect and treat these apparently premalignant cells as early as possible? Or might it not be better to wait until older ages when misdiagnoses seem to be less common? . . . The major weakness of cervical cancer screening programmes is that high-risk women rarely attend for testing. Those at high risk are women who have many sexual partners and are of low social class.' If these women were to attend screenings, then perhaps rates of cancer of the cervix might be reduced in the community generally.

At present one out of every four women under the age of 25 is getting a smear test in Britain – but these are not the women at high risk. The fact is that of the 2,000 deaths from cervical cancer each year, only 0.5 per cent (ie one in 200) are amongst women aged under 25.

One calculation shows, however, that if the first smear is carried out at age 35 and the test is repeated every five years until the age of 80, then 77 per cent of deaths might be prevented.[12] An editorial in the *British Medical Journal* recommends that women should be screened either at 25 if they obtain contraception, become pregnant or get VD or at age of 30 if they were sexually active and had not yet been tested. They should be re-checked every five years (and every three years after the age of 35, if possible).[12]

Amniocentesis – the fatal birth test

The technique of amniocentesis was introduced in 1967, yet it took a further eleven years (until 1978) before its safety was evaluated. Thousands of women may have unnecessarily lost their babies or given birth to needlessly handicapped children because of the reluctance of the medical profession to evaluate this test sooner.

What is the amniocentesis procedure?

The fluid present inside the womb which exists to protect the developing foetus can provide a whole range of vital information about the growing baby. If a sample of this amniotic fluid, as it is called, is extracted with a syringe, cells from it can be cultured and they can indicate if the

107

baby is handicapped in some way. The chromosome structure of these cultured cells can tell us the sex of the baby, whether it will suffer from Down's syndrome, or from a number of other genetically induced handicaps, spina bifida for example. If the test is carried out during the first 4 months of pregnancy an abnormal foetus, if discovered, can be aborted. Since the lifelong cost to the state of caring for a handicapped child is in the region of half a million pounds (at 1979 prices)[13] – there is considerable economic pressure to abort such handicapped foetuses. Apart from such pecuniary considerations parents must also consider the pain and misery of having to bring up a handicapped child. However, not all handicaps are of equal severity and the test is unable to distinguish the degree of a potential handicap. Added to this problem is the evidence described here of considerable damage caused by the test itself to normal healthy babies. 'Can the damage to normal infants be tolerated if its severity is less than that of the condition prevented by amniocentesis?' asked an editorial in *The Lancet*,[14] written after the Medical Research Council's investigation of the safety of amniocentesis was published.

The risks which the amniocentesis test may predict

(1) Spina bifida (a baby with deformed spine and nervous system)

(2) Anencephaly (a baby without a properly formed brain – no chance of survival)

(3) Hydrocephalus (water on the brain)

These deformities are generally associated with severe mental handicap.

These types of malformations occur in about 1 in every 200 births and are most common amongst poor, low-social class groups of women. The greatest risk is to women who have already had one affected child, for then there is approximately a 1 in 20 chance of having another such baby. Nowadays a blood test which measures the levels of alpha-fetoprotein in a pregnant women can indicate if she is at high risk, and this should always be performed before attempting the more hazardous amniocentesis test.[15]

(4) Down's syndrome or mongolism.

Two groups of women are at risk: (a) those having a baby at an advanced age of 35 years upwards – the table overleaf shows that the risk is increased more than ten times by the time a woman is in her mid-forties; (b) mongolism can be caused by an inherited gene, so women who have already had a mongol child or those who come from a family with a history of mongolism are at an increased risk. Under the age of 30 the risk of having a mongol child is about 1 in 1,000, rising to about 1 in 60 at the age of 45. The risk will be increased if women have been exposed to extensive doses of X-rays (see X-ray hazards, page 113).

(5) Sex-linked disorders.

Some unfortunate families have a history of diseases which may affect males only – for example, haemophilia and certain types of muscular dystrophy occur only in males. Women can still carry the gene which produces these disorders but it will not affect them or their daughters directly. Since the amniocentesis test can indicate the sex of a growing foetus it is possible therefore to prevent these disorders by aborting all male foetuses. However only 50 per cent of male foetuses are affected by these sex-linked diseases so healthy males may be unnecessarily aborted half of the time.

The hazards of the birth test

The considerable risks of the amniocentesis test for birth defects were discovered by a Medical Research Council investigation into nearly 2,500 women who had the test performed by skilled personnel, at nine different hospitals between 1973 and 1976.[16] The test was performed during the first four months of pregnancy and their subsequent pregnancies and births were compared to an equal number of pregnant women who did not have the test. Altogether the births of nearly 5,000 women were followed up by the researchers. The results of the survey make disturbing reading particularly as most of the problems and hazards of amniocentesis which they uncovered were not predicted or expected by the experts. Compared to similar but untested women, those women who underwent the test had more than double the number of miscarriages, more than three times as many cases of haemorrhage (needing a Caesarian delivery) and they suffered from more than

Why pregnant women had amniocentesis – the prenatal birth test. Results of the Medical Research Council's seven-year investigation

Reason for performing the pre-natal birth test (amniocentesis)	No. of women who had the test performed for this reason	% of pregnancies found to be abnormal
Previous child born with a genetic abnormality	34	29
Previous child born with a nervous system (neural tube) defect (spina bifida, anencephaly)	1,021	4
More than one previous child with a nervous system (neural tube) defect such as spina bifida or anencephaly	52	15
Where one parent is a genetic carrier of Down's syndrome (Mongolism)	39	10
Maternal age (risk of mongolism increases with age): Age of mother: 35–39 years	663	1
40–41 "	306	5
42–43 "	150	8
44–47 "	38	11
Mother's blood known to contain abnormally high levels of a protein called alpha-fetoprotein. This substance is known to be related to high incidence of neural tube defects (spina bifida or anencephaly)	110	22
Previous child born with a sex-linked abnormality; for example, haemophilia which only occurs in males	34	44
Previous child born a mongol where no parent is a genetic carrier of the condition	188	½
Family history of Down's syndrome (Mongolism)	72	0
Family history of neural tube defects such as spina bifida or anencephaly	93	2
Mother was worried about the normality of her baby	32	0

Adapted by the author from the results of the Medical Research Council's study.[16]

seven times the number of baby deaths shortly after birth. There were also three times more cases of unexplained breathing difficulties for up to 24 hours after birth. On every dimension the babies of women who had been subjected to an amniocentesis test suffered more than the babies of untested women. Major orthopaedic abnormalities requiring urgent surgery in the newly born were six times more common in the tested women – probably caused by the lack of protective fluid in the womb after the procedure was performed. One of the few *expected* side effects was that 50 per cent more babies whose mothers had rhesus-negative blood groups developed antibodies in their blood.

There is now a dilemma for both parents and doctors worried about whether or not a developing baby is normal. It has been calculated that the human cost of preventing the birth of some 555 deformed spina bifida babies each year in England and Wales (most of whom would die in early life) would be 120 dead or damaged *normal* infants.[17] Another calculation has shown that to prevent the birth of 329 seriously affected spina bifida babies (many of whom would not survive long either) it would be necessary to abort 95 *healthy* babies and 110 handicapped but not hopeless children.[18]

What did the test tell these women?
Just over 4 out of every 100 women who had the test performed were found to have a baby with some foetal abnormalities. Sometimes the test wrongly identified an abnormality – but this was very rare – only 1 case in 500.

The most common reason for having the birth test was where a pregnant mother had previously had a child with a neural tube deformity such as spina bifida or anencephaly. Of the thousand or so women who had this test 3.7 per cent *did* discover that their developing baby was deformed. The table gives the *other* reasons why women had the test and shows how often the test discovered an abnormal foetus.

High-technology clumsiness
One out of every ten women tested had to have the test performed again because inadequate cell tissue was obtained first time around. Sometimes the needle had to be inserted into the womb several times to obtain the specimen, but this occurred less often when the operator was

experienced and used an 'ultrascan' machine to find the best location for the needle. (An ultrascan can provide a picture on a TV screen of the inside of the womb, by radiating the foetus with high-frequency sound waves). This should make it possible to withdraw amniotic fluid from the womb without sucking up the foetus' precious blood. However, the survey reports that the frequency of bloodstaining was no lower with ultrasound scans. The test should be performed at the same time as the scan is made, not a few moments afterwards. The unborn baby can wriggle about quickly, making a *prior* scan a waste of time.

Risks to mothers of the screening test

The amniocentesis test has to be performed at a stage when the development foetus is reasonably mature, at about four months, otherwise there is insufficient fluid in the womb for a sample to be taken. Some women may have to wait several weeks longer until there is sufficient fluid in the womb for the sample to be taken. But the loss of amniotic fluid increases the pressure on the foetus and this is thought to be the cause of breathing problems and orthopaedic damage, which is found more often in the babies of mothers who have had an amniocentesis birth test. Once the fluid has been collected it then takes a further four to six weeks to culture the amniotic cells, which can then be examined under a microscope to determine if the developing foetus is normal or not. If an expectant mother is then told that the result is abnormal she has to decide on whether or not to have an abortion. Apart from the increased hazards to the mother of having such a late abortion (see page 31 for the risks of different kinds of abortion) it is not easy emotionally for a woman who at this stage can feel her baby kicking. In the Medical Research Council's investigation there was only 1 death from abortion amongst 143 abortions performed because of abnormalities found in the developing foetus.

'Parents must give careful prior consideration to the hazards of this test'

This is the main conclusion of the extensive Medical Research Council's investigation. For the benefit of parents faced with this difficult choice the risks of this procedure have been given here in detail, since it is considered unlikely that *all* of these factors will be explained to them. The sour reputation (see page 303) which obstetricians have gained for performing procedures of unproven benefit to both mother and child makes the public knowledge of these statistics all the more important.[19] This technique of amniocentesis was introduced in 1967, yet it took a further eleven years before its safety was evaluated. It had been hailed as the greatest advance in perinatal medicine for a generation.[20] Now its widespread use is being restricted and questioned. Faced with these results of the Medical Research Council survey, parents may be less enthusiastic than they were in the seventies during the unfettered heyday of amniocentesis.[14]

X-ray hazards – why you should refuse to be 'routinely' X-rayed

(See also X-rays on pregnant mothers, page 98, and Dental X-rays, page 123.)

One reason which the British Department of Health gives for its decision not to screen all women for breast cancer is the danger of raising the overall levels of cancer in the population by exposing millions of women to hazardous X-rays. X-rays change the basic structure of living cells: they can alter the structure of DNA, the genetic material present in all living cells; too much radiation and the cells will not reproduce properly – their self-regulating mechanisms go haywire: this is cancer.

The latest informed scientific opinions on radiation risks believe that *every* exposure to X-rays carries risks. There is no safe dose because the body accumulates or stores up X-ray radiation. In this way several 'safe' doses can add up to make one unsafe dose. Once a cell is damaged by an X-ray, it remains damaged and is a potential cancer. Some 90 per cent of the radiation to which the public is exposed comes from medical and dental X-rays.[21] The American government announced in 1979 a comprehensive radiation-reduction programme in 'the healing arts' because it was concerned about this public health hazard. (The remaining 10 per cent of radiation is caused by natural background radiation present in the earth and comes from the sun's rays, the nuclear power industry, fall-out from atomic weapon tests, and industrial users.)

American health officials believe that risky medical exposure can be halved at least by cutting out unnecessary X-rays. There is no plan in the UK to cut down the public's exposure to unnecessary X-rays even though the number increases yearly. Old equipment put patients at unnecessary risk, according to Professor Patricia Lindop, radiation biologist at St Bartholomew's Hospital. 'More than double the dose of radiation than necessary is given to patients in hospital examinations because worn-out intensifiers need to be replaced.' She wrote in *Doctor* magazine in 1977[22] that the cash shortage in the Health Service has forced radiologists to use higher voltages to obtain satisfactory results. 'Image intensifiers in X-ray equipment used in hospitals throughout the country need to be replaced sooner.' Figures are not obtainable in Britain, but in the USA where safety standards are generally far stricter than in Britain, nearly one-third of all the X-ray machines tested needed mechanical attention or improvements to reduce hazardous exposure to radiation.[23] The US surveys have found too that exposure from X-ray machines can vary by up to two hundred times from one facility to the next, and that between 5 per cent and 10 per cent of all X-rays have to be repeated because of poor technique.

They found that many doctors order X-rays as routine or because patients simply expect them. The US authorities question, also, the routine and indiscriminate X-raying of healthy people when they take up a new job – a very common practice in Britain, particularly in the Health Service!

US surveys show that 90 per cent of all medical X-rays are performed without protective shielding and that half of all conventional X-ray examinations expose patients to unnecessary radiation because the X-ray beam is larger than the area of the film. In one survey 15 per cent of radiologists were found to be using a beam area twice as large as the film.[24]

British X-ray dangers slammed by safety watchdog

In October 1980 the UK National Radiological Protection Board published a damning report on safety standards at X-ray departments in British hospitals. It found that many patients are receiving unnecessarily high doses of X-ray radiation.[25] After surveying over 80 hospitals, they found that the British public are receiving as much genetically-significant radiation as they did 20 years ago, despite the introduction of technical improvements which can reduce exposure. It was found that hospitals are failing to use *gonad shields*, particularly in adults where only 25 per cent of patients in their 20s are being given gonad shields. Children fare only slightly better with only one third receiving this vital shielding of their sex organs. Although the number of X-ray examinations performed is rising by 2 per cent each year, the NRPB maintain that hospitals could reduce the dangerous exposure by half if they made use of gonad shielding.

Two disturbing factors emerged from the survey, according to its director, Dr Stuart Rae: the enormous range of doses used in different hospitals, and the failure to reduce doses in the last 20 years with the aid of image intensifiers. 'I take the view that all ionising radiation is bad for you, and if doses can be reduced, they should be reduced'.[26]

The survey also confirmed that medical X-rays are the major source of radiation in Britain, and found that a 10 per cent reduction in X-rays could have as much effect as eliminating all other sources of man-made radiation.[27]

The hazards of low doses of radiation

Studies on the survivors of Hiroshima and Nagasaki, and recent studies on nuclear power workers, show that the old belief that risk increases in proportion to the dose of X-rays received is sadly incorrect. 'Unfortunately in most cases of human exposure there is no evidence of a safety factor at low doses,' says Professor Karl Morgan in an influential article which appeared in the *New Scientist*.[28]

One of the greatest risks of X-rays concerns unborn children (see page 98), particularly in women who may not even know that they are pregnant, between the 2nd and 7th weeks, when the various body organs are being formed inside the womb. A child exposed in the womb has a 50 per cent increased risk of dying from leukaemia. If a child has asthma in the first four years of life this produces a 5,000 per cent increase in the risk of leukaemia.[28] Professor Morgan states that if a million children each receive X-rays whilst in the womb we might expect 300 to 3,000 cases of leukaemia. He refers also to new investigations on nuclear fuel workers at the American Hanford Reprocessing Plant which show that 'low-level' radiation causes other forms of cancer which might double these rates – ie a further 600 to 6,000 cancers for every million children exposed to only 1 rad of X-rays (1 rad is used in just one X-ray to determine the age of a foetus, for example).

Professor Morgan, however, states that the real culprit for unnecessary population dosage of radiation is the medical profession. 'When we have stopped unnecessary medical exposure to ionising radiations (ie X-rays), which is 90 per cent of the problem, then, perhaps, I can see that the next step might be to reduce the maximum permissible exposure to workers (in the nuclear industry). A reduction of only 1 per cent in unnecessary diagnostic exposures in the United States would reduce the population dose of man-made sources of radiation more than the elimination of the nuclear power industry to the year 2000.'

Reducing the risk to your children

Every X-ray you have increases your risk of having diseased or handicapped children. The sex organs are the most vulnerable parts of the body to radiation risks because the reproductive cells can have their genetic potential permanently damaged. X-ray damaged sperm or X-ray-damaged eggs may mean that the damage is inherited by your children, and passed on to future generations. These cell mutations caused by X-rays do not produce dramatic damage but subtle changes, such as an increased predisposition to develop chronic illnesses, i.e. high blood pressure or schizophrenia, later on in life. 'The amount of radiation required to produce a single mutation in the reproductive cells is low, *certainly* within the dosage received in many diagnostic X-rays,' says the American Department of Health.[29]

In the USA the government is attempting to encourage the use of 'gonad shields' to protect reproductive cells from this form of X-ray damage. Few dentists and physicians use them although the National Academy of Sciences recommends shielding as a simple effective way to reduce exposure.

Mongolism or Down's syndrome is a thousand times more likely to occur in the babies of women who conceive in their forties because of the increased radiation damage that a woman of this age has suffered through the years compared to a younger woman. The longer an egg remains inside a woman the greater the amount of radiation damage it builds up over time (see page 110).

Skull X-rays

The American Food and Drug Administration found that it could safely eliminate 40–60 per cent of all skull X-rays. A project carried out at two Washington State hospitals found that more than half the skull X-rays normally performed were not needed.[30]

A study from Israel has shown that tumours (both malignant and benign) of head and neck were three times more common in 11,000 children irradiated for ringworm during the 1950s and 1960s.[31] Brain tumours, thyroid and parotid gland cancers were those involved.[32]

The body scanner: X-rays still a hazard

The 'brain-scanner', invented by EMI and for which one of their employees received the Nobel Prize for Medicine is a computerised X-ray machine hailed as a 'revolutionary development'[33] which makes it possible to obtain very clear pictures, revealing disease of soft body organs and blood vessels which previously could only have been seen after surgery. From the patient's point of view the advantage is that the scanner is a painless procedure without any obvious side effects. Particularly, the brain-scanner has reduced the need to inject radioactive dye into the bloodstream when doctors want to obtain X-ray pictures of the blood vessels in the brain, for example.

Scanners work by taking dozens of thin X-ray slices of the patient and the computer combines these slices together to make a composite picture of the inside of the body. Contrary to popular opinion it has been shown that brain- and body-scanners still expose patients to doses of hazardous X-rays which are as great as the old-style diagnostic methods. A report published in 1979 by the British National Radiological Protection Board,[34] which investigated X-ray doses produced by the latest range of EMI scanners, found that the 'eight scans typically needed for diagnosis' expose the patient to as much as the ordinary skull X-rays. Also EMI scanner 'slices' of the torso involve exposing a patient to more radiation than a usual chest X-ray. Furthermore, to obtain clearer pictures of internal organs scanners can be made to scan at a slower speed and in this way patients receive a further fivefold increase in radiation. The researchers concluded that before scanner patients are subjected to these increased risks of cancer with these slow X-ray scans the resulting improvements in picture quality must be fully justified.[35]

Hospital tests that make people ill

If you are allergic to some common foods such as corn or eggs, you may have problems taking some hospital tests. Dr Vicky Rippere of London's Institute of Psychiatry has shown that when allergic people are given glucose tolerance tests, they may suffer from tension, shakiness, abdominal cramps, sneezing and headache. Also, the 'fatty meals' given to people before an examination of the gall bladder may be 'disastrous for an acutely egg-sensitive individual', says Dr Rippere.[36] She claims too that when patients try to draw attention to these problems they are ignored, or worse, labelled as hypochondriacs.

Mild blood pressure: one test that may save lives

People who have been found to have mild blood pressure conditions (diastolic blood pressures between 90 and 104mm of mercury) will live longer if they are tested and receive treatment, according to the results of a five-year study involving 11,000 people carried out in the USA by the National Heart, Lung and Blood Institute. But drugs are not necessarily required to make these improvements in health. Instead weight control, reduced dietary salt, increased exercise, less smoking and so on were found to keep blood pressure under control.

The study involved people aged 35–69 who were split randomly into two groups. The first group received 'routine' treatment from their doctor in the community, but the second group were given intensive treatment at fourteen clinics around America. After five years there were 17 per cent fewer deaths related to high blood pressure in the intensively treated group. Reductions in deaths from heart disease and stroke, the two most common causes of death in the West, were even greater. They obtained a 45 per cent reduction in the number of deaths caused by strokes and 25 per cent fewer deaths from

118

heart attack.[37]

The interesting point to come out of this study is the variety of non-drug treatments which were used to combat these mild blood pressure conditions. Drugs on their own have not yet been shown to be capable of producing a reduction in illnesses and deaths in patients with mild to moderate blood pressure (see page 212 for information on this in connection with the drug Inderal).

6

Dentistry

Why six-monthly dental check-ups are unnecessary

The pun-artists had a field day in 1977 when Dr Aubrey Sheiham, a senior lecturer at the London Hospital Dental School, published a highly convincing article in *The Lancet*[1] which argued that six-monthly dental checks were both unnecessary and harmful. 'Dentistry can be a lot of rot' proclaimed the *Daily Telegraph*. 'New Cavity in dental lore' heralded the *Observer*. 'Dentists open their mouths' punned the *Guardian* in one of its less cringe-making moments.

Dr Sheiham posed the reasonable question: 'Is there a scientific basis for six-monthly dental check-ups?' – pointing out the fact that the dental check-up is the most frequently performed health-screening measure. His delightful paper made elegant use of no less than forty-one published research findings to back up his claims. For example he cites four investigations alone which have found that people who regularly attend the dentist's surgery have fewer healthy teeth than irregular attenders. 'They have had more teeth filled than irregular attenders have had decayed and this can only be a result of a tendency to overtreat,' says Dr Sheiham. Treatment can be made unnecessarily because of the tendency for initial cavities in the teeth to remineralise on their own, according to Dr Sheiham. He mentions one study which has shown that more than half of the holes found by dentists had remineralised without treatment; this especially occurs in places with fluoride in the water supply. In such places there is even less need for people to visit their dentists.

Part of the problem, suggests Dr Sheiham, is that all adults in Britain are entitled to *free* six-monthly check-ups. He points out that only one study, carried out in the USA in 1975, has tried to determine the *optimum* interval for dental check-ups. It found that for young adults age 15–19, two years was best.[2] This two-year interval was sufficient because dental decay ('caries' in the trade) is a very slow disease in the permanent teeth and takes that length of time to progress through the enamel. Dr Sheiham comments that the most striking and important finding is the long interval of 3–4 years between initial enamel lesion and its extension to dentine (ie the point where it is treated). He continues: 'As 28 of the 32 permanent teeth have erupted by the age of 12, the maximum incidence of caries (decay) will be over by the age of 16.' There is ample evidence too that both periodontal and gum disease (gingivitis) are no worse after one year has elapsed, according to Dr Sheiham.

The conclusion that Dr Sheiham reaches is that it is necessary for 12–16 year-olds to have a check up only every twelve months and those over 16 every eighteen months. In fluoridated areas the gap can be made even larger because of the tendency for holes in the teeth to remineralise of their own accord.

Shortly after his extensively researched articles appeared in *The Lancet* Dr Sheiham was, as he has been before, accused of maligning his own profession. The General Dental Practitioners' Association announced that they would report Dr Sheiham to the General Dental Council. Their spokesman said: 'What he says is nonsense; the reason for the bad state of the nation's health is government apathy'[3] – ever willing to shift the blame onto someone else. Yet these emotional outbursts at the time were not matched by any reasoned critique of Dr Sheiham's article. Moreover a look at the correspondence columns of *The Lancet* revealed that correspondents agreed with the general argument made by Dr Sheiham. Only two factors were repeatedly mentioned as good reasons to visit the dentist regularly; firstly, it was claimed that dentists may spot oral cancers which comprise 1 per cent of all cancer incidence; secondly, dentists could instruct their patients in oral hygiene which can prevent tooth decay.

Are you having unnecessary dental treatment?

When a journalist working for a London newspaper visited a variety of dentists for a check-up he was told by some that he needed as many as a dozen fillings or more and by other dentists that he needed only one or two fillings.[4] Whilst this is only anecdotal evidence, clearly an important principle emerges from this story. The need for a filling is often a subjective matter and can vary greatly between dentists; dental decay is not an all-or-nothing condition, just as the existence of a 'cataract' is a matter of ophthalmological opinion (see Cataract surgery, page 45). It has been claimed that widespread dental disease is caused by dental treatment and women have fewer teeth than men because they visit dentists more often. This was the disturbing conclusion reached in a report by five MPs and eight dental experts submitted in 1977 to the British Royal Commission on the National Health Service.[5] They described the dental service provided in the UK as 'often expensive, ineffective and counter-productive'. 'We are not managing to prevent dental diseases nor are we effectively treating disease when it does occur . . . the present mode of payment to dentists does little to promote the good will of dentists towards the NHS or guarantee the quality of care.'

Dentists are paid a fee for each item of service, which could encourage some dentists to sacrifice quality of treatment at the expense of a large turnover of patients. It can also tempt dentists who may be in doubt about the need for treatment to opt for expensive and profitable items such as crowning, rather than less expensive dentures[6] and to perform unnecessary dental X-rays for which they are paid an extra fee (see Hazards of unnecessary surgery, from page 31).

Since about half the population go to the dentist every six months there is a widespread over-treatment. The dentist says he can see teeth that are going to go bad so he fixes them at the first stages of decay. But it has been shown that dentists do damage teeth, so by going regularly it is probable that more things will go wrong and more unnecessary filling will be done. Also many treated cavities might have remineralised on their own accord as already explained. Using a high-speed drill often results in damage to adjacent teeth; sometimes the water-cooling system fails to work, resulting in what dentists call 'cooking the pulp', when the system cannot match the action of the drill. Food can get trapped inside badly prepared fillings. Sometimes the gum can be irritated by a piece of tooth that overhangs after a poorly drilled filling. There is also the possibility of some very serious injuries: infective hepatitis and kidney disease can be spread through bacteria carried by patients who pass through the dental surgery. Occasionally dentists may even kill their patients with the aid of intravenous anaesthetics. Anaesthetic deaths at the dentists are more likely to occur than in hospital because dentists do not employ trained anaesthetists (see page 125).

Dental treatment increases with the number of dentists

'There is one area in London which has more dentists than any other in the country and its children have more highly treated teeth than anywhere else' – Dr Aubrey Sheiham.[5] There is a new version of Parkinson's law: 'Fillings increase to provide employment for dentists.'

More dentists tend to work in middle-class areas but in the North many areas are short of dental personnel while in the South an increasing number of dentists are withdrawing from the NHS.[5] Only 1 per cent of the money spent in dental hygiene goes towards prevention, compared to 42.7 per cent on fillings.

The hazards of unnecessary dental X-rays

'Many believe today that no radiation exposure is so low that it cannot induce a health effect.'[7] Even though dental X-rays expose patients to a relatively small dose of radiation there is still real concern that they may be as hazardous as larger X-ray doses. The hazards include cancer, genetic mutations and diseases in the future children of people dosed with X-rays. A popular myth about these mutations is that they cause dramatic abnormalities, write

James Morrison and Mark Barnett in the American magazine FDA *Consumer* (February 1977). They point out that X-rays do not cause gross birth defects or extra fingers or toes but mainly subtle changes which are hard to identify at first. For example, mutations induced by X-rays can lead to an increased susceptibility to certain chronic diseases later in life such as diabetes or high blood pressure. The amount of radiation needed to produce such a single genetic mutation in a sperm or egg cell is low, certainly within the dosage received in many diagnostic X-ray examinations.[7] Since X-ray doses are cumulative, it means that two so-called 'safe' doses can add up to one unsafe dose.

In the USA the Bureau of Radiological Health has been running a campaign for a number of years to persuade dentists to use special metal shields, called 'gonad shields', to protect human eggs and sperm from exposure to radiation. These shields are placed in the laps of patients while they have their teeth X-rayed. Anyone who might wish to have children should always request that a lead apron be placed over the chest and lap, says Priscilla Laws, an Associate Professor of Physics and author of *Medical and Dental X-rays – A Consumer Guide to Avoiding Unnecessary Radiation Exposure.*[8] 'A dentist who aims the X-ray beams down through the top front teeth may be including your reproduction organs in the main beam,' says Dr Laws. Even in other exposure positions, there is a small amount of radiation to the ovaries or testicles resulting from scattered radiation, she adds. Lead aprons for children should not be forgotten either as they are potential parents too, warns Dr Laws.

Some dental X-ray machines are particularly hazardous. Dr Laws describes them as having short-pointed plastic cones. These plastic cones produce a scattering of the X-rays and expose dental patients' reproductive organs to twice as much radiation as the more modern lead-lined cylinders. The long open-ended lead-lined cylinder produces a narrow pencil-thin beam of X-rays with just as good, if not better, results. Dr Laws advises dental patients to ask their dentists to install long cylinders on their X-ray units, if they still use the plastic pointed cones. She maintains that this change does not involve much additional expense and is clearly a lot safer.

There are other ways of making X-rays safer for patients. It is possible to reduce by half the X-ray exposure a patient receives, with the aid of special 'rare earth screens' which reflect X-ray radiation back onto the X-ray film once it has passed through the organs of the body. In a survey carried out in the USA called DENT (Dental Exposure Normalisation Technique) it was found that some dentists were using fifty times more radiation than other dentists. The FDA estimates that between 5 and 10 per cent of X-rays are repeat examinations because the initial X-ray was not taken properly. A further 30 per cent of X-rays are taken when sets of film already exist. Some patients have the mistaken belief that X-rays are a necessary part of the routine treatment, but both the FDA and the American Dental Association state that X-rays should not be a standard part of every dental examination. Dr Priscilla Laws advises patients who change dentists to request that their X-ray records be transferred.[8]

Why anaesthetics are more likely to be fatal at the dentist's

As far back as 1967 an official report to the then Ministry of Health recommended that a dentist should not act as both operator and anaesthetist except perhaps in an emergency[9] but this recommendation has never been implemented. In 1979 the President of the Association of Anaesthetists of Great Britain, Stanley Mason, said that their association has campaigned for years for properly trained dental anaesthetists in dental surgeries. At present, dentists are neither properly trained in the administration of general anaesthesia nor in resuscitation.

About 12 people die each year as a result of receiving dental anaesthetics.[10] An investigation by Oliver Gillie of the deaths of 4 young people after receiving anaesthetics at the dentist's, and published in the *Sunday Times*,[9] reported that one dentist admitted having to resuscitate about 1 in 1,000 patients. Also it revealed that dental nurses are not required to have any special training and may be the only help for a dentist in an emergency. Dentists are as free as doctors to try out new types of anaesthetics, without any extra training.

Is the dental chair a hazard?

Deaths during dental anaesthesia usually occur when the patient receives the anaesthetic in the upright position sitting in the dentist's chair. Dr J. G. Bourne makes this observation in a letter to *The Lancet*[11] and suggests that dental patients should be treated lying down, to facilitate breathing. 'In some cases it may be more prudent to refer the patient to a hospital where he can be anaesthetized under ideal conditions,' comments Dr Iain Laws in *The Practitioner* in 1975.[12] Like Dr Bourne he also believes that it is difficult to maintain adequate anaesthesia, check vital functions and to support the head and jaw for any length of time with the patient *sitting* in a dental chair.

How to survive at the dentist's

One-quarter of all patients visiting the dentist have a medical problem which the dentist should know about before starting his treatment,[12] and as many as one-third have a disease which may seriously increase the hazards of a dental anaesthetic. Dr Iain Laws who published these figures maintains that few patients realise the vital importance of telling their dentist about the medical condition and of any drugs they may be taking. A simple tranquilliser like Valium could turn a safe anaesthetic into a life-threatening experience.

Information you must give the dentist

1 Respiratory disease such as asthma, chronic bronchitis or any lung condition.
2 Heart disease, high blood pressure.
3 Kidney or liver disease.
4 Pregnancy (the anaesthetic could injure the unborn child, see page 82 for details).
5 Diabetes.
6 *Any* drugs being consumed.
7 History of epilepsy.

Liver damage from anaesthetics

Since many dental patients will have a number of extractions or fillings in less than a year it is possible to suffer liver damage from repeated doses of anaesthetics. Dr Bill Inman investigated 130 cases of jaundice wich had been reported to the Committee on the Safety of Medicines from 1964–1972. Some 60 per cent of those who had been exposed more than once to an anaesthetic in a short period of time died from jaundice – whereas only 35 per cent of those who developed jaundice after one exposure to anaesthetic died from it.[13] A similar finding was made in the USA by the National Halothane Study.[14]

Corsodyl – drug for dental decay not recommended by 'Drug and Therapeutics Bulletin'

Corsodyl, a drug containing the chemical chlorhexidine and made by ICI to treat inflammation of the gums (gingivitis), cannot be recommended, says the authoritative independent guide to prescribing, the *Drug and Therapeutics Bulletin*.[15] 'In our opinion,' states the *Bulletin*, 'its promotion for this purpose should cease.'

More than 90 per cent of people with their own teeth suffer from gingivitis, caused by a film of bacteria (dental plaque) that begins to form within one hour of cleaning the teeth, says the *Bulletin*. For people over the age of 34, more teeth are lost from this condition than from ordinary dental decay because the infection eventually results in the loosening of the tooth.

There are various ways in which the bacterial dental plaque can be removed from the teeth and gums: by toothbrushing, dental floss, toothpicks and so on. The chemicals inside Corsodyl gel also inhibit these bacteria and users are advised to brush their teeth with it once a day. But in a controlled experiment to test the effectiveness of this drug it was found that established gingivitis was not reversible when mouth rinses were carried out with this drug. Gels of Corsodyl failed too to improve gingivitis but did reduce the amount of dental plaque. 'In addition,' says the *Bulletin*, 'the gingivitis and plaque worsened when the treatment was stopped, showing that it had no prolonged effect on children or young adults . . . Furthermore, it has little effect on gingivitis when it has progressed to chronic periodontitis unless the teeth are professionally scaled. As chronic periodontitis affects 90 per cent of adults in Britain chlorhexidine gel by itself has little use.'

Corsodyl stains teeth

Not only is this product largely useless, it also stains the teeth and fillings brown, and tastes bitter and unpleasant. It is pointed out that whilst ICI do recommend the brushing of teeth with an ordinary abrasive toothpaste to remove these stains it was still necessary to have the teeth professionally polished in 30 per cent of patients tested.

The question of fluoride

Internationally, Sweden, Finland, Denmark, France, West Germany, Holland and other European countries have opposed fluoridation. The House of Commons Expenditure Committee on Preventive Medicine has recommended against it. Yet an eminent body of doctors and dentists, under the umbrella of the Royal College of Physicians, in 1976 published a lengthy report which dismissed all the fears and dangers of fluoridation and recommended it.[16] Who can we believe?

Does fluoride cause extra cancer deaths?

Two distinguished researchers at the American National Cancer Institute claim to have proved a connection between fluoridation and cancer in ten of the largest cities in the USA. They have produced statistics that showed a city with fluoride in its water had greater numbers of deaths due to cancer than a non-fluoridated city. Drs J. Yiamouyainnis and Dean Burk have claimed that after studying cancer figures for twenty years they believe that 25,000 extra cancer deaths occur annually in the USA because of fluoride artificially added to the water supplies. But other experts like Sir Richard Doll, British Professor of Medicine at Oxford University and the man who first showed the relationship between smoking and cancer, disputes these claims. Sir Richard, as a member of the Royal College of Physicians' team that looked into fluoridation, believes that it should be encouraged.

Does fluoride really prevent tooth decay?

The possibility that fluoride in water might have some effect on tooth decay was first discovered forty years ago by an American public health official. He noticed that people with stained and mottled teeth seemed to have less tooth decay. Those people were found to live in places which had naturally abundant quantities of calcium fluoride in their water. Fluoride occurs naturally in almost all water. In Glasgow, for example, the water has naturally occurring levels of between 0.15 and 0.45 parts per million. But according to dental experts these levels are too low to

128

be of any benefit to teeth. By artificially raising the levels to just one part per million, the fluoride lobby say that they can create the so-called advantages of places which naturally have high fluoride in their drinking water. In Britain, Hartlepool has a naturally high amount of calcium fluoride and dentists claim that tooth decay in that area is reduced by half as a result. But what does this mean in practice? In fact, only 0.8 cavities per year are prevented in children aged 8–11. Fluoride does not guarantee a healthy or full set of teeth. It merely *postpones* tooth decay, according to a British Department of Health investigation.[16] In Scotland 44 per cent of the population over the age of 16 have had all their teeth extracted. By the age of 15, 97 per cent of children in Britain have tooth decay with 10 out of 28 permanent teeth decayed, missing or filled. Clearly, putting fluoride into the Scottish or English water supply is not going to make much difference, even with a 50 per cent reduction in decay.

The Royal College of Physicians' Report on fluoridation in 1976 admitted that the 'precise mechanism by which fluoride reduces caries (tooth decay) is not understood'. But on the other hand, they do admit that the cause of rotten teeth is our unhealthy diet. The Scots and the English have the highest consumption of sugar per person in the western world. During World War II, British teeth were much healthier than they are today, mainly on account of a balanced wartime diet containing fewer refined, processed foods.

Does a lack of fluoride cause tooth decay?
The Royal College of Physicians' Report states that they are concerned about the ethics of withholding a procedure if it is safe and of benefit. But the National Pure Water Association points out that another ethical question should be asked of the Royal College Committee: 'Knowing, as you do, that a major cause of tooth decay is children's over-indulgence in sticky sweets and other refined carbohydrates, is it ethical to condone and encourage this indulgence by holding out the false promise that fluoridation will prevent toothache?' The Royal College add weight to their 'concern' by stating that caries is not a trivial disorder but one that is responsible for a great deal of morbidity (disease) and for an appreciable number of

deaths from dental anaesthesia. But many dental deaths could be avoided if dentists were properly trained to use anaesthetics and required to have a separate anaesthetist present, according to the Department of Health's own reports.

The bias of the Royal College Committee on fluoridation

The National Pure Water Association also points out that the 1976 report is no more than the opinion of 18 members of the Royal College of Physicians and that a great many more equally or better qualified doctors and scientists including more than 60 members of the same college have given reasoned and unqualified opinions to the contrary. The Association itself has two professors and numerous doctors on its own committee. 'The arrogance of the (Royal College) Committee is astounding,' says the Association. It states that no authoritative medical opinion has previously been given on fluoridation yet more than 300 doctors, dentists, and scientists in the UK alone have for many years recorded their equally authoritative opinions against fluoridation.[17]

Is fluoride safe?

Fluoride occurs naturally in food and water, as calcium fluoride. Tea contains high concentrations of fluoride, and on average everyone consumes up to one milligram of fluoride in their food each day. The World Health Organisation has even said that it is one of the elements essential for life. If you drink a lot of tea each day you will be adding considerably to the amount of fluoride in your body. But the British government and others have banned the use of sodium fluoride as a food additive, yet sodium fluoride is one of the substances used to fluoridate water supplies. (Water is not considered a food by the government's food safety committee, so although we probably consume more water than anything else it can still have any banned *food* additives put into it).

Does fluoride cause bone disease?

Fluoride has a natural tendency to combine with calcium in our body; this means it accumulates in our bones and teeth. The first signs of fluoride poisoning are mottling of the teeth enamel. This occurs when there are only two parts per million of fluoride in the diet. Putting fluoride in our water supply will mean that everybody will be exposed to one part per million. The difference between a 'safe' level and a damaging level might easily disappear when it is remembered that we are constantly adding to the fluoride levels by using brands of toothpaste which contain fluoride. The average tube of fluoride toothpaste contains 200 milligrams of fluoride. Higher concentrations of fluoride can cause hardening of the bones and a hunch-back deformity, a condition known as 'fluorosis', seen in India and the Middle East, which is caused by levels of fluoride as high as forty parts per million.

Fluoride makes the bones more dense, and it has been used to treat people who suffer from a disease called osteoporosis. In this condition the bones become brittle and porous. It was noticed, however, that people who live in high fluoride areas suffered less from bone fractures so doctors started giving these fracture patients fluoride supplements in an attempt to strengthen their bones. But this practice soon stopped. Professor John Anderson of King's College Hospital said it was 'unscientific' and it is now believed that although it helps to improve bone condition at the beginning of treatment, in the long run fluoride is dangerous and actually makes bones worse. There is some evidence that long-term treatment with fluoride may also cause cancer. Kidney patients on kidney machines are particularly liable to suffer from fluoride-induced bone disease. This is because their diseased kidneys are unable to remove fluoride from the body and it gets retained in higher than normal quantities. The Royal College of Physicians' Report found that kidney patients in Britain and America tended to develop severe bone disease after using fluoridated water, but when pure, unfluoridated water was run through their dialysis machines their rates of bone disease dramatically decreased.

Does fluoride cause kidney disease?
The body's main defence against toxic substances is the kidney; all the waste products of our diet travel to the kidney to be purified and expelled from the body in our urine. Drugs like phenacetin and paracetamol have been shown to cause kidney disease. The *Journal of the American Medical Association* reported in 1972 that two teen-agers who had been drinking fluoridated water had

suffered kidney damage.

Does fluoride injure unborn children? Does it cause mongolism?

It has been suggested by Dr Ionel Rapaport of Wisconsin University that mongol children are twice as likely to be born in cities which have had their water supply fluoridated. Mongolism or Down's syndrome is caused by many factors, some genetic, some environmental, including damaged chromosomes, so no one is suggesting that fluoride is the only cause but it may be one of the factors involved. Again the Royal College of Physicians disagrees with these findings and quotes studies carried out in Birmingham (a fluoridated city) to show that mongolism is NOT increased by fluoride. It is interesting to note that Dr Rapaport was unable to publish his research in the United States where the pro-fluoride lobby is said to be very strong; he had to publish in France, a country which is against fluoridation.[18] A scientific issue has been transformed into a moral and political one. Each side in the fluoride war carefully chooses its facts and figures to suit its purpose and the public are left confused and dazed by the barrage of arguments for and against.

Why isn't there an anti-chlorine lobby?

Chlorine, as the fluoride lobby often points out, is also a poisonous chemical, yet there are no protests against the addition of chlorine to the water supply. But chlorine is very different: it is used to make the water drinkable, to make it clean. It works like a disinfectant, killing off germs. Without it, water would carry diseases. Chlorine also disappears by the time you turn on your tap. it is dispersed by the time you drink it. There will be none left in your glass of water. If, by any chance, there is any left, boiling will remove it, whilst fluoride is concentrated if you boil it. People who live in fluoridated areas are often advised not to use water that has been boiled more than once because of the increasing levels of fluoride that accumulate.

Will fluoridation be only the start of a mass compulsory medication?

In Tanzania and Chile, organochlorine chemicals have been added to the water supply in order to combat a disease called bilharzia, a parasitic disease that affects most of the population. In letters published in the *New Scientist* the managing director of Shell Chemicals, Lord Iliffe, advocated the 'harmlessness' of such measures.[19] But organochlorines are known to cause cancer and to affect fertility.

Also, a Dr M. Krieger has suggested that drugs that reduce the sex drive should be added to the water supply in order to curb the population explosion (again in the *New Scientist*).[20]

In *The Lancet* a Dr Voors suggested in 1969 that lithium be added to the water supply to 'improve the quality of life for the middle aged'. Lithium has been associated with birth defects in experimental animals, and serious kidney damage when given to mentally disturbed patients.[21]

Doctors and dentists who are really concerned about reducing tooth decay should take the obvious course and start a campaign to improve our diet, to lower sugar and sweet consumption. People who want fluoride can buy it in their toothpaste; it is even possible to put it into milk. In Edinburgh 44,000 school kids receive a fortnightly fluoride mouthwash, once their parents have signed a consent form. Fluoride could even be added to sweets; in that way the rot could be combated at its source. All these methods allow the public to choose whether or not to have fluoride in their diet. When it is put into the water supply that freedom to choose is taken from us.

7

Contraception

The top nine methods of contraception

No. of users in Britain

1	The Pill	3,100,000
2	Rubber condoms	2,700,000
3	Coitus interruptus	700,000
4	IUD or 'coil'	600,000
5	Sterilisation	600,000
6	Female barrier methods (eg cap)	500,000
7	Rhythm methods	200,000
8	Spermicides used alone	100,000
9	Depoprovera	33,000

The figures for the number of contraceptive users in Britain were provided by the Family Planning Association (FPA) in 1979 and since then it is possible that fewer women are taking the Pill because of the warning of increased risk of thrombosis for women over the age of 35.

There are some 11,000,000 women in Britain in the fertile age range of 15–44 and, of these, the FPA estimates that 8 million are sexually active and at risk of pregnancy. But the FPA points out that as many as 3 million of these sexually active women (or their partners) are not using any reliable form of contraceptive or are not using one regularly.[1]

Perhaps the most interesting statistic here is the large number of condom users. Despite its messiness and the lack of spontaneity associated with its use, it remains one of the few safe methods of contraception.

Methods of birth control are only as effective as those who use them. Forgetting to take the pill or apply a spermicide jelly turns an effective contraceptive into a useless one. Only sterilisation, the IUD and Depoprovera require no action by the user.

How effective are the different forms of contraception?[2]

Method	No. of women out of 100 who will become pregnant in one year
1 (a) combination pill (oestrogen plus progestogen)	less than 1
(b) progestogen-only pill	2–3
(c) Depoprovera injection	n.a. (but see p. 142)
2 IUD or coil	1–6
3 Diaphragm plus spermicidal jelly (ie cap)	2–20
4 Creams, foams and jellies (a) aerosol foam alone	2–29
(b) jellies and creams alone	4–36
(c) vaginal suppositories	no figures available but effectiveness estimated to be fair to poor
5 Rubber condom	3–36
6 Female sterilisation	none – (but see p. 64)
7 Male sterilisation (vasectomy)	none – (but see p. 71)
8 Rhythm methods: (a) calendar method	14–17
(b) temperature method	1–20
(c) mucous method	1–25
(d) temperature or mucous method with intercourse only after ovulation	1–7
9 Withdrawal method or 'coitus interruptus'	very high failure rate
10 Douching	useless

Quick guide to the risks of using the various contraceptives

The Pill

(a) RISKS TO ALL WOMEN
Tender breasts, nausea, vomiting, unexpected vaginal bleeding, more sugar and fat in the blood. Increased risk of diabetes and heart disease.

Blood clots: thrombosis. Greater risk of heart attack and stroke, increasing with age and amount of cigarette smoking.

Possible higher blood pressure. Higher risk of gall-bladder disease needing surgery. Small increase in risk of benign liver cancer.

(b) WOMEN ESPECIALLY AT RISK
Smokers on the Pill have a greater risk of heart attack. Women who have had a heart attack, stroke, angina, blood clots, any cancers, scanty or irregular periods.

In a woman who becomes pregnant while using it, the Pill can injure the foetus.

The Pill aggravates migraine headaches, depression, fibroids of the uterus, kidney and heart disease, asthma, high blood pressure, diabetes and epilepsy.

All risks increase with age. After the age of 35 other forms of contraception should be used.

(c) EFFECT ON THE ABILITY TO HAVE CHILDREN
The Pill does not make women infertile but it may delay conception. Women coming off the Pill should wait a short time before trying to have a baby, using an alternative contraceptive for several months. After childbirth the Pill should not be used immediately as the hormones in the Pill pass straight into the mother's milk, and the effect on the baby is not known, but unlikely to be safe.

IUD/Coil

(a) RISKS TO ALL WOMEN
Cramps and heavier periods. IUD can be expelled without woman knowing. Anaemia, pregnancy in the fallopian tubes, pelvic infection, perforation of uterus or cervix and septic abortion.

Serious complications if pregnancy occurs with IUD.

(b) WOMEN ESPECIALLY AT RISK

Women who are prone to pelvic infection, who have more than one regular partner, women with cancer of uterus, cervix or pelvis prior to IUD use, recent pregnancy, abortion or miscarriage, VD, severe cramps, copper allergy, anaemia, history of fainting attacks, unexplained genital bleeding or vaginal discharge, abnormal cervical smear.

(c) EFFECT ON ABILITY TO HAVE CHILDREN

Pelvic infection in IUD users may lead to infertility and ectopic pregnancy (in the fallopian tube) which always ends in miscarriage.

Diaphragm: no risks
Foam, cream or jelly: no risks
Vaginal suppositories: no risks
Rubber condom: no risks

Female sterilisation

(a) RISKS TO ALL WOMEN

Ordinary risks of surgery, infection, bleeding or injury to other organs. No women are *especially* at risk unless surgery is inadvisable.

(b) EFFECT ON THE ABILITY TO HAVE CHILDREN

The operation may be reversible with specialised microscopic surgical techniques, available only in rare instances. Generally should be considered permanent (but see page 64).

Male sterilisation

(a) RISKS TO ALL MEN

Not effective for the first few months. Minor complications of surgery such as infection, sperm-antibodies produced by some men (see page 71). No men are *especially* at risk unless surgery is inadvisable.

(b) EFFECT ON THE ABILITY TO HAVE CHILDREN

Only rarely is this operation reversible. Generally looked upon as permanent.

Rhythm method

Sexual frustration because of the extended time each month that sex must be avoided. Pressures on relationship as the couple must refrain from having sex except on certain days of the month. No other risk, apart from a low rate of effectiveness.

Withdrawal and douching

The major risk here is pregnancy and therefore these methods should not be considered practical means of birth control.

IUD (the 'coil')

'The most serious doubt about the use of the IUD is that it may impair ability to conceive or complete a subsequent pregnancy' *British Medical Journal* editorial.[3]

It is disturbing that British women have been kept in the dark about the risks associated with the IUD (the 'coil'), one of the most popular forms of birth control because of its simplicity of use and its apparent safety. In the USA doctors are required by law to inform women of these risks before fitting an IUD; British women have not been made aware of the risks.

The risk of becoming infertile with an IUD

IUDs were originally designed for women who had already had children. Fitting an IUD through the tight cervix of a woman who has not experienced childbirth was originally thought to be impossible. This problem was overcome with the aid of narrow-gauge IUD-inserters; nevertheless, the use of IUDs for women who have not had children has still always been questioned because of the possible long-term risks to fertility.[3] If a childless woman is fitted with an IUD she will have a higher risk of (a) pregnancy when she does not want it; (b) expulsion of the IUD; (c) bleeding and pain; (d) most harmful of all, a higher risk of pelvic infection which can affect her future chances of childbearing.

'IUDs should not be the first choice of method of contraception for women who have never had children,' concluded Dr R. Snowden and his colleagues after reviewing the hazards of IUDs in over 20,000 women.[4] 'The most serious doubt is that it may impair fertility,' says the *British Medical Journal*, adding that 'The evidence suggests that in most cases the ability to conceive after wearing an IUD is not unduly retarded, but the same cannot be said for women who have had pelvic infection, spontaneous abortion (a miscarriage) or an ectopic pregnancy (ie a pregnancy that takes place in the Fallopian tube resulting in a miscarriage), all of which are more likely with an IUD.'

Several investigations have shown that a woman wearing an IUD who has never had children is seven times more likely to suffer from an infection of the Fallopian tubes compared to a woman on the Pill.[5] 'What makes these findings the more worrying,' states the *British Medical Journal*, 'is the apparent relation between pelvic infection and subsequent infertility.'[3] It adds, 'When pregnancy does occur, the proportion who miscarry or who have an ectopic pregnancy is higher among IUD users than among non-IUD users. The effect of pelvic infection, spontaneous abortion and ectopic pregnancy on the outcome of subsequent pregnancies is a matter of especial concern to those who are using an IUD as a means of delaying their first pregnancy.' The editorial ended by making a plea for investigation of this hazard, which it believed was overdue.

'It is most important for the doctor to remember that women who present with an accidental pregnancy after more than three years' use of an IUD have about a one in ten chance of having an ectopic gestation.' These were the concluding words of a paper recently published in *The Lancet* by Professor Martin Vessey and his team at the Department of Social and Community Medicine at Oxford University,[6] who investigated a series of ectopic pregnancies in the Oxford area. In previous surveys they had already found that ectopic pregnancies were thirteen times more common in women using IUDs compared to women using other types of contraception. This latest analysis of IUD users has shown that the possibility of an ectopic pregnancy does not actually increase the longer this method is used, the risk remaining the same no matter how long a woman wears the IUD.

IUD risk related to age: younger girls at greatest risk
A new survey of women and young girls using IUDs has found that after two years of use, 16–19 year-olds had a pelvic infection rate more than ten times that of 30–49 year-olds.[7] The risk decreased the longer the IUD was used. Part of these findings can be explained by the fact that younger women are more likely to be exposed to

sexual infections because of a supposedly greater frequency of sex. Nevertheless, using an IUD increases the risk, and the researchers advise 'careful counselling before use of the IUD by women who have not had children, especially the very young'.

American warnings about the IUD

In July 1975 the American FDA decided that women contemplating the use of the IUD should be given a brochure by their doctors outlining the benefits and risks known to be related to its use as compared with other available methods of contraception. US doctors are also required to obtain the patient's written or oral consent before fitting the 'coil'. The following section is an illustration of the kind of information supplied to American women by the FDA and the companies who manufacture IUDs. [8]

'The IUD is a relatively safe and effective means of contraception but it does carry with it certain problems. Two of these problems are the risks involved if you become pregnant while wearing an IUD and an increased chance of developing pelvic inflammatory disease.

PREGNANCY AND IUD USE

If your period is late, or you think you might be pregnant, you should be checked by your doctor.

If you prove to be pregnant, the IUD should be removed if this can be done easily. Removal of the 'coil' early in pregnancy prevents serious complications from occurring.

If the IUD is not removed, you should be aware that there is an increased risk of infected abortion occurring when the pregnancy is allowed to continue. You and your doctor should discuss whether it is best to terminate or to continue the pregnancy.

If a pregnancy is allowed to continue, whether the IUD is removed or not, you should be examined very closely by your doctor for early signs of complication.

PELVIC INFLAMMATORY DISEASE AND IUD USE

Recent studies have shown that women who wear an IUD have a greater chance of developing pelvic inflammatory disease than non-users. Those who are most susceptible are women in the under-25 age group, those who have had PID before, and those who have more than one sex partner or who frequently change partners.

Pelvic inflammatory disease refers to a group of several pelvic infections that may affect the uterus, the tubes, or the tubes and ovaries, and which can be caused by gonorrhoea or certain other bacteria.

Symptoms of pelvic infection can include pelvic or abdominal pain, increasing pain with intercourse and/or menstruation, irregular bleeding (spotting, flooding, or passing clots), abnormal vaginal discharge, and occasional chills and fever.

If the tubes are affected and become sufficiently scarred, infertility may result. Also, scarred tubes may increase the chance of an ectopic (tubal) pregnancy. There can also be serious interference with or curtailment of a woman's ability to become pregnant.

If you wear an IUD and suspect that you may have pelvic infection, contact your doctor immediately – this condition requires early identification and proper treatment.

If you are considering an IUD as a method of family planning, discuss *all* the risks with your doctor.'

No equivalent warnings about the IUD appear in Britain.

In addition, American women are warned that the copper IUDs may cause allergy to this metal. These copper devices can also cause heat damage if the woman receives diathermy (ie microwave) treatment for back pain. Such heat treatment may be more likely in an IUD-user as one of the side effects of wearing the 'coil' is back pain.

Special hazard warning

One type of IUD called the Dalkon Shield, a small crab-shaped device, was withdrawn in 1975 in Britain and America because of extra hazards such as septic abortions, infection, cramps, bleeding and ectopic pregnancy associated with its use. But as over 100,000 of these particular IUDs were fitted in Britain, it is possible *but unlikely* that some women still have Dalkon Shield IUDs inside them. Any woman with this type of 'coil' should have it replaced with a safer IUD or use an alternative method of contraception.

Progestasert, another IUD device which is tipped with the female hormone progesterone, has also been withdrawn because of the unusually high rate of ectopic pregnancies associated with its use.

Depoprovera

This is a contraceptive injection of the female hormone progesterone that remains effective for at least three months. However, because of evidence from animal experiments of an increased risk of breast cancer with this drug it has been banned in the USA and its use has been restricted in Britain. Many doctors, however, have disregarded the UK safety guidelines on the use of Depoprovera; more than 30,000 women in Britain receive the injections.[9] The Planned Parenthood Federation distributes Depoprovera in more than forty-two countries, particularly in the Third World, where drug safety laws are less stringent than in the USA and Britain.

Does Depoprovera work as a contraceptive?

A study has been made of over 70 women who were given DP injections whilst they were awaiting sterilisation after having a baby. DP resulted in more than a quarter of these women having episodes of intermittent heavy bleeding – a well-known side effect of this contraceptive – but most of the women were happy to have had the protection.[10]

Another investigation, of nearly 1,000 women, found that a single six-monthly injection was as effective as the Pill and the IUD. Irregular bleeding was also common as was weight gain; however, most women were pleased to continue with further doses of DP.[11] But had they been informed of possible risks?

Why did the US government ban Depoprovera?

In March 1978 the FDA told Upjohn, the manufacturers of Depoprovera, that it would not allow the drug to be used as a contraceptive because the benefits did not justify the risks. This ban was the second occasion that the American drug authorities had taken action against this progesterone-only contraceptive. In 1970 long-term animal experiments revealed that beagle dogs developed both breast and uterine cancers after being given Depoprovera injections.

But before they finally banned Depoprovera, the American drug authorities allowed its use on the condition that any women who were given this contraceptive would have to be first informed of the increased risk of breast cancer and of the possibility that Depoprovera might make it difficult for them to conceive, as it can delay the onset of subsequent fertility. In addition the FDA stipulated that it was only to be given to women who were unable to tolerate any other form of contraception. Patients would be required to sign a consent form acknowledging that they had been warned of these adverse effects by their doctor before starting the treatment. Upjohn protested against such severe limitations on their product and have been fighting for a reversal of this decision ever since. However, not only did they fail to obtain a reprieve, but in 1979 the FDA again flatly refused the company's request for a licence to sell Depoprovera as a contraceptive in America, arguing that other, safer, methods of contraception were already available. Also the FDA stated, 'No clear evidence has been submitted to show that there are patients who particularly need this drug.'

One of the other side effects of Depoprovera is that it can cause painful periods (dysmenorrhoea) which may necessitate a woman having to take oestrogen pills. As these pills themselves carry an extra risk, any benefit that might be obtained from taking Depoprovera as a contraceptive would disappear since a combination of oestrogen pills plus Depoprovera is no different from taking the Pill. If Depoprovera fails to work, or if the injection is given once a women has already become pregnant it will expose the unborn foetus to a harmful dose of progesterone. This situation can greatly increase the risk of giving birth to a deformed baby with heart defects or limb deformities.

These reasons have kept Depoprovera away from the American public as a contraceptive although it is permitted to be used as an anti-cancer drug for cases of womb cancer.

Cancer found in monkeys after treatment with Depoprovera

One of the groups in the USA which has fought against Depoprovera's introduction is the American Women's Health Network and it has uncovered yet further evidence of the drug's potential to cause cancer. In August 1979[12] they produced evidence to counter the claim often made by Upjohn that the original beagle experiments were invalid because these animals proved too sensitive to progesterone. However, researcher Stephen Minkin discovered that the only beagles which survived this study had all undergone hysterectomies – in other words, the beagles did not have their own natural supplies of oestrogen. This makes sense as oestrogen is known to stimulate the growth of cancers, and hysterectomies are often performed to prevent cancer (see Unnecessary surgery, pages 57-60). In the beagle experiments the animals which died all had cancer of the uterus. Since all women who are given Depoprovera have intact wombs these results may be particularly significant.

Further evidence that Depoprovera may cause cancer in humans comes from a ten-year-long study of the effect of the drug in monkeys. It was found that 2 out of 16 monkeys given high doses of Depoprovera died of cancer of the uterus. The remaining monkeys had uterine disease proportionate to the dose of Depoprovera which they received. According to researchers at the National Institute of Health uterine cancer is extremely rare in rhesus monkeys, so this experiment provides the strongest argument that Depoprovera may induce cancer in humans. Deproprovera is a cancer drug and like most drugs used to *treat* cancer it may *cause* cancer as well. It has been shown that if mice are exposed to a known carcinogen (ie cancer-causing substance) the incidence of cancer of the cervix is increased when progesterone is given at the same time.[13]

Depoprovera in Britain – many doctors are ignoring government restrictions

The British Committee on the Safety of Medicines has given permission for Depoprovera to be used on a restricted short-term basis only for women who need short-term contraceptive protection. The two reasons officially permitted by the Department of Health are when a woman's husband/partner has had a vasectomy and needs a few months before all his sperm are completely blocked off, or where a woman has had a German measles vaccine and may need contraceptive protection for a short period as the live vaccine can injure the foetus. These are the *only* two circumstances in which the Committee on the Safety of Medicines has permitted Depoprovera to be used, but these restrictions (in strict legal terms, 'guidelines') are being widely ignored by doctors all over Britain.[14] If women are aware of the risks, but still request the drug, this may be acceptable, but the drug is being abused in its application according to MPs and a national group known as the Campaign Against the Use of Depoprovera. There is evidence that many doctors are giving Depoprovera selectively to black, Asian and white working-class women. These women are often *considered by their doctors* to be living in 'degrading poverty' and therefore 'too irresponsible' to be able to cope with other forms of birth control. It is unlikely that any of these patients are being informed of the associated risks.

Depoprovera affects the brain

Depoprovera is known to affect the pituitary adrenal cortex hormone system (ie the hormonal control centre of the brain), so it is possible that it may unbalance the very finely tuned hormonal controls of the entire body. Infertility and irregular periods are the consequences of such interference and they are known to be associated with the use of Depoprovera. Additionally both the oestrogen and progestorone hormones have been implicated as a cause of congenital heart defects in babies exposed in the womb.[15] Also as the manufacturers say in their warning sheet to doctors, 'Some instances of female foetal masculinisation (clitoral hypertrophy) have been observed on large doses', but they add reassuringly 'these have usually reverted to normal within a few weeks of birth'. The long-term effects are, of course, unknown, even if they do 'revert to normal within a few weeks'.

In February 1980 the British Committee on the Safety of Medicines turned down a further request from Upjohn for a licence to market Depoprovera without restrictions on its general use.

Morning-after pills: do they work?

In the first three days after intercourse, oestrogen hormones taken in high doses *can* prevent pregnancy. But nausea and breast soreness are common side effects and failures tend to occur when the hormones are taken after three days. The failure rate has been reported at up to 2 per cent with great hazards to any subsequent baby born.

Hazards

If the pregnancy is not terminated there is a strong risk of injuring the foetus (see page 148 for defects caused by the Pill, and page 253 on DES cancer). Ectopic pregnancies (ie those that occur in the Fallopian tubes) are relatively common (10 per cent of cases) where this type of morning-after pill fails, says the *Drug and Therapeutics Bulletin*.[16]

Other methods

The contraceptive pill can be used. Two tablets of the pill Eugynon 50 or Ovran taken once and then twelve hours later are effective and produce fewer side effects than oestrogens alone.[16] But product licences for Ovran and Eugynon do not include 'morning after' contraception, and this is not recommended by the drug companies.

If an IUD (coil) is inserted into a woman within seven days of unprotected intercourse it is an effective contraceptive. The *Drug and Therapeutics Bulletin* reports that nearly 300 women over a five-year period have successfully used this method.

Progestogens can also be used successfully but only in the first 24 hours. But there is a higher failure rate and menstrual problems are more likely too.

The Pill

'Users of the Pill have a 100 per cent risk of illness. Everybody in my experience eventually becomes ill. The only question is how long it takes to get ill' (Dr Ellen Grant, Former Chief Research Physician at the Family Planning Association).[17]

Does the Pill make women infertile?

'The evidence seems clear that on average there is some temporary impairment of fertility after the preparations are stopped.' This is the conclusion reached by Professor Martin Vessey and Sir Richard Doll of Oxford University,[18] two of the most distinguished researchers to have studied the effects of the Pill. They reviewed the matter in 1976 and then said that it had not yet been shown that the Pill could cause permanent infertility. One of their own investigations compared 17,000 users of the Pill, the diaphragm and the IUD (ie 'coil'). Pill users tended to have more trouble conceiving than either of the other two groups, in the first two years. After the first two years the

146

chances of conceiving were pretty good for women who had already borne children but not as good for the childless (ie most young women on the Pill). But for the vast majority, conception was likely either after a few months or within the first two years, after discontinuing the Pill.

There is one group of women though who are at special risk of infertility, according to some American investigators. Women who have irregular periods before going on the Pill are more likely to suffer from infertility or absence of periods (amenorrhoea) afterwards. The early use of the Pill combined with a late start to menstruation are factors which make this more probable, according to Dr Gideon and Barbara Seaman writing in their exhaustive book *Women and the Crisis in Sex Hormones*.[19] They refer to a study of over 300 women in Providence, Rhode Island, USA which identified the risk factors. 'This is another reason the Pill is so dangerous for teenagers – it can destroy their fertility for ever,'[19] comment the Seamans. In the USA women on the Pill have to be informed of this risk and many other risks linked with its use in specially printed 'patient package inserts'. In this particular context the Food and Drug Authority requires that women (not just doctors) are told that those 'with scanty or irregular periods should use another method of contraception since if they use the Pill they may have difficulty in becoming pregnant or may fail to have menstrual periods after discontinuing the Pill'.[20] British health authorities do not insist on any label warning for women using the Pill. However all UK companies now voluntarily provide a patient leaflet listing the Pill's side effects and contra-indications.

But in Britain the Committee on the Safety of Medicines *has* required doctors to be warned about the hazards of prescribing the Pill to young girls. Schering Ltd, who make the popular brand of the Pill known as Eugynon, tell doctors that 'oral contraceptives should not be given to young girls who have only recently experienced their menarch (ie begun to have periods)', adding that young girls should be checked after three months to see if their body temperature alters whilst they are off the Pill for a month.

The time taken to conceive has been investigated in a recent four-year study of thousands of Israeli women in Jerusalem[21] and published in 1978. The fertility of nearly 6,000 women was studied, 1,400 of these women having used the Pill prior to becoming pregnant. Drs Susan Harlap and Michael Davies, who conducted this vast investigation, found that 30 per cent fewer one-time Pill users conceived in the first month compared to women using other methods of contraception, but again they observed that this was only a temporary setback. However, the loss in fertility was found to be greater in older women and women who had been using the Pill for long periods of time. The dose did not seem to be related to any delay in fertility. Evidence is available from several sources that there is an increase in the numbers of deformed babies born to women who conceive immediately after coming off the Pill so this delay in fertility may be a blessing in disguise.

Do women on the Pill have a greater risk of having deformed babies?

'Women who stop using oral contraceptives (ie the Pill) should wait a few months before becoming pregnant to minimise the risk of birth defects associated with the use of sex hormones during pregnancy' (warning to American women contained in every Pill packet).

One of the reasons why the FDA instituted this particular warning in 1977 was because New York researcher Dr Dwight Janerich (after a study of 600 such cases) discovered that women who had given birth to a malformed child were 30 per cent more likely to have used the Pill immediately before conception or during early pregnancy. Another study published in the *New England Journal of Medicine* in 1977 also found that the chances of having a deformed baby were more than doubled in women who took hormones during early pregnancy. Normally the risk of having a heart defect was found to occur in about 1 in every 125 births, but with the Pill this risk was found to rise to about 1 in 55 births.[22,23]

Further evidence of this increased risk to unborn children comes from the Jerusalem study[21] which concluded that oral contraceptives are safe for women who plan to become pregnant at ages 20–34 regardless of parity

148

(ie whether or not they had any children), education, social class, ethnic group and height *provided that conception is avoided for a few months after stopping the Pill*. They had found an excess of major congenital malformations in male but not in female babies and an increase in the numbers of twins born and stillborn infants amongst mothers who did not take a reasonable break between discontinuing the Pill and conceiving. In the light of these findings the research team in Jerusalem recommended at least a *three*-month interval before attempting to conceive.

Women who discontinue the Pill for other reasons – for example, because of side effects or because of surgery where the Pill can aggravate any thrombosis that may result from surgery and so on – should be aware that they are likely to conceive, with the increased risk of producing a deformed child. Every woman suffering from amenorrhoea after stopping the Pill (ie absence of menstruation) should also take precautions against pregnancy. One interesting suggestion made by the Jerusalem team is that since the malformation risk seems confined to male babies, then perhaps the sex of the foetus could be determined with amniocentesis (see page 107 for details). If the sex of the baby were discovered in this way then male foetuses could be aborted and baby girls left to develop normally.

The female sex hormones which are used in the contraceptive pill have been identified as capable of causing birth defects from the various other ways in which they are used in medicine. For example, hormone pregnancy tests once sold in Britain as the product Primodos, were associated with increased risk of heart defects. Another hormone called DES or diethyl-stilboestrol (or just Stilboestrol) was the first synthetic oestrogen to be discovered, but its use resulted in an epidemic of vaginal cancers in the daughters of mothers who took this drug to prevent miscarriage. DES neither worked nor was it safe. There are thousands of DES daughters and sons in America and some 7,000 in Britain, too, who should now have annual check-ups to make sure their genitals are not diseased with a precancer state induced by this dose of oestrogen taken after conception.

The real risks of heart and blood diseases caused by the Pill
The Pill, because it contains oestrogen, can create blood clots (ie thrombosis). High blood pressure also results from use of the Pill and this condition in its own right is known to result in a greater risk of heart attack, stroke and kidney damage. Although these blood and heart diseases are reasonably rare they do kill about 60 otherwise healthy women each year. The risk of stroke is about 1 in 10,000 and since over 3 million women in Britain use the Pill, a simple calculation shows that 300 extra women will experience a stroke.[18] The risk of a fatal heart attack is about 1 in 30,000 or three times greater than normal.[24] The risks associated with the Pill become more serious (six times greater than for non-users) in women over the age of 35, especially if they smoke cigarettes. But the so-called 'mini-Pill', which contains only progestogen, may be safer than the combined Pill which contains *both* oestrogen and progestogen.

Pill hazards: New findings
The Royal College of GPs' long-term investigation of the hazards of the Pill amongst thousands of Pill-users produced a new report in 1981 confirming that their risk of death from heart disease or stroke was 4.3 times greater compared to women who had never taken the Pill. The massive survey of the health of Pill-users co-ordinates information from 1,400 GPs' surgeries. The new finding made was that the risk of death is *not* associated with the length of time a woman has been taking the Pill.

Women under 35 on the Pill seem to suffer no greater risk of death than those not taking it IF THEY DO NOT SMOKE. Below this age the risk is one in 77,000 for non-smokers and one in 10,000 for smokers.[25]

How a woman can protect herself from a fatal reaction to the Pill
'The occurrence of such events can be minimised by ensuring that patients with a history of naturally occurring thrombo-embolism (ie blood clots) are not given these preparations and by noting and acting on early-warning signs of thrombosis, such as pain in the calf of the leg, or of embolism – pain in the chest.' This is the advice provided by Drs D. R. Laurence and J. W. Black[26] in their book *The Medicine You Take*.

Schering, the manufacturers of one of the most popular Pills – Eugynon – advise doctors in their drug information sheets when the Pill should be discontinued. Under the heading *Reasons for stopping oral contraception* they include, 'The occurrence of migraine in patients who have never previously suffered from it, or exacerbation of pre-existing migraine, any unusually frequent or severe headaches, any kind of acute disturbances of vision (blood clots trapped in the network of blood vessels in the retina of the eye can cause partial or complete blindness). First signs of thrombo-phlebitis or thromboembolism (pain in the leg or chest as previously mentioned), jaundice, four weeks before elective surgery, and during immobilisation, eg after accidents, etc, significant rise in blood pressure, pregnancy.'

Does the Pill damage the skin?

'In particularly predisposed women, long-term use of the tablets can sometimes cause brownish patches on the face which are made worse by long exposure to the sun. Women who have this tendency should therefore avoid spending too long in the sun.' This again is the advice given to British doctors by the manufacturers of Eugynon, Schering Chemicals Ltd.

Dr Gideon and Barbara Seaman comment that after weight gain, fluid retention, breakthrough bleeding and depression, patchy skin discolouration is the most common side effect of the Pill.[19] It is imperative to stay out of the sun if these patches develop; they are often a permanent disfigurement. Some Pill users become so sun-sensitive that they get a rash just from light streaming in through a window.

The skin infection thrush, which can spread over the vagina, is also associated with the Pill. The hormones in the Pill reduce the acid secretions in the vagina and therefore make it easier for bacteria to thrive. Natural yogurt is often recommended as a cure for thrush because it increases the acid concentrations if applied vaginally. Tight clothing (eg tights) also increases the risk of this infection. The Seamans suggest that varieties of the Pill with a greater percentage of progesterone are more likely to produce skin reactions because there is a masculinising effect associated with their use. It produces complaints such as acne, hairiness, scanty periods and permanent weight gain. Examples of Pills with high progesterone concentrations are Ortho-Novim, Norlestrin, Norinyl, Norquen, Loestin, Zorane. Oestrogen-dominant pills (Enorid, Ovulen, Demulen) can improve acne, they say, but can cause fluid retention, heavy periods and breast swelling.

Breast cancer and the Pill: disturbing new evidence of increased risk to young women

'The implications are worrying: if this risk persists into old age – a possibility that cannot be proved or disproved – it might eventually produce groups of women with a one-in-five chance of developing breast cancer.' – The *British Medical Journal*, commenting on two new large-scale studies involving 40,000 women who have used the Pill.[27]

One of these studies, carried out by the Royal College of General Practitioners and involving 23,000 women, found that women aged between 30 and 34 diagnosed with breast cancer were three times more likely to have used the Pill. These results were statistically significant and lend support to the results from a study of Californian women (by Pike and his colleagues), which found double the risk amongst women under age 33 who had been on the Pill for four years or more. The risk was even greater for women on the Pill for more than eight years.

Breast cancer takes 20 to 30 years to develop, and as the Pill was introduced in 1960 (in the UK) and in 1959 (in the USA), the full risks of the Pill cannot be known until 1990.

The *British Medical Journal*, in its editorial on these findings, concluded that 'blanket reassurance [of the Pill's safety] might prove to be irresponsible. The "worst case" conclusion is that young girls should avoid prolonged use of the Pill before their first pregnancy, especially if they have a history of benign breast disease.'[27]

Does the Pill cause liver cancer?

More than three studies have confirmed that benign liver tumours are more common in women taking the Pill. They are mainly benign cancers (ie not invasive cancer) but still need to be operated on and may cause fatal haemorrhage.

The connection between liver cancer and the Pill was first spotted by Dr Janet Baum in 1973, who found 7 cases in five years.[28] A group of doctors in Kentucky found a further 13 cases of liver tumour, 4 of which were malignant (ie invasive cancer) and 3 of which died. A further 50 cases were discovered shortly afterwards.[29] The Pill causes other liver complications such as jaundice and this may be an early sign of potential tumour.

Normally liver cancer is extremely rare but now 'cases are popping up all over the country and in Europe' according to the American researcher Dr Janet Baum.[28] She points out that in the two years since the association with the Pill was discovered, almost as many cases have been announced as appeared in all the medical literature since 1913. 'We do not know the number of women who have died with these liver tumours undiagnosed; it is probably not as low as one might think. The risk is *not* related to the length of time a woman has been taking the Pill and the tumours are not immediately recognised in normal liver tests.'

The continuous use of the Pill for five years increases the risk of a liver cancer fivefold, according to a report in *The Lancet* in February 1980 by Dr James Neuberger.[30] He also says that after nine years the risk is increased twenty-five times – however, this still makes it a very unlikely event. However, Dr Neuberger says he was often struck by the variations in the tumours and the delay in reaching a diagnosis.

Cancer of the womb and cervix from the Pill?

Animal experiments have often shown that the oestrogens in the Pill can cause cancer of the womb. Equally, the same oestrogens when used in menopause drugs have been responsible for an increase in womb cancer of between four and thirteen times the usual incidence, amongst post-menopausal patients. But the combined Pill contains not only oestrogen, a cancer-causing substance, but also progesterone which is frequently used as an anti-cancer drug, so it is possible that the usual combination-type Pill used by most women both causes and prevents cancer simultaneously. Until 1975 another type of Pill was some-times used, called the sequential pill (because it gave a dose of oestrogen followed by a dose of progesterone – much like hormone replacement therapy), but two doctors, Steven Silverberg and Edgar Makowski, discovered that this type of Pill was linked to cancer of the womb (uterus).

They published details of 21 young women with this type of cancer who had been taking sequential pills.[31] Other reports have confirmed the risk of womb cancer with sequential pills.

'Something which is not widely known or publicised by the medical profession is that the Pill modifies the tissues of a woman's reproductive tract – specifically the cervix and the lining of the uterus. These changes are often described in the medical literature as hyperplasia' (Joe Graedon, writing in *The People's Pharmacy*).[32] Cell changes in the womb are a precursor of cancer and women who develop cancer of the womb nearly always have hyperplasia first.

Not enough time has passed yet to know if the Pill will be responsible for an increase in the incidence of cancer of the uterus. It took thirty years to discover that DES could cause cancer in the daughters of mothers who took this drug – so perhaps it will take until the late 1980s or early 1990s until the full pay-off of the Pill is known.

Does the Pill always work?

No. The most likely reason for the Pill not to work is the failure of the woman to take it. If more than thirty-six hours pass between tablet taking ovulation may occur, resulting in pregnancy, say the manufacturers.[33] Both the low-dose mini-Pills (eg Loestrin) and the progesterone-only Pills (eg Femulen) are less effective than traditional Pills and it is more important to take them at exactly the same time each day. Progesterone-only Pills also offer less protection against ectopic pregnancy. Women taking the former type of Pill are three times more likely to get pregnant than with the latter type.[34]

Some antibiotics given to women for TB (such as Rifamprin and Rimactant) can nullify the effect of the Pill (see below and page 176 for Hazards of antibiotics). Other such reputedly nullifying drugs include: antihistamines, barbiturates, butazolidin, Dilantin, Equanil and Miltown,[19] also drugs used to treat epilepsy.[33]

Despite all these drawbacks the Pill remains the most effective form of contraception barring sterilisation.[34]

Commonly used antibiotic also found to inactivate the Pill

'We should advise that women taking low dose oral contraceptives should take extra precautions against con-

ceiving in any cycle during which antibiotics are given. '[35]

Three cases of pregnancy have been recorded in women taking the Pill at the same time as taking Ampicillin (semi-sythesised form of penicillin).[35] Now two Australian doctors report another case of a 20-year-old student who became pregnant after taking Tetracycline antibiotics, although she had been regularly taking the Pill for four years. The pregnancy occurred after she took a five-day course of Tetracycline. Without realising she had become pregnant the woman continued to take the Pill for a further three months. When her pregnancy was discovered she was found to have a 12-week-old foetus.

It is believed that the Pill is inactivated by antibiotics because they destroy vital bacteria inside the gut which would normally react with the hormones in the Pill, resulting in lower than normal concentrations of the Pill hormones circulating through the body. 'With the widespread use of low dose oestrogen contraceptives such interactions may well occur more often,' say the authors of this report, Drs Janet Bacon and Gillian Shinfield. They point out that Tetracycline antibiotics are used for a wide range of infections which affect women, such as pelvic inflammatory disease and non-specific urethritis.

A recent editorial in the *British Medical Journal* concluded that ideally doctors should advise the use of alternative contraceptive precautions for all women receiving broad-spectrum antibiotics and using any oral contraceptives, but unfortunately there is still insufficient knowledge about these risks of drug interaction to give any definite advice. Certain groups of women may be especially susceptible, and generally women may be at greater risk if the antibiotic is given at a sensitive stage of the menstrual cycle.[36]

Does the Pill cause blindness?
A blood clot in the retina of the eye can cause partial blindness, blurring of vision and loss of some of the visual field.

Does the Pill cause gall-bladder disease?
Yes, women on the Pill are more than twice as likely to have a diseased gall-bladder which will require surgery, an operation carrying great risk.[37] The possibility of the formation of gallstones is increased because the Pill causes

cholestrol to be concentrated in the bile (see page 52 on gall-bladder surgery).

Does the Pill cause depression?

'Some people think that the leading cause of death from the Pill is suicide, from the depression and not from thrombosis.'[38]

Since the Pill alters the entire hormonal balance of the body, it is hardly surprising that the parts of the brain responsible for stabilising emotional and stressful reactions may be upset by an unnatural addition of hormones. The Royal College of General Practitioners found, for example, that women who successfully committed suicide were twice as likely to have been on the Pill.

Also accident proneness has been found to be double for women on the Pill.[39]

8

Drugs Prescribed by Doctors

The disturbing behaviour of the drug companies
'To my surprise a respected drug representative recently offered me money and a free trip to the Continent, in return for joining a drug trial organised by his company. The "trial" seemed to me to be designed to provide commercially useful data rather than medical information. (letter in *British Medical Journal,* 5 July 1980).[1]
'I have been so increasingly disgusted with the machinations of the drug companies that my only solution to the constant temptation to prescribe at the bchest of a drug company has been to cease to allow any representative to cross the threshold of my surgery and to have my name removed from all "medical mailing lists". (letter in *British Medical Journal,* 19 July 1980).[2]
'Unfortunately the information about overdosage in many data sheets is incomplete, vague, misleading or wrong, and in some the treatment recommended is frankly dangerous.' (*British Medical Journal*, 1980)[3]

Scottish pharmacologist Dr Larry Prescott of Edinburgh University and Dr R. Illingworth of Leeds General Infirmary, both experts in drug poisoning, analysed 1,035 drug manufacturers' data sheets and found that over a quarter (28 per cent) contained *no* information on the problem of overdosage, even though they are required by law to supply doctors with this type of information. Manufacturers of products containing the painkiller paracetamol were particularly negligent about informing doctors of the problems of poisoning; only 21 out of 40 (52 per cent) mentioned that liver damage may occur. 'Effective and specific treatment for paracetamol poisoning has been available since 1974', say the researchers, but less than half the manufacturers recommended it. As paracetamol poisoning can kill, these are vital omissions.[3]

Secret drug company reports hide side-effects

Whenever a drug manufacturer seeks to sell a new product he must submit research demonstrating its safety and effectiveness to drug-licensing authorities in each country. But this information is confidential and secret and is not even available to doctors. Recently, however, a Finnish researcher, Dr Elina Hemminki, was given permission to investigate the secret files submitted to the Finnish and Swedish drug authorities by drug companies between 1965 and 1975. Her findings revealed that these unpublished reports actually contain more information on side effects than the published reports. She also found that most of the drugs firms' experimental trials were designed to study only the short-term effectiveness of their drugs and were therefore not suitable for studying side effects. 'Most of the information on side effects was of poor quality', said Dr Hemminki.[4]

Questions which patients may want to ask the doctor about their treatment[5]

You will get most benefit from your treatment if you know why you are having it and how you should use it. So if there are any questions listed below that concern you and that you don't know the answer to, ask your doctor. *Hint*: Be diplomatic. Doctors are human too, and most are very willing to answer reasonable queries.

1. *What for and how?*
   What kind of tablets are they and in what way do you expect them to help?
   How should I take them?
   Will I be able to tell whether they are working?

2. *How important?*
   How important is it for me to take these tablets?
   What is likely to happen if I do not take them?

3. *Any side effects?*
   Do the tablets have any other effects that I should look out for?
   Do they ever cause any trouble?
   Is it all right to drive while I'm taking them?
   Are they all right to take with other medicines I may need?
   Will alcohol interfere with them?

4. *How long for?*
   How long will I need to continue with these tablets?
   What should I do with any that are left over?
   When will I need to see you again?
   What will you want to know at that time?

Tranquillisers: Valium

Brand name of drug: Valium (Roche).
Purpose of drug: To reduce anxiety.
Special warning: May be addictive and it may become ineffective after a period of time.
Main chemical used in the drug: Diazepam – belongs to class of drugs called the benzodiazepines.

Similar drugs:
Diazepam: Atensine (Berk), Evacalm (Unimed), Sedapam (Duncan Flockhart), Solis (Galen), Tensium (DDSA).
Chlordiazepoxide: Librium (Roche), Tropium (DDSA).
Lorazepam: Ativan (Wyeth).
Meprobamate: Equanil (Wyeth), Equagesic (Wyeth), Meprate (DDSA), Milonorm (Wallace), Miltown (Carter-Wallace), Tenavoid (Burgess).
Hydroxyzine hydrochloride: Atarax (Pfizer).
Clobazam: Frisium (Hoechst).
Medazepam: Nobrium (Roche).
Oxazepam: Serenid-D (Wyeth), Serenid-Forte (Wyeth).
Benzoctamine hydrochloride: Tacitin (CIBA).
Clorazepate: Tranxene (Boehringer Ingelheim).
Chlormezanone: Trancopal (Sterling).
Ketazolam: Anxon (Beecham).

Valium is the most widely prescribed drug in the world, and this record gives it the honour of a place in the

Guinness Book of Records. It states that there were 47 million prescriptions for Valium in the USA in 1973. Hoffman La Roche, the Swiss drug company that invented Valium, have also marketed a number of other very similar tranquillisers, all of which belong to the same chemical class known technically as the benzodiazepines. 'The tranquilliser is replacing tobacco,' says Dr Vernon Coleman[7] and warns that it may prove even more dangerous. He claims that Valium is said to be taken by 14 per cent of the population of Britain, 17 per cent in Belgium and France, 15 per cent in Denmark, 10 per cent in Italy, Spain and the USA and 14 per cent in Germany.

The astonishing success of this class of drugs has been achieved partly through heavy advertising and subtle promotion to doctors, thd free distribution of drugs to hospitals, and undercutting of rivals. Valium and Librium have been sold to doctors as aids to coping with the stress of modern life, with little emphasis on using Valium as treatment for specific illnesses. They were introduced in the early 1960s as very safe and non-addictive, and compared to the barbiturates that had been used as tranquillisers until that time they certainly were safer. Non-addictive? Well, there is now a lot of evidence that Valium and Librium are drugs of addiction as well.

Part of their success is no doubt due to their addictive properties and ordinary patients (not only Valium *addicts*) can suffer serious withdrawal effects. In long-term use they are of doubtful effectiveness as their effect can wear off after just a few days. The list of side effects that they produce is growing: they are associated with an increase in driving accidents, they can be fatal mixed with alcohol, they can produce paradoxical aggression and anxiety and may be responsible for some cases of baby batterings. They have been linked with increased incidence of birth defects, they get into breast milk, mothers given them during childbirth have difficult, injured and dopey babies, and many thousands of people are simply addicted to them, taking them for years on end. Some animal experiments suggest Valium and Librium may promote the incidence of breast cancer.

Does Valium actually work?

There is no evidence that after four months Valium or

Librium or any other of the mild tranquillisers actually have any effect, says FDA drug chief, Dr Richard Crout. After four months, or often less, the body has grown accustomed to the presence of Valium in the system and so it no longer reacts to it. In fact, it has been shown that the effects of Librium wear off in just a few days. Two researchers at the London School of Pharmacy, Sandra Velluci and Sandra File, have shown that rats are made anxious when they are placed in unfamiliar surroundings under a powerful light. This fear of the surroundings is directly related to the amount that rats will socialise with other rats. But when the rats were given Librium they became much more social than rats who had not been given the drug, but after only fifteen to twenty-five days the two researchers found that there was no difference between the behaviour of the drugged and the undrugged animals. When they examined the brains of the rats who had been drugged they found that the Librium had managed at first to reduce levels of a 'fear hormone' called serotonin, but after taking the drug for twenty-five days the levels of serotonin in the brain had climbed up to high, anxiety-associated levels once again. [8]

Seven American states have stopped paying for Valium and other minor tranquillisers because they are 'vastly overused, are largely medically unnecessary and are expensive', writes Dr Sidney Wolfe of the Public Citizens' Health Research Group (May 1979), adding that usually they are used as a substitute for care and solicitude on the part of the physician. 'These drugs do not cure anything but merely tranquillise to enable people to cope with the ordinary frustrations of modern living. The drug industry through heavy advertising has convinced the medical profession and the public that these problems are medical problems,' writes Dr Wolfe. He describes dramatic improvements which occurred at a hospital in Chicago (Cook County Hospital) following the decision to restrict the use of tranquillisers: 73 per cent of patients said they had a better relationship with their doctor and 69 per cent said they were getting better medical treatment; 90 per cent thought that the doctor was spending more time talking to them. 'The Doctor spends more time with me now and listens to me instead of just writing prescriptions,' one patient remarked.[9]

The problem of Valium abuse; are you addicted?

'The smartly dressed woman driving a sleek, late-model car could be the envy of her neighbours. She has a loving husband, bright children, a beautiful home in the suburbs and apparently no cares in the world. Except one. This woman is a junkie . . . She is dependent on legal drugs, the kind prescribed for her by a doctor.'[10] This is the way the US FDA tries to warn the public about the hazards of getting hooked on minor tranquillisers, such as Valium. Most addicts are women; almost twice as many women have tranquillisers prescribed for them compared to men. This is not a phenomenon limited to the sixties and seventies since the advent of Valium (which came on the market in 1963), but goes back to the days when women could freely take opium for menstrual pain in the early 1800s. The common availability of patent medicines laced with opiates and widely advertised for 'female troubles', contributed to their heavy use by women, writes Annabel Hecht.[10] She says that in the late nineteenth and the twentieth centuries women opium eaters outnumbered male drug users by three to one. As the FDA in America and Medical Acts in Britain limited the availability of these narcotics, they were replaced by other substances – first barbiturates then the Valiums and Libriums.

'While other physicians were reading their mail, I was eating mine.' (Dr Theodore Clark, reformed tranquilliser addict)[11]

'Millions of Americans who take tranquillisers such as Valium may become addicted to them and withdrawal can be extremely difficult,' former addicts told a US Senate Committee investigation into Drug Abuse in 1979. The problem was made worse because most doctors did not regard the minor tranquillisers such as Valium as truly addictive. One doctor who gave evidence described his own personal addiction problem: 'I had to take drugs to start the day,' he told the Senate Health and Scientific Research Committee. 'I was on alcohol and used the minor tranquillisers to stop drinking. I would anxiously wait for drug samples to be sent by drug manufacturers. It got to the point where I wouldn't see my patients until the mailman had arrived. While other physicians were reading their mail

I was eating mine.'[11] Another witness, a Catholic priest, said that after taking Valium things got so bad that 'emptying the wastepaper basket was a weeklong project'. But the president of Hoffman La Roche, the makers of Valium, said: 'I have to conclude that the slice of life seen here is not typical, otherwise we would be up to our necks in lawsuits, and that is not the case.' But these claims of addiction are not merely from the lunatic fringe of American life. Professor M. Rawlins, Clinical Pharmacologist at Newcastle University, has shown[12] that these drugs produce psychological and physical dependence even after short-term use. Professor Rawlins and his colleague Dr Andrew Smith, a GP, demonstrated that normal healthy volunteers displayed anxiety symptoms after only two weeks when the tranquillisers were stopped. An article in the *British Clinical Journal* describes withdrawal symptoms of Valium and Librium as: acute feelings of apprehension, agitation, accompanied by crawling sensation in the skin and nasal irritation.[7]

Dr Richard Crout, the Medical Director of the American Bureau of Drugs, said in September 1979 at a Senate meeting: 'It has become clear that all of the marketed diazepines (Valium, Librium etc) can cause physical dependence.' He described the symptoms as including agitation, insomnia, sweating, tremors, abdominal and muscle cramps, vomiting and even convulsions, ie fits. He said that while most cases have occurred in patients taking these drugs for months or years, those most at risk of addiction are those who take the drugs for longer than four months. In the USA, special warnings are now printed on the labels of containers of these drugs advising doctors to reassess patients at least every four months; without reassessment, said Dr Crout, this was a clear misuse of these drugs. But there is another, more important, reason for this warning. *Read the next section.*

Does Valium make some women batter their babies?
Dr Margaret Lynch of the Human Development Research Unit at Park Hospital, Oxford, has found that when mothers had been taking these tranquillisers many of them had been referred for child-battering. 'If a woman is isolated with an inconsolably crying infant outbursts of aggression occur,' says Dr Lynch.[13] She believes that the

link between aggression and the use of tranquillisers has major implications in the treatment of child abuse. 'We advocate extreme caution when prescribing tranquillisers and anti-depressants for mothers of young children, especially when the complaints include inability to cope with a baby's demanding and frustrating behaviour. It could well be that such complaints are in fact a warning that a child is at risk of abuse.'

Does Valium promote cancer?

It has been discovered that tranquillisers are used more often by women who suffer either from a recurrence of breast cancer or from the growth of secondary cancers after the initial diagnosis of breast cancer. There is also a two- to threefold increase in the use of tranquillisers amongst women diagnosed with breast cancer; perhaps this is not surprising considering the great fear of cancer that exists in society generally. But these statistics do raise a disturbing possibility: could Valium somehow increase the incidence of secondary cancer amongst women who have been diagnosed with breast cancer? Dr David Horrobin from the Clinical Research Institute of Montreal believes he has shown that Valium does have this effect, though the Director of the Institute, Dr Jacques Genest, does not approve of the way in which Dr Horrobin has announced his findings through the channels of the press and seems to suggest that these findings are open to question. Nevertheless, Dr Horrobin has claimed in a letter to *The Lancet* that cancer growth was three times greater amongst a group of rats fed amounts of Valium which were only two to three times the human dose. Dr Horrobin and his team wrote: 'We believe that for two reasons this tumour growth promoting effect may have been missed in the usual screening studies.' He then goes on to state that they believe that diazepam (ie Valium) *promotes* cancer, rather than directly causing it. This means that it will only be detectable as a cancer agent if it is tested with a known cause of cancer or if it is given to individuals who already have a cancer. This explanation certainly fits the information known about the incidence of breast cancer in women taking Valium. Dr Horrobin also believes that Valium has not been classified as a cancer agent because it has failed to produce cancers when given in large doses. But he points out that some substances only produce cancer when used in very small quantities. Dr Horrobin and his colleagues conclude that they believe 'this issue merits urgent investigation, in view of the very high levels of tranquilliser use in society'.[14,15] But his research in this area has been halted as a result of a failure to obtain funding from medical research organisations in Canada.

The Valium-cancer theory has since been widely reported and debated. The only drug safety authority to react to Dr Horrobin's findings has been the Canadian government's Health Protection Branch, who have ordered a one-year study into the possible cancer risk. They will perform animal and bacterial tests, according to a report in *New Scientist*.[16] 'We can't close our eyes and not investigate', one of the researchers, Dr Ian Henderson, is quoted as saying.

Roche deny that there is any risk and have attempted to argue that Dr Horrobin's work is scientifically flawed. Horrobin was asked to resign from his post in Montreal following the worldwide publicity his findings produced. But since that time some scientific support for Dr Horrobin's claims have come from several other cancer researchers.

Dr E. Boyland, of the prestigious London School of Hygiene and Tropical Medicine, wrote in *The Lancet* that 'although the widely-used tranquilliser diazepam (Valium) was synthesised twenty years ago, it does not appear to have been adequately tested for carcinogenic (cancer-causing) activity'. Boyland suggests that Valium may be similar to phenobarbitone in promoting tumours, but there may be safe levels of these drugs below which they are not harmful.[17]

Dr June Marchant of the Regional Cancer Register at Queen Elizabeth's Hospital, Birmingham, has suggested that Valium may increase cancer by stimulating the release of the hormone prolactin, which has itself been shown to promote cancer growth. She writes: 'When I worked with mice, the big placid ones believed to have high levels of prolactin seemed to be much more susceptible to breast cancer induction by chemicals than the jumpy, jittery ones, known to be low in the hormone, and I often wondered whether prolactin itself was the ultimate tranquilliser.'[18]

But a new large-scale American study by the National Cancer Institute, which compared 1,200 women with breast cancer to a matched equal number of women without the disease, found no link between Valium and cancer.[19] However, the question of whether Valium promotes growth of cancer is being further investigated by the study group, as they say their results were insufficient to fully assess this risk. Moreover, since breast cancer can take fifteen years or more to develop, only long-term studies can give a definite answer to the problem.

The hazard of birth defects caused by tranquillisers like Valium

At least three studies suggest that mild tranquillisers such as Valium and Librium may cause congenital birth defects such as cleft palate in babies of mothers who take these drugs for anxiety during pregnancy. One study looked at over 19,000 births and found that if Librium was taken in the first six weeks of pregnancy there were more than 11 birth anomalies for every 100 births. But if the drug was taken later in pregnancy no difference was seen.[19] A second study looking at 590 children born with cleft palates in Finland from 1967–71 found that Valium-taking (and related drugs) was significantly more common amongst their mothers compared to a control group of normal mothers and babies. A third study, of Atlanta mothers, found that mothers with a baby born with a cleft lip reported use of diazepam during the first three months of pregnancy, four times more often than other mothers. The American drug authority, the FDA, comment that whilst these surveys do not prove that tranquillisers cause birth defects, they do suggest an association. Since the use of tranquillisers is rarely an urgent matter during the early part of pregnancy it advises that their use should be avoided. In July 1976 the FDA ordered the manufacturers of these tranquillisers to warn physicians that they should always be avoided by women during the first three months of pregnancy. No emphatic warning appears on British brands of these drugs.

The damage caused by Valium to newly-born babies

It is not uncommon for mothers to be given doses of Valium during childbirth in order to make them more relaxed. It is healthier for a baby if the mother is not pumping masses of adrenalin into her bloodstream and therefore into the baby's bloodstream through the cord. But a study has shown that when Valium is given in the fifteen hours before birth it results in babies who have low scores on a test of mental and physical ability performed straight after birth (The Apgar test, see page 84). The survey shows that when mothers had received Valium the babies subsequently had low Apgar scores, low temperatures, needed feeding by tube because they were too sleepy to suck, and they lacked muscle tone and strength. It was also found that the concentration of Valium was greater in the babies' cord blood than in the mother's own blood. Hence the babies had received *more* than an adult dose of the tranquilliser; perhaps it is not surprising then that they showed all these extra symptoms immediately after birth. In a third of the babies studied the concentrations of Valium *rose* after delivery and they scarcely fell until a week later. As Valium can remain active for up to ten days this means that the baby's response and development at a critical period of its life can be affected by simply giving the mother a dose of Valium to calm her down before birth. It should also be pointed out that a mother's milk becomes contaminated if she is taking Valium whilst breast feeding her child, so the same effects will also apply in this instance.[20]

How Valium can make people more depressed: another paradox

Within days of starting a course of Valium, a group of patients suffered from tremulousness, confusion, marked apprehension, insomnia, nightmares, depression and a compulsion to commit suicide against their will. Dr Hall and J. Joffe, who describe this reaction in the *American Journal of Psychiatry*, point out that the patients returned to normal when Valium (diazepam) was withdrawn. When elderly patients showed this type of reaction to Valium, it occurred sooner and they took longer to recover after treatment was stopped.[21]

In another group, patients on diazepam (Valium) told of 'deepening depression'; in most of these patients there were suicidal thoughts and impulses following Valium treatment.[22]

Other side effects of Valium which have been reported

Low blood pressure (hypotension), nausea and vomiting, stomach and visual disturbances, rashes, water retention, headache, loss of libido, confusion and vertigo.[23]

Valium and alcohol: a fatal combination

'No deaths have ever been caused by Valium overdose alone, but taken in combination with other drugs, especially alcohol, it can be deadly'—*FDA Consumer*.[24] The American National Institute on Drug Abuse reports that Valium and similar drugs are commonly abused in conjunction with alcohol by women. Surveys conducted in eighteen states in 1973 and 1974 show that among women who were using drugs to relax and minor tranquillisers like Valium, two out of every five were regular drinkers and one was a heavy drinker.[24]

The disturbing way in which Valium has been sold to doctors

In order to cut out any competition Hoffman La Roche have given away supplies of Valium and Librium to both hospitals and the armed services. This practice shows that their prices were too high, commented the British Government Monopolies Commission Report on Valium and Librium. In Britain two other companies (DDSA and Berk) were granted licences in 1969 to manufacture their own versions of Librium and Valium – despite vigorous attempts by Roche to stop them. But still Roche managed to hold on to 99 per cent of the market for these drugs by persistently undercutting their rivals. In 1973, the Monopolies Commission found that Roche had been over-charging the British Health Service and they were ordered to pay back over £3 million in revenue from these drugs and to lower their prices; they were also instructed not to give drugs away to hospitals and the armed services.

Canadian authorities have prosecuted Roche for giving supplies of their product away to hospitals in order to drive out competition from rival manufacturers Frank Horner Ltd.[25]

Another, even more subtle, method which Roche has used to promote its products is through so-called 'medical education programmes'. In the USA in 1979, Roche Laboratories were underwriting the cost of an extensive programme on the *Consequences of Stress*, produced by a private firm and distributed to US doctors. But Dr Richard Crout; Chief of the American drug watchdog, the FDA, has said that they 'are not entirely comfortable about this programme . . . it is aimed at stress and it has the potential of subtly conveying the message that tranquillisers should be prescribed for many patients whose internal discomfort is much closer to that accompanying the normal pressures of life, rather than the medical disorders for which tranquillisers are indicated. From our perspective,' he added, 'the initial materials produced by this programme were oriented far too much towards drugs, particularly Valium, and not enough towards the fundamental biology of stress.' The company were also clearly linking an advertising campaign to tie in with this medical education programme, observed Dr Crout, and the FDA was 'most concerned by this development'.

Since the drugs are mildly addictive, patients who receive them in hospital will often insist on receiving these drugs from their GP after they have been discharged, and often only Valium will do – not just diazepam, the

The Big Business of stress.

chemical equivalent. This is the commercial sense behind the free supplies: they are loss-leaders for the bigger pickings in the future. Dr Alan Klass pinpoints the hazards of hospitals accepting free supplies of Valium: 'Young doctors at the threshold of their prescribing career become indoctrinated in the use of this drug while pursuing the hospital part of their training. The young doctor who has never prescribed Valium for his patients while continuing his training in hospital must be rare. This effectively shuts off any knowledge and experience that he might acquire about other drugs that have a similar tranquillising effect and have been accepted for many years prior to the arrival of Valium.'[26]

New warnings on hazards of Valium and other tranquillisers

In March 1980 the British Committee on the Review of Medicines demanded that much more stringent precautions be taken by doctors before prescribing Valium, Librium and similar benzodiazepine tranquillisers. Drug companies were also required to publish a much tougher and more comprehensive 'hazard' information sheet (called 'data sheets') for the benefit of doctors.

The watchdog body warned doctors that drugs such as Valium, Librium, Nobrium and Tranxene stay active for so long in the system (over ten hours) that they make people sleepy and therefore dangerous to drive the day *after* or evening *after* they have been swallowed, especially if combined with alcohol. Safer, short-acting drugs include products such as Halcion (triazolam), Euhypnos, Normison (temazepam), Serenid-D, Serenid forte (oxazepam) and Ativan (lorazepam).

The Committee decided that there was no difference between products such as Valium, which is sold as a tranquilliser, and, say, Mogadon, which is sold as a sleeping pill, in their ability to make people go to sleep or reduce anxiety. None of these drugs (called benzodiazepines) should be given to children to treat anxiety or insomnia, nor are they any good as painkillers or antidepressants. They should not be given for tension headaches or dysmenorrhoea, except when there is also anxiety, said the Committee. They also noted there was no evidence that these drugs are effective after four months of

170

continuous treatment. All patients receiving these drugs should be monitored, and prescriptions should only be given for short-term use.[27]

Sleeping pills: Mogadon

Brand name of drug: Mogadon (Roche)
Purpose of drug: To prevent insomnia.
Special warning: May become ineffective after a few days.
Main chemical used in the drug: Nitrazepam

Similar drugs:
Nitrazepam:
Nitrados (Berk), Remnos (DDSA), Somnased (Duncan, Flockart), Somnite (Norgine), Surem (Galen)
Flurazepam:
Dalmane (Roche)
Others:
Doriden (CIBA) = Glutethimide
Euhypnos (Farmitalia) = Temazepam

Halcion (Upjohn) = Triazolam
Heminevrin (Astra) = Chlormethiazole edisylate
Mandrax (Roussel) = Methaqualone diphenhydramine
Noctec (Squibb) = Chloral hydrate
Noludar (Roche) = Methyprylone
Normison (Wyeth) = Temazepam
Welldorm (Smith & Nephew) = Dichloralphenazone

Are you addicted to a useless drug?

Most sleeping pills lose their sleep-promoting effect after as little as three days of continuous use; at the very most they continue to work for about a fortnight. This was the shock finding made by the US Institute of Medicine in April 1979.[28, 29] It was a shock because these drugs are often prescribed for years to millions of so-called insomniacs.

Sleeping pills cause insomnia!

When Mogadon and later Dalmane were introduced they were hailed as an answer to the problem of addiction to the deadly barbiturate drugs, but now it is apparent that many people can become physically dependent (ie hooked) on Mogadon and Dalmane as well. Coming off these sleeping pills causes painful withdrawal symptoms, one of which includes – guess what? – insomnia and disturbed sleep. The absurdity is that these sleeping pills can actually *cause* insomnia.

Why Mogadon and other sleeping pills may fail to work

Why can't you sleep? Worried about your job, your love life, an exam/interview, or money problems? Maybe you just drank too much coffee or too many cups of tea before going to bed. Perhaps you need a new mattress – one that doesn't sag like a hammock, or perhaps you sleep too much and don't need eight hours sleep a night. There are so many ways in which you can become an insomniac that it seems rather odd that one type of drug can apparently 'cure' all these problems. Well, in fact, sleeping pills, as everyone knows, do not *'cure'* any of these problems because they are all examples of the way in which daily living stresses us. But stress from daily living is not a medical disease! Stress will only disappear if the individual makes changes to his/her life, not by consuming a Mogadon. The enormously complicated problem of insomnia clearly must be tackled at its roots, and not by merely treating the symptoms.

Is Mogadon the same substance as Valium?
It will not surprise the reader to discover that the chemicals inside Mogadon or Dalmane are virtually identical to the chemicals put into the famous drugs Valium and Librium, which are prescribed for anxiety. One of the first stated *side effects* of Valium or Librium is drowsiness. This should not be called a 'side effect' at all because this is the effect which the drug is designed to have, ie to make people sleepy, when it comes packaged under its other name of Mogadon or Dalmane. This explains why Valium and Librium are a factor in road-accident figures. The fact is that all these drugs – Valium, Librium, Mogadon and Dalmane – are benzodiazepine chemicals. 'There is no convincing evidence that one benzodiazepine is more effective than any other in relieving anxiety or inducing sleep,'[30] says the highly respected *Drug and Therapeutics Bulletin.* Since both Mogadon and Valium are equally good at sending people to sleep it has been pointed out that the government wastes millions of pounds on prescriptions for Mogadon tablets, which are three times more expensive than Valium.[31]

How long does an insomniac sleep?
Research inside sleep laboratories has shown that people who think they are insomniacs and are convinced that they stay awake all night, in fact sleep almost as much as everyone else. Most insomniacs sleep from seven to eight hours a night. Sleeping pills reduce the time needed to fall

asleep by only ten to twenty minutes, and have been shown to lengthen sleep by a mere thirty to forty minutes.[32]

Why sleeping pills fail to work after a few days

The American Institute of Medicine's investigation into the use of sleeping pills warns doctors not to prescribe them for more than two to four weeks, until more is known about the effects of their long-term use. Their survey showed that the effect of most sleeping pills was gone within three to fourteen days of continuous use. Unless the body gets larger and larger supplies the sleeping pills fail to work. The human body, in this case, the brain, quickly adjusts to the presence of these drugs so that they are made ineffective; to use the medical jargon, *tolerance* develops. However, it is inadvisable to suddenly stop taking sleeping pills if you have been taking them for some time, as you will suffer severe withdrawal effects.[33]

Are you suffering from Mogadon Confusion Syndrome?

Sleeping tablets do not just make you sleep at night; unfortunately their effect often lasts well into the next day. When ten healthy young volunteers were given Mogadon or similar sleeping pills, it was found that they had difficulty in performing the simple task of sorting out cards, for a period of up to thirteen hours after having a good night's sleep.[34]

Dr J. Evans described a syndrome which he regularly came across amongst old people put on sleeping pills, which disappeared when Mogadon was withdrawn. It included mental confusion, low blood pressure when standing up, uncontrollable jerky movements and even incontinence. He said that he came across six or seven cases of this syndrome each month. Other doctors have reported vivid nightmares related to earlier disturbing events with patients on sleeping pills.[35,36]

One of the most disturbing side effects of sleeping pills is their tendency to cause more accidents. Sleeping pills are often to blame for old people falling at night and breaking their legs, according to a report by Drs J. B. and E. T. MacDonald,[37] of Nottingham. They found that when they looked into the causes of falls in nearly 400 elderly patients, almost all (93 per cent) had been taking barbiturate sleeping pills. Similar side effects can occur with Mogadon-type sleeping pills. The US Institute of

Medicine's report on sleeping pills has found that Dalmane or Mogadon can impair driving skills even more than barbiturates if taken for a week. Mogadon tends to accumulate in the bloodstream, so that after it has been taken for seven consecutive days there can be four to six times as much in the blood as there was on the first morning after commencement. These pills may still be active fifty to one hundred hours after taking them, according to the Institute of Medicine's research. This explains why they can have side effects long after they are taken.[32]

Does Mogadon alter your dreams?

A great deal of emphasis has been put by the makers of these drugs, Roche, on the fact that they do not suppress the amount of time spent dreaming. Through the night there are periods of a special kind of sleep which is always accompanied by rapid eye movements (REM) which are thought to be a sign of dreaming. One of the disadvantages of barbiturate-type sleeping pills is that they suppress the amount of time spent having dreams or the rapid eye movements which seem to accompany most dreams. The human body does appear to need to dream for minimum periods each night, for it has been shown that when people stop taking barbiturates they experience a rebound and start to spend more time dreaming – as if they need to catch up. Also it has been shown that if normal people are deprived of dreaming sleep (by waking them up every time their brain waves show they are dreaming) they tend to go mad.[28] For these reasons it was originally thought that Mogadon was a great advance. But although Mogadon and Dalmane may not suppress dreaming sleep it has now been found that they reduce two other vital stages of sleep – stages 3 and 4, as they are called.[28] There is now evidence that dreaming is not only confined to stage 1 of sleep as was originally thought but that it can occur in all the four stages of sleep. Even if dreaming does not occur in stages 3 and 4 (which is unlikely) there are still hazards about suppressing any of the stages of sleep: no one yet knows which stages of sleep are the most important for healthy and sane survival, so any drug which upsets the pattern of sleep (as the sleeping pills all do) is a potential hazard.

How to get off sleeping pills if you are hooked

Are any of the following symptoms familiar after you have been taking sleeping pills for a period of time? Do you suffer from: apprehension, weakness followed by anxiety, headache, dizziness, tremors, vomiting, nausea, cramps and insomnia? Rarely, some people may suffer from low blood pressure or even convulsions, hallucination, DTs and the need for a deep sleep. These are the withdrawal symptoms of Mogadon, Dalmane or barbiturate sleeping pills. They can occur if the tablets are suddenly stopped, but can be avoided almost totally if the tablets are discontinued *gradually*.[23] *Martindale's Guide to Drugs* says that all these symptoms can be dramatically reversed by taking almost any sedative and then withdrawing the sleeping pills over a period of days or weeks.[23]

There is a tendency for many Mogadon sufferers to increase the size of the dose and to have a strong need to continue with the drug in order to maintain its levels in the body's system. In this way it is a drug of addiction as much as heroin or morphine because there is a mental and physical need to keep taking it (see addiction to Valium, on page 162, for details of a similar problem).

Deadly barbiturates

Barbiturate sleeping pills

Evidorm (Winthrop), Gerisom (Winthrop) (removed UK 1979), Medomin (Geigy), Nembutal (Abbott), Sodium Seconal (Lilly), Phanodorm (Winthrop), Sodium Amytal (Lilly), Sonergan (May & Baker), Soneryl (M&B), Tuinal (Lilly)

Barbiturates are still commonly prescribed as tranquillisers and sleeping pills despite the availability of less harmful alternative drugs (Valium and Librium) (but see pages 159-75). However the British Committee on the Review of Medicines investigated barbiturate drugs in 1979 and took steps to reduce their availability. Barbiturates are relatively ineffective, addictive and fatal in overdose. They are responsible for more than a quarter (27 per cent) of all the deaths (2,900) caused by poisoning, and the product Tuinal alone causes one-third of these deaths, says the *Drug and Therapeutics Bulletin*.[38]

Another hazard of barbiturates is that they can cause unwanted pregnancies because they accelerate the way the body metabolises the hormone used in the pill. They also suppress breathing and may worsen asthma or bronchitis.

Barbiturates: fatal and ineffective

There is no convincing evidence that barbiturates reduce anxiety in any way other than making patients feel sleepy, according to the *Drug and Therapeutics Bulletin*. They also tend to make painkillers ineffective. They do not significantly reduce blood pressure either. The US Food and Drug Authority maintains that the barbiturate sleeping pills have not been shown to be effective beyond fourteen days of consecutive use, yet surveys reveal that they are frequently prescribed for months or years.[39] One study published in the *Journal of the American Medical Association* in 1974 found barbiturates were relatively ineffective when taken by insomniacs over a two-week period.[40]

Hidden barbiturates

The names of many products give no hint that they contain a barbiturate drug. Some doctors may not be aware that they do and patients' requests for repeat prescriptions tend to be too readily accepted, says the *Bulletin*.

How to get off barbiturates

Barbiturates produce mental and physical addiction. Patients must be withdrawn gradually from their drugs over a period of at least two weeks.

Conclusion

'Barbiturates are obsolete for most purposes, but they are still available in dozens of products,' says the *Bulletin*. The Committee on the Review of Medicines has asked manufacturers to withdraw products which contain barbiturates combined with other drugs.

Antibiotics: Penicillin

Brand name of drug: Penbritin

Purpose of drug: To kill bacterial infections.

Special warning: All antibiotics hazardous to sensitive individuals. May become ineffective if overused.

Main chemical used in the drug: A semi-synthetic penicillin called ampicillin.

Similar drugs:

Amfipen (Brocades)	Pentrexyl (Bristol)
Ampiclox (Beecham)	Vidopen (Berk)
Magnapen (Beecham)	

176

Other penicillin

Cuprimine (MSD)
Crystapen G (Glaxo)
Penidural (Wyeth)
Havapen (Wyeth)
Broxil (Beecham)
Bicillin (Brocades)
Crystamycin (Glaxo)
Crystapen (Glaxo)

Triplopen (Glaxo)
Apsin VK (APS)
CVK (Compocillin VK) (Abbott)
Distaquaine (Dista)
Icipen 300 (ICI)
Stabillin VK (Boots)
Tonsillin (Winthrop)
V-Cil-K (Lilly)

Antibiotics: the miracle pills with a fatal sting

Antibiotics – the word alone often means instant cure for most people. Antibiotics still have a magical quality and connotation which puts them above all other drugs. Yet this idea that antibiotics will make almost anything better has no doubt contributed to their being dangerously overused. Their needless use has resulted in the proliferation of many antibiotic-resistant strains of deadly bacteria. Thousands of people died in Mexico in 1972–4 from a typhoid epidemic that was resistant to Chloramphenicol, the only antibiotic which can normally cure typhoid.[41] The uncontrolled and haphazard use of this particular antibiotic in Mexico created strains of bacteria which could survive in the presence of the drug.

Some commonly used antibiotics cause deafness, others discolour teeth and attack the bones, some cause kidney damage. Some people suffer fatal reactions if they take penicillin. Few doctors bother to test patients before prescribing antibiotics, with the result that they are often prescribed incorrectly. Antibiotics are fed to chickens to make them grow more quickly and as a result more resistant strains of bacteria are created by this all-embracing use of antibiotics. Some antibiotics cause liver damage, others cause fatal inflammation of the bowels (colitis). Some antibiotics are inactivated by stomach tablets such as antacids. Others can stop the contraceptive pill from working. *Vital they are, but harmless they are not.* Many books could be written about the dozens of antibiotics that are commonly prescribed. Over 40 million prescriptions are made out for antibiotics in Britain each year. [23] This section will only attempt to highlight the main dangers of specific antibiotics and to show how they are being used unnecessarily.

How antibiotics become useless: incurable VD hits Liverpool!

Some very tough little VD germs caused something of a panic in Liverpool in 1975, because they were capable of producing an enzyme that could destroy penicillin. The germs got into Britain through travellers entering the Port of Liverpool from West Africa. The uncontrolled and wholesale use of penicillin in West Africa has led to the development of penicillin-resistant strains. When penicillin or any antibiotic is used too freely there is greater opportunity for rare varieties of bacteria to multiply and gain a foothold. Once there is room for penicillin-resistant germs to spread in an environment, they can replace other germs and become a health hazard.

Supersonic germs

Jet travel has provided not only a greater mingling between peoples but also between germs. Since many Third-World nations permit the open sale over the counter of powerful antibiotics these drugs are often taken as freely as aspirin is in the West. Drug-resistant epidemics of typhoid in Mexico and dysentery in Guatemala may be just the tip of the bacterial iceberg. Many other countries in the Third World may be encouraging the creation of drug-resistant germs which no antibiotic can kill. The international transit of these germs and their accompanying diseases is steadily increasing as more and more people jet around the globe. Antibiotic-resistant dysentery caused thousands of deaths in Guatemala in 1973 because of the overuse of antibiotics in that country. Britain has managed to avoid disasters on this scale but resistant bacteria are still common, especially in hospitals. When Dr R. Shooter tested sixty-six strains of bacteria, which he had found present in a hospital canteen and in school food, he found four strains which were resistant to Ampicillin (a popular version of penicillin), one strain resistant to Tetracyclines, another to Sulphonamides and another to Nitrofurantoin.[42] It has also been found that about 5 per cent of all hospital patients are resistant to the Tetracycline antibiotics. Three-quarters of the staphylococci, which are the commonest cause of blood poisoning, and more than half the cases of gonorrhoea in large towns, cannot be cured with penicillin.[42] Natural selection has favoured the few resis-

Salmonella Airways Ltd – the jet-set, duty-free bacteria line.

tant strains, once an insignificant minority, at the expense of the others.[13]

Antibiotics at the butcher's shop

The use of antibiotics to promote growth and to prevent infection in chickens and turkeys and other intensively reared animals has created strains of salmonella bugs which resist many types of antibiotics. Salmonella is a cause of food poisoning which can be very hazardous to young babies or older people.[41] Ninety-five per cent of all cases of food poisoning are caused by meat contaminated with bacteria.

In Britain a committee of medical experts under the guidance of Sir Michael Swann in 1968 banned the use of antibiotics (used in medicine) for animal feeds. But antibiotics such as lincomycin are still permitted and they are often fed to poultry to make them put on weight rapidly. Despite official assurances that these are quite safe there are residues of this antibiotic found in the eggs and tissues of such drugged poultry. One study has shown that whilst cooking did destroy all residues in the muscle of these

179

birds, the livers retained half of their uncooked concentrations of antibiotic.[44] A study by the Poultry Research Station at Houghton has found that the use of antibiotics has seriously increased the level of salmonella (the bug responsible in food poisoning) in factory chickens. One survey showed that 35 per cent of raw carcases from four English packing stations were contaminated with these bugs.[45] It is possible, then, that the regular eating of chicken livers may make someone resistant to certain antibiotic treatment. For a similar reason some authorities in the United States advise women not to eat chicken or beef liver because of the concentrations of sex hormones they contain. In both Britain and the USA many animals are fed with artificial female sex hormones to make the animal grow faster. Some of these hormone additives have been linked with cancer (see page 253 for cancer-causing substances such as DES).

Why your antibiotic may be unnecessary

Antibiotics are frequently prescribed to people who do not need them. For example, doctors will prescribe antibiotics for colds or for flu, but both of these illnesses are caused by viruses. Antibiotics work only against bacteria and leave viruses totally unharmed. Chicken pox and measles are two other illnesses caused by viruses for which patients often expect an antibiotic. 'Ideally the choice of antibiotic is made on the results of sensitivity tests which should be carried out on specimens (of urine for example) from every patient,' advises the Pharmaceutical Society's guide to drugs *Martindale's Pharmacopoeia*.[23] It adds that if it is necessary to provide treatment before tests can be performed they should still be done to confirm a choice or to indicate a change. By taking an antibiotic without any real reason the individual allows potentially harmful bacteria which are resistant to that antibiotic to multiply freely inside the body.

Hospitals also prescribe unnecessary antibiotics on a large scale. It is common practice in hospitals to give doses of antibiotics to patients undergoing surgery especially where there is a high risk of infection developing, for example, in bowel surgery. But several investigations have shown that such treatment can not only fail to reduce infection rates but *increase* the risk of infection developing. In one study in the USA over 1,000 patients undergoing this surgery took part in an examination of the usefulness of such antibiotic treatment. Dr F. Herter found that inflammation of the colon was far more frequent amongst those given antibiotics compared to those who received no drugs at all.[46] Another study published in *The Lancet* in 1975 found that there were three times *more* cases of wound infection amongst those surgical patients who *had* been given penicillin or tetracycline antibiotics, compared to those who had not been given any antibiotics at all.[47] Since antibiotics can upset the delicate balance of microbes in the body these higher rates of infection may have been caused by the multiplication of germs resistant to the antibiotics used.

Penbritin

This is the most popular antibiotic prescribed by doctors. It is a semi-synthetic form of penicillin and has all the same toxic side effects as penicillin. It contains a substance called Ampicillin which is closely related to traditional penicillin. It will cause sensitivity reactions in the same way as penicillin.

Hazards of antibiotics in pregnancy

Penbritin and all antibiotics are unsafe during pregnancy as they cross into the baby's bloodstream through the placenta. It has been found that between 25 and 75 per cent of the mother's concentration of penicillin or Tetracycline crosses into the baby. Fifty per cent of the mother's dose of Streptomycin, Chloramphenicol or Erythromycin have also been found in foetal blood. One antibiotic, Tetracycline, is particularly harmful to the teeth of unborn babies (see pages 188-90 for details of this hazard).[48]

Three main hazards of Penbritin and other antibiotics are:

(1) They can irritate the lining of the stomach and cause sickness, nausea and vomiting. This can occur with Ampicillin, Clindamycin, Lincomycin, Tetracycline.
(2) Since some bacteria naturally present in the gut are responsible for manufacturing the body's vitamins, antibiotics can interfere with vitamin production. Vitamin B can be insufficiently absorbed when taking some antibiotics. Since antibiotics can provoke

diarrhoea it means that food may not be properly absorbed; these risks especially apply to Neomycin.

(3) Antibiotics can alter the pattern of germs present in the intestines by suppressing some bugs and allowing others to multiply and produce a new infection, growing over the old one. In this way yeasts and fungi can multiply at great rates, producing a type of 'super-infection' such as thrush.

Are YOU sensitive to penicillin?

Some people are so sensitive to penicillin that if they were given the drug they could collapse and die within a few minutes. But don't be panicked into not taking this drug, as this sensitivity is rare and can sometimes be predicted (but not always) if a doctor asks the right questions. The risk is less than 1 in 100,000 so it is a pretty remote possibility.[49] Signs of sensitivity include rashes, fever and swelling around the face or joints. Anyone who has a history of allergy to any other drugs should be given penicillin with great caution, advises the Pharmaceutical Society's encyclopaedic guide to drugs, *Martindale's*. A review of over 150 deaths which had occurred after taking penicillin found that 70 per cent of the penicillin victims had received the drug before and one-third of these people had shown some sort of evidence of an allergic reaction towards it. It noted that where death did occur, the side effects of the drug generally appeared immediately or within 15 minutes. Death occurs because the penicillin forms antibodies which release poisonous chemicals into the bloodstream. Someone who has shown penicillin sensitivity has a store of such antibodies which can be triggered into a fatal combination with further doses of penicillin.[49]

The important point perhaps to learn from this possibly fatal reaction is that penicillin should not be given for trivial infections, especially if the patient is known to be hypersensitive to drugs in general. There are plenty of other types of antibiotics outside of the penicillin group which can be safely prescribed instead, but note that it is also possible to be sensitive towards other types of antibiotic as well.

A doctor should always ask a patient if he/she is sensitive to penicillin; patients should be careful to check too whether *any* drug they are given contains penicillin.

Many penicillin preparations have names which could confuse the unwary.

The antibiotic that may cause fatal blood disease

Chloramphenicol, which is the only antibiotic that works against the bacteria that cause typhoid, can have a very dangerous side effect. Between one in 20,000 and one in 100,000 people who take this drug will suffer from bone-marrow disease, called aplastic anaemia (an often fatal condition where the marrow fails to make new red blood cells). It may not develop for months or weeks after taking a dose and there is no way of identifying in advance which people will be susceptible to this risk. In 80 per cent of cases this disease is fatal but survival is considered more likely if the condition develops early, though even then it may later turn into fatal anaemia.

As a result of this fatal side effect, this drug should be reserved only for very serious conditions, and the Pharmaceutical Society's guide to drugs, *Martindale's,*[23] advises that regular blood counts are performed whilst it is taken.

Chloramphenicol is commonly used in eye and ear drops. The ear drops should be avoided as they can cause hypersensitivity skin reactions in as many as one in 10 patients.[50] Products include Chloromycetin (Parke Davis) and Otopred (Typham). The eye drops are not hazardous, although it is occasionally possible for the chloramphenicol to be absorbed into the general circulation which then could lead to side effects. Products include Chloromycetin (Parke Davis), Minims Chloramphenicol and Snophenicol (Smith & Nephew).

Britain and the USA have strict rules regarding the use of this antibiotic and have banned its use as an ingredient in over-the-counter preparations. But other Western countries such as Spain, France and Portugal and most of the Third World still allow it to be used in cough mixture that can be bought freely in chemists' shops and supermarkets. Every now and then tragic reports appear in British newspapers of holiday-makers dying from taking innocent-looking cough mixtures, containing, for example, Chloramphenicol. As a rule any over-the-counter medicines bought abroad should be treated with great caution. It may be best to take a supply from Britain when going to some countries with lax drug regulations.

Brand names of Chloramphenicol:
Actinac (Roussel)
Chloromycetin (Parke Davis)
Kemicetine (Farmitalia)

Needless deaths caused by British inertia? Lincomycin and Clindamycin – the case of antibiotics that can cause fatal inflammations

A disturbing example of the inertia of the British drug authorities can be illustrated by the way they delayed warning doctors of the dangerous and often fatal side effects caused by the two antibiotics, Clindamycin and Lincomycin. In January 1975 the American FDA warned doctors in its regular drug bulletin that these antibiotics were linked with an increase in the number of cases of fatal intestinal disease known as pseudomembranous colitis. The FDA stated then that the incidence of this drug-induced disease could be as high as 1 in 10 of all patients treated with these antibiotics. The FDA did not know how often this condition resulted in death but reported that in January 1975 a total of 28 deaths which they knew about seemed to be related to colitis that had been caused by these drugs. As a result of this information the FDA ordered a revision in the warning labels that appeared with the drugs and so restricted its use to only serious cases, where the use of other antibiotics (such as penicillin in the case of allergic reactions) was not possible.

But it took another 18 months for the British Committee on the Safety of Medicines to put out the first alert in the UK. Finally in 1979 their 'yellow peril' warning went out to all doctors, stating that between 1964 and 1978 the Committee on the Safety of Medicines had received 174 reports of colitis attributed to antibiotics; 42 deaths had resulted from these cases, ie a 25 per cent risk of death with Lincomycin or Clindamycin. The Committee had noted that 80 per cent of these cases had been treated with Lincomycin or Clindamycin.[51] 'It is not always clear when to use these drugs and there is evidence that they are often being prescribed for minor conditions,' said the Committee on the Safety of Medicines. They advised doctors that these two drugs should be used only for serious or life-threatening conditions where other therapy is ineffective or undesirable, especially if the bacterial organisms being treated have been shown to be sensitive to these two drugs.

How many deaths could have been avoided in Britain if the Committee on the Safety of Medicines had acted at the same time as the US authorities? A four-and-a-half-year time lag may have accounted for needless deaths, especially since many cases of drug-induced disease are not reported to the Committee.

Brand names of Lincomycin: Lincocin (Upjohn), Mycivin (Boots).

Brand names of Clindamycin: Dalacin C (Upjohn).

The usual side effects in addition to colitis include severe and persistent diarrhoea.

The antibiotic that causes liver damage

Five years after the British Committee on the Safety of Medicines reported in 1973 that Ilosone caused dangerous liver damage, there were in 1978 still over half a million prescriptions made out for this product. Ilosone is a brand of Erythromycin made by Dista, the American drug company owned by Eli Lilly and Co. Ilosone differs from other brands of Erythromycin in that it contains Estolate which makes it potentially more hazardous than other varieties of this antibiotic group. Ilosone is particularly damaging to adults in whom it may cause attacks of jaundice; children do not seem to be affected as badly, but some liver damage is still caused.

Ilosone may cause jaundice if it is given for more than 14 days, but other forms of this erythromycin antibiotic do not have this side effect.[50] One possible advantage of Ilosone is that it is absorbed more quickly, but American pharmacologists do not believe that it has any therapeutic advantage over the less dangerous forms of erythromycin. In 1979 the US government watchdog body the FDA proposed a ban on Ilosone because of this danger. A special committee was established to look into the controversy, as there is disagreement on whether the hazard really exists. Erythromycin is a useful antibiotic with a broad spectrum of activity for people who are sensitive to penicillin.

Each year thousands of Americans are needlessly injured by Ilosone, says the Washington-based Public Citizens' Health Research Group, a medical branch of

Ralph Nader's consumer organisation. This group has evidence that about 1 per cent of the patients receiving the drug suffer from liver damage characterised by jaundice, hepatitis, and liver-function abnormalities leading, in some cases, to unnecessary surgery because of the severe abdominal pain which often accompanies the side effects of the drug. In Britain these statistics imply that over 5,000 people each year may suffer for no medical reason from liver damage caused by Ilosone. The US Public Citizens' Health Group is demanding that the drug be banned in the USA in order 'to stop the outrageous annual toll of thousands of avoidable drug injuries'. They point out that a number of hospitals (New York Hospital of Cornell University School of Medicine and the National Institute of Health Medical Centre) have discontinued stocking Ilosone in their pharmacies because of its toxicity and lack of therapeutic advantage over other Erythromycin drugs. They have found that it is responsible for a twentyfold increase in the risk of liver damage.

Harvard Medical School professor, William McCormack, in a recent review article,[52] asked 'whether there is any justification for the continued availability of the potentially toxic form of erythromycin . . . there is no convincing evidence that erythromycin estolate offers any clinical advantage.'

Mt Sinai Medical School professor, Dr Peter Nicholas, has stated,[53] 'Since there is no evidence of superiority of the estolate over other erythromycin preparations with respect to clinical efficacy in the treatment of infections, it is difficult at this writing to justify exposing patients to the risks associated with this drug . . .'

The antibiotic that causes deafness: Neomycin

Whether it is given by injection, mouth, enema, or applied to open wounds or damaged skin. Neomycin can cause irreversible deafness. The severity of the deafness this antibiotic can cause is dependent on the dose used; someone with damaged kidneys or liver will suffer from even more damage to the hearing. Even after stopping a course of these drugs the hearing can become progressively worse. The risk of deafness is about 1 in 100, which may seem a small number, but for someone who goes deaf it is a major disaster.[23] The Boston Collaborative Drug Survey found that of 495 patients who received Neomycin by mouth 6 became deaf, which represents a risk of just over 1 per cent.[54] The risk is much greater if the antibiotic is applied to the skin, so this risk percentage represents probably the lowest possible associated with this drug. The risk of deafness is made nearly fifty times greater if the drug is given to someone suffering from liver disease. When 13 patients with liver disease were given Neomycin 6 of them (ie 46 per cent) developed irreversible deafness, reports Dr J. Ballantyne.[55]

This antibiotic is often used in aerosol form to prevent infections following skin burns. At first it was thought that hearing damage only occurred when it was given by injection, but now it is known that damage can arise no matter how it is administered. Dozens of drugs on the market contain Neomycin; it is often combined with steroid hormones in skin creams (see page 204, hazards of Betnovate). The British Committee on the Safety of Medicines put out a 'yellow peril' warning in May 1977 advising doctors that this drug can cause deafness if applied to damaged or burned skin. Considering its widespread use in many different types of drugs, Neomycin may be responsible for thousands of cases of deafness or hearing losses each year.

The following drugs contain Neomycin:

Adcortyl with Graneodin (Squibb)	Maxitrol (Alcon)
Audicort (Lederle)	Minims neomycin (SNP)
Betnesol N (Glaxo)	Mycifradin (Upjohn)
Betnovate N (Glaxo)	Myciguent (Upjohn)
Biomydrin (Warner)	Naseptin (ICI)
Chymacort (Armour)	Neo-cortef (Upjohn)
Cicatrin (Calmic)	Neomedrone acne lotion
Decaspray (MSD)	(Upjohn)
Dermovate NN (Glaxo)	Neosporin (Calmic)
Dexa Rhinaspray (Boehringer	Neosulfazon (Wallace)
Ingelheim)	Neovax (Norton)
Donnagel with neomycin (Robins)	Nivemycin (Boots)
Graneodin (Squibb)	Otoseptil (Napp)
Gregoderm (Unigreg)	Otosporin (Calmic)
Halcicomb (FAIR)	Polybactrin (Calmic)
Hydroderm (MSD)	Predsol-N (Glaxo)
Hydromycin (Boots)	Rikospray Antibiotic (Riker)
Ivax (Boots)	Silderm (Lederle)
Kaomycin (Upjohn)	Synalar N (ICI)
Lomotil with neomycin (Searle)	Tampovagan N (Norgine)

Tri-Adcortyl (Squibb)   Uniroid (Unigreg)
– Otic (Squibb)   Vibrocil (Zyma)
Unidiarea (Unigreg)

Another antibiotic drug that may cause deafness

Streptomycin is another antibiotic that may cause deafness. It can attack the nerves responsible for hearing,
causing either vertigo, tinnitus (constant buzzing in the
ears), or sometimes even deafness. Like Neomycin the
chances of this happening are related to dose, age and the
health of the kidneys and the liver. People who have
damaged livers or kidneys should have regular blood
counts to see that poisonous concentrations of the antibiotic are not being built up. A damaged liver means that
the drug will not be excreted very efficiently.

Women who are pregnant should avoid this drug as it
will pass into the foetal bloodstream and could therefore
cause deafness in the unborn child.[23] Although streptomycin is now used almost entirely to treat TB, it is still
included in two anti-diarrhoea products: Cremostrep and
Sulphamagna. These products should be strictly avoided as
they may well prolong an attack of diarrhoea and are
considered to have no evidence of effectiveness, according
to the doctors' guide to prescribing, the *British National
Formulary*.[50] (See page 276 for Useless anti-diarrhoea
products list.)

The following brands contain Streptomycin:

Cremostrep (MSD)   Streptotriad (May & Baker)
Crystamycin (Glaxo)   Sulphamagna (Wyeth)

Antibiotic hazards for your children: 'The children who dare not smile'

One commonly prescribed antibiotic has the distasteful
side effect of discolouring children's teeth, so that they
turn irreversibly yellow. Tetracycline antibiotics are able to
deposit themselves permanently in teeth and bones, yet a
number of products specially made for children contain
this drug. It has been estimated by Dr J. Stewart, writing in
the *British Medical Journal*,[55] that more than 1 in 5 of all
children up to the age of 12 have teeth discoloured by this
antibiotic. Tetracyclines are rarely needed nowadays as
they have been replaced by safer and more effective
antibiotics.[55] They are only essential for a handful of

extremely rare diseases such as Rocky Mountain Fever, psittacosis and some forms of pneumonia. Nevertheless they are commonly prescribed by GPs for minor throat infections, encouraged no doubt by the large number of special paediatric preparations on the market.

The British Dental Association has frequently appealed to the drug manufacturers to stop making these children's syrup versions of Tetracyclines. 'The syrup makes it nice and sweet to encourage children to take these medicines', says Dr Edward Renson, Chairman of the British Dental Association, 'but this is quite wrong. The staining can vary from pale yellow through to purple just like bruising and it can have a severely damaging psychological effect on the growing child . . . I have known a number of cases where the child has become withdrawn, refusing to converse or smile and naturally this has had an effect on the parents and other members of the family.'[56]

Tetracycline-stained teeth cannot be polished white again. The only solution is to cap them, an expensive

'We'll either have to get her teeth capped, or change the wallpaper.'

treatment not usually obtainable on the NHS. Also it cannot be done until the adult teeth are in set position, so the child has to grow up with yellow teeth.

There is a great problem in convincing GPs of the dangers of these drugs, despite frequent reminders of the hazards. Surveys show that they are still being prescribed indiscriminately. One study involved analysing hundreds of teeth which had been extracted by dentists from children. By grinding up these extracted teeth it was possible to see how often children had been prescribed Tetracyclines; the drug was found in a highly significant number of the teeth tested.

Teeth of unborn children also stained by this drug

Tetracycline drugs are also absorbed by the developing bones and teeth of unborn children. This drug can easily cross the placental barrier so it will also damage the teeth of the baby developing in the womb. Tetracyclines cause a reduction in enamel-formation, increased susceptibility to caries (ie tooth decay) and the yellow staining. Since Tetracyclines can be taken up by bones too, they may cause a period of delayed growth, writes Dr Timothy Pickard in the *Guardian*.[58] He suggests that as more and more children are having their teeth damaged by these drugs, there is a strong case for restricting their use to hospital consultants only and banning their use by general practitioners. Parents can protect their children by making sure they do not consume any of the following products which contain Tetracycline: Chlortetracycline, Oxytetracycline, Doxycycline, Clomocycline, Methacycline. At the end of 1979 the American government announced a ban on paediatric (children's) versions of Tetracycline antibiotics.

Brand names:

Pharmax: Megaclor syrup; *Boots Company:* Totomycin mixture; *Lederle Laboratories:* Achromycin syrup, Aureomycin syrup, Deteclo syrup, Ledermycin syrup; *Berk Pharmaceuticals:* Berkmycen syrup, Tetrachel syrup; *Glaxo Laboratories:* Clinimycin syrup, Clinitetrin syrup; *ICI*: Imperacin syrup; *E. R. Squibb & Sons:* Mysteclin syrup, Steclin syrup; *Pfizer*: Rondomycin syrup, Sigmamycin syrup, Vibramycin syrup, Terrramycin syrup, Tetracyn syrup; *Bristol Laboratories:* Tetrex syrup; *Upjohn:* Albamycin; *Armour:* Chymocyclar; *MCP:*

190

Sustamycin; *Organon:* Tetrabid. (Some products are no longer available in the UK.)

More Medicines that rot children's teeth

Not only Tetracyclines cause problems. Most liquid medicines given to children will rot their teeth, because they contain up to 80 per cent sugar! It has been found that children who take syrup-based medicines have four times more dental decay compared to children who take tablets or who are taking no medicines at all. These were the findings of a disturbing study published in the *British Medical Journal* in 1979.[58] Some children who need to take prolonged drug treatment (eg those suffering from asthma or epilepsy) cannot avoid doing permanent damage to their teeth as a result of drug firms' obsession with sugar flavouring. Admittedly some drugs are unpleasant to taste unless sweetened, but there are safe alternatives to sugar which do not rot the teeth. Dr J. M. Smith of Newcastle's Regional Drug Unit says that sweeteners that do not damage teeth are available, but the drug firms simply don't bother with them.

Children of anxious mothers receive unnecessary antibiotics

'At many of these consultations the mother rather than the child should have been treated as the patient.' (*British Medical Journal*, Dr J. Howie and Dr A. Brigg, 22 March 1980)[59]

A ten-year study of 50 families attending a general practice in Aberdeen has shown that mothers who receive an abnormally high number of tranquillisers have children who receive an unnecessary number of antibiotics for respiratory complaints.

The survey found that the prescription of antibiotics to these children acted almost as a substitute for the mothers' own tranquillisers. The researchers showed that the times of the greatest use of antibiotics in the children coincided with the time when the mothers had the least number of tranquillisers prescribed!

Tetracyclines can cause more infections such as thrush

Sometimes Tetracyclines are so successful at killing off bacteria that they upset the balance of the normally harmless bugs, which live in harmony with the rest of the body inside the gut. The drug can upset this delicate balance of life inside the intestines by massacring the bacteria which ordinarily keep down the number of moulds, yeast or fungi present in the intestines. This massacre of bacteria gives the fungi a sudden new freedom to expand their territory all over the human body, resulting in 'superinfections' (as they are called) – thrush for example. These moulds can infect the mouth and other body openings such as the anus and the vulva. [23]

Sometimes it is not only fungal-type infections which suddenly undergo this sort of population explosion after the taking of Tetracyclines, but it is also possible, in hospitals particularly, to have superinfections of other bacteria – staphylococci, for example. These particular germs may be resistant to Tetracyclines and so they can cause new dangerous 'superinfections', which may result in serious inflammations of the intestines and possible dehydration. Occasionally these infections can be fatal.

Other side effects of Tetracyclines include liver, kidney and eye damage.

Special extra hazards of tetracyclines with food

Tetracyclines will not work if you consume any milk products, antacids (such as aluminium hydroxide) or any other alkalis at the same time as taking these drugs. Such substances prevent the Tetracyclines from being absorbed in the gut.

Tetracycline antibiotics must be reasonably fresh since they can break down into poisonous substances if taken after the date recommended on the container.

Which antibiotics can stop the Pill from working?

The antibiotics chemically known as the Rifampicins have the unusual and hazardous property of being able to create enzymes in the liver which can reduce the action of oral contraceptive pills. Patients on oral contraceptives should be advised to use alternative non-hormonal methods of birth control during Rifampicin therapy, say the manufacturers of one of these types of antibiotics – Lepetit Pharmaceuticals Ltd, makers of Rifadin. Since these antibiotics are mainly used against TB infections, they should not be a common hazard for women taking the Pill.

The following brands of antibiotics contain rifampicins: Rifadin (Lepetit Ltd); Rimactane (CIBA); Rimactazid (CIBA); Rifinah (Lepetit Ltd). A recent report also claims that *Tetracyclines* can also de-activate the Pill (see page 154).

Septrin

Brand name of drug: Septrin (Wellcome).
Purpose of drug: Destroys urinary-tract infections.
Special warning: May cause serious side-effects. Safer alternatives available.
Main chemical used in the drug: Co-Trimoxazole.
Brand name of drug with similar contents and hazards as Septrin: Bactrim (Roche).

This is a powerful drug which frequently produces serious side effects. It works like an antibiotic but, in fact, contains two substances neither of which are real antibiotics. Septrin contains two artificial chemicals. One is a *sulphonamide*, a substance derived originally from red dye which in the 1930s was discovered to kill off bacteria. The second substance, called Trimethoprim, works by also stopping the growth of bacteria. A number of distinguished drug experts have criticised the way in which Septrin has been promoted to doctors by the manufacturers (Burroughs Wellcome) since it can have such very serious side effects. As this product contains two drugs combined into one tablet there are twice as many possible side effects when taking Septrin.

Why Septrin is unnecessary

The major objection to the use of Septrin (or Bactrim) is that it is totally unnecessary to subject a patient to the risks of two drugs when one drug on its own is perfectly adequate. 'In acute or chronic urinary tract infections many consultants prefer to use older drugs such as sulphonamides alone, or antibiotics.' This was the verdict of the highly respected and independent US *Medical Letter*.[26] It also pointed out that Septrin was a waste of money costing ten times more than these alternative drugs. Clearly a simple antibiotic may be a much safer choice than Septrin. One-half of Septrin (or Bactrim) consists of a sulphonamide-type drug and 'these have been largely replaced by antibiotics in the treatment of infections' says the Pharmaceutical Society's guide to drugs, *Martindale's Pharmacopoeia,* adding that they *may* be of value only in treating those people who cannot tolerate antibiotics. One of the toxic hazards of Septrin (and Bactrim) is that it can form crystals in the urine and so lead to kidney damage; it is important, therefore, to drink extra fluids when taking a course of these tablets. *Martindale's* adds that it is doubtful that mixtures of sulphonamides have any advantage over more soluble ones. It particularly points out that Septrin (and Bactrim) are not very soluble in the urine – which means that they could cause kidney damage. But the problem is that *unless* the drug does become concentrated in the urine it will not be effective against a urinary-tract infection, a complaint for which Septrin and Bactrim are prescribed.

Do you need to be exposed to the hazards of Septrin?

It has recently been shown by researchers at Turku University in Finland[60] that just *one* of the drugs used in Septrin (and Bactrim), called Trimethoprim, has definite advantages over the *two* drugs that are used in these products. The Finnish researchers obtained samples of bacteria which had been collected from over 1,000 patients who were suffering from urinary-tract infections, eg cystitis. They tested their 'bugs' to see if they would be killed off by various commonly used drugs. Comparisons were therefore obtained between the medical effectiveness of plain Trimethoprim, Bactrim and Septrin-type drug combinations, and ampicillin (a popular version of penicillin). They found that Trimethoprim alone was just as effective as all of these other drugs which are commonly prescribed for urinary infections, even after five years' constant use. This means that the germs that cause urinary infections do not readily develop bacterial resistance against Trimethoprim, a common problem when antibiotics are used too frequently. On the basis of this research it would seem totally irrational to take preparations like Septrin (and Bactrim) which offer no more protection but create many more side effects than Trimethoprim alone. In January 1981 a new product was launched on the British drug market called Monotrim, containing just Trimethoprim. Although the sulphonamide ingredient in Septrin (and Bactrim) does have a wide range of antibiotic action against infectious bacteria it can often be made ineffective, especially in hospitals, by pus and dead tissue, according to Professor Peter Parrish. He adds that before using Septrin (and Bactrim) tests should be made to see if bacteria are sensitive to both of the chemicals used in the drug, to make sure that it is really vital to use a drug which has so many serious side effects.[61]

Is it too poisonous for minor infections?

This is the question posed by the *Drug and Therapeutics Bulletin*.[62] 'Co-trimoxazole was implicated in 13 out of 17 deaths from agranulocystosis (bone-marrow disease) during 1974–5 – only one of which was reported to the Committee on the Safety of Medicines,' says the *Bulletin*. Yet they point out it is 'no more effective than ampicillin or amoxycillin for chronic bronchitis. Also for uncomplicated urinary infections there is no evidence that co-trimoxazole (ie Bactrim and Septrin) is any better than antibiotics or sulphonamide drugs alone.'

The hazards of Septrin treatment

'Close supervision of the patient should be maintained since the onset of serious intoxification is unpredictable,' warns the Pharmaceutical Society guide to drugs.[23] Blood counts are necessary when having these drugs for more than seven to ten days, as sulphonamides can cause bone-marrow disease, which is dangerous and unpredictable. Trimethoprim, however, does not cause this side effect.

Kidney damage, as mentioned earlier, can be also caused by Septrin (and Bactrim) forming crystals in the urine. Allergic reactions include skin rashes and a fever is not uncommon, particularly in people who have been previously sensitised to these drugs, says *Martindale's Guide*. A doctor should always be told of any reaction to this drug that has occurred on a previous occasion.

Direct exposure to sunlight can increase the risk of dermatitis caused by Septrin.[23]

Skin rashes and nasty ulcers of the mouth in a particularly dangerous form known as Stevens–Johnson syndrome can also occur (25 per cent of cases of this syndrome are fatal). Septrin should be avoided at all costs during pregnancy or when breast feeding a baby. One survey of over 400 mothers with congenitally deformed children found that the use of sulphonamide drugs during pregnancy was significantly more common, compared to mothers with normal babies.

Other common side effects reported include:
nausea, vomiting, loss of appetite, fever, drowsiness, lowered mental ability, headache, diarrhoea, fatigue, insomnia, nightmares, confusion, depression and psychosis, vertigo, tinnitus and persistent hiccups!

The promotion of Septrin
'Only the blind, the deaf or the dead in the medical profession could have avoided receiving this barrage, with its message of something really splendid.'[26] This is how Dr Alan Klass describes the manner in which Septrin was promoted in the USA when it was introduced on to the market there in 1973. Despite the opinions of expert drug panels who believe that Septrin should not be widely prescribed, it has achieved a remarkable success, there being over 5 million prescriptions annually in Britain alone.

Another criticism has been levelled at the two companies that manufacture the two brands of this drug. Roche make Bactrim and Wellcome make Septrin, yet both these products are the same in every respect apart from their brand names. It would usually be expected that since they are rival companies, they would try to compete with each other. Yet the *Drug and Therapeutics Bulletin* claims that these two firms have a mutual marketing arrangement so that the prices of the two 'competing' products remain the same. This 'pseudo-competition' results in unnecessary confusion for consumers, greater promotional costs (double that necessary), and is unlikely to lead to new and better drugs because both companies are capitalising on the same pool of knowledge, says the article. There are many other examples of pseudo-competition in the drug industry, eg the birth pills Eugynon and Ovran, or Microgynon and Ovranette: these contraceptive pill brands pretend to compete but the two companies involved, Schering/Wyeth, have a pricing agreement, so there is no real competition at all, says the *Drug Bulletin*.[63]

Flagyl
Brand name of drug: Flagyl (May & Baker).
Purpose of drug: To cure urinary and other kinds of infections.
Special warning: May cause cancer.

Main chemical used in the drug: Metronidazole.

'It should be regarded as potentially dangerous . . . it should not be used for infections that could be treated by other means and should generally not be used in pregnant women' – *US Medical Letter.* [64]

'It must be considered a potential human carcinogen (cancer-causing substance) . . . every effort should be made to limit the use of the drug' – *US Food and Drug Administration.* [65]

Despite these hazards Flagyl remains the most commonly used drug to treat infections of the vagina and penis (trichomoniasis, technically). It is also used to treat certain gut and mouth infections. But it has been shown in animal experiments on both rats and mice to be capable of causing significant increases in the incidence of lung cancers and cancers of the breast. In April 1976 the American Food and Drug Administration, concerned over this cancer risk, ordered manufacturers of the drug to print a special boxed warning on the drug data sheets and advertisements sent to doctors. No similar warning has yet been made by the British Committee on the Safety of Medicines. Furthermore, the American authorities require that doctors are told that this drug passes into the placenta rapidly, and is also secreted in breast milk, and they state there may be a possible effect on a developing foetus. 'Therefore Flagyl should not be used in the first trimester of pregnancy,' say the FDA. In addition they recommend that during the other stages of pregnancy and during lactation (breast feeding), the use of Flagyl should be restricted to those in whom local treatment has been inadequate to control symptoms. Again no warning about its hazard in pregnancy is printed in Britain, two years after the US warning.

Often a woman may be re-infected after successful treatment if her partner (who may not show any symptoms) has not also been treated. Flagyl has no effect on thrush (Candida species of yeast).

The FDA has also stopped the marketing of Flagyl vaginal inserts on the grounds that there is not adequate data to support their effectiveness. However, some American doctors do not agree that there is a risk with this drug. For example, Dr Peter Goldman writes in the *New*

England Journal of Medicine that it is a very effective drug. 'Human studies indicate that the risk of cancer is almost certainly not large and is probably negligible.'[66]

Side effects of flagyl include: stomach upsets, loss of appetite, nausea, a furry tongue, dry mouth, unpleasant tastes, skin rashes and headaches.

Painkillers: Distalgesic

Brand name of drug: Distalgesic (Eli Lilly & Co's subsidiary, Dista, manufacture it).
Purpose of drug: Painkiller.
Special warning: May cause addiction and can be fatal with small overdose, especially if combined with alcohol.
Main chemicals used in the drug: Propoxyphene and Paracetamol.

Similar drugs:

Cosalgesic (Cox-Continental)	Dolasan (Lilly)
Depronal SA (Warner)	Doloxene (Lilly)
Dolasan (Lilly)	Doloxene Compound (Lilly)
Digesic (Australian version)	Napsalgesic (Dista)

Distalgesic is the top-selling painkiller in the UK, with 10 million prescriptions per year; 1 in 3 of all painkillers prescribed is a Distalgesic.
In the United States Darvon (the US equivalent of Distalgesic) is associated with more deaths than any other drug sold; an estimated 1,800 deaths were related to its use in 1977. Two or three times the recommended dose can cause death, especially if the drug is mixed with alcohol, tranquillisers or sleeping pills. The British version is in fact a combination of paracetamol and a chemical called *propoxyphene* which is closely related to morphine. Just twice the recommended daily dose of Darvon can lead to addiction, say the manufacturers. It makes people euphoric, having the same properties that 'dope' addicts look for in heroin or morphine. Finally it is no more effective a painkiller than either aspirin or paracetamol alone and several investigations show that it is less effective than cheaper and safer drugs obtainable over the counter.

It is not difficult to see why Distalgesic and Darvon have become Britain and America's top-selling painkilling drug: (1) in Britain it is manufactured to contain paracetamol so that its weak effect as a painkiller goes unnoticed by

The case against the continued widespread use of dextropropoxyphene (Distalgesic) seems overwhelming – Dr R. J. Young and Dr A. H. Lawson in 'Distalgesic Poisoning – Cause for Concern', *BMJ,* April, 1980.

The drug companies' most profitable drugs are those which are gently addictive, for after all, such drugs are assured of a regular and enthusiastic clientele. – Dr Andrew Malleson in *Need Your Doctor be so Useless?*[67]

Dextropropoxyphene, alone or in combination with paracetamol (Distalgesic etc), is less potent than codein. It should be prescribed with caution because death from respiratory depression may occur rapidly following overdose and there is an increasing problem of drug abuse. – *The British National Formulary*, the doctors' guide to prescribing.

If Darvon (US name) were being considered for approval as a new drug today – knowing what we know about its strong record of killing people and relatively weak record of killing pain, it is unlikely the drug would get on the market. – Dr Sidney Wolfe of the US Public Citizens' Health Research Group at American Government Hearing.[68]

patients because paracetamol is an effective painkiller in its own right; (2) it has been advertised widely to doctors; (3) its addictive properties and the euphoria it brings to patients make it difficult for patients to stop taking it, so that it remains high on the list of repeat prescriptions. Although the makers, Lilly & Co, launched it in 1957 as a 'safe' and 'non-narcotic' painkiller 'as effective as codeine', the company later admitted that the main ingredient of the drug was a narcotic which was addictive at just twice the normal dose used in America.

Already public health departments in more than ten separate states in the USA refuse to pay for this drug because of its hazardous properties and its relative lack of effectiveness. Dr Wolfe of Public Citizens' Health Research Group (a medical offshoot of Ralph Nader's consumer organisation) has demanded that the drug be withdrawn from the market because of the public health hazard it poses. This consumer group has already presented a barrage of powerful evidence against propoxyphene to the US Food and Drugs Administration, and the US Secretary of Health Education and Welfare is considering these petitions.

Is Distalgesic no better a painkiller than aspirin?

'There remains no conclusive evidence that this drug has any superior analgesic (pain-killing) efficacy when compared with other manifestly less dangerous alternatives.' (Dr Robert J. Young and Dr A. Lawson[69])

A study of patients at the Mayo Clinic in New York compared the effectiveness of two tablets of aspirin to all other painkillers on the market at the time, including narcotics. It was found that patients reported that aspirin was superior to every other painkiller even though at the time they did not know which drug they were taking. Propoxyphene, the main ingredient of Distalgesic, was not only inferior to plain old simple aspirin, it was also no better than a sugar pill. This was the eighth study to make such a finding about propoxyphene.[70,71] The FDA state, on the basis of many experiments, that propoxyphene is no better than paracetamol, so for people who are sensitive to aspirin, they are better off taking paracetamol alone.

As a result of the way in which Eli Lilly & Co advertised their product Darvon, they were forced to send out the following letter to all US doctors: 'There is no substantial evidence to demonstrate that Darvon is more effective than two tablets of aspirin and the preponderance of evidence indicates that it may be somewhat less effective.' (In Britain, Distalgesic in fact contains 32.5 mg of propoxyphene, making it even *less* effective than Darvon with 65 mg.)

At an American government hearing in April 1979, the FDA's own outside expert on drug effectiveness stated again: 'It is now more doubtful than ever that propoxyphene provides an analgesic (painkilling effect) equal to two tablets of aspirin.'

Furthermore, no one has ever identified a group of people who obtain any unique benefit from propoxyphene, ie a group of patients who could use neither aspirin nor paracetamol for whom the drug would be of some special use. In fact, in both Britain and the USA the vast majority of prescriptions for propoxyphene drugs are for those drugs which are combined with paracetamol or aspirin anyway.

Are you addicted to Distalgesic?

'When taken for an extended period of time propoxyphene (the major ingredient of Distalgesic) produces physical and psychological dependence of the morphine type. Dependence may occur if patients take as few as 8 to 12 pills a day (of Darvon)' – advice put out by the American Food and Drug Administration. Abuse of this drug among American servicemen in Germany[72] resulted in 13 deaths. When a group of patients at Harvard Medical School were given Darvon four times a day (which is less than the maximum recommended daily dose) 3 out of 19 patients developed withdrawal symptoms suggesting addiction after a three-month course of treatment.[73] Physical addiction has been repeatedly shown to occur with this drug with just over the daily dose. Mental disturbance and epileptic fits have been caused by a dose which is just twice the recommended daily dose, say the manufacturers, Eli Lilly, in their American labelling. A survey of soldiers in West Germany found 1 in 5 took the drug for non-medical reasons, ie they were taking it to get 'high' and were probably addicted.

In the United States the FDA warns doctors and patients (on the labels for the drug) not to prescribe or take the drug during pregnancy because of the possibility that the baby will be born suffering from withdrawal effects. One baby was born suffering from tremors, irritability, high-pitched cry, diarrhoea, weight loss and a ravenous appetite and occasional seizures. In one case a young man who took it for 'confidence, aggressiveness, euphoria and a relief of tension', suffered from two epileptic fits. When the drug was taken away from him he complained of a craving for it. He was gradually taken off the drug but later resorted to illicit use and suffered a third epileptic fit.[74]

'The evidence is very strong that propoxyphene is a narcotic drug which will produce moderate to severe psychological dependence and a moderate degree of physical dependence,' says Dr William Martin, the ex-head of an American Addiction Research Centre.[68]

The fatal crise de coeur! Deaths from Distalgesic

'Anyone taking a small overdose of the painkilling drug Distalgesic especially in combination with alcohol may lose consciousness and die before medical help can be summoned,' wrote Birmingham's Coroner, Dr R. M. Whittington, in the *British Medical Journal*.[75] He was trying to alert British doctors to the fact that Distalgesic compared to all other painkillers kills in a very short time. Dr Whittington described 26 deaths in the West Midlands, mainly among young people whom he believed had taken an overdose without really intending to commit suicide. 'Some were suicidal, but many were more in the nature of crise de coeur.' In almost half the cases Dr Whittington examined an appreciable amount of alcohol was an additional factor. The fact that the victims were so young compared to average age for other types of overdose particularly struck Dr Whittington. The age of his cases was on average 36, compared to 57 generally for overdose victims, 'thus emphasising the danger for young people'. He adds that Distalgesic is currently the commonest cause of death referred to forensic science laboratories in Britain. Figures obtained from the government's statistical office show that the numbers of deaths from Distalgesic are climbing each year. Dr Whittington writes that Distalgesic has been advertised for 'everyday aches and pains' and that there is a popular belief that it is safe and that it may be prescribed with increasing frequency, often at doses above those recommended by the manufacturers. Many American coroners too have attacked the continued use of this drug. In the USA it was associated with more deaths than were heroin or morphine in the first half of 1977.[68] Figures in the USA show that in 1977 Darvon caused more than twice the number of deaths compared to codeine, nearly four times the number of deaths caused by aspirin poisoning, and nearly eight times more deaths than paracetamol.[76]

In the US in July 1979, the FDA forced the manufacturers of Darvon, Eli Lilly & Co, to distribute a consumer leaflet warning of the hazards of taking the drug in excess, or with alcohol or other drugs. Doctors were also given an extra warning about the need to carefully choose the patients who receive Darvon and particularly to advise them about the fatal hazards of combining it with alcohol. 'These actions are part of a major effort by Lilly and the Government to bring to the public attention the risks associated with the overuse, misuse and abuse of Darvon,' said the FDA. The US Commissioner for Food and Drugs said at the time: 'I am pleased that Lilly has taken action to bring this problem to the attention of physicians and consumers.' In March 1979 Lilly's UK Medical Director, Dr Bryan Gennery, warned doctors of the signs and symptoms of Distalgesic overdose and of the dangers of prescribing it with central nervous system agents (eg tranquillisers) and to patients with a history of mental illness or those known to abuse alcohol. But, unlike Americans, the British public received no warnings about these hazards. The British Department of Health too has failed to make any public warnings on the hazards of this best-selling drug. In the USA, pharmacists have also been brought into the campaign to prevent deaths due to Darvon; special stickers are put on to prescriptions for these drugs. In addition, every package of tablets contains a leaflet for patients warning of the hazards. The FDA is particularly concerned as it says: 'Apart from deaths amongst addicts, *other* deaths appear to have occurred amongst people who are not habitual drug users and who took propoxyphene with alcohol, tranquillisers or sedatives without understanding the danger.' They warn that there is increasing concern that some of these accidental deaths occurred at doses only slightly higher than the upper limits of the recommended dose.

Fortral

Fortral or Fortagesic (Pentazocaine) is a powerful painkiller but there is a risk of addiction. In a number of American cities, particularly Chicago, it is being used by drug addicts as a substitute for heroin, according to the US Food and Drug Administration. Experiments show that Fortral is addictive even in low doses and that babies born to women dependent on the drug experience withdrawal effects immediately after birth.[77] The same precautions should be applied as are applied to morphine says *Martindale's* (the Pharmaceutical Society's Guide to prescribing)[78], though Fortral does not have as much potential as morphine for producing addiction.

Fortral causes hallucinations, according to a report in the *British Medical Journal*, in as many as 10 per cent of the patients taking this drug.[79] Fortagesic contains a combination of paracetamol and another painkiller, pentazocaine, and as a result its use is NOT recommended by the doctors' authoritative guide to prescribing, the *British National Formulary*.[80]

How to choose a painkiller: which ones to avoid
Stick to simple aspirin, or paracetamol or codein on its own. Avoid mixtures, especially those with caffeine which has no painkilling effect and which may aggravate the stomach irritation caused by aspirin, according to the *British National Formulary*.[80]

The *BNF* suggests avoiding the following mixtures because they complicate the treatment of overdosage – ie they are more dangerous in overdose than simple painkillers and they rarely offer any advantage: Codis, Cosalgesic, Distalgesic, Dolasan, Doloxene, Equagesic, Fortagesic, Hypon, Lobak, Medocodene, Napsalgesic, Norgesic, Onadox 118, Panadeine compound, Paracodal, Parahypon, Paralgin, Paramol 118, Para Seltzer, Parazolidin, Safapryn, Solpadeine, Tandalgesic, Trancoprin and Veganin.

Steroid skin creams: Betnovate

Brand name of drug: Betnovate (Glaxo).
Purpose of drug: To treat inflamed skin.
Special warning: Can be addictive and make the skin thin and red.
Main chemical used in the drug: Betamethasone valerate (corticosteroid).
Steroid skin creams are divided into four groups, representing four levels of potency and strength. The most potent steroid creams (in Group 1) have the most severe side effects, and the least potent (in Group 4) are associated with the least number of side effects.

Group 1 (Very Potent): Propaderm Forte (A&H), Dermovate (Glaxo), Halciderm Topical (Squibb). *Mixtures in Group 1:* Dermovate NN (Glaxo), Halcicomb

(Fair). *Group 2 (Potent):* Propaderm (A&H), Betnovate (Glaxo), Tridesilon (Dome), Nerisone (Schering), Temetex (Roche), Topilar (Syntex), Synalar (ICI), Halcort (FAIR), Locoid (Brocades), Adcortyl (Squibb), Ledercort (Lederle). *Mixtures in Group 2:* Betnovate C and N, Propaderm A and C, Synalar C and N. *Group 3 (Moderately Potent):* Alphaderm (Eaton), Eumovate (Glaxo), Synandone (ICI), Metosyn (Stuart), Ultradil (Schering), Ultralanum (Schering), Haelan (Dista). *Group 4 (Weak):* Hydrocortisone (Brocades), Calmurid HC (Pharmacia), Cobadex (Cox Continental), Cortril (Pfizer), Dioderm (Dermal), Domecort (Dome), Efcortelan (Glaxo), Hydrocortistab (Boots), Hydrocortisyl (Roussel), Hydrocortone (MSD).

'Steroids suppress the inflammatory reaction while in use *and are in no sense curative*' (my italics)—*British National Formulary,* 1981.[80]

Are you suffering from the 'Bright Red Betnovate Face'?

The condition is so striking that it can be recognised as the patient enters the room. On close questioning the patient usually reveals that the trouble began with a trivial eruption of the face. Then the patient almost invariably admits to having applied potent topical steroids (ie Betnovate and similar drugs) over long periods of time.

This is how an editorial, in *The Lancet* in January 1980 entitled 'Perioral Dermatitis', reports about the hazards of Betnovate-type skin creams. It adds that researchers have shown that these skin problems are *not* caused by fluoridated toothpaste, moisturisers or other common contact allergy-causing substances, but by products like Betnovate. A study by Dr D. S. Wilkinson of 259 patients with skin eruptions of the face found that 258 had been applying steroid creams, such as Betnovate – although some were reluctant to admit using them at first.[81]

Hazard warnings should be printed on the containers of these products, demands Dr J. A. Cotterill, another dermatologist alarmed at the widespread injury drugs such as Betnovate produce.[82]

Hormone skin creams such as Betnovate, Dermovate and Propaderm can appear to rapidly cure skin disorders such as dermatitis, eczema or psoriasis. But the fast relief they bring may not last very long since these creams only suppress or hide skin problems; they do not cure them.

'All who prescribe them should be aware of the possible dire consequences of injudicious and prolonged administration' – so concludes an editorial in *The Lancet*[83] on the hazards of the steroid skin creams like Betnovate or Dermovate. Dr J. N. Burry who has made a study of people injured by these drugs says that the application of these creams over a period of years, in some instances can prevent the healing of established skin conditions. The problem with these drugs is that they can cause permanent skin damage and after a long period of use the skin wastes away or stripy lines appear. It is perhaps difficult for most users of a skin cream to imagine that these drugs will enter the bloodstream through the skin and will then have the same serious side effects as drugs that are taken by mouth, but they do have all the toxic effects of other hormone drugs.

'These steroid drugs are wondrous drugs indeed and it is probably for that very reason that they are overprescribed by physicians and overused by laymen,' claims Dr Albert Klugman in the *Journal of the American Medical Association*.[84] He states that sunburn, insect bites, burns and especially acne should not be treated with these creams.

The manufacturers (Glaxo), however, tell doctors that Betnovate can be used for the management of insect bites and skinburn. Dr Klugman and other experts say that the main hazard of these drugs comes from their repeated use for months or even years on a particular part of the face. What can often happen is that when an adult woman (the most common users of these preparations are middle-aged women) starts using the cream, there is usually a quick and dramatic relief of the skin problems, but this is followed by worsening of the condition of the skin when the patient stops applying the cream. This happens because the hormone cream merely hides the symptoms of the skin disorder. At this stage the patient thinks that she has only to increase use of the steroid cream to secure again the benefits of the drug. So the patient takes some more cream, and at first it gets better but then gets worse again, and after repeating this process a number of times the patient becomes totally dependent on the cream, using it almost continually. 'Patients seem to be *addicted* to these agents,' says *The Lancet,*[83] because in the short term they do relieve the discomfort associated with inflamed skin. But the skin of such patients is particularly prone to being worn or wasted away by these powerful hormone drugs. In turn, this wasting away exposes the tiny blood capillaries beneath the surface layer of the skin. As a result the skin and the complexion becomes much redder in colour. 'This rebound may explain why patients once having started the treatment find it so difficult to stop,' suggests *The Lancet.* It is ironic that steroids are frequently illicitly obtained in order to treat the type of skin problems that they are responsible for causing in the first place, such as acne and rosacea (a form of acne in adult women). Steroids are unsuitable for acne because they *cause* acne, says Dr Klugman. 'Acne can only be brought under control by stopping steroid cream treatment and giving antibiotic treatment, if anything at all.'[84]

A survey of 73 patients who were suffering from skin disorders found that when they stopped using these steroid creams their skin usually healed on its own accord. But there was a period lasting from 8 to 10 days during which their skin conditions got worse. This worsening was controlled with the aid of antibiotics. The only patient who experienced a severe recurrence of his skin condition was discovered to have started using the hormone creams again.[85]

Not only are these creams not recommended for use in trivial skin inflammations of the face, but it is also considered by Dr J. A. Milne[86] that there is a danger of dependency developing (ie addiction) if they are used continually to treat more serious problems such as psoriasis.

Sales of Betnovate exceed those of Dermovate although it has been found that most patients, if given the choice, prefer Dermovate for the treatment of psoriasis and eczema. An investigation involving over a thousand patients found that Dermovate was considered the more beneficial of these two steroid creams.[87]

It should be remembered that these skin creams have exactly the same toxic effects as the other powerful corticosteroid drugs, which include: the retention of water and salt, corneal ulcers and cataracts. There is a case of two young women aged 17 and 20 who developed cataracts with permanent damage to their eyesight after prolonged use of steroid skin creams to relieve skin irritations around the eyes, caused by contact lenses.[88]

Corticosteroids can also increase the loss of calcium from the bones leading to a greater likelihood of fractures. Growth in young children can be stunted. 'Moon Face', hirsutism, buffalo hump, acne, bruising, amenorrhoea, mental and neurological disturbances are possible also simply from the use of corticosteroid creams over a prolonged period of time.

Cough mixtures: Benylin

Brand name of drug: Benylin (Parke Davis).
Purpose of drug: Cough treatment.
Special warning: Probably useless, but may make you sleepy.
Other similar cough medicines:
Actifed (Wellcome), Benafed (Parke Davis), Flavelix (Pharmax), Histalix (Wallace), Bronchotone (Wade), Dimotane Expectorant (Robins), Guanor (R P Drugs), Linctifed (Wellcome), Rubelix (Pharmax), Pholcomed (Medo), Sudafed (Calmic), Valledrine and Vallex (M & B).

The following advertisement for Benylin appeared in 1981 in the British publication *The Pharmaceutical Journal*: 'Why these three important products earn your recommendation' (referring to a photograph of bottles of Benylin Expectorant, Benylin Fortified Linctus and Benylin Paediatric syrup): 'They're established, well accepted by your customers and an important source of profit to the pharmacy. No wonder they're clear leaders in the field.'

'Most of the coughs that present for the first time in general practice will have settled within a week no matter what treatment is prescribed' – Professor E. Wilkes, *Prescriber's Journal.*[89]

There are over 5 million prescriptions each year for Benylin, a cough mixture whose every ingredient has been demonstrated to be useless or present in too small a concentration to be of any use. The dilemma for the manufacturers is that by increasing the concentrations of those chemicals which could do something, they would cause very serious side effects. In one of the Department of Health's rare attempts to cut down the prescribing of useless medicines a fascinating leaflet, which mentions Benylin and other cough mixtures, was posted to all British doctors. It stated that in 1975 little short of 4 million litres of cough mixtures were prescribed in England and Wales at a cost of £11½ million. On the flip side of this little leaflet was a delightful quotation snipped out of the *British National Formulary*, which is one of the most orthodox guides to medical prescribing in the world. It stated: 'Many cough preparations contain both expectorant and sedative drugs (ie contradictory substances) and perhaps this reflects the lack of evidence that the ingredients have any effect.'

What this little quotation was getting at was the fact that Benylin, and other cough mixtures too, contain one chemical designed to make you cough and another one designed to stop you coughing.

Let us go through the ingredients inside a bottle of Benylin. It contains an antihistamine yet 'there is no support at all for the popular belief that antihistamines are of any use in treating coughs,' says Professor of Pharmacology, Peter Parrish,[90] adding that they may produce sedation which may help at night, so they may help you fall asleep, but so will a glass of wine or a cup of Horlicks. Professor Wilkes points out that the dose of antihistamine used in popular cough mixtures is too low to be effective, and that for children it is difficult to achieve the required sedative effect without a risk of overdose. 'Antihistamines are added in the hope . . . without good evidence that they may lessen inflammation,' says Professor Wilkes, but concludes that their value in controlling a cough is 'negligible'.

The American Department of Health, unlike its British counterpart, has *attempted* to protect the innocent consumer from drinking millions of gallons of ineffective cough mixtures. It has published the conclusion of a panel of drug experts who have considered the effectiveness and safety of this and many other drugs sold over the counter in the USA. When they looked at cough and cold remedies they also found that the antihistamine would stop coughing but only when it is present in almost double the concentration used in Benylin.[91]

The next major ingredient is the so-called expectorant (which makes you cough), a chemical called ammonium chloride. This chemical irritates the lining of the stomach and in theory it is supposed to make your sputum more watery and therefore easier to cough up. But the dose actually needed to do this would not only make you cough up but also give you stomach pains and make you sick says Professor Parrish.[90]

'Some of us feel that the pharmacy of the modern cough mixture still belongs to an era from the days when the doctor dealt largely in reassurance through the bottle of medicine. This was carried away as a talisman, a piece of the doctor, its colour and taste being chosen as carefully as its active constituents,' writes Professor Wilkes.[89]

According to the American FDA, 'There is substantial lack of evidence that this drug [Benylin] has the effect purported.'

One final word on this useless ingredient, ammonium chloride (the expectorant): 'It is doubtful whether its irritant contributes to any expectorant action,' says *Martindale's Extra Pharmacopoeia,* an encyclopaedic survey of drugs published by the British Pharmaceutical Society.[92]

The third ingredient in Benylin is sodium citrate: all this does is to provide a lemon taste and smell. In fact, large concentrations of this substance were thought to have some effect on a cough but sodium citrate has been found to be useless even at high doses. 'There are no well controlled studies documenting the effectiveness of sodium citrate as an expectorant,' reports the American government panel. 'It is probable that the water ingested with them is the basis for any beneficial effects.'[93] In small doses it is not an active ingredient and no labelling claim should be made for it as it is being used only as a flavouring agent, adds the American report.

The fourth useless ingredient put into Benylin is chloroform: 'There is no evidence that chloroform is effective as an expectorant or that it ameliorates cough' – US government findings. One report states that 'It is probably harmless as well as useless in the dosages used.' One hazard is that chloroform has been found to cause various types of cancer in experimental animals.[94] As a result its use has been banned in food and drugs. It has now been removed from Benylin.

Finally, another useless flavouring agent is added to Benylin, the ever-present *menthol*. 'There are no well controlled studies documenting the effectiveness of menthol as an antitussive (something that stops coughs) or as an expectorant. Its effectiveness is uncertain due to lack of properly controlled studies of the substance by itself,' reports the American government study[95] yet again.

So what have we got in a bottle of Benylin? Five substances which do not work but which add some flavourings and might make you feel sleepy! In the USA the label on a bottle of Benylin warns you not to take Benylin when breast-feeding or if you suffer from glaucoma, peptic ulcer or a prostate gland condition. None of these warnings appear on the British labels, which only tell you not to drive or operate machinery.

The side effects of antihistamines include: drowsiness, nausea, vomiting, diarrhoea, constipation, headache, blurred vision, tinnitus, elation and depression, nightmares, irritability, loss of appetite, dryness of the mouth, tightness of the chest, tingling, heaviness and weakness of hands.[92]

So what should you do about a cough? Advice from the real experts

It seems that one of the problems about most cough mixtures on the market is that they fail to distinguish on their label which type of cough they are best for. This is because they try to cater for *all* types of cough with the result that they contain contradictory substances (eg Benylin contains both something to stop you coughing *and* something to make you cough). So if you have a dry throaty cough you do not need to take an expectorant like Benylin. 'Anything that may be chewed or sucked will help,' says Professor Peter Parrish;[90] 'there is little point in taking cough lozenges or mixtures.' For a really bad cough on the chest a cough suppressant such as codeine is often advised. A productive cough is best treated with a warm drink or steam inhalations; simple salt water may also work as an expectorant. Steam inhalations are good for any type of cough, in fact. 'If a cough mixture is to be prescribed simple Linctus BPC or codeine linctus can be as helpful as any and when it is necessary to prescribe an antibiotic for infection then there should be no need for a cough mixture' (Professor E. Wilkes in *Prescriber's Journal*).[89]

'Most people derive great satisfaction from cough remedies, even when it has been objectively shown that the chemicals used do not work. Cough remedies work by altering the patient's emotional state in such a way as to reduce the anxiety about the cough and to induce a belief that objective improvement has resulted. If a person with a cough believes in a remedy that person can probably obtain as much relief from a simple inexpensive product as from the most elaborate and costly one.'[96]

'A simple linctus which is both harmless and cheap', suggests the doctors' guide to prescribing, the *British National Formulary*.[97]

Blood pressure and heart drugs: Inderal

Brand name of drug: Inderal (ICI).
Purpose of drug: To reduce blood pressure and angina.
Special warning: Possibly unnecessary and dangerous for some people.
Main chemical used in drug: Propranolol.

Similar drugs:

Beta Cardone (Duncan, Flockhart) = *sotalol*	Sectral (M & B) = *acebutolol*
	Slow Trasicor (CIBA) = *oxprenolol*
Betaloc (Astra) = *metoprolol*	Sotacor (Bristol) = *sotalol*
Betim (Leo) = *timolol*	Tenormin (Stuart) = *atenolol*
Blocadren (MSD) = *timolol*	Trasicor (CIBA) = *oxprenolol*
Lopresor (Geigy) = *metoprolol*	Visken (Sandoz) = *pindolol*

Inderal is widely prescribed for high blood pressure and angina. It can be very effective in reducing the pain of angina by blocking the nerves that make the heart pump more blood; this is why it is called a 'beta-blocker'. For the same reason it can also reduce blood pressure and as a result it may reduce the risk of having a stroke or a heart attack. But it is a drug with a number of serious side effects and there is evidence that it may be prescribed too widely and unnecessarily for people who do not need any heart drug at all. Another hazard is that if this drug is suddenly stopped, its cessation can cause fatal heart attacks. Treatment for high blood pressure is one of the main causes of drug-induced illness in the elderly, according to an editorial in the *British Medical Journal*.[98] There is no evidence that people with moderate to mild blood pressure obtain any benefit from this and similar blood pressure-lowering drugs. Other drugs also used to lower blood pressure include: Aldomet (see page 218), Moduretic, Lasix, Navidrex (see page 223 for details of these drugs).

Are blood-pressure drugs unnecessarily prescribed?

In 1973 a group of doctors from all over Europe joined together to find out whether or not elderly people suffering from high blood pressure would benefit from being given drugs to reduce their blood pressure. Although it is a well-known and established fact that high blood pressure is associated with heart disease, stroke, artery disease and a reduced life expectancy, no one has actually shown that reducing blood pressure with the aid of drugs reduces the incidence of these diseases or actually prolongs life.[98] The European Working Party of 1973 set up an investigation involving 600 patients over the age of 60 who were suffering (if 'suffering' is the correct word) from mild to moderate blood-pressure conditions (hypertension, as the doctors often call it). Half of these 600 people were given drugs to reduce blood pressure and the other half were not given real drugs at all, just placebos or sugar pills, but which the patients thought were the real thing. Before this experiment was started it was agreed by all the doctors involved in the research that if the treatment was shown to confer either significant benefit or disadvantage the experiment would be stopped. However, over five years later, in 1979, an editorial in the *British Medical Journal* reported that the experiment was still going on. There had been a fall in blood pressure amongst those people taking the real drugs but since the experiment had not been stopped, the article pointed out that it could be deduced that no other benefit had occurred. 'We can take it therefore that the substantial fall in blood pressure has not as yet been accompanied by a significant reduction in stroke, heart attacks or deaths.' The *Journal* concluded that there was no evidence yet that a reduction of blood pressure in the elderly by means of drugs alters the course of the disease. Of course it is possible that an effect may be noticed after another five years, but that is a long time to take pills. One of the problems of these drugs is that generally they have to be taken for life.

Another massive study, involving 36,000 people, was started in 1978 by the Medical Research Council to see if these drugs did anything for moderate blood pressure. An editorial in the *New Scientist*, in February 1978, questioned the sense of such a vast undertaking, pointing out that the famous physician Sir George Pickering has said that 'if this sort of blood pressure is a disease at all, it is a disease hitherto unrecognised by medicine, a disease characterised by a quantitative not a qualitative deviation from the norm'. The late Professor Henry Miller also remarked that we do not know whether the rigorous treatment of mild blood pressure without any symptoms of illness prolongs life or not. He added that from the experience of insurance examinations it is known that the detection of such mild blood pressure causes disabling anxiety (see Useless and Hazardous Tests, page 102).

In the face of all these uncertainties and the possibly dubious benefits of these drugs, a thorough investigation is just what is needed, suggests the *New Scientist*, at the same time posing the awkward question of how are doctors to deal with the unfortunate guinea pigs who are now testing these drugs. Thousands of people will receive a drug that may cause serious side effects, and since they could be long-term toxic effects that may not show up for years no one can know what they will be. The anxieties raised by participating in these experiments could alter the results so long as the doctors in charge are *honest* in explaining the possible side effects of the drugs. Can the guinea pigs in such a trial be given a briefing that is ethically proper and yet does not produce meaningless results? asks Dr Bernard Dixon.[99]

Already, in the USA, an investigation into the value of these drugs, which involved over 5,000 patients who were followed for years, has proved to be of no value in assessing the effectiveness of the drugs. The US Hypertension Detection and Follow-Up Programme recently announced that there was a 17 per cent reduction in deaths amongst these people, who received care at special clinics. But Drs Peart and Miall who are coordinating the British MRC study have pointed out[100] that since there was no control group of patients taking a placebo it was as much a trial of medical care as of anti-hypertensive drugs. The results fall far short of proving whether or not in the UK we ought to be giving drug treatment to all middle-aged people with mild hypertension.

It is commonly believed amongst experts that research will eventually discover that mild or moderate blood pressure is something which would need to be treated in young children in order to forestall later disease. One American researcher who has followed up children who had slightly raised blood pressure has shown that the predisposition to high blood pressure in adulthood can be identified in the early years of life. The implications of his findings are worrying. For it means that vast populations of young people may be considered suitable cases for lifelong treatment with these anti-hypertensive drugs.

Hazards of Inderal and similar drugs

One of the problems of Inderal is that it works by blocking nerve messages to the heart, but it does not only block nerves going to the heart, it can also block the bronchial tubes. So people with asthma or bronchitis may suffer from increased breathing problems with Inderal. Although all beta-blocking drugs carry the risk of inducing bronchial asthma, three drugs are linked with less risk than Inderal. They are Atenolol (Tenormin), Metoprolol (Betaloc and Lopresor) and Acebutol (Sectral). Unfortunately there was a drug that worked selectively on the heart called Eraldin (also made by ICI; it is chemically very similar to Inderal – so much so that you may have noticed that Inderal is an anagram of Eraldin), but Eraldin has gone out of use because thousands of patients who took it suffered from serious skin, eye, stomach and lung damage, after using the drug for a number of years. ICI has had to pay out hundreds of thousands of pounds in damages to victims of Eraldin.

Eraldin caused permanent damage to thousands in Britain, yet it did not injure any Americans. The reason is simple: the American drug authorities require much stricter proof that these types of drugs are safe before they allow the public to be given them. The British public at large was used as an experiment to see if Eraldin was safe. ICI thought the drug *was* safe and it certainly was more effective than Inderal which has now returned to replace it. The Americans did not suffer Eraldin damage because the US watchdog for drugs, the FDA, requires long-term human and animal research before it approves these types of drugs. The FDA points out that these extraordinary requirements are based on the question of safety that has been raised about these drugs.

The Americans have particularly good reason to be cautious: their scrupulous attitude has prevented the use of Thalidomide and Eraldin. Also, two other beta-blocking drugs which were being used in Europe for some time were later discovered to be cancer-causing. Eraldin itself and another drug (Alprenol) also gave some indication that they might cause cancer, and two further drugs of this class have been proven to cause cancer in animals (Pamatolol and Tolamolol). The possible risks associated with these types of drugs have been considered so great in the USA that the FDA has limited clinical investigations of these drugs to a maximum of 30 days initially. US government approval for use is withheld until experiments with animals demonstrate that there is no increased risk of cancer associated with their use.[101]

The fatal hazard of withdrawing Inderal suddenly

If you stop taking Inderal suddenly you may have a heart attack and die as a result. It has been found that the more the drug benefits a patient the more pronounced is the damage that follows its sudden withdrawal. The US Food and Drugs Authority warns physicians of this special risk and advises that the dose should be only gradually stopped. It even suggests that when a doctor believes that a patient may be unreliable in taking the drugs he should consider alternative treatment.

One report published in the *American Journal of Cardiology* describes what happened when 20 patients had their supplies of Inderal taken away abruptly. Five of them suffered attacks of angina which were worse than they had ever experienced, and one died. A sixth patient died of a heart attack.

The FDA makes the point, too, that this drug should only be tried after other drugless measures have failed. For example, dieting, rest, giving up smoking, and avoidance of stressful situations all contribute to the reduction of angina and high blood pressure.

Other side effects of Inderal

One can get a good picture of the side effects generally caused by Inderal by looking at a survey carried out in 1974, of nearly 800 patients who were on this drug from anything between a few weeks and six years.[102] The most common side effect experienced by more than 1 in 10 of all patients were stomach upsets, including nausea, vomiting and diarrhoea. Next came the complaint of coldness in the extremities of the body due to the reduced pumping action of the heart. The fingers, toes and so on remained cold in more than 1 in 20 of the patients on Inderal. As many people again suffered from congestive heart failure, a very serious complication, requiring special treatment with digitalis, for example. Attacks of dizziness and sleep disturbance occurred in almost 1 in every 20 patients. But only 3 per cent suffered from tiredness or fatigue. Breathing problems caused by the drug's effect on the bronchial nerves occurred in 1 in 50 patients. Nearly the same proportion again suffered from depression. Fewer than 1 in 100 suffered from a slow pulse and dangerously low blood pressure, hallucinations or skin rashes.

Other side effects which have been reported include: blood disorders, fluid retention and consequent weight gain, muscle cramps and dryness of the mouth.

ICI (the manufacturers of Inderal) also warn doctors that the drug should not be given to women who are pregnant nor should patients who are taking it have surgery unless special precautions are taken by the anaesthetist or unless the drug is withdrawn before the operation.

Some heart drugs to avoid

There is a whole family of drugs derived from the rauwolfia plants which should be avoided because, according to the *British National Formulary,* they are generally ineffective and cause an unacceptably high incidence of depression. The drugs include the following products:[50]

Reserpine, Abicol (Boots), Decaserpyl and Decaserpyl

Plus (Rousell), Enduronyl and Harmonyl (Abbott), Hypercal and Hypercal B (Carlton), Hypertensan (Medo), Raudixin, Rautrax and Rautrax Sine K (Squibb), Rauwiloid (Riker), Seominal (Winthrop), and Serpasil and Serpasil Esidrex and K (Ciba).

Apart from depression they can also cause a dry mouth, blocked nose, drowsiness, low blood pressure, fluid retention and a slow pulse.

The safe alternative to drugs for blood pressure

'It is time to consider whether the amount of salt we eat is doing us more harm than good, and whether reducing it would do more good than harm' – Editorial, *Lancet* Aug. 1980.

You don't need to take drugs for years on end to achieve significant and permanent reduction in your blood pressure, according to an editorial in *The Lancet*.[103]

It claims that 'at least two studies have shown that moderate salt restriction will lead to a lowering of blood pressure in hypertensives'. In both studies a salt-restricted diet (difficult to follow unless food labels list ingredients) was found to reduce blood pressure as much as, and sometimes more than, drugs were able to do so – and without any side effects. Not everyone's blood pressure responds to a lowered salt intake, but there are also other avenues to try – scores of investigations show that blood pressure will drop when weight goes down, especially if dieting is accompanied by exercise!

'Salt and calories are not the end of the matter', says *The Lancet*. 'There are more differences between a Polynesian islander and a hypertensive Londoner than their respective diets.' It goes on to declare that meditation and relaxation can lower blood pressure permanently using techniques such as biofeedback – pioneered in Britain by Dr Chandra Patel and Dr Malcolm Carruthers.

Aldomet

Brand name of drug: Aldomet (Merck Sharp & Dohme).
Purpose of drug: To lower blood pressure.
Special warning: May have serious side effects including dangerously low blood pressure and depression.
Main chemical used in the drug: Methyldopa.
Similar drugs: Dopamet (Berk), Medomet (DDSA) and

Hydromet (MSD)

This is another of the many drugs used nowadays to reduce high blood pressure. Like many of these drugs it may be unnecessary (see page 212 on Inderal, top-selling drug used for angina and blood-pressure reduction) and it may also have the effect of reducing the blood pressure excessively, so that patients may begin suffering from the problems of low blood pressure. Frequent measurements of pressures are needed to prevent this happening. This drug is particularly hazardous for people with liver or kidney problems and should not be taken by those who suffer mental depression as it will make them even more depressed.[23]

Does Aldomet really work?

It sometimes works, but not always. Aldomet lowers the blood pressure by reducing the concentration of a hormone called noradrenalin which naturally increases blood pressure. Noradrenalin usually works to constrict the blood vessels, but a dose of Aldomet reduces the effect of this hormone resulting in lowered blood pressure. But the makers of Aldomet warn doctors that the effect may wear off after a couple of months. Larger doses may be necessary and other blood-pressure drugs (diuretics, for example) may be needed as well to maintain a lowering in blood pressure.

A survey of 100 patients suffering from high blood pressure found that 49 per cent of these patients had a good blood-pressure reduction with Methyldopa (Aldomet), but 51 per cent had only a poor or a fair response to the drug.[104]

Side effects of Aldomet

In the survey of 100 patients mentioned above, as many as 72 per cent suffered from side effects. The most common reported were drowsiness, listlessness, dryness of the mouth, nasal congestion and fluid retention – leading to high blood pressure again. A more recent survey of a group of men being treated with Aldomet in Australia found that more than a quarter suffered from depression and 1 in 5 suffered from tiredness. One in six had their blood pressure excessively reduced, particularly when standing (this is called postural hypotension) and the same proportion suffered from nasal congestion. Other side effects included diarrhoea, jaundice (liver disease) and impotence.[105] Sexual problems with Aldomet are not uncommon; some surveys have found that after persistent questioning as many as 53 per cent of men admit to being impotent whilst on this drug. It is interesting that only 7 per cent of these patients initially volunteered the information that they were having such problems.[106] Another study which compared the effect of Aldomet with other types of drugs used to lower blood pressure (diuretics like Navidrex or Moduretic) found that whilst Aldomet caused sexual difficulties in about a quarter of the men using it, the other drugs did not cause any such problems.

Special precautions needed with Aldomet

During the first six or twelve weeks of treatment, or if patients at any time develop an unexplained fever, it is advisable to perform liver-function tests and to take blood counts, warns the Pharmaceutical Society's guide to drugs (*Martindale's Extra Pharmacopoeia*). Generally speaking, people suffering from liver or kidney damage should not take this drug. Like most drugs that lower blood pressure Aldomet can cause problems if a patient is having an anaesthetic (that includes dental anaesthetics as well). Dentists and surgeons should take special precautions with such patients.

Atromid-S

Brand name of drug: Atromid-S (ICI).

Purpose of drug: To reduce cholesterol levels in the bloodstream.

Special warning: Double hazard: ineffective, increases risk of cancer and gall-bladder disease.

Main chemical used in the drug: Clofibrate.

Similar drugs: Liprinal (Bristol) (withdrawn UK 1980)

Cholesterol madness and the margarine myth

One of the greatest 'wonder drug' fiascos of the last twenty years revolved around a drug – still available, but largely now abandoned – which was designed to reduce cholesterol. Clofibrate (made by ICI under the brand name of Atromid-S) was in fact rather effective at reducing levels of cholesterol. Unfortunately, it also had the slight drawback of killing people – giving them cancer, gall bladder disease and heart attacks. *The Lancet* summed up the findings as: 'The treatment was successful but the patient died.'[107]

The treatment was successful, but the patient died.

Only after this drug was widely used on thousands of people did these side effects surface; fortunately it was put under scrutiny by the World Health Organisation, which co-ordinated an investigation on 10,000 patients. 'This should spell the end of the use of Clofibrate, except maybe in the desperate problem of gross hypercholesterolaemia (ie very high amounts of cholesterol in the bloodstream)', wrote *The Lancet*.[107] One of the most disturbing discoveries of the WHO survey was that there were one third more cancers amongst men taking this drug, and animal studies have found increased rates of liver cancer in rats and mice.

Now an American study has found that having *low* blood cholesterol levels in itself puts people at an increased risk of developing cancer. From a study of 3,000 Americans, Dr J. D. Kark has shown that people who developed cancer had low levels of cholesterol before they got the disease. This is not an isolated finding, and it places a disturbing question mark over the efforts of the margarine industry to advertise some of their products as health-promoting. Another editorial in *The Lancet* points out that 'if there is any likelihood that dietary changes reduce the risk of one common fatal condition but increases the risk of another, policies must be based on good data.'[109]

Cholesterol is not a poison (it is naturally produced inside a healthy body), and scientific trials have also shown that *low* cholesterol is linked with *higher* rates of heart disease! In New Zealand, the Maoris have very low blood cholesterol levels but have the highest death rates from heart disease.[110] So enjoy your butter and cheese, but take plenty of exercise and stop smoking!

Lanoxin

Brand name of drug: Lanoxin (Digoxin) (Wellcome).
Purpose of drug: To treat heart failure and irregular or rapid heart beat.
Special warning: As many as 1 in 3 patients poisoned. Often unnecessary.
Main chemical used in the drug: Digoxin.

Since primitive times the leaves of the purple and white flowering foxglove have been used to cure people from heart failure. But digoxin, the modern refined version of this ancient remedy, accounts for much doctor-induced drug poisoning in hospitals. 'Despite our knowledge of the adverse effects and despite the fact that every medical student is taught about them, a high proportion of adverse drug effects take place in hospitals and are due to intoxication with digitalis-related drugs,' says Professor of Pharmacology, Peter Parrish.[61] More than one-third of all the patients treated with Digoxin in hospitals suffer from poisonous effects, according to some reports.[111]

Why Lanoxin or Digoxin may be unnecessary in the first place

'Digoxin is unnecessary and many patients do just as well without it,' according to an editorial in the *British Medical Journal* on the subject of drug poisoning.[112] Another comment, in *The Lancet,*[113] expresses a similar view: 'whatever the explanation, it seems that many patients are being asked to take Digoxin tablets and expose themselves to the risk of potentially serious side effects for no therapeutic gain'. The trouble with Digoxin is that the difference between a poisonous dose and a safe dose is very small. The controversy over Digoxin's effectiveness centres around those patients who are being treated with water pills – diuretics. It is not known whether people on these pills gain anything at all from taking Digoxin.[114]

It is still often prescribed by intuition or in a fixed regular dose, although as long as ten years ago a reliable method for measuring its concentration in the body was discovered. This offered fresh hope that Digoxin would be prescribed more scientifically and that its use in medicine would become more rational. Unfortunately, this hope has never been fulfilled, reports *The Lancet*.[113]

Up to 4 out of every 10 patients who receive Digoxin from their doctor are not taking sufficiently large doses to have any effect on their hearts.[113] The drug is under-prescribed probably because doctors are frightened of poisoning their patients, suggests *The Lancet*. These patients are getting no benefit at all, only side effects, from such under-prescribing.

One other reason which suggests that this drug may not be necessary in the first place is the discovery in two surveys that almost half of the patients given tablets of Digoxin were not actually swallowing them! Many patients took fewer tablets than the number prescribed by their doctor. *The Lancet* comments that this practice undoubtedly protected many people from being poisoned! Further evidence that Digoxin is often unnecessary has come from reports that over 90 per cent of patients taking maintenance doses of Digoxin therapy (for sinus rhythm) can have the drug withdrawn without any ill effects.

The side effects of Digoxin

The first signs of an overdose are stomach upsets: diarrhoea, nausea, vomiting and loss of appetite; tiredness and headache can also occur. The heart beat is increased; extra heart beats appear as the rhythm of the heart becomes upset by the drug. If the heart rhythms are allowed to get out of control unchecked they could be fatal.

Diuretics: Navidrex

Brand name of drug: Navidrex (CIBA).

Purpose of drug: To reduce water content in the body and to reduce blood pressure.

Special warning: Possibly addictive. Can be hazardous and useless in pregnancy.

Main chemical used in the drug: A Thiazide compound: cyclopenthiazide

Similar drugs:

Trasidrex (CIBA) = cyclopenthiazide + oxprenolol
Lasix (Hoechst) = Frusemide
Diumide K Continus (Napp) = Frusemide + potassium
Dryptal (Berk) = Frusemide
Frusetic (Unimed) = Frusemide
Frusid (DDSA) = Frusemide
Lasikal (Hoechst) = Frusemide
Lasix + K (Hoechst) = Frusemide + potassium
Moduretic (MSD) = hydro-chlorothiazide
Aldactide (Searle) = a thiazide + spironolactone
Aldactone (Searle) = Spironolactone
Aprinox (Boots) = a fluazide
Baycaron (Bayer) = mefruside
Berkozide (Berk) = a fluazide
Brinaldix (Sandoz) = clopamide
Brinaldix + K (Sandoz) = clopamide + potassium
Burinex (Leo) = Bumetanide
Burinex + K = Bumetanide + potassium
Centyl–K (Leo) = fluazide + potassium

Direma (Dista) = a thiazide
Diurexan (Merck) = xipamide
Dyazide (SKF) = a thiazide + triamterene
Dytac (SKF) = triamterene
Dytide (SKF) = a thiazide + triamterene
Edecrin (MSD) = ethacrynic acid
Enduron (Abbott) = a thiazide
Esidrex (CIBA) = a thiazide
Esidrex + K (CIBA) = a thiazide + potassium
Hydrenox (Boots) = a thiazide
Hydrosaluric (MSD) = a thiazide
Hygroton (Geigy) = chlorthalidone
Hygroton + K = chlorthalidone + potassium
Metenix (Hoechst) = metolazone
Metopirone (CIBA) = metyrapone
Nefrolan (M & B) = clorexolone
Neo-naclex (Glaxo) = bendrofluazide
Neo-naclex + K = bendrofluazide + potassium
Nephril (Pfizer) = a thiazide
Saluric (MSD) = a thiazide

Dieters beware! Are you addicted to diuretics?

Diuretics are drugs that reduce the amount of fluid and salts in the body. Excessive fluid retention (called oedema by doctors) can be accompanied by high blood pressure, and for this reason these drugs are given for high-blood-pressure problems –particularly as they enhance the effects of other blood-pressure drugs. But it has recently been discovered that diuretic drugs can actually make women become *more* overweight and retain some fluids, rather than *reduce* their weight as is often supposed. Some women appear to get hooked on these drugs in the mistaken belief that they will help them solve their weight problems.

Although doctors often prescribe them to reduce oedema in pregnancy, it has been found that these drugs have no effect. In fact, their use to reduce weight in pregnancy is possibly harmful to the unborn child as these drugs rapidly pass into the baby's bloodstream.

Since diuretic drugs reduce the amount of fluid and salt in the body it is often advised by doctors to take supplements of potassium, but recent research has shown that this practice may make no difference to the salt-content ratios in the body and may damage the stomach.

How these drugs can make women gain weight

For many years doctors have been puzzled by a condition in which for no reason at all some women appear to suddenly put on weight due to the water which they retain in their bodies. This oedema, or retention of fluids, was given the grand and disturbing title of 'idiopathic oedema'. When doctors have no idea what causes an illness they call it 'idiopathic'; it makes it sound as if they know what they are talking about when a disease is prefixed with this awful word. Nothing is further from the truth –idiopathic means 'of no known origin'. The problem of 'idiopathic oedema' now appears to have been solved by Professor G. MacGregor and his colleagues at Charing Cross Hospital. With the aid of some clever detective work Professor MacGregor found out that there was a special group of women who continuously took these diuretic drugs; often they were nurses who perhaps had easy access to these drugs. The distinguishing factor about these women was that they were obsessively concerned about their weight and appearance. If they stopped taking these drugs they would immediately put on weight and become full of water, says Professor MacGregor. He writes, 'They had convinced themselves that diuretics were essential to prevent this problem. This concern was shared by their doctors who on occasions had tried to stop them taking the drugs only to be faced a few days later by a distraught water-filled patient'! But Professor MacGregor found that if these patients were forced to stop taking the drugs, they did indeed put on weight, but in an amount which was directly proportional to the dose of the diuretic drugs that they were taking. He showed that their weight gain after stopping the drugs was caused by a build-up of two chemicals (renin and aldosterone) inside the body. The

The distraught water-filled patient wants more water pills.

build-up of these two chemicals resulted from taking diuretic drugs for a longer period of time. He showed that diuretic drugs can upset the body's own delicate chemical mechanisms for maintaining and regulating its own water levels. Although these women put on weight at first, by keeping them off the drugs for a week Professor MacGregor managed finally to lower their weight and after a further five to ten days it was back to normal. Until the levels of the two chemicals had subsided, weight loss could not occur in these women.

How dieting can make you bloated

But why do women, who are concerned about their weight, start taking these drugs in the first place? Since they were so obsessive about their appearance they would sometimes go on crash diets, says Professor MacGregor, and starve themselves for a few days and then eat a large meal to recover. It is known that the sudden intake of carbohydrates caused by eating a large meal after fasting can cause the retention of body salts and subsequent retention of water (oedema). This process has been demonstrated in normal women. It is probable then that a crash diet or fast followed by a large meal really makes people become bloated. These women who were studied had gone initially to their doctors with genuine symptoms of fluid retention, but each doctor was probably unaware that his patient had been fasting and then eating abruptly. Once a GP starts to prescribe diuretics a woman can become hooked on the drugs, as whenever she tries to come off the treatment, she gains weight fairly quickly. Some women had been addicted to diuretics in this way for years, Professor MacGregor found.[115]

Diuretics useless in pregnancy and harmful to baby

Pregnant women are sometimes given diuretics because of high blood pressure and oedema (retention of fluids) or 'toxaemia' as it may be sometimes called. But there is a great deal of evidence that such drugs are totally unnecessary for these conditions, have no effect and that these conditions are in fact the body's natural and healthy response to pregnancy itself.

In an experiment which was performed on over 150 pregnant women, half were put on a course of diuretic drugs and the remainder were left untreated. There was no difference found in the amount of weight gain or blood-pressure disease in those treated with the diuretic drugs compared to the women who were not treated at all.[104] As a result of findings like these, in the United States the FDA has obliged manufacturers of these drugs to point out to doctors on the drug labels that they have virtually no use during pregnancy.

The FDA has stated that there is growing recognition among obstetricians and gynaecologists that the use of diuretics in pregnancy is excessive and should be curtailed. Oedema (bloating) in pregnancy is very common and the routine use of diuretics exposes the mother and the baby to unnecessary risks, warns the FDA. The warning says: 'The routine use of diuretics in an otherwise healthy woman is inappropriate and exposes mother and fetus to unnecessary hazard . . . Diuretics do not prevent development of toxemia in pregnancy and there is no satisfactory evidence that they are useful in the treatment of developed toxemia . . .'

In addition the FDA warns that these drugs can cross the placenta and may result in jaundice (liver disease) in the unborn or newly born child, and a blood-cell condition called thrombocytopenia which causes a lowering of the number of vital platelet cells in the blood.[116, 117] The British drug authorities have failed to impose similar warnings on these drugs.

Are potassium supplements with diuretics necessary?

When diuretic drugs are taken it is common practice to prescribe supplements of potassium salts in an attempt to make up the loss of this mineral caused by the drugs. Some drug companies have even combined diuretic drugs with potassium in the one tablet. You can generally tell if this has been done – there is a 'K' suffix after the name of the drug. The letter K is the chemical symbol used for potassium. But this addition of potassium is unnecessary, as Dr H. Dargie has shown in an experiment with two groups of patients. The first group took diuretics with potassium and the second group took only the diuretics. In both groups Dr Dargie found that the total concentrations of potassium in the body remained unchanged. Unless a patient is suffering from heart failure or kidney disease there is no need to take potassium supplements, according to this finding.[118] According to the latest edition of the BNF, very few patients getting these drugs actually need potassium, and for those that do need it, the drugs are a waste of time because there isn't enough potassium in the products to help them![119]

There is a real hazard from taking some forms of potassium: slow-release tablets have been found to damage the stomach lining and to cause ulcers. Tablets such as 'slow K' are dangerous and should not be used, say letters in the British Medical Journal:[120] they can cause ulcers in the bowel. The authors of the letters recommends the addition to the diet of potassium-containing foods as the safest way to prevent a potassium deficiency. The following are suggested: fruit and vegetable juices; apricots, avocados, bananas, cherries, dried fruits and tomatoes.[23] A rich diet in these foods should obviate the need for extra potassium.

Side effects of the diuretic drugs

Diuretics can cause allergies, skin rashes, loss of weight (this may explain why they are popular amongst women trying to lose weight), stomach pain, nausea, vomiting, diarrhoea, constipation, sensitivity to sunlight, dizziness, headache and weakness. The diuretic brand containing Frusemide which is sold as 'Lasix' may, in addition to those side effects already mentioned, also cause a dangerous reduction in blood pressure (called *hypo*tension; contrast this with *hyper*tension, which is excessively high blood pressure). Frusemide may also cause gout (a painful joint disorder); a dangerous reduction in white blood cells – bone-marrow disease which can be fatal –also occurs rarely. Patients with kidney deficiencies may suffer from tinnitus (painful and continuous buzzing noises in the ears) or even deafness after taking Frusemide.

Diabetes drugs: Diabinese

Brand name of drug: Diabinese (Pfizer) and other diabetic drugs.
Purpose of drug: To control diabetes.
Special warning: Double hazard. May be both useless and dangerous.
Main chemical used in drug: Chlorpropamide.

Similar drugs:

Melitase (Berk) (chlorpropamide)
Rastinon (Hoechst) (tolbutamide)

Dibotin (Winthrop) (phenformin hydrochloride)
Pramidex (Berk) (tolbutamide)

Others
Daonil (Hoechst), Euglucon (Roussel), both contain *Glibenclamide*
Dimelor (Lilly) contains *Acetohexamide*
Eudemine (Allen & Hanburys) contains *Diazoxide*
Glibenese (Pfizer), Minodiab (Farmitalia CE), both contain *Glipizide*
Glucophage (Rona) contains *Metformin*
Glutril (Roche) contains *Glibornuride*
Gondafon (Schering) contains *Glymidine*
Tolanese (Upjohn) contains *Tolazamide*

'In general the treatment of "mature" diabetics would seem to be an example of the large scale use of ineffective and possibly dangerous therapies in a particularly inefficient way' – Professor Archibald Cochrane, *Effectiveness and Efficiency*.[121]

Most people suffering from diabetes are overweight and can improve their condition simply by going on a diet without the aid of any prescribed drugs. This was the conclusion that shocked doctors and drug companies after an eight-year-long study into the safety and effectiveness of drugs used to lower sugar levels in the blood of mature diabetics, ie those over the age of 40 or so.

It should be pointed out that there is a rarer kind of diabetes which can effect young people, often referred to as 'juvenile-onset diabetes'. This variety of diabetes generally has to be controlled with insulin injections, and its treatment is a totally separate subject compared to the treatment of older diabetics who are given the type of drugs to be examined in this section.

The drugs considered here include: Diabinese, Dimelor, Rastinon, Tolanese, Daonil, and Euglucon which all belong to the same chemical group and they can all make the body produce greater amounts of insulin but, unfortunately, though they may work initially for a short while, they do not actually reduce blood sugar level in the long term.[122]

There is another even more dangerous drug used in mature diabetes: Phenformin, sold under the name of Dibotin, made by Winthrop in Britain. It is so dangerous that it was banned from sale in the USA in 1977. Phenformin has been linked with a large number of deaths from a condition known as 'Lactic Acidosis' which is fatal in 50 per cent of patients who suffer from it. However, Phenformin remains freely available on prescription in Britain. The vast majority of patients who take this drug do not really need it, as experiments have shown that diet alone can alleviate their diabetes.

Despite the evidence that all these diabetes drugs do not work for long periods, that they may increase heart-disease deaths and that diet alone can help most patients, over one and a quarter million prescriptions for these drugs are still dispensed each year in Britain (1978 figures). There has been a long controversy over whether or not diabetes drugs increase the risks of heart disease. The Americans tend to say yes. Some British doctors, however, say the case is not proven. Diabetics who need to take drugs are overweight, and this fact and their diabetes alone make them prime candidates for heart attacks anyway.

Diabetes drugs do not even work

The American university clinic's diabetes investigation which took 1,000 patients suffering from diabetes and compared the use of these drugs with placebos (fake pills) and a diet, found that placebos were just as good at reducing sugar in the blood as the real drugs. All drug treatments which they looked at failed to maintain a lowered blood sugar level after five years of treatment.

Some failed to work after just one year of treatment because the sugar level in the blood rose once the body had got used to the drugs. Before these findings, many doctors used to believe that these drugs helped patients to lose weight; again, this was found to be a misconception when investigated scientifically.

In fact one drug, Tolbutamide, significantly increased weight. Three other studies, involving hundreds of patients, have also come up with the same result – that at first these drugs have an effect, but after a while they are no better than a placebo and increase the risk of dying from a heart attack or stroke.

An article in the *New England Journal of Medicine* commented about these useless drugs: 'There is no reason to use a drug that does not work . . . even the safest drug is of no value if it has no efficacy . . . diabetes can probably be controlled in many patients with diet alone. Those whose disease is not controlled by diet alone should be treated with insulin.'[123]

Do diabetes pills cause heart disease?

A massive study costing more than 7 million dollars which was carried out in the USA between 1961 and 1969, was the first to claim that diabetics who took drugs to reduce the sugar levels in their bloodstream suffered from more fatal heart attacks. Even before the study was completed, doctors felt morally obliged, in 1969, to stop giving patients one particular drug (Tolbutamide, still sold as Rastinon in Britain) because they believed that it was endangering patients' lives. In the patients on this particular drug they found a large increase in the number of deaths compared to those on a sugar pill, containing no active drug. There were also two and a half times more cases of heart disease amongst those taking this particular drug. In statistical terms, these were highly significant results. Another drug being tested, Phenformin, was found to be responsible for over 60 per cent more deaths and also to be connected with more than four times the usual incidence of heart disease. This discovery made the researchers abandon the use of this type of diabetes drug in 1971, whilst the investigation was still proceeding. But this premature withdrawal of two of the drugs being investigated provoked angry criticism of the results within the medical community, and a controversy over these alarming findings has continued ever since then. Almost as soon as the results were published in the USA a row blew up and there were suggestions of errors in the recording of the medical data and the interpretation of the results. British drug expert Professor Michael Rawlins points out that the American results are flawed because many of the American patients who received Tolbutamide had heart disease *before* they started taking the drug – so he says no firm conclusions can be drawn from the study.

Several other investigations of these diabetic drugs carried out in England, Sweden and California had failed to find evidence of increased heart disease amongst diabetics taking the drugs,[124] but it has been pointed out that they were all conducted for shorter periods of time and were less comprehensive than the original university clinic's investigation. A review of the controversy published in 1977 in the *New England Journal of Medicine* had this to say about the original study: 'The probability that these drugs cause premature death from heart disease remains valid and cannot be dismissed on the basis of other evidence. The University Group Diabetes Programme is the most comprehensive and most adequately controlled study published today.'[123]

Recently the American drug watchdog body, the FDA, took the trouble to sift all the original results from the University Group Diabetes Project and came to the conclusion that the original findings remained completely valid.[124] But since both diabetes and obesity predispose people to heart disease anyway, the debate continues.

Worldwide evidence of side effects of drugs

Numerous other investigations throughout the world *have* supported the conclusions originally made by the American team. For example, at a Belfast hospital it was found that heart attacks were twice as common amongst drug-treated diabetic patients compared to those simply on a diet.[125] Another study carried out in Birmingham by Dr N. Soler and his colleagues in 1974 found that patients on the diabetic drugs suffered from fatal heart attacks nearly three times more often than diabetes patients who were on diets.

An even more convincing demonstration of the damage

these drugs cause came from some fascinating animal experiments. A group of monkeys were fed on an average American diet (which causes heart disease in its own right). After two years the monkeys on this diet who received diabetes drugs (Tolbutamide) had three times more coronary artery disease than those not given the drugs.[126] Also when diabetic dogs (presumably over-weight dogs who have eaten too many sugary dog biscuits!) were treated with the drug they too suffered damage to the heart.[127] Since the introduction of these drugs in the late fifties, the international death rates for diabetics in the past twenty years have risen in England, Wales, Germany, Japan and Israel, probably because of the use of these drugs.[128,129]

There is now a clue as to why these drugs increase the frequency of heart disease. It's simple – they strain the heart! Dr Roger Palmer, an American pharmacologist, has shown that Tolbutamide increases the heart's force of contraction, thus straining that organ and forcing it to use up more oxygen. When the oxygen supply fails or is limited this means that the drug will cause extra damage to the heart muscle. These drugs also have been shown to disturb the electrical rhythm of the heart, says Dr Palmer, causing an increased risk of a heart attack.

American authorities ban fatal diabetes drug still sold in Britain

In July 1977 the US Secretary of Health, Education and Welfare banned Phenformin, a diabetes drug still sold in Britain in 1980, because of the 'unacceptably high risk' of a disease called lactic acidosis associated with its use. The US authorities had discovered that the risk of this disease was much higher than was generally appreciated. Up to four cases per thousand users of the drug occur each year, the FDA reported. As 50 per cent of victims die, this meant that as many as 700 deaths per year were being caused by the drug in the US alone.

The FDA emphasised that the disease can even occur in patients who show none of the usual warning signs, even if the drug is taken in the proper small doses. Since the chance of women dying, say from the Pill, are at worst about one in thirty thousand, the risks of death from this drug turn out to be over a hundred times greater. This type

233

of risk, says the FDA, is 'not compatible with the continued unrestricted marketing of this drug', especially in view of its limited role in treating diabetes, and the availability of alternative drugs. The very tiny proportion of patients for whom this drug is possibly needed still get their supplies, despite the general ban of this product throughout the United States.

It is both typical and ironic that the first demand for the removal of this drug came from two English doctors at Nottingham General Hospital in the *British Medical Journal*, yet Britain continues to allow the sale of this product.[130] Even before the American ban was imposed, doctors had been specially informed of the hazards of this drug in package inserts since 1974. The US ban was finally effected by a petition from Ralph Nader's Public Citizens' Health Research Group, after a slow response initially by the FDA. It took nine months after a US government advisory committee had found that Phenformin should be removed from the market. The main reason given for the ban was that there was no way of identifying which patients would die from using this drug. Phenformin is still available in the UK as Dibotin (Winthrop). Metformin is not as hazardous as Phenformin but still carries this risk.[50] It is available as Glucophage (Rona).

Ulcer drugs: Tagamet

Brand name of drug: Tagamet (Smith Kline & French).
Purpose of drug: To relieve symptoms of duodenal ulcers.
Special warning: Relieves pain and other symptoms, but does not *cure* ulcers.
Main chemical used in the drug: Cimetidine.
'We know that over 80 per cent of Cimetidine-healed ulcers relapse if no further treatment is given' - *Lancet* Editorial.[131]

This new drug has revolutionised the treatment of people suffering from ulcers; it has resulted in fewer ulcer operations being performed and is now the first drug to treat millions for ulcers. But, and there is always a 'but', though Tagamet has been shown to quickly heal a bleeding ulcer and relieve all the pain that goes with an ulcer, it does not actually *cure* it. In other words, once treatment with the drug is stopped, the majority of ulcers reappear within weeks or months and the only solution is to continue therapy with the drug for a further period of months and possibly years. Although it is a safe drug for short-term treatment it is not yet known how people will cope or react to such long-term courses of this drug.

The limitations of Tagamet

Four out of every five patients treated with this drug suffer again, once treatment is stopped. Many hundreds of patients have been involved in clinical investigations of the effectiveness of Tagamet and it is clear that between 60 and 90 per cent of all duodenal ulcers heal within a month of treatment.[131] Unfortunately the ulcer heals but the patient is not always cured. *The Lancet* comments that this 'success' has stimulated the drug industry to hunt for new ulcer-healing drugs, as GPs are prescribing them with great enthusiasm. Where there are ulcers there are large profits to be made. Tagamet is a very expensive product, four times more expensive than conventional remedies such as liquorice-containing drugs, like Caved-S, that can also heal ulcers fairly effectively. Tagamet has caught on because it is mainly free of side effects (so far) and because it has been shown to rapidly relieve the pain of an ulcer. 'Unfortunately,' says the *Lancet*, reporting in December 1978, 'it has not yet been shown to be capable of *curing* the ulcer disease.' Between 70 and 90 per cent of ulcers relapse within weeks, or at most within months of the initial bleeding. There is no agreement within the medical profession about how to deal with ulcers that start bleeding again. Some doctors prescribe more Tagamet pills until the ulcer heals once more, but it has been found that ulcers which relapse rapidly when treatment stops do seem to relapse equally rapidly after further treatment. Other doctors give the drug continuously for many months on end. One survey of patients given Tagamet at night for up to a year has shown that only a quarter of them started to bleed again within this form of continuous night therapy. But the major problem of giving people continual doses of this drug, even if only a nightly dose, is that once again when the maintenance treatment is stopped most patients begin to rapidly suffer from bleeding again.

In 1978 *The Lancet* reported that so far it has not been shown that this type of *long-term* treatment for up to a year is any better than no treatment at all. It added that it seems that for about three-quarters of the patients with duodenal ulcers, Tagamet only delays making a medical decision.[131]

But more recent results offer some hope. In January 1980 a letter appeared in *The Lancet* from Linköping Hospital in Sweden, reporting a two-year investigation into ulcer patients successfully treated with Tagamet. It described an experiment in which ulcer patients had been treated with either the drug for one year or with a placebo (a non-active pill). They found that twice as many patients taking Tagamet were symptom-free after two years compared to those taking the placebo. Nevertheless over one-fifth of the patients taking Tagamet still needed surgery for their ulcers, but on the other hand more than half of those on a placebo required surgery. Clearly these results suggest that Tagamet may be more beneficial than *The Lancet* editorial of 1978 suggests. But it should be mentioned that this survey only studied the effects of the drug on 32 people compared to 36 patients on a placebo, and the follow-up lasted only for two years. 'Cures' are generally considered only to have been achieved after five years' absence of disease. With such an unreliable history behind it. Tagamet has still to prove itself as a cure for ulcers for most patients.

Does Tagamet make ulcers bleed?

This suggestion at first sight may sound absurd, since the drug has been shown to heal most ulcers very rapidly. But the evidence also shows that most ulcers start to bleed again after treatment with this drug. Recurrences of ulceration in the form of pain, bleeding or perforation may show themselves within days, or just hours after treatment. Perhaps there is a causal connection between these relapses and the use of the drug? asks *The Lancet*.[131] There is evidence that treatment with the drug has resulted in more rebleeding than treatments with a totally non-active placebo. A team of doctors at St James' Hospital found that 8 per cent more patients suffered rebleeding when given Cimetidine compared to those given a placebo. They had excluded patients whose bleeding was so severe as to require immediate surgery. They concluded that the routine use of Cimetidine for duodenal or gastric ulcer was not supported by their results.[132]

Does Tagamet cause sterility?

Long-term-treated male patients have been found to have reduced levels of male sex hormones in their bloodstream, a finding that has also been made in animal experiments. In practice this may cause sterility.[133] One American researcher, Dr David Van Thiel of Pittsburgh Medical School, has reported halved sperm counts in about 10 per cent of the men who take it. Normal fertility returns six weeks after coming off the drug, says Dr Van Thiel.[133]

Does Tagamet cause cancer?

'Cimetidine has been greatly overused for patients without ulcers,' according to Dr Peter Reed of the Royal Post-graduate Medical School. He has found that half of the patients treated with this drug develop abnormally high levels of a known carcinogen (cancer-causing chemical) in their stomachs.[134] This substance, nitrosamine, is also formed from the nitrates and nitrites used as food preservatives in processed meats, so it is not uncommon in our environment. Reed believes that Cimetidine has been used too freely by doctors on patients who are merely suffering from simple tummy upsets. The *Sunday Times* reported in 1981 that 11 million people in 100 countries have been put on Cimetidine!

There has been controversy over whether or not Cimetidine is a cause of cancer. It is accepted that the symptoms of stomach cancer can be relieved by Cimetidine and its use may seriously delay the use of correct anti-cancer treatment. It is possible therefore that the presence of cancer will be masked by a course of treatment with this drug. Considering its widespread use, it is not surprising that some people using it will also have cancer of the stomach. The latest evidence about Tagamet (Cimetidine) still leaves a question mark over its cancer-causing potential. Cimetidine can sometimes cause pernicious anaemia because it reduces absorption of vitamin B_{12}. It is known that patients with this form of anaemia are two to four times more prone to gastric cancer.

An editorial in April 1981 in the *British Medical Journal* considered that the evidence that Cimetidine may cause cancer was still 'weak' – though it admits that only long-term follow-ups of thousands of patients will reveal the true situation.[135] It warns that, like any other drug, it should be used with caution because there is at present only limited knowledge about its long-term effects. However, the editorial concludes that 'patients may be reassured'.

Is Tagamet necessary?

Many doctors are using Cimetidine as a drug of first choice for a duodenal ulcer, but *The Lancet* recommends that it should not be used in an uncomplicated ulcer. Instead, they recommend the use of a simple antacid to neutralise the acid in the stomach (eg sodium bicarbonate) and perhaps a day or two in bed.[131]

For a troublesome ulcer, however, they suggest that a short healing course with Tagamet might work. A quarter of the patients treated in this way will be healed for some time. The remainder may need continuous treatment of 400mg nightly. Doctors may try to stop continuous treatment after a year or two, but patients must be closely monitored to see if there is any recurrence of symptoms. 'No patient must be submitted to a prolonged course of treatment with a powerful and expensive drug like Cimetidine without unequivocal confirmation of the diagnosis,' says *The Lancet*. It also warns that standard barium meals are not sufficient for diagnosis as they can give positive results of an ulcer when there is not one really there. Instead an 'endoscopy' probe is suggested for a definite diagnosis of a duodenal ulcer.

Despite all the limitations of Cimetidine, *The Lancet* concludes that it is preferable to surgery because even more problems are associated with surgery than with the drug.

Asilone

Brand name of drug: Asilone (Berk).

Purpose of drug: Antacid to protect stomach lining and prevent flatulence.

Special warning: May prevent absorption of antibiotics.

Chemicals used in drug: Dimethicone, aluminium hydroxide and magnesium oxide in some formulations.

Other similar antacids: Mucaine (Wyeth), Aludrox (Wyeth), Gaviscon (Reckitt & Colman)

This is an antacid that can be used to treat the symptoms of an ulcer. Its main ingredient is aluminium hydroxide

238

which neutralises the acid in the stomach. Antacids like Asilone do not actually cure ulcers (neither does the widely prescribed drug Cimetidine or Tagamet), it only relieves the pain. They tend in fact to increase the amount of acid inside the stomach but reduce the action of the acid so that it causes less pain. The net result though is that when treatment is stopped the ulcer flares up again because of the increased amount of acid in the stomach.[119] The amount of pepsin in the stomach is inhibited by the aluminium hydroxide ingredient of Asilone. For peak efficiency these drugs are best taken directly after meals when gastric acidity will be at its greatest.

Special risks of Asilone and other antacids

Since it contains aluminium hydroxide there is a hazard that vitamins and antibiotics such as Tetracycline being taken at the same time will not be properly absorbed. A person who needs to take these antibiotics should not continue with the antacid. Another side effect is constipation, caused by aluminium hydroxide, but the magnesium oxide ingredient which is also put into some versions of Asilone works (as a laxative) so it should counteract this effect.[23]

Birth defects from antacids

A survey has shown that the mothers of deformed babies have taken larger amounts of antacids during pregnancy compared to mothers giving birth to healthy babies.[136]

Iron preparations: Feospan

Brand name of drug: Feospan (Smith Kline & French).
Purpose of drug: To treat iron deficiency.
Special warning: Double hazard – may be unnecessary and dangerous.
Main chemical used in the drug: Ferrous sulphate.

Similar drugs:

Fefol (SKF)
Fefol vit (SKF)
Feospan (SKF)
Ferraplex (Bencard)
Ferrlecit (Wade)
Ferrograd C (Abbott)
Ferrograd Folic (Abott)
Ferro-Gradumet (Abbott)
Fesovit (SKF)
Folicin (Paines & Byrne)
Folvron (Lederle)
Iberol (Abbott)
Irofol C (Abbott)
Pregfol (Wyeth)
Pregnavite Forte (Bencard)
Pregnavite Forte F (Bencard)
Slow Fe (CIBA)
Slow Fe Folic (CIBA)

Ferrous fumarate
BC 500 with iron (Averst)   Fersamal (Glaxo)
Co-ferol (Cox Continental)   Folex 350 (Rybar)
Ferrocap (Consolidated)   Galfer (Galen)
Ferrocap F 350 (Consolidated)   Galfer FA (Galen)
Fersaday (Glaxo)   Pregaday (Glaxo)

Ferrous glycine sulphate
Fe-Cap (MCP)   Gastrovite (MCP)
Fe-Cap C (MCP)   Kelferon (MCP)
Fe-Cap Folic (MCP)   Kelfolate (MCP)
Ferrocontin Continus (Napp)   Plesmet (Napp)
Ferrocontin Folic (Napp)

Ferrous gluconate
Ferfolic (Sinclair)   Fergon (Winthrop)
Ferfolic SV (Sinclair)   Sidros (Potter & Clarke)
Fergluvite (Sinclair)

Ferrous succinate
Ferromyn (Calmic)

'In a modern society I am opposed to 95 per cent of
patients getting treatment when only 5 per cent need it.'
(Dr Tom Lind, Consultant Obstetrician and Gynaecologist, on iron tablets given to pregnant women)[137] He
continues, 'What we've learnt over the past few years is
that a pregnant women is not the same as a non-pregnant
woman with a baby inside her. Her whole chemistry is
different and the two simply cannot be compared. As a
result, doctors have been diagnosing diseases in pregnant
women which do not exist because they have failed to
appreciate this basic fact . . . We normally only absorb 10
per cent of the iron in food – the body does not need any
more iron. But pregnant women absorb 40 per cent of the
iron in their food, if they need to do so. So the last thing
they need is iron tablets to make them feel sick . . . Many
symptoms of anaemia are perfectly natural and healthy
reactions to pregnancy—such as fatigue, breathlessness
and a rosy complexion.'[137]

He is not alone. 'Most notable was the apparent lack of
benefit from iron, the least questioned of all supplements.'
This is how Professor Barbara Starfield of Johns Hopkins
University School of Public Health and Hygiene and her
co-worker, Dr Elina Hemminki,[138] summed up their
worldwide investigation of the use of iron supplements in

pregnancy. They tried to uncover every study that has ever looked into the supposed benefits of giving healthy women iron and vitamin supplements during pregnancy. They managed to uncover as many as seventeen studies that have been performed in the West. Their review of all these investigations shows that iron therapy benefits neither mother nor their babies. 'None of the studies reported any improvement for important outcomes such as low birth weight, pre-term births (ie premature births), infant disease or deaths, or maternal disease or deaths,' say Professor Starfield and Dr Hemminki.

Despite the overwhelming evidence that *routine* iron in pregnancy is unnecessary, it remains widely prescribed in Britain and elsewhere. There is evidence that it may cause birth defects and it can cause considerable side effects in women who consume it for months on end. There is also substantial evidence that iron therapy fails to reduce fatigue, and other symptoms normally thought to be associated with anaemia in non-pregnant women.

How the myth began

Most women who are pregnant do have iron and vitamin levels which are lower at first than in the non-pregnant state, and so it has been assumed that they need extra supplies of iron. (The fall of iron in the body is measured by a decrease in the number of haemoglobin cells, commonly called 'the red blood cells'. They contain iron and it is their job to carry oxygen around the body.) But the reduction in iron levels is a natural process in pregnancy and results not from a disease or deficiency but simply because the mother's blood volume is increased in order to supply the growing baby. It can therefore *appear* that there is a lower concentration of iron in the blood during pregnancy. But to make up this difference the heart of a pregnant woman pumps more than normal. Also the human body has large reserves of iron in the liver and bone marrow and during pregnancy these stores are used up. After the baby has been delivered the reserves are topped up again quite spontaneously by the body's own self-regulating mechanisms. *Whether or not iron tablets are taken in pregnancy these iron stores still remain low.*

It has been shown that this so-called 'iron deficiency' during pregnancy does not lead to iron deficiency later on in the newly born baby.[139] It has also been demonstrated that when a woman is given iron during pregnancy only her blood levels of iron rise, whereas her vital stores still remain below normal, despite the tablets. This lack of benefit from iron supplements that Professor Starfield observed is 'not surprising', says an editorial in the *British Medical Journal*, since the spontaneous and natural changes in the heart and the blood vessels that accompany pregnancy are more than adequate to compensate for 'anaemia' of this degree. In brief it is simply not necessary to maintain non-pregnant levels of iron in pregnant women, says the *British Medical Journal's* editorial.

Moreover, there are signs that iron supplements in pregnancy may actually harm the unborn baby, according to Dr Tom Lind, a British Medical Research Council consultant. He has shown that the consumption of iron tablets can lead to the development of enlarged red blood cells. The danger of having much larger-than-natural red blood cells is that they become too large to penetrate the very small and narrow capillaries in the mother and those in the growing foetus. This could lead to oxygen starvation and resultant brain damage. The implications of this are disturbing, suggests Dr Lind, for growth may be impeded generally and as a result iron supplements may cause low-birthweight babies to be born[140] with all the hazards that implies.

The false sense of security with iron tablets

A mother who takes iron tablets and vitamins may well have less motivation for maintaining a good diet, which is an essential requirement in pregnancy, comments Professor Barbara Starfield, so the tablets may cause an unjustified feeling of security. Also any genuine mineral deficiency present in a pregnant woman that *does* require special treatment may be masked and less easily diagnosed if iron is being taken. The cost of the drugs (unless prescribed free of charge in the UK) may also decrease the amount of money available for real food. The physical side effect of iron pills such as nausea and constipation may also reduce the appetite and cause extra psychological distress.

Iron drugs may not even work

Britain's most widely prescribed iron supplements

(Feospan, Fefol, Ferrogradumet and Fesovit) are not recommended by the medical profession's most authoritative guide to prescribing, the *British National Formulary*. The *BNF* says that these slow-release products may not work as claimed. They are supposed to release iron slowly over a 24-hour period, but they have no advantage over simpler drugs to justify their cost.[141]

Side effects caused by iron therapy

As many as 15 per cent of patients taking iron therapy have stomach upsets such as diarrhoea, vomiting and nausea. These side effects can be reduced by taking the tablets with or directly after meals, or by taking 'slow release' tablets.

Patients who are not suffering from iron-deficiency anaemia are at risk of iron overload. Iron also reduces the absorption of the Tetracycline antibiotics, so they may not work if iron is being taken at the same time[23] – but these should never be taken in pregnancy anyway (see page 188).

Birth defects possibility

A slightly higher rate of birth abnormalities occurred in children whose mothers had received iron during the first two months of pregnancy, compared to those who did not take iron.[142] But the *British Medical Journal* says that this risk has now been refuted.[139]

Asthma drugs: Ventolin, Intal and Zaditen

Brand name of drug: Ventolin (Allen & Hanburys).
Purpose of drug: Asthma treatment.
Special warning: May be hazardous in overdose.
Main chemicals used in the drug: Salbutamol

Similar drugs:

Sodium Cromoglycate:	Isoprenaline:
Intal (Fisons)	Aleudrin (Lewis)
Lomusol (Fisons)	Brontisol (Brocades)
Nalcrom (Fisons)	Duo Autohaler (Riker)
Opticrom (Fisons)	Intal Compound (Fisons)
Rynacrom (Fisons)	Iso autohaler (Riker)
	Medihaler duo (Riker)
	Medihaler iso (Riker)
	PIB (Napp)

During the 1960s at least 3,500 young asthma sufferers *died* after giving themselves accidental overdoses of a powerful asthma drug that could then be bought by anyone in a chemist's shop. In those days a drug called

Isoprenalin was commonly sold over-the-counter in a pressurised aerosol spray. Unfortunately the hormone drug present in these aerosols not only widened the bronchial tubes to ease breathing for asthmatics, but also had the undesirable effect of stimulating the muscles of the heart, so as to produce very rapid heart beats. A severe attack of asthma would be commonly treated with a few squirts of the aerosol, but if the attack got worse there was often a temptation for young people to squirt yet more drugs into their lungs. Sudden death could then occur as the heart could no longer take any more stimulation with this drug. Safer drugs such as Ventolin and Intal are now available only on prescription but many brands of the fatal Isoprenalins remain on the market. They were put on prescription only in 1968, after 3,500 young people had died.[143] Patients should take great care with these products and never use them in excess; if in trouble seek professional medical treatment.

Ventolin

The tragic number of deaths caused by the early asthma drugs has boosted the search for alternative, safer therapies. The most commonly prescribed drug in Britain is a substance called Ventolin, made by Allen & Hanbury's. Doctors prescribed over 6 million courses of this drug in 1978.[144] It accounts for the majority of the asthma-drug market. Unlike the fatal drugs used in the sixties, Ventolin contains a substance, called salbutamol, which does not effect the heart to any great extent; it mainly works on relaxing the bronchial muscles which produce the symptoms of asthma when they become tightened . But Ventolin is still not without its own risks; the overuse of Ventolin can also cause heart disorders and sudden death but this occurs somewhat less often as compared with Isoprenalin. Ventolin can also cause palpitations or muscle tremor, especially in the hands. An important advantage of Ventolin is that it can be used both to treat an asthma attack and to prevent an attack from occurring in the first place.

Intal

Intal is another drug that is fairly effective at *preventing* asthma attacks, which are caused by allergy; but Intal is useless for an attack that has begun. Since Intal only prevents attacks of allergic asthma it will not cure them.

Unless this drug is taken continuously, recurrences of asthma may occur.[23]

Does Intal work?

Not all asthma sufferers respond to Intal; a controlled trial of severely asthmatic children found that as many as 20–25 per cent showed no benefit at all.[145] One investigation of the effectiveness of Intal has found three different types of reaction to the drug. Almost one-third of patients tested found it no better than a placebo (ie a totally non-active drug), but over one-third did obtain some benefit, while the remaining third obtained prolonged benefit.[146] One of the problems of Intal is that it has to be taken with the aid of a device called a spinhaler which delivers the drug into the depths of the lungs. Fisons, the manufacturers, themselves admit that up to one-fifth of the Intal-users do not know how to use these devices properly.

New American warning on Intal

The American drug authority, the FDA, announced in May 1978 that the manufacturers had issued new warnings on Intal. Several years of experience with this drug have revealed the repeated occurrence of a number of side effects. The FDA pointed out that most doctors mistakenly believe that Intal has few harmful effects, but this recent discovery may make a doctor decide that the risks of Intal are greater than the supposed benefits.

The most frequently reported side effects were: sudden constriction of the bronchial tubes, ie bronchospasm, cough, nasal congestion, irritation of the pharynx, wheezing. Other less common reactions reported include: angiooedema, dizziness, painful and frequent urination, joint swelling and pain, weeping, nausea and headache, rash, swollen salivary glands and urticaria. Also use of the spinhaler device carries the risk of inhalation of gelatine particles or of the mouthpiece of the propeller.

The latest asthma drug: Zaditen (Ketotifen)

Zaditen (Ketotifen), a brand new asthma drug manufactured by the Swiss drug company, Sandoz, was launched at the end of 1979 to try and grab some share of the market currently dominated by the two products Intal and Ventolin, both of which necessitate the use of special inhaler devices. Sandoz have come up with an even more dramatic innovation than a spinhaler: the asthma pill! But even before the new drug had been on the market for a few weeks there were signs that it was not all that the manufacturers were claiming it to be.

'The Swiss drug company, Sandoz, has already been visiting GPs to promote a new asthma "wonder drug" released this week. But there is reason to question whether the drug is effective at all, let alone a wonder', is the way the *New Scientist* began a somewhat cynical report about the launching of this new drug. Two weeks after this statement appeared, the manufacturers wrote to the *New Scientist* to protest that they had never called it a 'wonder drug'. Of course they had not, presumably the words 'wonder drug' must have been used by members of the press who had been entertained by Sandoz and flown, all expenses paid, to Switzerland in order to hear about Zaditen at Sandoz' Swiss HQ.[147] Sandoz is naturally aware that it is against the rules of the Association of the British Pharmaceutical Industry to make exaggerated claims for drugs to the press.

The *New Scientist* report causes some strong doubts about the use of Zaditen which is being heavily promoted to doctors. Dr Donald Lane, an outside drug expert hired by Sandoz, said, 'It is not by any means a cast iron statement that this drug will have a permanent place in the treatment of asthma.' 'Not enough homework has been done with Zaditen,' commented Dr Ian Gregg, a clinical epidemiologist, director of the Cardio-Thoracic Institute of the Brompton Hospital.

According to the *New Scientist*, Sandoz' promotional literature suggests that Zaditen is better than Intal, but Professor Jack Pepys, one of the doctors whose research is cited by Sandoz as evidence of its superiority, does not agree with the way in which his work has been used by Sandoz. 'I don't think Sandoz have proven that the drug is better than Intal but I believe that is what they're trying to claim,' he told the *New Scientist*. The article reveals that two trials of Zaditen published in a journal called *Clinical Allergy* found that it worked no better than a placebo.[148]

More doubts about the new asthma drug Ketotifen (Zaditen) in adult asthma

The effectiveness and safety of the new asthma drug Ketotifen (Zaditen) were recently evaluated against a placebo (sugar pill containing no active drug at all) with the help of 50 patients suffering from asthma. The researchers concluded that 'Ketotifen's beneficial effect on asthma appears slight and must be balanced against the effect of drowsiness which was severe enough to cause 7 patients (14 per cent) to withdraw from treatment or to reduce their dosage'.[149]

When Dr Keith Prowse tried Ketotifen on 17 patients at the Stoke City General Hospital, 11 of them had to be withdrawn because of severe drowsiness. Two patients had attacks of sudden and unpredictable loss of balance causing them to fall over, but the symptoms disappeared after stopping treatment. 'The high incidence of side effects appears a high price for a marginal benefit,' says Dr Prowse.[150]

Sex hormones: Premarin

Brand name of drug: Premarin (Ayerst).

Purpose of drug: Hormone replacement therapy.

Special warning: May induce cancer, may cause psychological addiction.

Main chemical used in the drug: Oestrogen.

Similar drugs: Harmogen (Abbott), Progynova (Schering), Menophase (Syntex). Both Ayerst and Schering have brought out versions of their products with an added anti-cancer ingredient (progestogen) called Prempac (Ayerst) and Cyclo Progynova (Schering).

They were hailed originally as 'Happiness Pills', promising an end to the menopause and its hot flushes, a revitalised sex life, better sleep, wrinkle-free skin and an end to the blues. Instead what many women got was a far cry from happiness, but a misery pill that gave them cancer (see Cancer risk, p. 250). Some experiments have even shown that hormone replacement therapy is no better than a placebo (a sugar pill) at controlling hot flushes, the most commonly mentioned symptom of the menopause.[151] In addition, HRT can be psychologically addictive,[152] for it only delays the onset of menopausal symptoms, so unless the woman stays on HRT indefinitely (very hazardous as the risk of cancer increases with the length of exposure to the drug) she cannot avoid having the menopause.

Perhaps more than any other drug treatment HRT has

demonstrated the way in which the press can be abused to promote products available only on prescription, contrary to the drug industry's own code of conduct. An organisation called 'Women's Health Care' in Britain and 'The Information Center for the Mature Woman' in America, were established and financed initially by Ayerst Ltd, the manufacturers of Premarin, the top-selling hormone replacement product. Later four other manufacturers of hormone products also gave financial support to 'Women's Health Care'. Women with menopausal complaints who made inquiries at WHC received circulars which suggested they obtain hormone treatment even if their own doctors were against it. When the British Medical Association was asked for an opinion of the letters sent out to these women a spokesman commented on a 'World in Action' programme made in 1978. 'This is a commercial letter from a commercial organisation and it doesn't seem to me to have any great health education value so in that sense, I think it would be of little value to the people who received it.'[153] Apart from financing 'Women's Health Care' to promote the use of hormone replacement therapy, the drug companies have also financed a whole network of 'menopause clinics' in NHS hospitals, so that their products could be evaluated and tested for safety by 'guinea pigs' sent to these clinics by Women's Health Care.

Drug company's unique method of reducing cancer risk

When the first reports were published in the *New England Journal of Medicine* (in December 1975) of HRT causing cancer, sales of Ayerst's top-selling drug were seriously threatened. But some remarkable documents obtained secretly by a New York feminist magazine called *Majority Report* reveal that Ayerst were busy hatching a plot to reassure women using Premarin that they had little to worry about. This exposé was entitled 'But you'll make such a feminine corpse' and was written by Sharon Liebermann. It revealed the contents of a letter sent by an international public relations firm, Hill & Knowlton Inc, to the President of Ayerst Laboratories in New York which suggested that journalists should be encouraged to write favourable articles on Premarin in *Reader's Digest, Ladies' Home Journal, Family Circle* and *Redbook* in order to counterbalance the adverse publicity caused by the rising cancer incidence amongst HRT takers.[154]

Dr Denis Hawkins, Professor of Gynaecology at Hammersmith Hospital, described the promotional literature published by the companies manufacturing hormone replacement products as scare advertising:

> You don't have to feel like a senior citizen just because you're near the age of 40 or 50 [or] You may suddenly find yourself concerned about obvious changes in your appearance . . . is all scare advertising, it's quite subtle but it's none the less that.[153]

The natural hormones myth: Premarin, the top-selling brand of hormone replacement therapy, does contain natural hormones – but they are only natural to horses! Premarin is extracted from horse urine; in fact the name is derived from letters contained in the words PREgnant MARes' urINE = PREMARIN. The effects of horse hormones on women are obscure, says the *Drug and Therapeutics Bulletin.*[152]

Hormone therapy no better than a placebo? – the hot flushes fallacy

'Of course there are a lot of women who need to consult a doctor about symptoms which they may connect with the menopause but that doesn't mean they should walk out of the surgery with a prescription for oestrogen. There are a lot of other things that doctors can do and do do. And one of those is just to listen to the patient and to discuss her problems and to help her to understand them and in many cases that helps a great deal' – Dr Andrew Herxheimer.[153]

'There is no evidence that oestrogens are significantly better than placebos in treating hot flushes. We suggest that as oestrogens carry a significant risk we should stop prescribing them for a condition which we do not fully understand.' So say Professor J. R. A. Mitchell and Dr G. Mulley.[151] On the other hand, Dr Malcolm Whitehead and Professor Stewart Campbell claim they have produced 'definitive' evidence of oestrogen's superiority over placebos in treating hot flushes.[155]

A study carried out by Drs Jean Coope and L. Poller in 1975 and published in the *British Medical Journal*[156] found that there were equally dramatic improvements in menopausal symptoms with either Premarin or a totally fake drug, a placebo sugar pill. Dr Poller also found that Premarin has similar dangerous blood-clotting effects as the Pill. They write: 'Our findings are disturbing because after only three months there was a pronounced acceleration of clotting . . . this must cause concern . . . These findings were similar to those observed with oral contraception.'

The cancer risk associated with hormone replacement therapy

In 1975 the first of twelve investigations[157] was published in the USA demonstrating that HRT increased the risk of cancer of the womb between four and fourteen times. The studies show that the risk increases with the length of treatment. There is some evidence that the risk of cancer can be reduced by combining the oestrogen hormone with a progestogen – an anti-cancer drug. A study of 745 women reported in the *British Medical Journal*[158] found that the frequency of women getting hyperplasia (abnormal cells that may be precursors of cancer) was reduced if they took progestogens. Pre-cancerous cells were absent entirely if they took progestogens for more than ten days per month whilst taking oestrogen replacement therapy. The authors admit that the length of their treatment – up to two years – was too short to allow any definite conclusion, but believe progestogens may reduce the risk of womb cancer.

An important by-product of this research project was the discovery that women with pre-cancerous hyperplasia may not necessarily suffer from any symptoms such as unusual vaginal bleeding. So however healthy women may seem whilst on HRT they need a six-monthly curettage check-up to make sure they are not developing cancer.[158] It was also found that the longer women stayed on HRT the greater was the incidence of pre-cancerous hyperplasia. Over 40 per cent of the women on HRT for between 18 months and 2 years developed these abnormal cell changes.

However, this combination of hormones carries risks of its own – it may still have the same dangerous blood-clotting effects as the contraceptive pill, particularly for women in their 40s and 50s. These progestogens given with low doses of oestrogen may be associated with increased risk of stroke and heart disease, according to a recent editorial in the *British Medical Journal*[160] It adds that, since the dangers increase with age, so the risks need to be assessed very carefully. Also this combination is very similar to the now-abandoned sequential contraceptive pills. The sequentials were found by researchers Drs S. Silverberg and E. Makowski [161] to increase the incidence of womb cancer. Also by taking these combined preparations menopausal women will experience 'periods' once again. The shedding of cells in the womb caused by the progestogen results as monthly bleeding.

Breast cancer risk also increased

Dr Robert Hoover has shown that hormone replacement therapy certainly does not protect against breast cancer, as some studies have claimed, but slightly increases the risk – 1.3 times.[162] He looked at nearly 2,000 women who had received six months or more of treatment with Premarin. A study by Dr Malcolm Whitehead and Professor Stuart Campbell conducted at Chelsea Hospital for Women also discovered a higher than expected number of breast cancer cases amongst women on HRT.[159] But Dr Whitehead says that these results are not reliable and that a later study showed no increase in the number of breast cancers.[163] Out of twelve investigations into the breast cancer risk three have found an increased risk with HRT.

Women in the United States must by law be informed of the increased risk of cancer associated with HRT before treatment is started. No similar warnings are required in Britain.

Duphaston

Brand name of drug: Duphaston (Dulphar).

Purpose of drug: To ease pre-menstrual tension.

Special warning: Possibly ineffective and hazardous.

Main chemical used in drug: Dydrogesterone (an artificial sex hormone).

'The continuing uncertainty over the cause of pre-menstrual tension is reflected by the many treatments offered' – editorial in the *British Medical Journal*.[164]

Duphaston is a synthetic version of the female hormone progesterone and it is commonly prescribed for the condition that has come to be called pre-menstrual tension (PMT). There is no accepted definition of PMT – it consists of a cluster of wide-ranging symptoms which include weight increase, breast tenderness, irritability, headaches and fatigue. The only common factor about any of these conditions is that they are said to occur before menstruation. But this very broad description of the condition makes it ripe for treatment with any number of drugs. Of course all women suffer from some of these conditions some of the time, just as it has been shown that the traditional symptoms of the menopause occur throughout life and not simply after the menopause. It is quite probable that tension also is not restricted to just before menstruation and that many of PMT's symptoms have little to do with hormone levels.[164]

Is Duphaston yet another drug in search of a disease?

The assumption behind giving women suffering from PMT a dose of progestogen in Duphaston is that their problems are brought about by a deficiency of this hormone at certain times of the month. Indeed, a group of doctors working at St Thomas's Hospital have shown that in the second half of the menstrual cycle 30 per cent of women with PMT did show a lack of progesterone when they were compared to a group of symptom-free women. But what about the remaining 70 per cent of women with PMT? The majority, it was found, did not have any hormone deficiency. It follows that doses of the drug Duphaston will probably be no more effective for PMT than a harmless sugar pill and they may carry the risk of side effects without any real benefit.

'Treatment with progesterone is probably illogical,' concluded Professor E. M. Symons and his team at Nottingham City Hospital recently,[165] 'unless a deficiency is detected.' They had measured the amount of progesterone in the bloodstream of women suffering from PMT and compared them to symptom-free women. They found that a deficiency of progesterone was largely unconnected with symptoms of pre-menstrual stress.

Duphaston and pre-menstrual tension

The *Drug and Therapeutics Bulletin* has examined the whole question of drug treatment for pre-menstrual tension and reports[166] that Duphaston synthetic progestogens have been found to cause an actual reduction in the amounts of progesterones in the blood! According to the

Bulletin: 'In two trials from one centre[167] it appeared to cause some improvement, though the presentation of the results leaves room for doubts. Other trials have shown no evidence that synthetic progestogens are effective.' 'Its value remains unproved,' says the report.

Some investigations claim to have shown that Duphaston can relieve some of the symptoms of pre-menstrual tension in about 70 per cent of women, but there is also evidence that it may be no more effective than other treatments such as pyridoxine. This may be a safer drug, if any must be used, for it is vitamin B_6. The *British Medical Journal* comments on this and other pre-menstrual tension 'cures' that 'there is no evidence indeed that any one treatment is more effective than the others'.[164]

Not only is the use of Duphaston questioned but Pyridoxine too comes in for some sharp criticism. The claim is far from proven that it is useful for dealing with depression for women on the Pill, says the *Bulletin*. They conclude that: 'The results of one small trial of pyridoxine (vitamin B_6) and PMT[166] are unimpressive and a meagre basis for its use.'

'What we need,' pleads the *British Medical Journal*, 'is a more precise definition of the syndrome, with well-planned carefully controlled trials of various treatments, including simple reassurance, mild sedation or tranquillisers.' It adds, 'Whatever else we offer these patients, they are likely to appreciate an understanding and sympathetic approach to the problem and this is where husbands and relatives and friends, as well as doctors, can be of help.'[164]

Unethical popular promotion of this drug

Unfortunately several TV programmes, books and articles in the British popular press have sold the idea to many women that the answer to their monthly problems lies with this form of progesterone treatment. The evidence how-ever does not support this type of wholesale promotion. In some ways the selling to the public of these drugs compares with the way in which hormone replacement therapy (HRT) was promoted (see page 247).

Diethyl-stilboestrol

DES and breast cancer

Diethyl-stilboestrol, DES for short, the synthetic oestrogen hormone given to vast numbers of women in the 1950s to allegedly prevent them having miscarriages, has now been linked with an increase in breast cancer incidence. A University of Chicago Survey in 1978 of DES mothers found that breast cancer was three times more common amongst them than in control mothers who did not suffer DES exposure.[168] DES was originally found to be the cause of an epidemic of a previously rare form of vaginal cancer in the *daughters* of the women who took it to protect them against their miscarrying. Up to 90 per cent of all those DES daughters today suffer from an abnormal cell pattern in the vagina called 'vaginal adenosis'. These abnormal cells – whilst not cancerous themselves – are precursors of cancer and therefore DES daughters are strongly advised to have regular, annual check-ups to make sure their 'adenosis' has not become malignant. DES sons have also been found to have abnormal cells in their testicles – but no one knows yet whether they are a sign of a later, more serious, disease state, such as infertility or cancer.

In the USA hundreds of thousands of women were given DES, in the hope of protecting them against miscarriage, but in Britain only 7,000 women have been estimated to have received DES. The irony of DES treatment and its horrific aftermath is that DES has never been shown to be effective at preventing miscarriage.[168] As a result of these findings women who took DES and their daughters are advised by the US Food and Drug Authority to avoid all other oestrogens.[169] DES is also used as a morning-after contraceptive (see p. 145) and also to promote growth in poultry and cattle (see p. 177).

DES cancer hits Britain

A new British investigation into the effects of DES on a group of 80 women diabetics who were given it between 1950 and 1953 to prevent miscarriage has found six times as many tumours of the reproductive organs amongst these hormone-treated women compared to a group given placebos. Four cases of breast cancer were found in the DES-treated group and none amongst the non-treated women. These findings show that oestrogen can cause breast cancer as many as fifteen years or more after treatment, say the researchers, Dr Valerie Beral and Linda

Colwell of The London School of Hygiene & Tropical Medicine.[170]

Whilst admitting that the hormone doses these women were given were massive, the researchers say that nonetheless the incidence of breast cancer was high – 5 per cent of the DES-treated group. All the women who received DES in this experiment also received a progesterone-like substance – ethisterone (see also pages 142 and 251).

Slimming drugs and amphetamines: Tenuate

Brand name of drug: Tenuate (Merrell).
Purpose of drug: To stop you feeling hungry.
Special warning: Addictive, ineffective and hazardous.
Main chemical used in the drug: Diethylpropion hydrochloride (an amphetamine-type compound).

Similar drugs:

Apisate (Wyeth)	Ionamin (Lipha)
Duromine (Carnegie)	Ponderax (Servier)
Durophet (Riker)	Teronac (Wander)
Filon (Berk)	

'The use of amphetamine-like drugs in the treatment of obesity is not justified, as any possible benefits are outweighed by the risks involved.'[171] It may come as a shock to many people that over 2 million prescriptions are still made out annually in Britain for slimming drugs which contain pep pills.[172] Amphetamine-type drugs are still used in brands such as Tenuate, Ponderax and Duromine. The Department of Health regularly tells doctors not to prescribe these drugs as they do not work after a short period of time and cannot replace willpower for someone who eats too much. They are also potent drugs of addiction – yet they are still prescribed by thousands of GPs.

How the nation got hooked on amphetamines

It was a chance discovery in the thirties that gave birth to the idea that amphetamines could suppress the appetite. They were originally given to the small number of people who suffered from uncontrollable sleepiness (narcolepsy). These patients noticed that the drug made them lose their appetite as well, and to their delight they also found it made them feel euphoric and full of energy. This 'amazing' property made the drug very popular during World War II. They were handed out in bulk to both

German and Allied troops to make the poor soldiers stay awake and feel happy about hurling bombs at each other.

Shortly after the war the Japanese began to hand them out to their workforces to boost production in their factories – the post-war Japanese industrial miracle was founded partially on amphetamine pills. Large stockpiles of these drugs were sold over the counter in Japan to eliminate drowsiness and aid the repletion of the spirit.[173] But by the early fifties the amphetamines were becoming a pusher's drug, often sold illicitly to housewife addicts. In Britain in the fifties and early sixties they were favoured particularly by women who were anxious about their weight, and soon the weight neurosis led to addiction.

It is ironic that in 1954 they were still described as non-addictive and free of side effects by Britain's Chief Medical Officer at the Ministry of Health. 'Many middle aged women had taken to forgery so that they could keep getting their supplies,' writes Dr Vernon Coleman in his book *The Medicine Men*.[174] He points out that an authoritative American drug manual written in 1958 and the *British Medical Journal* in 1963 both described the problem of amphetamine addiction as 'extremely rare and not satisfactorily substantiated'. It is interesting to note that nowadays, at the beginning of the eighties, the evidence that Valium or Librium are also addictive is being dismissed in a similar way. At least the problem of amphetamine addiction has now been recognised and in the USA abuse of amphetamines has resulted in the FDA proposing that their use for weight reduction be banned.

US government to ban slimming pills (amphetamines)

In July 1979 the American FDA proposed to ban amphetamines for weight reduction. But the proposal allows the drugs to remain available for two other reasons: the treatment of hyperactive children (see page 260 for details of Ritalin) and also of the rare condition of narcolepsy (uncontrollable sleepiness). The FDA had come to the conclusion that amphetamines were being abused much more than any other drugs used to control weight – they present a 'a severe risk of dependence'. They say too that alternative drugs are available which have equal effectiveness and less risk.

Since 80–90 per cent of the amphetamines produced in

the USA are used for weight reduction, the FDA ruling will force the manufacturers to reduce their output by up to 90 per cent. The Director of the FDA, Dr Richard Crout, has said that these drugs 'make only a minor contribution to weight reduction in the treatment of obesity'.

Do Tenuate, Ponderax, Duromine etc (amphetamines) really make people lose weight?

In 1977, the British Department of Health sent a circular to all doctors stating that 'appetite suppressants have little place in the management of the obese patient and there is no substitute for willpower'. It went on to say that the NHS paid out over £3½ million for amphetamine drugs in 1975. Figures in 1978 showed that still over 2 million prescriptions were made out for these drugs, and more than half of these were for one product, Tenuate. Tenuate contains a chemical called diethylproprion which although it is not chemically an amphetamine substance has exactly the same toxic effects.[61] 'Their power to suppress appetite soon wears off and they may produce drug dependence of the amphetamine type,' comments Professor Peter Parrish on this top-selling drug.[61]

Other popular brands of amphetamine-type slimming drugs are Duromine, which sells over a quarter of a million prescriptions, and Ponderax, selling over 200,000 per year.[146] These drugs should only be given for short periods of time as tolerance frequently develops, says the Pharmaceutical Society guide to drugs, *Martindale's*.[23] In other words, after a few weeks they have no effect and larger doses are needed. It is then that there is a danger of addiction. Although some success has been found with these drugs in suppressing appetite, several properly controlled scientific experiments have found that they do not work at all. It has been repeatedly shown that they are no better than a placebo sugar pill in producing weight loss.[175,176]

Side effects of Tenuate

Tenuate has the same toxic or poisonous effects as pure amphetamines and also has the same capacity to make people into drug addicts.

Side effects of Ponderax (fenfluramine)

Nausea and diarrhoea, headache, dizziness and sedation, hallucination, distortion of sense of time. Abuse of the amphetamine-type drug has occurred because of the euphoria Ponderax can produce.[177] After withdrawing the tablets there is a typical depressed state.

Are you addicted to Tenuate or another amphetamine-type drug?

You are addicted if you have a desire or need to continue taking these drugs in larger doses to obtain greater excitement or feelings of euphoria. If you need these drugs to combat depression or fatigue then you are already addicted. Since some parts of the nervous system do not get used to the drug as the dose is increased, nervousness and insomnia may persist with increasingly large doses. Anyone who is dependent on these drugs will suffer from increased accident proneness and will show aggressive, anti-social behaviour. They may also suffer from delusions and hallucinations. The World Health Organisation has recommended that these drugs should be brought under international control because of the risks. They say that they have little to offer as medicines and pose a substantial risk to public health.[23]

Drugs to control children: Tofranil

Brand name of drug: Tofranil (Geigy).
Purpose of drug: To stop bedwetting.
Special warning: Double hazard – largely ineffective and dangerous.
Main chemical used in the drug: Imipramine.

'If such drugs were safe their low success rate might be acceptable. But reports show that these drugs are potentially lethal: they are now the commonest cause of poisoning in children under 5 and should not be given to young children' – editorial in the *British Medical Journal.*[178]

Powerful anti-depressant drugs are commonly prescribed for young children to stop them wetting in their beds. The drugs are unnecessary, rarely work and kill many children each year. Yet with all these devastating properties the commonly prescribed brands are sold in special fruit-flavoured syrup to encourage children to swallow this largely useless and often fatal drug.

Why Tofranil will probably be a waste of time

Many parents worry unnecessarily when their child wets the bed: the *British Medical Journal* points out that once parents are informed of the normal rates for bedwetting in other children many accept that the problem will disappear of its own accord. The facts are that only 50 per cent of children are dry by the age of 2, 75 per cent by the age of 3 and 90 per cent by the age of 5. After the age of 5, 14 per cent of children spontaneously stop wetting the bed.

Most experts agree that bedwetting after this age is probably caused by some emotional upset; for example, trouble at school or at home (do the parents quarrel?) or a new baby in the family.[178] Generally most psychological difficulties of this nature clear up on their own as the environmental situation improves. Despite the psychological origins of bedwetting, doctors themselves have turned it into a new disease which they can therefore treat with a pill. They have given it a pompous title: enuresis. Even the *British Medical Journal*, the voice of the medical establishment, disapproves of this creation of clinical jargon. 'Use of the word enuresis has raised bedwetting to the status of disease that requires a drug to cure it when, in fact, in most cases the child is normal,' comments their editorial.[178]

Sometimes, of course, bedwetting may be caused by a physical problem such as a urinary infection, sugar in the urine and so on, and a doctor should always check for these conditions before considering any further treatment, advises the *British Medical Journal*.

Does the drug work?

Clinical experiments have shown that Tofranil and similar drugs produce a cure in only 30 per cent of children who take the drug[179] and within three months many children are wetting again. This high failure rate is even acknowledged by one manufacturer of the drugs, who includes special books of paper stars to be awarded to children when they have a dry night. But perhaps the most alarming fact to be revealed is that most children receiving this hazardous drug are too young to obtain any benefit from it. Many doctors fail to realise that Tofranil is ineffective in children under the age of 7 or 8 but it is often prescribed for children much younger. They risk all the hazards which this treatment implies, without any of the alleged benefits.

The side effects of Tofranil include: between 1 in 8 and 1 in 10 of children on these drugs become nervous, irritable and have difficulty in sleeping. In addition they may suffer from dizziness, nausea, difficulty in class, tearfulness and restlessness.[180]

Tofranil: 'an avoidable cause of childhood deaths'

'These drugs are now the commonest cause of poisoning in children under five', ie children for whom the drug would not be effective anyway, says the *British Medical Journal*.[178] It adds that 'Every year a score of doctors probably regret writing a lethal prescription for a benign condition which usually resolves spontaneously.'

A much more successful way to stop a child wetting the bed is to obtain a little device that wakes him up as soon as he starts to wet the bed. After a while the child begins to wake up before the buzzer goes off and in no time at all he is cured of wetting the bed. This form of conditioning borrows an idea from classical psychology discovered by Pavlov and his salivating dogs. These devices can produce an 80 per cent cure rate according to several surveys.[179] Since they work by closing an electrical circuit they are more effective if the child can be persuaded not to wear his pyjama bottoms so that the warning goes off as quickly as possible. Many school clinics keep supplies of these devices as do paediatric outpatient clinics, says the *British Medical Journal*.[178] They can also be purchased but a good GP should know where one can be borrowed. But 'doctors find it easier to write a prescription for an anti-depressant than to persuade a district supplies officer to buy, supply and service this type of equipment', complains the *British Medical Journal*.[178]

Ritalin

Brand name of drug: Ritalin (CIBA).
Purpose of drug: To control overactive children.
Special warning: Hazardous and may be ineffective.
Main chemical used in the drug: Methylphenidate.

Millions of American children have been prescribed potent amphetamine drugs to make them behave better in the classrooms.[181] The drugs are marketed in Britain but fortunately have never caught on very much on this side of the Atlantic. Suitable cases for treatment with this drug are said to be 'hyperactive', or in America: suffering from 'hyperkinesis'. The medical jargon used to refer to this condition, if it is a condition at all, is *'minimal brain dysfunction'*.

Is Ritalin a drug in search of a disease?

Many young Americans have been diagnosed as suffering from hyperactivity and minimal brain dysfunction and over one million of them are being treated with amphetamine-type drugs such as Ritalin. 'This is a terrible state of affairs,' say Peter Schrag and Diane Divorky, because as they point out, there is no universally accepted syndrome of hyperactivity. They say that parents are made to feel uneasy about children who are just slightly out-of-the-ordinary.[181] Once pseudo-scientific jargon can be made to fit the situation, their guilt about their children vanishes. Instantly a social or a psychological problem is magically transformed into a physical problem by doctors who pronounce that a child is suffering from 'minimal brain dysfunction'. This so-called 'dysfunction' can then be treated with the aid of a pill.

Does the drug work?

The authoritative *Drug and Therapeutics Bulletin* points out that there have not been any investigations of the long-term effects of Ritalin treatment.[182] Preliminary studies suggest the drug does not provide long-term improvement in children's behaviour, but that it may work for some children in the short term.

One five-year study of 'hyperactive children' who were given Ritalin at Montreal Children's Hospital discovered that these children did not differ in the long term from 'hyperactive' children who were not given the drug. Initially drug-treated kids were more manageable but at the end of five years their improvement and their level of adjustment was no better than untreated kids.[182]

Many children may fail to respond at all; benefit is more likely in children who show abnormal brain-wave patterns, neurological disorders and uneven scores on IQ tests. In those who do respond positively to treatment there is less disruption in the classroom, greater attention span and less activity generally. It is a widely held but mistaken belief that amphetamines *stimulate* adults but *sedate* children. The *Drug and Therapeutics Bulletin* claims that both adults and children show increased stimulation, vigilance and attention with these drugs. Insomnia and lack of appetite are also a problem at all ages.

The *Bulletin* warns that Ritalin should only be considered for children when tests and clinical examination reveal the existence of a clear neurological disorder with abnormal brain-wave patterns. The opinion of a child psychiatrist is essential before drug treatment starts. A health visitor, child psychologist, GP, teachers at school, parents and psychiatrist should all be involved in monitoring the effects of these drugs.[182]

Side effects of Ritalin treatment

These drugs can result in stunted growth; a child may lose up to 20 percentile points of height over a three-year period of treatment. This means he may lose several inches in height. If treatment is stopped there is generally a spurt of growth. 'It is clearly important to maintain growth charts for children taking a stimulant,' says the *Bulletin*.[182] The most common side effects of Ritalin treatment are insomnia and loss of appetite. Some children also become excitable, or more commonly they become irritable, oversensitive and depressed. Reversible psychotic episodes have also occurred with ordinary doses and occasionally there are tremors and facial tics. In some circumstances Ritalin can increase the likelihood of epileptic fits, warns the manufacturer, CIBA.

What are the real causes of hyperactivity?

There is a large body of evidence that children who have high levels of lead in their blood suffer from hyperactivity. Some parents in Britain have tried to sue the big oil companies for injuring their children with the lead put into petrol. Lead levels permitted in UK petrol are amongst the highest in the world.

Food additives too have been incriminated as causes of brain damage which can show itself as hyperactivity.

What is the effect of Ritalin on learning?

Dr Barbara Sahakian asks what is the cause of overactivity in children? Some factors seem to precipitate this problem, but no single cause has been identified. 'It is possible,' writes Dr Sahakian, 'that these children have sustained some brain damage during pregnancy or birth, but the data is not compelling and does not justify the label "minimal brain dysfunction".' Environmental pollution, social and genetic factors may also be responsible, she says.[183]

Contrary to popular mythology, amphetamine-type drugs do not actually reduce activity in children but increase it; however, they reduce the *variety* of behaviour. 'This kind of increased focusing of behaviour or attention can be seen in the behaviour and speech of amphetamine addicts. Addicts have been described as persistently combing their hair, constantly polishing their finger nails and even repetitively performing more elaborate behaviours. For example, an addict was observed to continually dismantle and build his car,' writes Dr Sahakian. Amphetamine drugs given to overactive children therefore result in an increased focusing of behaviour which is not a paradoxical reaction to the drug, says Dr Sahakian. This also means that the side effects found in children on these drugs are not paradoxical either; they include loss of appetite, rapid heart beat, insomnia, irritability and fearfulness. An example of this speeding up of behaviour was noticed by Barbara Sahakian when she found that Ritalin produced severe facial tics in one child. Before treatment the rate of tics had been very low. The most disturbing implications of Dr Sahakian's findings are that these drugs may produce real deterioration, particularly in learning new skills at school. Animal experiments have already shown that amphetamine reduces responses to new tasks and to novel situations where changes of behaviour are necessary. 'While hyperactive children treated with amphetamine might improve in simple repetition tasks they often do not show improvement in long term school performance,' says Dr Sahakian.[183]

Miscellaneous hazards: Lorexane, Tartrazine
Lorexane (Gamma Benzene Hexachloride) made by ICI
Lorexane is an insecticide used to get rid of lice, skin parasites, mites and scabies. It is rubbed into the skin but unfortunately since it penetrates *through* the skin it can do more damage than merely kill off lice. It could damage the nervous system. It has been found to cause convulsions and death in young rabbits. 'The veterinary literature contains numerous reports of deaths of young animals, dipped in the insecticide,' says the Food and Drug Administration.[184] It concludes that high doses are 'potentially dangerous, particularly in children, and should be

avoided'.

Tartrazine – yellow dye hazard in pills and food

Tartrazine is a yellow dye used to colour food and drugs. Some people are particularly sensitive to this colouring additive, generally those who are also sensitive to aspirin. Presence of this colouring in drugs and pills can cause bronchial asthma, urticaria (skin rash), angioedema and nasal symptoms in sensitive individuals. In Britain it is almost impossible for a hypersensitive person to find out if the food or drug he is taking contains this additive. But in the United States the Food and Drug Administration requires that all foods and drugs be labelled accordingly. The FDA points out that this is important because some drugs used to treat allergy contain the dye, so someone might find themselves in the following ridiculous situation: 'A patient sensitive to Tartrazine could, in the absence of the labelling requirement, continue to take drugs containing the colour additive to treat conditions or symptoms that may be the result of previous ingestion of the dye'![185] This dye is often used in drug products taken by asthmatics, such as antihistamines, antibiotics and bronchodilators.

9

Some of our Favourite Over-the-counter Drugs

Cold remedies: Night Nurse

'Nothing you can take will make your cold go away' – *Which? Magazine,* March 1976.

Night Nurse (the highly popular cold remedy) made by Beecham contains a mixture of drugs which includes a potent antihistamine (called Promethazine Hydrochloride) and a dose of paracetamol. The antihistamine may be not only useless but hazardous too. This is how the American Public Citizens' Health Research Group described the use of antihistamines in cold preparations, in a letter to the US Food and Drug Administration, complaining about their continued marketing.[1]

'Not only is there little evidence to substantiate their usefulness for runny nose, sneezing, itching and watery eyes, but the evidence is to the contrary.' Dr Philip S. Norman, Professor of Medicine, Johns Hopkins University, stated at the Nelson hearings on cough and cold medicine: 'Careful comparisons between patients treated with antihistamines and patients treated with placebos showed no evidence that antihistamine usage either relieved the symptoms of a cold or shortened the duration of the illness. The extensive nature of the work and the expertise of the investigators deserve to be emphasized; few subjects have been so carefully studied or results so consistently negative.'[2]

Another expert view from what Joe Graedon calls 'the most authoritative text book on medical pharmacology in the world'[3] says, 'despite early claims and persistent popular belief antihistamines are of little value in combating the common cold'. The Public Citizens' Health Group also warns about the hazards of antihistamines, 'allowing marketing of antihistamines for unproven benefits is unsafe because they have side effects, such as drowsiness, incoordination, mental inattention, dizziness, which make them dangerous for a consumer who is not staying in bed. Blood disorders have also been reported with antihistamines.'[6]

Beecham's Night Nurse is the most widely bought night cold remedy and Vick Medinite is its major competitor, according to a business analysis of over-the-counter drug sales in 1978.[4] Demand for these 'remedies' reached 16 million doses in the year ending June 1978 and Beecham took 60 per cent of those sales. British experts also agree that these products have little value. Night Nurse and similar drugs were discussed in the Pharmaceutical Society's *Guide to Drugs (Martindale's)*.[5] They wrote: 'Few of the drugs in this section have been shown to be effective by controlled trials.' The most effective ingredient in Night Nurse is probably the dose of paracetamol – a proven painkiller. But why pay a lot of money for a questionable combination of drugs, when simple paracetamol BP may be just as good and cause fewer side effects? Antihistamines are of equally dubious value for coughs, according to Professor Peter Parrish, who says 'they are of very doubtful and unproven value in cough medicines . . . they may have undesirable effects because they dry the lining of the nose and respiratory tract, impairing natural defence systems . . .' He adds that 'apart from providing some relief from a running nose, they are of no benefit in treating the common cold'. 'There is no point in spending money on any preparations because they fizz or taste fruity,' says Professor Peter Parrish.[7]

Lemsip and Contac 400

Lemsip contains (amongst other ingredients) paracetamol and a chemical called phenylephrine which is supposed to work as a decongestant. This substance has been found to be ineffective in doses up to 40 milligrams according to

Consumers' Union (the American equivalent of the Consumers' Association).[8] Yet Lemsip contains only 5 milligrams of phenylephrine.

Another cold product with a decongestant chemical is the widely advertised Contac 400. This product has 'tiny time capsules' which are supposed to gradually release the ingredients over a period of several hours. The US Consumers' Union however point out that with Contac's timed release formula the dosage is theoretically spread out over twelve hours – so the user gets too small a dose at any one time to be effective against cold symptoms. Contac only contains 50 milligrams of the decongestant (phenylpropranolamine hydrochloride) which is only effective for a few hours at doses of 25–50 milligrams, say Consumers' Union.[9]

Not only is this product likely to be ineffective, it can also seriously raise blood pressure to dangerous levels. For this reason it should not be taken by people suffering from heart disease, hypertension, angina, etc. One experiment has shown that when two young men took Contact they were found to have blood pressure of 180/110 – which returned to normal when they stopped taking the product.[10]

Other serious side effects with this drug have been reported after eating a meal which included cheese. Severe headache, visions of coloured lights, tightness of chest and heart pounding, and increased blood pressure have been reported by a patient who took 64 milligrams of phenylpropranolamine (the decongestant present in Contac).[11] Also 'temporary acute psychotic episodes have occurred in three people who took it as a nasal decongestant'.[12]

The US Public Citizens' Health Research Group also report that the American Medical Association Council on Drugs 1971 described a similar combination of drugs as those used in Contac as 'irrational'.[6] They also say that, 'a number of FDA medical officers over the years have expressed concern about the safety of this product, due to the lack of thorough information about its safety'. They point out that animal studies have shown that when the ingredients of Contac are taken in combination there is an increase in the harmful effects of individual ingredients.[6]

Another popular product: Alka Seltzer

'Over the years Consumers' Union's medical consultants have frequently advised against the regular use of Alka Seltzer as an antacid. In their judgement its continued popularity is a clear defeat for public health education' – the American Consumer Organisation Consumers' Union in the *Medicine Show*, 1976.[13]

Alka Seltzer is a very popular product widely advertised and hence widely used for stomach upsets, but the aspirin used in it could make it a danger to people with any stomach problems. The manufacturers (Miles) claim on their packets that it is 'for fast and effective relief of headache with upset stomach and particularly when due to too much to eat or drink'. But the combination of drugs, aspirin, citric acid and sodium bicarbonate used in Alka Seltzer could aggravate an ulcer and stomach pains. Aspirin irritates the stomach and makes it bleed in 75 per cent of people taking it. One in four of people who take aspirin find that it causes indigestion. Also, aspirin combined with alcohol produces twice as great a risk of serious stomach bleeding – so anyone who takes Alka Seltzer after a heavy drinking bout may be more likely to suffer stomach bleeding.[14] An indication of the possible hazards of aspirin in Alka Seltzer can be gleaned from the fact that in the United States the manufacturers have marketed a product which they call 'Alka Seltzer without Aspirin'! They claim, however, that when ordinary Alka Seltzer is dissolved it becomes a buffered solution which protects the lining of the stomach from the hazardous effects of aspirin. One possible advantage of taking aspirin in Alka Seltzer is that being in liquid form it passes through the stomach quickly. Alka Seltzer also contains high concentrations of sodium which may be dangerous to people who need to keep to a low salt diet,[13] eg, those with high blood pressure. In the US the FDA requires that Alka Seltzer be labelled with the following warning: 'Do not use this product if you are on a sodium-restricted diet', but there is no equivalent warning in Britain.

The great laxative scandal

'There can be no doubt that laxatives have contributed

more to the ills and discomforts of mankind than the condition they are supposed to remove.'[15]

Many people mistakenly believe it is vital to have a daily bowel movement and so when they don't have one – they resort to laxatives. The trouble with laxative drugs is that if they are regularly used they can have the effect of stopping the bowel working on its own. They can also mask the vital signals indicating appendicitis.

Laxatives can empty the bowel so completely that it takes several days to fill up again. During this period the poor patient can easily be misled into thinking that he or she is suffering from further constipation. As a result more laxatives are consumed and a vicious circle is created: the drugs become useless and the patient becomes addicted to them.

If over-used, some laxatives can dangerously lower the body's levels of potassium salts, which can in turn lead to heart failure. Anyone on diuretics, blood pressure or heart drugs may be at special risk in this situation. The *British National Formulary* says that 'laxatives should generally be avoided' under normal circumstances since simple constipation can usually be relieved by increasing the amount of fibre (fresh fruit, vegetables and bran) in the diet.[16] Substituting genuine wholemeal bread for white often does the trick.

There is an enormous variety of laxatives available at the chemists and as many as one in every three households stock them – yet only one in ten of the population claim to be regular sufferers from constipation.

The trouble with stimulant laxatives such as Ex-Lax and Senokot

Ex-Lax contains a stimulant chemical call phenolphthalein which stimulates movements of the gut (called peristalsis) and can thereby cause painful cramps. The American Consumers Union says that products like Ex-Lax and Senokot should be avoided, and the *BNF* warns that prolonged use should be avoided. They may also cause dangerous loss of fluid, pink urine and allergic skin rashes. Professor Peter Parrish warns that the effect of such stimulants is unpredictable: response to dosage varies tremendously, and what may produce stomach cramps and diarrhoea in one person may have no effect in another.[7]

Fynnon Salt, Milk of Magnesia, Andrews Liver Salts, Eno's Fruit Salt and other 'health salts'

These harmless-sounding 'health salts' may be potentially dangerous. For example, those containing sodium (check the label for details of ingredients) may be harmful to people suffering from heart disease as they cause the retention of fluid in the tissues (Eno's, for example, contains sodium bicarbonate). Also, if you are taking diuretic drugs you must not take sodium salts, as one drug will cancel out the effect of the other. Fynnon Salt's main ingredient is a laxative, yet it is sold mainly for rheumatism. 'There is no evidence that regular bowel movement is any more important for rheumatism sufferers than for anyone else', says *Which?* magazine, published by the UK Consumers Association. They also say that there is no evidence that the ingredients in Fynnon Salt have any direct effect on rheumatism.[18]

Another problem, with salts containing magnesium is that they may cause magnesium poisoning in people with kidney damage. Signs of such poisoning include low blood pressure and breathing difficulties.

Finally, if you do take these salts, always drink lots of water or fruit juice as they can cause dehydration. Professor Peter Parrish neatly sums up the scandal of the continued promotion of these drugs as 'health salts': he says it is reasonable enough to call them 'health salts' if you define health as 'bowel movements and belching'![7]

Paracetamol
Fatal liver hazard with common painkiller

The Lancet asked in 1975: 'Surely the time has come to replace paracetamol with a drug which cannot cause liver damage?'[19] Paracetamol crops up in over forty different products including the dangerous and relatively ineffective prescription drug 'Distalgesic' (see page 198). 'If paracetamol was discovered today it would not be approved by the Committee on Safety of Medicines and it would certainly never be freely given without prescription.'[19]

Although paracetamol is commonly advertised to the public as a 'safe' painkiller, just a very small overdose can cause liver damage. 'The apparent safety is deceptive, it causes liver damage which may be fatal, paracetamol is one of the commonest causes of liver failure in Britain', according to a team of investigators reporting in *The Lancet*.[20]

'Do not exceed the recommended dosage because severe liver damage may occur.' This is the American warning label that appears on all products containing paracetamol (called Acetaminophen in the USA). No warning about liver damage appears in Britain; instead it has been advertised (until recently) 'for safer relief of pain'. This referred only to the fact that, unlike aspirin, it does not cause stomach bleeding.

After studying over 2,000 cases of liver poisoning, Dr Laurence Prescott of Edinburgh University believes that liver damage can occur at overdose levels of just 7.5 grams, or even at lower levels in some susceptible individuals.[21] This is not much more than the recommended daily dose of 4 grams per day. Once consumed, paracetamol is changed into a toxic substance that the liver can only deal with in small quantities and a slight overdose cannot be tolerated. The toxic substance builds up, and for three days after an overdose there *appears* to be no damage. But four to six days later, acute liver failure occurs.

What to do with an overdose

A small overdose can produce liver damage, but as the makers of Panadol (Winthrop) say, 'a patient suffering from an overdose may appear quite well for the first three days and then succumb to liver damage'. Successful treatment of an overdose depends on speedy action. Do not delay to take the patient to a hospital for emergency treatment *no matter how well the patient appears*. An antidote does exist to paracetamol: cysteamine has been successfully used on overdose victims, but it has to be administered within eight to ten hours of the paracetamol overdose. If it is administered later, it can produce coma.

Does paracetamol damage the kidneys?

Paracetamol is chemically similar to phenacetin which was banned in 1974 from general sale to the public. People who took large quantities of drugs containing phenacetin over a period of years have developed kidney disease. A survey in Britain has found that 500 cases of kidney failure a year were related to phenacetin intake.[22]

(Phenacetin is now banned in Britain.)

Often these victims develop a psychological dependence on their drug cocktails, and it is only after intense questioning that they admit taking these painkillers; so these figures might hide the real situation.

Australian research shows that one-third of the patients needing kidney machines have been hooked on painkillers containing phenacetin, but most of the products taken also contain aspirin.[23] The problem is that aspirin too has been shown to cause kidney damage and aspirin often is combined with paracetamol in over-the-counter medicines. No one yet knows whether the combination of aspirin and paracetamol will be as harmful in the long term as phenacetin mixtures.

Since phenacetin breaks down into paracetamol within two hours of being taken, the possibility remains that paracetamol may also be dangerous to the kidneys, Australian researcher Dr Priscilla Kincaid-Smith has said. 'The implication that preparations are safe because they contain no phenacetin should be avoided. Patients taking mixtures containing paracetamol may relapse in the same way as those taking phenacetin. This is not surprising as the substance concentrated in the papilla (of the kidney) after administering phenacetin is in fact paracetamol.' In 1972 Kincaid-Smith found that kidney failure recurred in a group of patients following the replacement of phenacetin by paracetamol in analgesic mixtures which were advertised in Australia as 'safe'. It is now generally agreed that combinations of painkilling drugs are more harmful than the single ingredients. There is a synergistic (ie additive) effect, for example between aspirin and paracetamol: the side effects of aspirin reduce the blood supply to the kidney, making it less able to cope with the toxic substances contained in paracetamol.

Dr Elizabeth Mollond at the London Hospital has shown that rats fed with mixtures of aspirin and paracetamol suffered much greater kidney damage than those fed the single drugs. This discovery and others like it illustrate the possible need to restrict the sale of drug cocktails containing paracetamol. At present 46 UK products include paracetamol. These include:

Askits (paracetamol + aspirin and codein)
Calpol (children's version of paracetamol)
Codein co (paracetamol + aspirin and codein)
Feminax (paracetamol, codein and caffeine)
Hedex
Panadol
Panadol co (paracetamol + codein)
Solpadeine (paracetamol + codein)
Panadol Elixir
Panasorb
Paragesic (paracetamol + pseudoephedrine and caffeine)
Safapryn (paracetamol + aspirin)
Veganin (paracetamol + aspirin and codein)

Are you sensitive to aspirin?

'Paracetamol is less potent a painkiller than aspirin and has only weak anti-inflammatory properties, but it is less irritating to the stomach', according to the *British National Formulary*.[24]

Apart from the fact that it makes most peoples' stomachs bleed, as many as 20 per cent of asthmatics are sensitive to aspirin. They can develop dramatically increased breathing problems due to blockage of the airways, including wheezing, a running nose and sometimes flushes on the face and a rash just from taking a single aspirin tablet.[25] Other painkillers, including paracetamol, can also produce this reaction in some asthmatics, says an editorial in the *British Medical Journal*.[25] (See also Tartrazene, page 264).

Listerine

Bad breath is caused by many different conditions including throat and tooth infections, food trapped in the teeth, inadequate dental hygiene; and even diabetes, liver and lung disease may result in a certain mouth odour. No mouthwash is going to successfully banish any odours caused by any of those conditions which all clearly need specific and appropriate treatment.

Listerine contains alcohol, benzoic and boric acid and various flavouring substances such as menthol. The first three ingredients may work to reduce the number of bacteria in the mouth, but this effect is very short-lived as the mouth quickly fills up again with bacteria.[26] The dry and furry feeling in the mouth experienced on waking is due to the action of bacteria in the mouth which have been able to get to work overnight whilst the anti-bacterial mechanisms of the mouth have not been active. Otherwise the actions of swallowing, talking and chewing remove bacteria from the mouth during waking periods. Plain water can wash away the 'morning bacteria' just as well as a mouthwash, say US Consumers' Union.[26] They also point out that the alcohol present in Listerine and similar products may damage the mucous membranes in the mouth thereby aggravating any pre-existing inflammation or infection. The use of mouthwashes may therefore increase the likelihood of having a sore throat or a cold. The US FDA does not permit the manufacturers of the mouthwashes such as Listerine to claim that they are of any use for bad breath. In the UK the label on Listerine bottles states, however, that the product is for bad breath.

The garlic trick

Anyone who tries Listerine or a similar mouthwash to get rid of the smell of garlic will not have much success. The odour of garlic does not originate in the mouth and no amount of mouthwash will counter it. Garlic is absorbed into the bloodstream from the intestines. The blood flow through the lungs forces the garlic odour to be exhaled through the breath.[26] Chewing a sprig of parsley is said to be a good way to get rid of unwanted garlic odour, but mouthwash will only make the breath smell fresh for a few minutes.

Hexachlorophene: banned in USA, still available in Britain

Products containing this substance: Phisohex and Phisomed (Winthrop).

Despite a large body of evidence that the antiseptic hexachlorophene is absorbed through the skin and may cause brain damage, paralysis and deaths in the newborn, it remains in 1981 on sale over the counter in Britain. The product called Phisohex contains 0.75% hexachlorophene, and a stronger, prescription-only product called Phisomed (which is also used in hospitals) contains 3% hexachlorophene. In the United States the Food and Drug Administration banned the sale of hexachlorophene over the counter in 1972, and in 1978 advised surgeons, nurses and others to use alternative antibacterial scrubs following reports from Sweden of birth defects after hexachlorophene had been applied to the skin.[27]

Although hexachlorophene has been widely used since the 1940s it was not until the early 1970s that it was discovered that repeated use of this drug led to significant amounts passing into the bloodstream. The major shock finding came from France in 1971 when more than twenty babies died after being dusted with baby powder containing more than 6% hexachlorophene.[28] Winthrop claim their product is safe and cannot cause brain damage. It is a cream, not a powder as in the French cases.

Hexachlorophene accumulates in the blood and the margin of safety between toxic and non-toxic blood levels in humans and animals appears to be narrow, says the American FDA.[29] During the 1960s and 1970s many soap, toothpaste and deodorant products contained hexachlorophene, so that total absorption from all these sources was considerable. Few products were labelled, especially those used on the skin such as deodorants, so the consumer could not choose to avoid this chemical. The FDA also said in 1978 that 'published literature fails to provide assurance that hexachlorophene is safe for use in women who are or could become pregnant.'[29]

Typically, like so many other potentially hazardous products, hexachlorophene is also ineffective. It offers no protection against what are called gram-negative infections (eg the salmonella bug responsible for food poisoning) and its antibacterial action depends on repeated use.[29] In fact, its use has been shown to lead to an *increase* of infections by certain germs like salmonella and it has also been shown to be ineffective against staphylococci bacteria. Studies by Dr I. J. Light and Dr J. Sutherland prompted them to comment that 'routine bathing of infants with hexachlorophene could result in an *increase* in disease caused by gram-positive bacteria eg staphylococci'.[30]

The manufacturers, Winthrop, state in data sheets for doctors that their product Phisomed is to be used for bathing mothers and babies as a measure against cross-infection. They warn later in the data sheet that it is 'not recommended for washing a child under two years of age except on medical advice'. The only indication that it may be absorbed through the skin and cause damage to the nervous system comes with the bold type warning: 'It is important that the baby should be thoroughly rinsed before drying.' Apart from this bland and uninformative warning, there is no hint of the nervous system hazards that hexachlorophene may cause in babies.

Traveller's diarrhoea

'With the wealth of antibiotics and chemotherapeutic agents available at present, it seems difficult to believe that none can be recommended for treating traveller's diarrhoea, but this is indeed so.' – Dr Norman Noah of the UK Public Health Lab.[31]

Not only are antibiotics useless for diarrhoea, they may also be dangerous and they will prolong the agony, says Dr Noah. The *British National Formulary* agrees with him and also states that there is no evidence that antibiotics, sulphonamides or clioquinol are effective in preventing traveller's diarrhoea.[32] The following products (not many of which can be bought over the counter) should be *avoided*, says the guide: Cremostrep (MSD), Enpac (Aplin & Barrett), Flar (Consolidated), Furoxone (Eaton), Guanimycin (A & H), Ivax (Boots), Kaomycin (Upjohn), Lomotil with Neomycin (Searle), Neo Sulfazon (Wallace Mfg), Neovax (Norton), Sulphamagna (Wyeth), Unidiarea (Unigreg) and Uniflor (Aplin & Barrett). People taking these products may also develop resistance to the antibiotic ingredients, which may themselves *cause* further diarrhoea![22]

Some anti-diarrhoea products such as Lomotil, codeine, Kaolin and morphia have the property of reducing the natural reflex movements or contractions of the gut (peristalsis). 'These drugs may do more harm than good', says Noah. He accepts that a business traveller may need them occasionally to attend a vital business meeting but warns that not more than three doses should be taken.

How to treat diarrhoea

Most cases of diarrhoea clear up without the need for any intervention; like colds and flu, they are mostly self-limiting conditions. But it may be advisable to drink plenty of fluids to prevent dehydration. Dr Noah recommends simply adding 5 grams of salt to a litre of water to treat moderate dehydration. Even better, add it to a fruit juice which is rich in potassium and therefore of double benefit.

How to avoid the big 'D' in tropical countries

Drink only bottled water or bottles of Coke, Pepsi, 7-Up or similar. They may rot your teeth, but your stomach will stay in one piece. Avoid raw, unpeeled fruit, vegetables or salads and cooked food unless it is served piping hot. Boil tap water and cover it whilst cooking.

NB An attack of diarrhoea may reduce the effectiveness of oral contraceptives (the pill). (See page 154 for how antibiotics can inactivate the pill.)

The vitamin business

There is a popular myth that since vitamins are 'natural' they are harmless, no matter how large a quantity is consumed. But vitamin A for example taken over a long period of time can, according to the US Food and Drug Administration, 'cause liver and spleen enlargement, painful swelling under the skin, and, in its most serious form, permanent liver damage and stunted bone growth'. Also high doses of vitamin C can cause kidney and bladder problems. Excess amounts of this vitamin can interfere with a common test for sugar in the urine of diabetics. Some studies indicate that doses of vitamin D greater than 1,000 to 1,200 IU (International Units) may contribute to kidney stones and heart attacks.

The American Food and Drug Authority require warning labels to be placed on all vitamin preparations sold over the counter. No such warnings appear on British vitamin products.

Professor Peter Parrish in his book *Medicines – a Guide for Everybody*, echoes the same warning when he says: 'The clear but wrong and misleading message which is being given by the manufacturer and promoters is that if 100 units of a vitamin does you good, then 1,000 units will do you even better.' Later he states also: 'There is no evidence that minor deficiencies of vitamin cause debility or increased risk of getting colds and other infections.'[33]

The Pharmaceutical Society's *Guide to Drugs (Martindale's)* says: 'Many vitamins, often as multivitamin preparations, have been given as "tonics" or with minerals as dietary supplements.' It adds that 'large doses (megavitamins) are sometimes claimed to be effective in cardiovascular (ie heart) and other degenerative disorders', but maintains that there is 'little justification for the use of vitamins for these purposes and vitamin supplements are only indicated if the dietary intake is inadequate'.[34] (See unnecessary *iron* preparations, page 239.)

Typically, it is the unproven and ineffective drug like vitamins which provide the industry with their largest profits. According to a drug trade study of over-the-counter medicines carried out by Euro-monitor of the UK Health Markets in 1978:[35] 'Vitamins and tonics and indigestion remedies emerge as the main areas of real growth.'

Vitamin A – ineffective against most complaints

'There is no justification for the claim that it is the anti-infective vitamin, or that it is of value in the prevention of colds, influenza and other infections', says the Pharmaceutical Society's Guide to prescribing, *Martindale's Pharmacopoeia*.[34] They add that 'neither is there sufficient evidence to warrant claims that it will prevent the formation of kidney stones or that it may be useful in the treatment of anaemia, degenerative conditions or sunburn'.

In the USA the Food and Drug Authority have stated that vitamin A in very high levels can cause acute toxicity, characterised by severe headache, dizziness, nausea, and red and swollen skin. Long-term use of vitamin A can cause enlarged liver and spleen, painful swelling under the skin, and, in its most serious form, permanent liver damage and stunted bone growth. 'As little as 8–16 milligrams daily for as little as thirty days could induce signs of intracranial [in the skull] pressure.'[36] *Martindale's* say 'the incidence of vitamin A poisoning was increasing and might be increased by the use of bizarre highly fortified health foods'.[34]

'There is no proof that vitamin A is of any value against warts, acne and other skin diseases, dry and wrinkled skin, stress ulcers, respiratory infections, or eye disorders. Nor is there any evidence that naturally-occurring vitamin A is superior to the synthetic kind. Labels making such claims

278

should not be permitted,' stated the US Food and Drug Authority.[36]

Also there is 'no convincing evidence' that a product named Sylvasun containing vitamin A and calcium carbonate gives any protection against sunburn, according to the *Drug and Therapeutics Bulletin,*[37] adding that there is strong evidence it does not protect against sunburn. In a trial involving seventy-four Australians who took Sylvasun the night before and also one hour before exposure to the ultraviolet radiation, Sylvasun was found to be no more effective than an inactive placebo drug.

Hazards of vitamin A acne treatment: Retin-A

Retinoic acid sold as Retin-A (by Ortho Ltd) and containing the chemical called Tretinoin may cause an increased risk of skin cancer when used as a treatment against acne. Retinoic acid is a chemical derived from the breakdown of vitamin A and is applied to the affected skin. But in September 1978 the American Food and Drug Authority warned doctors that patients using this product should avoid direct exposure to the sun or sun-ray lamps. Research on mice at Temple University revealed that multiple skin tumours developed in 80 per cent of mice treated with retinoic acid when exposed to simulated sunburn, compared to only 6 per cent of mice left untreated. This increased risk of skin cancer with sunlight is enhanced by retinoic acid, though there is no evidence that the acid on its own will cause skin cancer.[38] Several studies have also shown that large doses of vitamin A are no more effective than a placebo in preventing or curing acne.[39]

Does vitamin A prevent cancer?

'We must take seriously the notion that low vitamin A intake makes people susceptible to cancer.' This was the conclusion of an editorial in *The Lancet*[40] which examined the latest important discoveries about vitamin A and cancer. There is now evidence that vitamin A in massive amounts can inhibit cancer growth in some animal experiments, and that some people who get lung, bladder and stomach cancers have an abnormally low intake and low blood level of vitamin A, and lower than usual consumption of fresh vegetables. But *The Lancet* warns that before smokers are advised to buy vitamin A pills with every

279

packet of cigarettes they should know that some animal experiments also show that vitamin A enhances tumour growth.

Although the application to human disease of results obtained in a laboratory with animals is notoriously difficult and uncertain, says *The Lancet*, nevertheless the animal work is tantalising and exciting. Not only are animals deprived of vitamin A more susceptible to cancer-inducing chemicals, but extra vitamin A has been found to reduce human cancers of the bladder and pre-cancerous developments in the mouth, tongue and larynx. However high doses of vitamin A can produce an illness called hypervitaminosis involving skin changes, liver dysfunction and headache.

It is possible that vitamin A may not itself be a protection against cancer: large increases in the intake of vitamin A only cause a small increase of concentration in the blood stream, says the *British Medical Journal*.[41] British cancer experts Dr Richard Peto and Sir Richard Doll suggest that attempts to increase concentrations of carotene may therefore be more useful. Carotene is a chemical contained in green vegetables and carrots which can be converted into vitamin A by the liver. Most of the promising cancer research on the usefulness of vitamin A applies equally to carotene, say Peto and Doll.

Vitamin B: Niacin or nicotinic acid

Although it reduces cholesterol levels Niacin has been shown to be both useless and dangerous as a treatment for heart disease (see also Atromid-S, page 220). In a five year-long investigation of the effectiveness of Niacin and other cholesterol-reducing drugs it was found that Niacin was no more effective than a placebo (sugar pill) in reducing deaths due to heart disease. However, it did produce a lowered incidence of non-fatal heart attacks, but also an increase in cardiac irregularities (ie non-regular heart beats) and stomach problems.[42]

Niacin is the drug under investigation at present for the treatment of schizophrenia.

Vitamin B6: pyridoxine

The US Food and Drug Authority have declared that there is no evidence that vitamin B6 is useful for preventing kidney stones or controlling vomiting in pregnant women.[43]

Vitamin B6 is also probably ineffective in treating pre-menstrual tension and depression. In one admittedly small study involving thirteen women suffering from these conditions only one woman improved significantly with vitamin B6.[44] It is reported that unless there is a deficiency present it probably has no effect. But some reports show up to 80 per cent success. Judy Lever writes, 'you will probably only feel an improvement when you reach the right dosage', but she warns that more than 200 mg a day can cause gastric acidity.[109]

Do women on the pill need vitamin B6?

Women on the pill *do* have lowered levels of vitamin B6 (as well as lower levels of vitamin B2, C1, folic acid and B12). A deficiency of B6 is thought to be linked with depression and other psychiatric problems – hence its use in pre-menstrual tension and depression. In the USA a contraceptive pill was marketed at one time which was combined with vitamin doses in the hope that it would prevent depression associated with pill use. Professor Victor Wynn writing in *The Lancet* questions this practice and states that a biochemical, as opposed to clinical, evidence for vitamin deficiency is not the same as a nutritional lack of vitamins. 'It is possible that the biochemical changes observed in pill-users are necessary adaptations by the body to the pill,' suggests Professor Wynn. Furthermore pill users would need to take ten times the recommended daily dose in order to obtain normal levels of vitamin B6. 'This may result in dangerous toxic effects of vitamin overdose,' says Professor Wynn.[45]

Does pyridoxine/vitamin B6 hinder breast feeding?

'Most prenatal and other multivitamin preparations include B6. There is now solid research evidence that pyridoxine blocks lactation; it inhibits the secretion of breast milk in nursing mothers . . . one cannot escape the haunting thought that the too frequent failure of present day nursing mothers in developed countries to provide adequate milk for their babies may be due in part to the widespread use of the lactation-inhibiting vitamin B6.'[46]

This provocative letter in the *New England Journal of Medicine* in 1979 brought a chorus of critics down upon its author, Dr Leonard Greentree. They pointed out that only huge pharmacological doses used as drugs may inhibit lactation but that the doses naturally needed by the body (physiological doses) do not cause any harm. Dr Greentree retorted that since most foodstuffs contain this vitamin the deficiency in any case only occurred rarely. He also said that good nutrition was most important for feeding mothers. Reliance on vitamin supplements can make people less careful about what they eat because of the mistaken belief that the supplements will be adequate on their own.

Vitamin B12

A deficiency of B12 can cause pernicious anaemia and psychiatric problems. Strict vegans (ie people who eat only unrefined cereals, pulses, nuts, fruit and vegetables) may need supplements of B12 and vitamins D to prevent any deficiency occurring. It has been shown that a great deal of vitamin B12 is prescribed unnecessarily by doctors for all sorts of conditions for which vitamin B12 is totally ineffective. Professor Archie Cochrane has demonstrated that at least twenty times as much B12 is prescribed than is actually needed by the small number of patients suffering from pernicious anaemia. 'The effect of publishing the article was disastrous,' said Professor Cochrane. 'There was a rapid increase in B12 consumption!'[47]

Stomach surgery may cause inadequate B12 to be absorbed and it has been found that 25 per cent of patients with a history of gastric surgery admitted to mental hospital are suffering from B12 deficiency.[48] The deficiency was believed to be a prime cause of psychiatric illness in 80 per cent of these patients.

'Vitamin' B15 (pangamic acid)

'There is no good evidence that it has any value in the prevention or treatment of any human disorder, or even that it is safe' – this is how the authoritative US *Medical Letter* described 'Vitamin' B15, pangamic acid.[49] It has been promoted as a cure for heart disease, diabetes, cancer, high blood pressure, autism, alcoholism, ageing and fatigue. It is not really a vitamin either. It was misnamed a vitamin by Dr Ernst Krebs who isolated it in apricot seeds. He named it a vitamin because he thought it occurred in all seeds, but in fact it does not.[50]

Laetrile: 'Vitamin B17' – Cancer cure or quack medicine?

Laetrile, or 'vitamin B17' as it is called by its enthusiasts, is an extract from apricot pips which is claimed to be capable of curing cancer. Although laetrile has never been the subject of much controversy in Britain, it has been fiercely and passionately debated in the United States – a country which is more open, some people may say 'obsessed', about cancer, and 'cures' for cancer.

Laetrile enthusiasts tend to view the actions of the US Food and Drug Administration against laetrile as protecting the vested interests of the drug industry. The FDA declared lactrile illegal because of it being worthless and dangerous – capable of causing fatal cyanide poisoning – in 1977, though some American states still permit its sale,[51] as does Britain. There may be some truth in the claims of laetrile supporters, particularly as most orthodox medical treatments against cancer are largely ineffective and highly toxic too (see breast and lung cancer surgery, page 36 and page 62). In America the laetrile controversy is political, long and bitter, and the interested reader is advised to read, for the pro-laetrile view, a book entitled *World Without Cancer – the Story of Vitamin B-17* by G. Edward Griffin, published by American Media but available in Britain from Thorsons or Health Food shops. But to get a balanced view of the debate is very difficult. *New Scientist* has, over the years, reported the issue fairly from both sides. Their Index lists articles on this subject under the heading 'Laetrile'.

It is true that unscrupulous businessmen are selling laetrile at great cost to cash in on a very vulnerable section of the public who may well need protecting. On the other hand, conventional cancer therapy may have failed for these cancer victims and already cost those patients (in the USA) a great deal of money anyway. Who is to say they should be denied a treatment which they believe in – particularly as there *does* seem to be a strong psychological element in some successful cancer cures (see page 39). But in the absence of proof that laetrile really works, and with evidence that it can sometimes cause fatal cyanide poisoning, perhaps the FDA is perfectly justified in taking its strong anti-laetrile policy. They say: 'Diversion of cancer patients from effective therapy remains the major hazard in the promotion and use of laetrile. Tragic results of its use are seen in patients who could have been helped had they continued or undertaken effective therapy.'[51] However, 'effective therapy' is often not available to many cancer patients within the confines of conventional treatment. Unfortunately, it does not exist.

One study, admittedly with a number of shortcomings, published in the *New England Journal of Medicine*[52] in 1978 has given some support for laetrile. It was conducted with the assistance of the US National Cancer Institute who, in view of its results, voted to recommend a proper clinical investigation of laetrile cancer treatment. American doctors were asked to submit cases of patients successfully treated with laetrile. Few doctors responded, as use of the drug is illegal in the US, although immunity from prosecution was guaranteed. Nevertheless of the twenty-two laetrile case histories examined by cancer experts, six patients improved; two experienced a complete disappearance of their cancers, and the other four cases had a 50 per cent improvement. Significantly, perhaps, these six patients had cancer which ordinarily is not known to disappear spontaneously (ie have spontaneous remission). A report in *New Scientist* on this survey comments that the cancer experts used to evaluate these cases were, 'if anything, biased against laetrile'. When they were asked to guess whether a laetrile case had been treated conventionally or with laetrile, no more than three of the twelve panellists ever guessed laetrile.[53]

Does vitamin C stop colds?

Ever since Nobel-winning scientist Linus Pauling published his book *Vitamin C and the Common Cold*, people have been consuming tons of vitamin C tablets in the belief that it will either stop their colds from occurring in the first place, or that vitamin C will reduce the cold symptoms. But nine years after the publication of this book numerous investigations carried out amongst thousands of cold sufferers have failed to show that vitamin C has much effect even in the massive doses recommended by Pauling, though some general improvement has been found in a few experiments. A normal diet should contain at least 30 milligrams of vitamin C daily, according to an editorial in the *British Medical Journal*.[55] It points out that blood cell

Vitamin C

'As has been the case with the other vitamins some people have assumed that if a little is good, a lot will be better. In the case of vitamin C this does not appear to be true . . . the body uses only the amount it needs and eliminates the rest in the urine' – The American Food and Drug Authority 1979.[54]

The *British Medical Journal* wrote in 1976: 'Major advances in treatment are usually apparent after a few well-conducted studies and at present no strong evidence can be found to support the prophylactic (ie preventive) use of vitamin C. Apart from the possibility of long-term side effects it is difficult to escape the conclusion that most of the administered vitamin will be lost in the urine within a few hours of eating it.'[55]

leucocyte levels of vitamin C are reduced when the body is stressed, but that levels return to normal as the symptoms of a cold disappear, on around the fifth day. The fall in vitamin C in blood levels has not been shown to be prevented by taking 1 gram of vitamin C per day, according to the *British Medical Journal*, but the editorial does state that colds can be limited by taking large doses of 6 grams per day from the onset of symptoms.

Aspirin has also been shown to reduce blood cell levels of vitamin C. As many cold sufferers are prone to take aspirin tablets it may make some sense to combine aspirin doses with vitamin C. It is unlikely though that the low levels of vitamin C put with over-the-counter cold remedies will make any substantial difference. Unfortunately, the addition of vitamin C has an effect on the aspirin as well; it slows down its elimination from the body, prolonging and intensifying its effect, says Joe Graedon in his book *People's Pharmacy.*[56] This might be distressing for someone with indigestion or ulcer trouble, conditions which aspirin aggravates.

Scurvy, the vitamin C deficiency disease, can be prevented by eating fruit and vegetables, preferably fresh, raw and uncooked, as cooking destroys about 50 per cent of the vitamin.

Professor Pauling, the patron saint of vitamin C, says that there is nothing to be gained by buying so-called natural vitamin C . 'So-called' synthetic ascorbic acid (the chemical name for vitamin C) is natural ascorbic acid, and is identical to vitamin C in oranges. There is no advantage in buying 'all natural vitamin C', wild rose-hip vitamin C or similar preparations, says Professor Pauling.[57]

The US Food and Drug Authority recommend a daily intake of between 50–100 milligrams of vitamin C to prevent deficiency. But Professor Pauling recommends a minimum daily intake of at least ten times this level to maintain optimal health, rising to over 300 times this level for illness. Who is right? Contrary to popular mythology, large doses of vitamin C can cause serious side effects (see page 288), but on the other hand vitamin C may have a beneficial effect on cancer (see page 289).

The vitamin C cold experiments

Many different experiments involving different doses of vitamin C have been conducted and they are described here so that the reader can decide if any are personally relevant. There is a confusing array of results. One of the earliest full-scale experiments into the effectiveness of vitamin C against colds was conducted in 1967. Ninety-one volunteers were split into two equal groups, and one group took *three* grams of vitamin C daily, whilst the other group took a placebo that looked and tasted like vitamin C, but contained no drug at all. After three days on vitamin C or placebo each volunteer was given nasal drops containing a cold virus. After the resulting colds had run their course it was discovered that there was no difference between the groups in the severity, number and duration of the colds they experienced. This experiment was published in the *British Medical Journal* by Dr G. H. Walker and colleagues and a similar result was published in the *Practitioner* in 1968.[58, 59] This experiment could be criticised on the grounds that these volunteers had not been taking the vitamin C for long enough. This point was taken up by a much more successful Canadian study carried out in 1972 by Dr T. W. Anderson and his team, which must have given a huge boost to vitamin C sales.

Over 800 people took part in a two-month-long study in which half were given *one* gram per day of vitamin C or a placebo (the experiment was double blind, ie neither doctors nor the volunteers knew who was really receiving vitamin C). Anyone who had a cold was instructed to increase their dose to *four* grams during the first three days of illness. The results found that vitamin C *did* reduce illness. It was found that 26 per cent of those on vitamin C remained free of illness, compared to only 18 per cent of those not taking the vitamin; a significant positive finding. The vitamin C group spent 1.3 days 'confined to their house' because of illness, compared to 1.87 days for the placebo group. Also one-third of the patients who increased the dose to four grams once their cold began did not experience any nose or throat symptoms. It seems from this experiment that vitamin C did have some significant effect on the general symptoms of illness rather than preventing the cold itself. It has been suggested that the vitamin may help reduce the body's reaction to stress, or that only certain types of individuals will respond positively to vitamin C, and others will get a cold anyway no matter how much vitamin C they consume. The authors of this investigation refused to make any firm recommendation until more was known about appropriate dosage levels and the safety of prolonged ingestion of vitamin C.[60]

The positive finding, however, stands out almost alone as one of the few successful studies. Unfortunately Dr Anderson himself, when he repeated the experiment in 1974,[61] found on this occasion that 250 milligrams, one gram or two grams daily, did not appear to have a greater preventive action than a totally non-active placebo, against colds and flu. Another two studies reported in the *British Medical Journal* in 1974,[62] found that when over 150 adults took placebo or vitamin C doses of one gram for eighty days there was no difference in the incidence of colds. Several further studies involving doses of vitamin C varying from 50 milligrams daily to three grams daily also failed to find any positive effect of the vitamin.[63, 64] One other study on the effect of vitamin C on over 600 Navajo Indian school children which originally found that one or two grams seemed to result in fewer days off school, was later shown to be inconclusive.[65] Further investigations showed that 'if anything symptoms lasted longer in children with high vitamin C levels in their bloodstream'.

One particular type of bacteria was lower amongst those taking vitamin C, but it had no effect on the incidence of cold symptoms. 'All in all, it seems that the harder researchers look at the vitamin C question the less evidence there is that it does any good,' commented *The Times* science report in 1976.[66]

The just-in-case principle!

These results do not seem to have dampened the general enthusiasm shown by the drug companies and the public for vitamin C cold remedies, and it is possible that many people are taking large doses of vitamin C 'just in case' it works. However it is by no means proven that large doses are as harmless as Professor Linus Pauling and other enthusiasts maintain; a number of serious side effects have been reported in the medical literature. In the US in 1979, the Food and Drug Authority declared that manufacturers should not claim that vitamin C is useful for treating the common cold, after an expert panel had examined all the relevant evidence.[67]

The toxic effects of large doses of vitamin C

The most common and immediate effect of taking large doses of vitamin C is diarrhoea. This is perhaps the least worrying side effect. Kidney stones are also more likely to be formed if one gram or more is ingested daily for several months.[67] The chemical name for vitamin C is ascorbic acid, and if large doses of the acid are excreted through the kidney and bladder there is a tendency for oxalic acid crystals to form in the kidneys. This is especially the case amongst people prone to gout, or in those who eat large quantities of foods high in oxalic acid, for example spinach, rhubarb, chocolate and tea.[67]

Vitamin C may cause infertility

Infertility is another hazard caused by the acid nature of vitamin C. The acid in vitamin C may actually dissolve the mucous tissue in the cervix and make it less permeable to sperm, according to an article in *The Lancet* by Australian Dr M. H. Briggs.[68] He describes cases of women who took more than one gram daily who failed to conceive until they stopped taking high doses of vitamin C (ie 2 grams per day). Dr Briggs recommends that women should take no more than 500 mg per day in order not to reduce their chances of conceiving. Another pregnancy-related hazard has occurred with mothers who have taken between 500 and 1,500 mg per day during pregnancy. A number of newborn babies have been born with scurvy because their system had adjusted to very high concentration during their embryonic development in the womb. This hazard had been discovered originally in animal experiments with guinea pigs. (Incidentally, human milk contains four times as much vitamin C as cow's milk, so babies who are not breast fed do need supplements of vitamin C, in the form of orange juice or other *un*sweetened fruit juices.) Products like Del-Rosa Syrup and Ribena contain a very high proportion of sugar which will rot the milk teeth – even though they do contain vitamin C. Other possible hazards of large doses of vitamin C include scurvy, after abrupt withdrawal of the vitamin. Bone disease can also occur because vitamin C can lead to an increased turnover of bone minerals. Dr Briggs also points out that one of the major breakdown products of vitamin C has been shown to cause diabetes in animal experiments.[68] Vitamin C can also interact with other drugs in a harmful way. It has already been mentioned that the effect of aspirin is increased with vitamin C. The ascorbic acid of vitamin C can also destroy the effect of the erythromycin antibiotics. One glass of orange juice contains enough acid to affect the antimicrobial action of these antibiotics.[69]

'Each of these potential hazards requires proper evaluation, and until such evidence is available the administration of ascorbic acid in doses many times the recommended nutritional requirement seems unjustifiable,' writes Dr Briggs.[70]

Does vitamin C cure cancer?

Several studies have found that cancer patients are severely depleted of vitamin C and that surgery, which they often undergo, further reduces their blood levels of vitamin C. No one disputes that this vitamin is essential for the development of cartilage, bones, teeth and for the healing of wounds. But according to Professor Pauling and one of his co-workers, Dr Ewan Cameron of the Vale of Leven Hospital, Loch Lomondside, Scotland, if people maintained a reasonable intake of vitamin C we would see a diminished incidence of cancer generally. Several uncontrolled studies conducted by Cameron and Pauling on terminal cancer patients do show superficially impressive rates of cancer regression. For example, in one study those patients on vitamin C therapy survived 293 days on average compared to a group of controls who survived only 38 days. In a similar study vitamin C patients survived for 210 days against only 50 days for the control group.[71]

Generally they found that 90 per cent of patients live longer than normally expected and about 10 per cent live a 'remarkably long time with vitamin C. By about the fifth day of treatment most of them report they are feeling better, and their appetites increase. Many of these people come into hospital to die. They are apathetic, on drugs, in bed and they are sick. But many will improve to the point where they will go home and enjoy a significant period of health before they die,' says Dr Cameron.[72] There is evidence that vitamin C maintains the body's immune system, ie it strengthens the body's ability to resist disease, to cast out infections, bacteria and viruses. Will vitamin C therefore help patients injured by the usual drug and radiation therapies used in cancer treatment? The studies carried out in Scotland and similar investigations elsewhere have not been randomised, double blind controlled studies, and for this reason they have been criticised as non-scientific. When an American investigation led by Dr Edward Creagen and his colleagues did perform a strictly double blind experiment with vitamin C therapy on terminal cancer patients,[73] they failed to obtain any significant improvement amongst the vitamin C-treated group. Over 120 terminal cancer patients were studied, half of whom received vitamin C. Ninety per cent of these patients had previously received conventional drugs and radiation therapy, and it was thought that vitamin C might restore their immunity system injured by this previous treatment. On the basis of this result vitamin C may not necessarily have any effect on cancer in patients given conventional treatment previously. But patients received ten grams of vitamin C per day, a dose that Pauling may consider too low to be of benefit, and they also received it at a very late stage of the illness.

New Scientist reported in May 1979 that vitamin C had been found to destroy mouse nerve tumour cells and that it boosted the effects of some anti-cancer drugs, and lowered the effects of other drugs. From some fascinating research findings the report concludes: 'One thing is clear; ascorbate may be useful in the treatment of certain types of cancer, but its indiscriminate use with other drugs is not to be encouraged, as maybe it reacts with other pharmacological agents.'[74]

Further support for the Vitamin C cancer therapy has recently come from Professor J. W. Dickerson of Surrey University, who says that cancer patients do have an abnormally high need for vitamin C. Breast cancer patients, he says, given 3 grams of vitamin C per day, showed no increased levels in their blood, compared to cancer-free patients.

Another factor supporting the theory is that this vitamin has the ability to stop nitrites and nitrates (food preservatives used in processed meats) from turning into the cancer-causing chemical nitrosamine which is believed to be capable of inducing stomach cancer.[75]

Vitamin D

Vitamin D is found in fish (cod liver oil for example) and dairy produce, and can also be made by the body after exposure to sunlight. A deficiency of vitamin D can result in rickets. It has been used in ointments and dressings in the hope of accelerating healing in burns, ulcers and superficial wounds, but controlled experiments have not shown it to be any better than other preparations, according to Martindale's *Guide to Drugs*.[76]

Some studies indicate that doses greater than 1,000 to 1,200 IU (International Units) daily may contribute to kidney stones because of calcium deposits, and heart attacks due to increases in cholesterol urea. There is no reliable evidence that vitamin D lowers blood cholesterol levels or prevents or cures osteoporosis (thinning of the bones) in the elderly according to an expert panel set up by the FDA.[77]

Excessive vitamin D can result in loss of appetite, nausea, headache, diarrhoea, sweating, thirst and vertigo.

Vitamin D and birth defects

A relationship has been found between exposure to excessive amounts of vitamin D during pregnancy and facial and dental abnormalities in babies.[78]

Vitamin E

'Although safe, vitamin E has no proven therapeutic value as a single ingredient drug. However, at a daily dose of 30 IU (International Units) it may be added to combination drugs designed to prevent multiple vitamin deficiencies. But there is *no* evidence that it increases fertility or is useful against cardiovascular disease, peripheral vascular disease, or leg cramps,' according to the American Food and Drug Administration. Its use by athletes is also unlikely to make them win any more medals. There is 'no convincing evidence of improved performance' according to a report in the *British Medical Journal*.[78]

Another report in *The Lancet* found no effect on oxygen consumption either.[80]

'Much of the evidence for the clinical use of vitamin E is inconclusive and in many cases ccnflicting,' says Martindale's *Guide to Drugs*.[51]

Do suntan lotions promote cancer?

Bergasol suntan lotion and many other suntan products contain an oil which has been shown to promote skin cancer in mice when they are exposed to sunlight's ultra-violet rays. This product, which alone accounted for 20 per cent of the market in suntan lotions in 1980, contains bergamot oil, a natural substance derived from citrus fruits. Unfortunately, this oil contains a cancer agent called psolaren. But it is at present at very low levels, say the manufacturers, Chefaro Ltd – just 25 parts per million. At such low levels they hope it won't promote cancer – but it probably won't help a tan either.

It is extremely doubtful that this potentially cancer-causing chemical does anything to enhance a tan, as one researcher, Ingrid Hook of the Dublin School of Pharmacy, has pointed out in the *British Medical Journal*. She says that tan enhancement is only achieved at a psolaren concentration of one per cent, 400 times greater concentration than is used in suntan lotions.

'Products containing bergamot oils should carry a warning that their use could cause cancer in fair-skinned people', says Professor Thomas Fitzpatrick of Harvard University,[81] who believes that the risk is too great to justify their use.

Psolarens may induce cancer by decreasing the body's own immune response – the antibody system that normally protects us from infection and disease. In Britain Professor Ray Bridges of Sussex University, who has shown that psolarens cause or promote cancer in mice, has appealed unsuccessfully to the government to investigate the use of psolarens in suntan lotions.[81] The UK Board of Trade says there is no evidence of cancer effects in humans. British products are not required to label their ingredients, but some say 'oil of bergamot' or that they are made from 'tropical fruit essence', which is also a source of psolarens.

Suntan lotions with a high *skin protection factor* are most affective at screening out the sun's potentially harmful ultraviolet (UV) rays.

Do you really need your glasses?

'It was difficult to understand why glasses with one plain lens and the other weakest in the box were ever prescribed.'[82] These were the comments of two doctors, Catherine Peckham and P. A. Gardiner (a consultant ophthalmologist), who have made a revealing study of why London schoolchildren were prescribed glasses. A national survey of British adolescents showed in 1979 that as many as one adolescent in six could see well without the glasses they had been prescribed.[83] Why are all these glasses being prescribed?

The national survey found that low-power glasses are most frequently prescribed in the more affluent south of England than in the north. 'The central problem is the combination of the professional, offering a diagnosis and a prescription, with the salesman in one individual', explains an eye-opening editorial in the *British Medical Journal*.[84] 'The justification offered by opticians for their closed shop is that before every purchase they can check there is no damaging eye disease', but says the editorial, 'no other country has thought such legislation worthwhile'. Admittedly, some opticians can recognise eye disease at an early stage, particularly glaucoma (raised pressure in the eye) – but routine screening for eye disease is a waste of time except for the relatives of those who already have glaucoma, according to surveys performed in the 1960s.[84] But even if there *were* grounds for routine eye testing, 'it should be done in its own right and not be tied vicariously to the routine selling of spectacles', argues the *BMJ*, 'any more than the sale of toothbrushes should be the monopoly of dentists'!

You cannot damage your eyes even if you have the wrong lenses fitted or if you haven't got glasses at all when you really *do* need them – although of course you will have poorer vision and/or some discomfort in the eyes.[84] 'Yet reminders sent out regularly by many opticians carry the implication that the eyes may be damaged if glasses are not regularly updated.'

Are your children's glasses really necessary?

Why don't adolescents *wear* their glasses? This simple question was asked by London researchers Catherine Peckham and Dr P. A. Gardiner when they investigated the wearing of glasses by 14- and 15-year-olds in the Merton, Sutton and Wandsworth (London) Area Health Authority.[82] The answer they found was that many did not really need their glasses in the first place. When they analysed the prescriptions of 80 pairs of glasses they found that one third seldom or never wore their glasses – but over 70 per cent of the non-wearers had been given glasses of such low power that they made virtually no difference to their vision.

Soft contact lenses

Although soft contact lenses are easier to wear at first for people who have never worn contact lenses, they do have a number of serious disadvantages – quite apart from the bother of having to sterilise them each night by boiling them. There are also now available 'permalenses' which can be left in the eyes, without sterilising, for up to six months or more. Some people find these very acceptable. But a survey of over 1,000 wearers of contact lenses conducted by *Which?* magazine published in June 1974[85] repeatedly came across certain problems with the soft lenses: more than 3 times as many people suffered poor vision, 2½ times as many (soft lens wearers) had sore or inflamed eyes and there were 8 times more cases of damaged lenses amongst the wearers of soft lenses. The report said that it was 'disturbed' to find from the survey that soft contact lens wearers were 2 to 3 times as likely to go back to their practitioners in the first three months because their eyes were sore or inflamed.

The Consumer Association point out that: 'There is no body in this country which like the FDA in the USA insists on manufacturers' evidence and long term clinical trials before soft lens material are available for general use.'

Twice as many soft lens wearers resorted to wearing spectacles on occasions compared to hard lens wearers, and again twice as many soft lens wearers felt that their 'experiment' with soft lenses had been unsuccessful compared to hard lens wearers. Vision was worse, and 10 per cent of soft lens wearers were not happy about the close vision provided by their lenses.

As soft lenses are made from water-attracting plastic which will snap unless it is kept wet, people with particularly dry eyes will not be able to tolerate them. Also a dry atmosphere – as provided by many centrally heated buildings – may dry up the lens and make it uncomfortable. Another hazard is that the water in the lens is the perfect site for bacteria to multiply – hence the increased number of infections or inflammations caused by these lenses. Also the water will absorb fumes and chemicals present in the environment and keep them in long-term contact with the highly sensitive eye tissue.

A further limitation is that although some modern lenses may be able to accommodate 'astigmatism' soft lenses cannot always correct for an irregularly shaped cornea, which is the cause of astigmatism.

The vaccine controversy

Vaccines do not always work and some may not be worth the risk or the bother involved.

The body has to develop its own antibodies once a vaccine is given, and this process can take several weeks to occur. In emergencies patients can be directly injected with antibodies.

Before having any vaccine a doctor should be told of any necessary history (or any relevant family history) of sensitivity to drugs and vaccines, ie bad reaction to a vaccine, allergy or of any ongoing illnesses, or pregnancy.

Hazards of unnecessary smallpox vaccination

Vaccination against smallpox is totally unnecessary nowadays as the disease has been eradicated worldwide. However, some countries still require a certificate of vaccination and this should be avoided as there is considerable risk of complications. A report in the *British Medical Journal* in November 1979 reviewed forty-four cases of patients with complications. The most common hazard was the accidental vaccination elsewhere on the body, mostly on the finger, face and eye. One woman was vaccinated when twenty weeks pregnant: 'She went into spontaneous labour at twenty-eight weeks and was delivered of a baby covered with ulcers, who died,' says the report. There have been no cases of smallpox since 1971 apart from the Birmingham Laboratory outbreak in October 1977. The authors recommend that doctors should consider issuing 'waiver' letters to travellers who are still required (by outdated regulations) to have a certificate of vaccination.

Whooping cough vaccine: Does it work?

This vaccine remains the most controversial vaccine of all because of the possible brain damage it can cause. An accurate assessment of the risk is impossible, says *Martindale's Guide to Drugs*, and estimates that there are about twenty-five cases of brain damage per year in the UK. Risks of brain damage between one in 20,000 and one in 300,000 have been quoted. When damage in the form of convulsions occurs twenty-four hours after the vaccine is given it is difficult to exclude it as a cause. Perhaps the greatest argument against the vaccine is not the side effects, but its lack of effectiveness.

Several studies indicate that whooping cough vaccine is not very effective. A report in *The Lancet*[86] claimed for example that over one-third of all whooping cough patients *had* been previously immunised. A study in Glasgow by leading anti-whooping cough vaccine campaigner Professor Gordon Stewart has shown that the attack rate was influenced three times as strongly by social class than by the 'vaccine acceptance rate'.[87] During the 1970–74 years of the whooping cough epidemic Professor Stewart found there was no difference in the duration, complications and so on whether or not children had been immunised. Low social class, poverty and bad nutrition are the major determinants of the disease. Other surveys have shown that whooping cough vaccine makes no difference to the incidence of whooping cough. For example, Professor Wolfgang Ehrengut found that Hamburg, where little vaccination is done, has the lowest number of whooping cough deaths in W. Germany. But Berlin has a vaccination rate 2½ times as great and a correspondingly higher death rate.[88] The number of deaths from whooping cough in Britain has varied from two to thirteen each year (three in 1976 and eight in 1977) yet the number of cases of brain damage is as high as twenty-five per year.[89]

Precautions that can be taken before having the vaccine
Any child whose family has a history of convulsions or epilepsy, allergy or any infection or illness at the time of vaccination, should avoid this vaccine.

Professor Stewart has found that in many vaccine-damaged children the damage was caused by the second or third injection. Doctors and parents are apparently unaware that a bad reaction is a sign to halt any further vaccinations. Professor Stewart has identified the following signs of vaccine reaction: '. . . persistent crying, or fits lasting up to two days after the injection; shock, rigidity of the body and pallor of the skin the day after the injection; abnormal irritability and interrupted sleep; refusal to eat, or vomiting after food, changes in response to parents; localised paralysis; convulsions'. Babies who are small or premature, or are ill or not feeding well, and babies who suffer from allergies such as eczema or nettlerash, may also be at greater risk.[90]

A campaign led by Jack Ashley, MP, has ensured that British victims of vaccine damage receive financial compensation from the government.

Whooping cough vaccine: latest advice
'The questions surrounding whooping cough vaccination have formed one of the most complex public-health issues of modern times.' Editorial in *The Lancet*.[91]

In May 1981 no fewer than six important new reports were published by the British Dept. of Health on the risks and benefits of whooping cough (pertussis) vaccine. Unfortunately, no clear conclusion emerges from this mass of scientific data. As *The Lancet* puts it: 'One of the few certainties is that the search for a vaccine that is both safe and fully effective must continue.'[91] It adds that, according to government advisers, the balance of risks is in favour of vaccination with stringent attention to conditions which warn against it (see below). 'It would be unjustified, however, to believe that no substantial dilemma exists.'[91]

Do not give your baby a whooping cough vaccine if there is: 'History of seizures, convulsions, or cerebral irritation in the neonatal (during the first month of life) period; history or family history of epilepsy or other diseases of the central nervous system; children with developmental neurological defects; any feverish illness, particularly respiratory, until the patient has fully recovered; *any severe local or general reaction to a preceding dose*. A personal or family history of allergy has in the past been regarded as a contraindication to vaccination, but there is now a substantial body of medical opinion which no longer considers this to be so. Nevertheless, doctors should use their own discretion in the individual case.'[92]

Finally, if you still cannot decide, here is the conclusion of an editorial in the *British Medical Journal*: 'The balance between risks and benefits to the individual tips strongly in favour of the vaccine when vaccination acceptance rates are low and the disease is common; it tips the other way as vaccination rates climb and the disease declines'[93] (ie if there is a local epidemic, it makes sense to vaccinate).

Triple vaccine

This is designed to immunise children against diphtheria, tetanus and whooping cough in one jab.

Again, the incidence of serious side effects is the main worry for parents. In one Swedish investigation of over half a million babies inoculated with triple vaccine, one in three thousand suffered a serious reaction. There were 167 neurological reactions altogether out of a total of 516,276 vaccines administered. They included:

3 cases of brain damage
80 cases of convulsions
14 cases of uncontrollable screaming
2 cases of serious meningitis[94]

The protective effect of diphtheria vaccine is enhanced by whooping cough vaccine, but parents can obtain a diphtheria and tetanus double jab without having the more hazardous whooping cough vaccine.

NAME OF VACCINE	EFFECTIVENESS AND SAFETY
BCG vaccine (the anti-tuberculosis vaccine)	The effectiveness of BCG vaccine against TB is highly variable. In a major trial in India, involving 260,000 people, not only was it proved to be totally ineffective but more cases of TB occurred in those vaccinated than in the placebo group! In England, on the other hand, 78 per cent of people were successfully immunised in a Medical Research Council trial. 'BCG has yet to prove its worth in the Third World where it is most needed.'[95]
Cholera vaccine	A course of two injections (with at least a week's interval) may immunise 50 per cent of patients for up to six months, says *Martindale's Guide to Drugs*.[96] But the vaccine is ineffective in controlling cholera amongst the family contacts of patients.[97]
Cold vaccine	'Though there is little evidence that the vaccines have any preventive value they have been widely used,' says *Martindale's*.[96] The vaccine consists of mixtures of several species of bacteria.
Diphtheria vaccine	Vaccine is highly effective but can sometimes, but rarely, cause polio. It should not be given during an outbreak of polio. 'Except in children aged ten or under, a "Schick test" should be performed to determine if any strong reaction is likely,' advises *Martindale's*.[96] Three doses are needed and should be completed by the age of four months.
Influenza vaccine	In 1976 President Ford authorised a nationwide vaccination programme against swine flu. The project ran into difficulties from the start and was abandoned after the vaccine was found to be causing paralysis and deaths amongst the elderly. Since flu can be caused by a collection of diverse viruses, it is quite possible to be successfully vaccinated against Hong Kong strain and then still succumb to England strain. Protection lasts two or three months and may be effective in 70 per cent of those immunised according to *Martindale's*.[96] In one study at a boys' school 26 per cent of those

NAME OF VACCINE	EFFECTIVENESS AND SAFETY
	vaccinated still got flu compared to 35 per cent of those who did not receive a vaccine.[98] A report in *The Lancet* states that after two years a study of 50,000 people showed that influenza vaccine made no difference to absenteeism.[99] One study reports moderate success. Those vaccinated had fevers which were half as long as those who remained unvaccinated.[100] It would appear that on the whole the vaccines are still more trouble than they are worth. In Britain members of the General and Municipal Workers Union have called for a full inquiry (into the effects of the vaccines) after nine of its members suffered persistent and distressing side effects of a flu vaccine. Tiredness, cramp, heaviness in limbs, dizziness and nausea were not uncommon symptoms.[101]
Measles vaccine	This vaccine is effective in 90 per cent of children and lasts about eight years, and is best given in the third year of life. This vaccine is killed by disinfectants and antiseptics so it will not work if they have been used to sterilise a syringe before use. Strong reactions to the vaccine are not uncommon. In one survey 32 per cent of children had a general reaction (such as fever and skin rash), which was severe in 6 per cent.[102] But the risk of neurological disorders, ie brain damage, is very low according to an American survey of 51 million children vaccinated. It occurred about once in every 600,000 cases. It should not be given to children sensitive to egg protein or those with a history of convulsions, TB or cancer.
Mumps vaccine	Works in 90 per cent of cases and protects those vaccinated for six years. It should not be given to children less than a year old because any antibodies still present from the mother might make it ineffective.
Hepatitis vaccine	An injection of immunoglobin a week before travelling to a suspect area provides immunity for about six months according to a report in *The Lancet* on over a thousand overseas volunteers.[103]
Polio vaccine	'Live' polio vaccine (of the 'Sabin' variety) is highly effective. It has virtually no risks attached to its use. Unvaccinated parents should receive a dose of vaccine when their baby is vaccinated because the vaccine given to a baby can cause

NAME OF VACCINE	EFFECTIVENESS AND SAFETY
	severe reactions in parents. Excreted live vaccine can become virulent. The risk of polio is greatest in young adults and adolescents.[104] Pregnant women should not be vaccinated as the vaccine has been found to cause a 20 per cent increased risk of stillbirths during the first four months of pregnancy. Also because polio vaccine may contain small amounts of antibiotics it should be given with care to those people who are sensitive to antibiotics. The risk of getting polio from the vaccination is very remote, equal to one in 4 million.[105]
Rubella vaccine – to protect against German measles	Rubella vaccine is routinely offered to all girls over the age of eleven, and to women who have given birth to babies who are found to be not already immune. If German measles is caught by a woman during pregnancy it can result in a physically or mentally handicapped baby. For similar reasons, following vaccination, women must not get pregnant for two months afterwards. It is disturbing to discover that it is standard practice in some hospitals to routinely give women doses of the injectable contraceptive Depoprovera at the same time as vaccinating against rubella.[106] Depoprovera is thought by some authorities to increase the risk of cancer (see page 142).
Smallpox vaccine	SEE MAIN TEXT.
Tetanus vaccine	A highly effective vaccine that can also prevent the disease occurring in the newborn. It was so effective in preventing tetanus during World War Two that there were only twelve recorded cases amongst 2,785,819 hospital admissions for wounds and injuries! Of these, six were not properly immunised and two received no booster shots at the point of injury.[107]
Triple vaccine	SEE MAIN TEXT.
Typhoid vaccine	Protection takes a month to develop, lasts for two years and works in about 70 per cent of people vaccinated. Two doses are needed 4–6 weeks apart and reinforcing doses every three years, according to *Martindale's Guide to Drugs.*[108] Paratyphoid is much less effective than typhoid vaccine.

NAME OF VACCINE	EFFECTIVENESS AND SAFETY
Typhus vaccine	Vaccine does not protect completely against typhus, but does reduce the severity of the disease. Two or three doses are needed at 7–10-day intervals.[108]
Whooping cough vaccine	SEE MAIN TEXT.
Yellow fever vaccine	Immunity takes ten days to develop and should last for up to ten years.[108]

Health Shock Post-script

The medical hypocrisy: the flight from science

In a bitter editorial attack on alternative medicine in the columns of the *British Medical Journal* at the beginning of 1980, the following complaint was made:

'What is wrong is the refusal by the critics and the fringe practitioners to accept the standards of proof that medical scientists have developed in the past hundred years.' It is claimed that orthodox medicine has a proud record, and it continued:

'Not for nothing has the concept of the randomized, double blind controlled trial been described as one of Britain's most important contributions to medicine since the war.'

Headed: 'The flight from science', the editorial managed somehow to equate opposition to nuclear power with fringe medicine and the growth of medical consumerism. It went on in the same way:

'Outside medicine, the public mood has swung away from the unquestioning admiration of science and technology that reached its peak at the time of the NASA flights to the moon. Nuclear power is now seen as a threat, not a hope for the future. The motor car is evil, jet aircraft are noisy, polluting and unsafe'[1] and so on. Environmentalists, consumerists, *and* fringe practitioners are seen together as a threat to science and orthodox medicine, in particular.

But is it really true that fringe practitioners have failed to evaluate their treatments, and has orthodox medicine any right to be proud of its controlled trials? According to the one man who has been most responsible for evaluating medical treatment in Britain, the medical profession's record is not all that impressive. Professor Archibald Cochrane, former head of the Medical Research Council's Epidemiology Unit in Wales, recently described why he bestowed his wooden spoon award on gynaecologists and obstetricians.[2] In his opinion, they have forced upon thousands of women and their babies unproven and possibly harmful treatments. They failed to see if low-risk pregnant women needed to have their babies in hospital. 'This was followed by a determined refusal to allow "Pap smears" to be randomized (evaluated) with disastrous results for the whole world. Then having filled the emptying beds by getting nearly all pregnant women into hospital the obstetricians started to introduce a whole series of expensive innovations without any rigorous evaluation . . . the speciality reached its apogee in 1976 when they produced 20% fewer babies at 20% more cost. G & O stands for gynaecologists and obstetricians, but it could also stand for GO ahead without evaluation! After due thought and meditation (but without prayer) I awarded them the wooden spoon.'

Professor Cochrane is not a lone critic; when two rheumatologists from Manchester University published an investigation into alternative forms of treatment for rheumatism and backache they also observed that: 'The theoretical foundation for much orthodox practice is either frankly pragmatic or as dubious as that of heterodox (alternative) practice.'[3] They found that *conventional* medical treatment for rheumatism and backache was largely ineffective and that as many as 200,000 people were happy to *pay* to see an osteopath or chiropractor each year. This is the same number as those who go to out-patients' clinics, free of charge, within the NHS. Drs Hewitt and Wood who carried out this survey observe that petty prejudice against fringe medicine is often irrational. 'Most orthodox medical practitioners are suspicious and sceptical of heterodox (ie alternative) activities because of their apparent dependence upon unsubstantiated theories. But this is to neglect the prior question. Both types of practitioners need to recognise that what matters is whether a procedure is effective; why it may be so is immaterial, until one is assured that it is effective.'[3]

After 'The flight from science' editorial was published, the *British Medical Journal* printed several letters from doctors who defended the record of alternative medicine. Four doctors from the Royal Free Hospital wrote: 'We were surprised to read your attack on alternative medicine . . . despite your statement to the contrary it does read rather like the reflex action of a defensive and autocratic profession.'

'You mention none of the papers which begin to provide the scientific proof you claim to be seeking, nor any of the journals or other publications in this area. You mistakenly group all the "alternatives" together despite the fact that they are as diverse as any collection of medical sub-specialities. Few in fact claim the universality of which you accuse them. The public's questioning of medicine should be both encouraged and educated, for it indicates active interest in taking responsibility for one's illness, which is surely still a basic requirement for healing. It is a pity that some so-called medical scientists take flight from science under the excuse of respectability when they themselves refuse to examine the available observations. That is not science; it may be prejudice. Why is reaching out into the unknown such a threat? It may be out of a desire to protect patients; that is commendable, for certainly some alternative medicines are either useless or dangerous, but then so are some orthodox ones.'[4]

A Nottingham doctor, Shah Ebrahim, also wrote: 'One possibility is that these practitioners are charlatans peddling their skills on an innocent public. Another possibility, which I favour, is that these practitioners are giving people something that they want and something, moreover, that orthodox medicine seems to have forgotten in the scientific age – that is, a humane, listening ear, a sympathetic understanding and a degree of hope.'[5]

Likewise it is often suggested that people who have a natural capacity to heal either through their own personal charisma, personality, warmth or 'healing power', call it what you will, should be the ones who treat patients. 'Successful practice does not necessarily mean that one has altered the natural history of the patient's condition. It may signify that one has been kind or sympathetic or that something concrete has been done and that you have projected your own confidence,' say Drs Hewitt and Wood in their perceptive article.[3] Does this not mean that the techniques of selecting doctors for medical school training should be made to take these 'charisma' factors into account? Could it also mean that many 'doctors' are not qualified in this sphere, whereas many 'fringe practitioners' may be highly gifted in this matter? (See placebos, page 9.)

Almost every account of the various types of alternative medical treatments begins by pointing out that people turn to these treatments after everything else has failed. But why should alternative medicine only be tried as a *last* resort? If it has been shown to be effective and safe surely many people would want to turn to it first, and not last. Contrary to popular belief a number of alternative medical treatments have been scientifically tested under controlled conditions and have been shown to be effective. Today's fringe or alternative therapy is often tomorrow's orthodoxy. Herbalists in 'primitive' societies have been using quinine, digitalis and plants to control infection and sexual cycles for thousands of years. Now refined and processed by the drug industry, they have become part of modern pharmacology. Biofeedback, transcendental meditation, acupuncture and homoeopathy have been investigated by scientists and evidence of their effectiveness and safety has been published in reputable medical journals, but they are virtually ignored by orthodoxy despite the published evidence that they work. There are admittedly a large number of alternative medical treatments which have never been evaluated and probably never will be, but a few notable exceptions are clearing the path and putting homeopathy, acupuncture and others on the medical map.

Unfortunately, there is no room in this present book to describe the scientific successes of alternative medicine.

The author hopes that the evidence accumulated in *Health Shock* has shown that orthodox and fringe medicine through history to the present day have both been dependent on fads and fashion. Slowly the process is becoming open and objective. The medical profession's awakening consciousness must surely be matched by a public responsibility, by patients, to remain equally open and objective. But the ill are illogical.

Perhaps the only way to avoid this trap is to prevent ourselves becoming patients, by changes in lifestyle, diet, environment and our personal relationships. As Eric Cassell, MD, says in his perceptive essay, *The Healer's Art*: 'People are not healthy because they became sick and were made better, but because they didn't get sick in the first place.'[6]

Cheers.

The *Health Shock*
Gossip Column

A review of the year 1981

'Why don't you come over to Switzerland for a few days so that you can get these criticisms in perspective?' This generous offer was made by an internationally famous drug firm to the *Daily Mirror* after the paper had decided to serialise the first edition of *Health Shock*.

'Many newspapers would have been intimidated by the drug industry's barrage of legal and psychological pressure designed to stop publication,' admits Michael Hellicar, the *Mirror*'s special writer in charge of serialisation. 'Constant phone calls at home, threatening cables and telexes sent to the *Mirror*'s chief lawyer and editor put immense pressure on the newspaper, but this just encouraged us to go ahead.' In 25 years of journalism Hellicar said he had never come across an industry so defensive and bullying as the drug industry.

'On a worldwide scale the drug industry must be intimidating many hundreds of editors with the result that the public rarely hears about useless and hazardous drugs', says Hellicar. Indeed in Australia, where *Health Shock* was widely acclaimed by the press, legal threats made by the drug industry prevented its nationwide syndication.

As long as many 'medical journalists' remain public relations consultants to the drug firms, it is unlikely that the situation will improve. Many magazines sent to doctors 'free of charge' depend on drug company advertising and thereby are unable to discuss drug safety and effectiveness in any independent way. The result is that many doctors haven't a clue about the side effects of the drugs YOU are prescribed.

The biggest bombshell of the year was undoubtedly the publication, by the British Medical Association and the Pharmaceutical Society, of a doctor's guide to prescribing which black-listed over 600 drugs, many of them top sellers.

BBC's *Man Alive*'s riveting investigation into the ethical practices of the drug industry in Switzerland was delayed by legal moves but finally hobbled bravely onto the screen with certain bits missing. The BBC's devastating *Panorama* programme on 'brain death', entitled 'Are the Donors Really Dead?', though definitely one-sided, evoked a general refusal by British doctors to admit that UK criteria for brain death might possibly be inadequate compared to the much tighter standards in the USA and elsewhere. The medicalisation of life portrayed by Ian Kennedy in the BBC's Reith Lectures series, entitled 'Unmasking Medicine', included the suggestion that we must become the masters of medicine, not its servants.

The UK Dept of Health scrapped (on the grounds of cost) two vital safety monitoring schemes recommended by the government's own safety advisors. The *British Medical Journal* reported that many drug firms still provide doctors with 'incomplete, vague, misleading and frankly dangerous' information on drug side effects (see page 157).

A. H. Robins Ltd finally advised doctors in October 1980 to remove any remaining Dalkon shields (IUD-type contraceptive devices), five years after they stopped distributing these products (see page 138 for details of the hazards of this IUD). A damning report from the UK's National Radiological Protection Board published the same month revealed that safety standards had not got any better for 20 years despite the availability of safety-protection devices (see page 114 for full report).

The World Health Organisation has drawn up a list of 220 essential drugs, and meanwhile we are still surrounded by many thousands of dubious drug products that go on selling . . . drugs banned in the UK and USA still turn up in Third World countries. In February 1981 it was widely reported that the US-owned Squibb drug company continued to sell a dangerous anti-diarrhoea drug (Quixalid) despite repeated evidence that it caused blindness. A woman who obtained the drug in Saudi Arabia received damages from Squibb after going blind. Read Charles Medawar's excellent *Insult or Injury?* and his later *Drug Disinformation* (published by Social Audit, London W1) for more drug horror stories in the Third World.

A TV documentary screened in 1981 interviewed an executive of an American-owned private clinic in Britain, who admitted that his company was primarily interested in quick, fast-turnover, high-profit operations such as surgery on tonsils and hernias. As Bernard Shaw said many years ago, 'of all the anti-social vested interests, the worst is the vested interest in ill health' (*The Doctor's Dilemma,* 1911, from the Preface on Doctors). Take care!

Basic Sources

Medical jargon is much like any other language; once you have mastered the basic vocabulary, the veil of secrecy disappears. No one should be intimidated by medical language. It is a precise technical language because medicine by its very nature needs to be precise and technical.

Once you have unravelled an article in *The Lancet* or the *British Medical Journal* you may feel, as Bernard Shaw observed in 'The Doctor's Dilemma', that 'all professions are a conspiracy against the laity'. All you need is an inexpensive medical dictionary (see below), and the closed doors of pages of medicine miraculously open with ease.

Here's a tip if you decide to follow up any of the 500 or more references in *Health Shock*. Go to the most recent reference, since it will always carry a list of previous references you may be interested in following up on that subject.

If you haven't got a reference to follow, you can look up any medical subject in *Index Medicus*, a monthly summary of everything published in the world concerned with medicine! It is collated into an annual volume at the end of every year. If you get totally stuck, write to the authors of any medical papers you can find (an address is always provided on the front page of medical papers). Alternatively, some public libraries have computer links which take the slog out of searching for information. A small fee is charged for this service, but it is very good value for money. Remember to use your librarians – they are very knowledgeable people who really seem to enjoy finding facts that aren't easily available. The beaming smile on a librarian's face who has just found a paper that no one else could find is a very joyous sight to behold!

If there were one book above all others that I believe is worth owning, it is *The British National Formulary* (1981 edition, or the latest edition available). It was written for doctors to advise them how to prescribe, and as a result it is very simply and clearly written and is probably the most authoritative guide to drugs in the world, published by the British Medical Association and the Pharmaceutical Society. The great asset of the *BNF* is that it tells you which drugs to avoid and offers you the better, safer alternatives.

Medical dictionary

Livingstone's pocket medical dictionary by Nancy Roper is inexpensive and very useful. It will help you decipher the most jargon-filled editorials in any medical journal. Armed with this or a similar dictionary, you will be able to do your own research into unnecessary or hazardous treatment.

Medical journals worth reading or checking for information

(All these journals have an annual or six-monthly index.)

The British Medical Journal (BMJ)
The Lancet
The Drug and Therapeutics Bulletin
Prescriber's Journal
The New England Journal of Medicine (NEJM)
Medical Letter

There are also many 'give-away' medical newspapers and magazines such as *Pulse, Doctor, World Medicine* and so on. Sometimes they do have very good features in them, but as they rely on drug company advertising they tend not to write about useless, hazardous or unnecessary medicine. Much better is to go to *independent* sources, particularly the *Drug and Therapeutics Bulletin,* which is published by the Consumer's Association. The DHSS pays for all GPs to receive copies of the bulletin, and it does not have to please any advertisers. But don't ignore journals full of drug company ads – they are most revealing, showing some of the drug firms at their worst as they often use sexist or one-sided messages to sell their dubious products to YOUR doctor!

Further Reading

Drugs

Best drug guide available (very strongly recommended): The British National Formulary (1981), jointly published by the BMA and the Pharmaceutical Society (new updated editions will be published twice a year)

Medicines – a Guide for Everybody by Professor Peter Parrish (Penguin, 1976).

The Medicine Men by Dr Vernon Coleman (Arrow, 1977).

Martindale's Extra Pharmacopoeia, published by the Pharmaceutical Society. Ultimate work of reference, but may be hard to obtain.

The Medicine Show, US Consumers' Union (Pantheon, 1976). Only available in USA, but well worth a trip to obtain it!

The People's Pharmacy by Joe Graedon (Avon, NY, 1976) (volumes 1 and 2). (Again only available in USA)

General

Effectiveness and Efficiency by Professor Archibald Cochrane (Nuffield Provincial Hospitals Trust, 1972).

Medical Nemesis – the Limits to Medicine by Ivan Illich (Penguin, 1975).

The Doctor's Dilemma by George Bernard Shaw (Penguin, 1979).

The Role of Medicine by Professor Thomas McKeown (Nuffield Provincial Hospitals Trust, 1976).

Prevention and Health: Everybody's Business (DHSS, 1979).

The Healer's Art by Eric Cassell MD (Penguin, 1979).

Man, Environment and Disease in Britain by G. Melvyn Howe (Penguin, 1976).

The Medical Risks of Life by Dr Stephen Lock and Dr Tony Smith (Penguin, 1976).

Particularly for Women

The New Women's Health Handbook edited by Nancy MacKeith (Virago, 1978).

Fat is a Feminist Issue by Susie Orbach (Hamlyn Paperbacks, 1978).

Our Bodies, Ourselves edited by Angela Phillips and Jill Rakusen (Penguin, 1978).

The Good Health Guide for Women by Cynthia Wentworth Cooke MD and Susan Dworkin (Hamlyn Paperbacks, 1981).

Childbirth

The Experience of Childbirth by Sheila Kitzinger (Penguin, 1978).

Living with Your New Baby by Elly Rakowitz and Gloria S. Rubin (Hamlyn Paperbacks, 1981).

Psychotherapy

Psychology and Medicine by S. J. Rachman and Clare Phillips (Penguin, 1978)

The Handbook of Psychotherapy and Behaviour Change edited by Garfield and Bergen, 2nd edition (Wiley, USA, 1978).

A Complete Guide to Therapy by Joel Kovel (Penguin, 1978).

In Our Own Hands by Sheila Ernst and Lucy Goodison (The Women's Press, 1981).

Alternative Medicine

Natural Medicine by Brian Inglis (Fontana, 1980).

Alternative Medicine by Robert Eagle (Futura, 1978).

Try Being Healthy by Dr Alec Forbes (Langdon, 1976).

Rights of Patients

Health Rights Handbook by Gerry and Carol Stimson (Prism Press, 1978 and Penguin, 1980).

Acknowledgements

I believe that this book owes most to the librarians and press officers who helped me find the material quoted throughout the book. I wish particularly to thank the librarians and press officers of the British Medical Association and the Pharmaceutical Society. I owe a special mention to Angela Shivers, Press Officer at the Pharmaceutical Society.

I wish to thank my friends Dr Chas Todd and Dr Amanda Howe and (my wife) Lynn Maddern for reading my early drafts and making invaluable comments (though they are in no way responsible for any errors or omissions). During my research for the book I visited many medical institutions in Britain and the USA, talked and corresponded with numerous medical specialists. There is no room to thank them all but I am particularly grateful for advice from the following people.

In Britain: Dr Andrew Herxheimer, Editor of the *Drug and Therapeutics Bulletin*, Professor Denis Hawkins of Hammersmith Hospital, Dr Jonathan Kersley, Dr Charles Du V. Florey of St Thomas's Hospital, Dr Jean Weddell, Mr Anthony Steel of Moorfield's Eye Hospital, Professor Archibald Cochrane and Dr Peter Ellwood of the MRC Epidemiology Unit in Cardiff, Dr Alan Long of the Vegetarian Society, Dr Sheila Peace of MIND, Rosemary Fost of the National Childbirth Trust, Mrs J. Burton of the Office of Population Censuses and Surveys, Dr Richard Mackarness, and the Family Planning Information Service. Also a special thanks to my friends: Dr Walia Kani of Durham University, Dr Elahe Madjd and Dr Betty Groves and Professor Philip David, who went out of their way to help answer my questions.

In the USA: The Press and Information Officers of the Food and Drug Administration (the FDA) in Washington DC and Rockville, Maryland. Dr Sidney Wolfe of the Public Citizens' Health Research Group, Prof. John McKinlay of Boston University, Prof. Mark Field of Harvard University, Dr John Stoekl of Massachusetts General Hospital, Dr Philip Cole and Prof. Benjamin Barnes of Harvard School of Public Health, Dr Samuel Shapiro and Dr Dennis Slone of Boston University Drug Epidemiology Unit. A special thank you to my friends Bob

Richards and Anne Wheelock of Boston for moral and practical support.

A very special thanks to Elaine Levine for transforming my scrawl into a typewritten manuscript and the Editor and Deputy Editor of the *Sunday Mail*, Clive Sandground and Noel Young, for originally publishing my 'Health Versus Medicine' series and for suggesting that I write this book.

Also to my literary agent Michael Sissons of A. D. Peters & Co for advice and encouragement throughout the period of writing this book. I wish to thank particularly Jack Angell, John Shillingford and Sarah Wallace of David & Charles for their patience, skill and ability in coping with the problems of producing this book.

Many thanks to the hundreds of researchers and authors whose works I have quoted through the book who I hope will accept a citation of their work in lieu of an acknowledgement.

Last, but not least, I must thank the brilliant cartoonist ffolkes for adding some sparkling touches of humour with his drawings.

London, July 1980

In addition, I would like to thank the following people for their help in the preparation of this revised paperback edition of *Health Shock*: Professor Michael Rawlins of Newcastle-upon-Tyne University, Judy Graham, Professor Gordon Stewart of Glasgow University, Dr David Ryde, Dr Andrew Herxheimer, Dr Vicky Rippere of the Institute of Psychiatry in London, Michael Hellicar of the *Daily Mirror*, Carol Pengelly and Tony Mullicane, Dr Paul Schatzberger and finally Nina Shandloff of Hamlyn Paperbacks for her patience and understanding in dealing with my endless revision. I would also like to thank the many other individual readers who have written to me since the publication of the first hardback edition.

Martin Weitz
London, November 1981

REFERENCES

Introduction
1. Marty, C. R. *BMJ,* no. 6199, 10 Nov. 1979, p. 1194.
2. Editorial. *Lancet,* 13 Dec. 1975, pp. 1189-91.
3. *The British National Formulary,* no. 1, 1981.
4. Doll, R. *Nature,* vol. 265, 17 Feb 1977, p. 589.
5. McKinlay, J. B. *Soc. Policy,* vol. 8, no. 29, 1978.
6. Owen, D. *In Sickness and in Health.* Quartet, London, 1976.
7. DHSS. *Prevention and Health: Everybody's Business,* 1976.
8. *Which?,* Jan. 1974.
9. Wade, O. L. *Adverse Reactions to Drugs.* Heinemann, 1970.
10. Lesser, E. *New Scientist* (editorial), vol. 1053, 26 May 1977, p. 442. See also M. Muller, vol. 1025, 4 Nov. 1976, pp. 288-9
11. Cochrane, A. L. *Effectiveness and Efficiency.* Nuffield Provincial Hospitals Trust, 1975
12. Herxheimer. A. 'How to make the most of your doctor,' *Lancet,* 11 Dec. 1976, p. 1294.

Part One: Doctors
1. Korsch, B. *Scientific American,* vol. 227, 1972.
2. Editorial. *BMJ,* no. 6199, 10 Nov. 1979, p. 1168.
3. Rachman, C. and Philips, C. *Psychology and Medicine.* Pelican, 1978.
4. Shapiro, A. and Morro, L. (Garfield and Bergin, eds.) *Handbook of Psychotherapy and Behaviour Change.* Wiley, 2nd edn., 1978.
5. Rosenthal, R. *Experimenter Effects in Behavioral Research.* Appleton Century Crofts, NY, 1966.
6. Cochrane, A. L. *Effectiveness and Efficiency: random reflections on health services.* Nuffield Provincial Hospitals Trust, 1972.
7. *New Scientist,* vol. 85, no. 1196, 28 Feb, 1980, p. 653.
8. Dunnell, K. and Cartright, A. *Medicine Takers, Prescribers and Hoarders.* Routledge & Kegan Paul, 1972.
9. Office of Health Economics. *The Health Care Dilemma, or 'Am I Kranken Doctor?'* OHE, 1975.
10. Holmes, T. and Rahe, R. *Journal of Psychosomatic Research,* vol. 11, 1967, pp. 213-18.
11. *See* reference 3 above.
12. Janis, I. *Stress and Frustration.* Harcourt Brace, NY, 1971.
13. Lazarus, R. *Psychological Stress and the Coping Process.* McGraw-Hill, NY, 1966.
14. *See* reference 3 above.
15. Egbert, L. et al. *NEJM,* 270, 1964, p. 825.
16. *See* reference 3 above.
17. Rutter, M. *Maternal Deprivation Reassessed,* Penguin, 1972.
18. Melamed, B. G. (Rachman, S. ed.) *Contributions to Medical Psychology.* Pergamon Press, 1977.

Part Two: Hospital Hazards
1. Mather, H. et al. *BMJ,* vol. 3, 1971, p. 334.
2. Cochrane, A. L. 'A critical review with reference to the medical profession', *Office of Health Economics. Medicine for 2000.* London, 1979.
3. Cochrane, A. L. *Effectiveness and Efficiency.* Nuffield Provincial Hospitals Trust, 1972.
4. Bunker, J., Barnes, B. and Mosteller, F. (eds.). *Costs, Risks and Benefits of Surgery.* OUP, NY, 1978.
5. Wolfe, S. Public Citizens' Health Research Group, before US Subcommittee on Oversight and Investigations on Unnecessary Surgery, 15 July 1975.
6. McKinlay, J. B. *Social Science & Medicine,* vol. 13A, no. 5, Aug. 1979, pp. 541-58.
7. Crile Jnr, G. *Hospital Physician,* vol. 11, 1975, p. 34.
8. Spodick, D. et al. Letter. *Lancet,* vol. 1. 1978, p. 1214.
9. Barnes, Benjamin. *See* reference 4 above, p. 109.
10. Barsamian, E. *See* reference 4 above, p. 212.
11. Cobb, L. A. *NEJM,* vol. 260, 1959, p. 1115.
12. Dimond, E. G. *Circulation,* vol. 18. 1958, p. 712.
13. Smithells, R. W. *Post Graduate Medical Journal,* vol. 15, 1975, p. 39.
14. Editorial. *World Medicine,* 2 May 1980, p. 5.
15. See reference 5 above.
16. McCarthy, J. *NEJM,* vol. 291, 1974, p. 1331.
17. *Drug and Therapeutics Bulletin,* vol. 18. no. 2, 1980, pp. 7-8.
18. Adler, M. W. et al. *Journal of Epidemiology and Community Health,* no. 32, 1978, pp. 136-42.
19. Eagle, Robert. 'Hospitals that won't let go.' *Sunday Times Magazine,* 19 Sept. 1976, p. 19.
20. Franco, J. A. *Clin. Orthop.,* vol. 122, 1977, p. 231.
21. Editorial, *Lancet,* 17 Mar. 1979, p. 593.
22. OPCS, Personal communication, 1979.
23. Editorial. 'Fit for anaesthesia?' *Lancet,* 23 and 30 Dec. 1978, pp. 1350-1.
24. Singh, P. and Hancock, K. Letter. *Lancet,* vol. 2, no. 8155, 15 Dec. 1979, p. 1307.
25. Vessey, M. P. and Nunn, J. F. 'Occupational Hazards of Anaesthesia', *BMJ,* vol. 281, 13 Sept. 1980, pp. 696-8.
26. Lunn, J. L. *Lecture Notes on Anaesthetics.* Blackwell Scientific Publications, 1979
27. *Nursing Standard,* 8 May 1978.
28. Doctor, 13 Apr. 1978, p. 20.

Part Three: Surgery
1. Editorial. *Lancet,* 13 Mar. 1976, pp. 573-4.
2. Muldoon, M. J. *BMJ.* vol. 1, 1972, p. 84.
3. Neil, J. R. *Lancet,* vol. 2, 11 Oct, 1975, pp. 699-700.
4. Braunwald, E. Editorial. *NEJM,* vol. 297, no. 12, 22 Sept. 1977, p. 663.

317

5. Rosati, R. A. et al. *Postgraduate Medical Research Journal,* no. 52, 1976, pp. 749–756.
6. European Coronary Surgery Group. *Lancet,* vol. 1, 28 Apr. 1979, p. 889.
7. Stoll, B. A. 'New aspects of breast cancer.' *Chicago Year Book.* Medical Publishers Inc. 1975.
8. Faulder, Carolyn. *Breast Cancer: a Guide to Early Detection.* Pan, London, 1979.
9. Editorial, *Lancet,* vol. 2, 1969, p. 1175.
10. McPherson, K. Bunker, J. Barnes, B. and Mosteller, F. (eds.) *Costs, Risks and Benefits of Surgery.* OUP, NY, 1978, pp. 308-22.
11. Crile, G. *What Women Should Know about the Breast Cancer Controversy.* Macmillan, NY, 1973.
12. Zelen, M. *Cancer Research,* vol. 28, 1968, p. 207.
13. Peyster, R. et al. *Radiology,* vol. 125, Nov. 1977, pp. 387–91.
14. Stjernsward, J. *Lancet,* vol. 2, 1974, p. 1285.
15. Atkins, Sir H. *BMJ,* vol. 2, 1972, p. 423.
16. Gilden, D. *Fact Sheet on Breast Surgery.* Feminist Women's Health Centre, Los Angeles, California, 1973.
17. Greer, S. *Lancet,* vol. 2, no. 8146, 1979, p. 785.
18. Cousins, Norman. *NEJM,* vol. 295, 23 Dec. 1976, pp. 1458-63.
19. King, H. Cancer risk and lifestyle. AAAS Annual Meeting, Boston, 1976.
20. Cutler, S. J. *Persons at High Risk of Cancer.* Academic Press, 1975.
21. Cutler, S. J. Third national cancer survey. Nat. Cancer Inst. Mono., 1975.
22. Reid, M. *BMJ* (letter), vol. 1, 16 Apr. 1977, p. 1031.
23. Steiner, P. E. *Cancer, Race and Geography.* Williams & Wilkins, USA, 1954.
24. Kalache, A. et al. *BMJ,* 26 Jan. 1980, pp. 223–4.
25. Ratner, H. *BMJ,* letter, 1 March 1980, p. 646.
26. *Drug and Therapeutics Bulletin,* vol. 19, no. 3, 30 Jan, 1980.
27. Harris, R. J. C. *Cancer.* Penguin, 1976.
28. Roe, F. J. C. *Proc. of Royal Soc. of Med.,* vol. 66, no. 1, Jan. 1973.
29. Doll, R. *Nature,* vol. 265, 17 Feb. 1977, pp. 589-96.
30. Hoover, R. *NEJM,* vol. 295, 1976, p. 401.
31. Calman, K. Personal communication.
32. Christopherson and Mays. *J. Nat. Cancer Inst.,* Feb. 1977.
33. Doll R. *Am. J. of Epidem.,* vol. 104, Oct. 1976.
34. Burkitt, D. *Lancet,* vol. 2, 1969, pp. 1229-31.
35. Wynder, E. L. and Reddy, B. S. *J. Nat. Cancer Inst.,* vol. 54, 1975, pp. 7–10.
36. Seidman, H. *Environ. Research,* vol. 3, 1970, pp. 234–50.
37. Hirayama. *Cancer Research,* vol. 35 (no. 11 Pt 2), 1975, pp. 3460–3.
38. DHSS. *Prevention and Health: Everybody's business.* 1976.
39. Duncan, W. and G. Kerr. *BMJ,* vol. 2, 2 Oct. 1976, p. 781.
40. Editorial. *NEJM,* vol. 289, 6 Dec. 1973, pp. 1249–51.

41. Lichter and Pflanz. *Medical Care*, vol. 9, 1971, p. 311.
42. Barraclough. *J. of Psychosomatic Medicine*, vol. 11, 1967, pp. 203–6.
43. *Drug and Therapeutics Bulletin.* 'Appendicitis Surgery', vol. 18, no. 2, 1980, pp. 7–8.
44. Editorial, *Lancet,* vol. 2, Sept. 1978, p. 618.
45. Bradley, E. L. *Archives of Surgery,* vol. 113, 1978, p. 130.
46. Wolfe, Dr Sidney. Evidence before the Senate Subcommittee on Oversight and Investigations on Unnecessary Surgery, 15 July 1975.
47. Harlap, S. *NEJM,* vol. 301, no. 13, 27 Sept. 1979. p. 677.
48. Lane Committee, *Report on Working of the Abortion Act.* HMSO, 1974.
49. Kline, J. et al. *J. of Epidemiology,* vol. 107, no. 4, 1978, p. 290.
50. *Family Planning Perspectives,* vol. 10, no. 1, Jan./Feb. 1978, p. 34.
51. Bracken M. *Am. J. of Epidemiology,* Apr. 1979.
52. Clarke, Sir C. *BMJ,* vol. 1, 22 Apr. 1978, pp. 1016-18.
53. Editorial, *BMJ,* no. 6089, 1977, p. 715.
54. Editorial, *BMJ,* vol. 1, 5 May 1979, p. 1163.
55. Harris, R. J. C. *Cancer.* Pelican, 1976.
56. Editorial. *Lancet,* 29 March 1980, pp. 687-8.
57. Reported in *New Scientist,* no. 1243, 5 March 1981, p. 603.
58. Editorial. *Lancet,* 20 Sept. 1980, pp.625-6.
59. Banta, H. D. *Costs and Benefits of Electronic Foetal Monitoring.* US Department of Health Education and Welfare (PHS), 79–3245, Apr.1979.
60 Goldenberg, R. *Am. J. of Obstetrics and Gynaecology,* vol. 123, no. 6, 15 Nov. 1975, pp. 617-19.
61. Jaffe, N. *NEJM,* vol. 299, 1978, p. 235.
62. Editorial, *BMJ,* vol. 1, 25 June 1977, p. 1616.
63. Wong, W. *Archives of Ophthalmology,* vol. 96, Mar. 1978, pp. 526-8.
64. Gilkes, M. J. *BMJ,* vol. 1, 23 June 1979, pp. 1681–3.
65. Editorial, *Lancet,* vol. 1, 2 June 1979, p. 1174.
66. Lubbers, J. A. *Acta Obstet. Gynaec. Scand. Suppl.,* vol. 62, 1977, p. 1.
67. Editorial, *Lancet,* vol. 1, 4 Mar, 1978, p. 482.
68. Franco, J. A. *Clin. Orthop.,* vol. 122, 1977, p. 231.
69. Bainton, D. et al. *NEJM,* vol. 294, 1976, p. 1147.
70. Seltzer, M. H. *Surg. Gyn. Obstet.,* vol. 130, 1970, p. 64.
71. Hogan, J. *Ir. Med. J.,* vol. 70, pp. 608-11.
72. Fitzpatrick, G. *See* reference 10 above, pp. 246-61.
73. Editorial. *NEJM,* 6 Dec. 1973, p. 1249.
74. Neuhauser, D. *See* reference 10 above.
75. Abramson, J. H. *B. J. Epidemiology,* 32, 1978, pp. 59–67.
76. Editorial, *BMJ,* vol. 2, 21 June 1975, p. 651.
77. Ferguson, J. et al. *Adv.* Surg., vol. 2, 1978, pp. 111–15.
78. Editorial. *Lancet,* vol. 2, 4 Oct. 1975, p. 642.
79. Steinberg, D. M. et al. *Brit. J. of Surgery,* vol. 62, 1975, p. 144.
80. *See* reference 10 above.
81. Vayda, E. *NEJM,* vol. 289, 1973, p. 1224.
82. Bunker, J. *NEJM,* 9 May 1974, p. 1051.

319

83. Wennberg, J. and Gittelsohn, A. *Science,* vol. 183, 1973, p. 1102.
84. Robinson, J. MacKeith, N. (ed) *New Women's Health Handbook.* Virago, London, 1978.
85. Barker, M. G. *BMJ,* vol. 2, 1968, pp. 91–5.
86. Richards, D. H. *Lancet,* vol. 2, 1974, p. 983.
87. Editorial. *Lancet,* 12 Aug. 1978, p. 357.
88. *JAMA,* vol. 238, 1977, p. 1616.
89. Smith, T. *Times,* 28 Nov. 1979.
90. Calne, R. et al. *Lancet,* 17 Nov. 1979.
91. *BMJ,* 8 Dec. 1979, p. 1461.
92. Editorial. *Lancet*, 17 Feb. 1979, p. 366.
93. Gardham and Davies. *The Operations of Surgery.* London and Churchill, 1969.
94. Galton, Lawrence, *The Patient's Guide to Surgery*, Avon, NY, 1977.
95. McNeil, B. et al. *NEJM,* vol. 299, no. 25, 1978, pp. 1397-1401.
96. Wennberg, J., Bunker, J. and Barnes, B. *The need for assessing the outcome of common medical practice.* Harvard School of Public Health, 1979.
97. McFarland, John (ed.) *Basic Clinical Surgery*, Butterworths, London, 1973.
98. Anderson, et al. *JAMA,* vol. 155, 1954, p. 1123.
99. Vianna, N. et al. *Lancet,* vol. 1, 1971, p. 431, and 16 Aug. 1980, pp. 338-9.
100. *See* reference 83 above.
101. Office of Population and Census Surveys. *Hospital Inpatient Statistics,* 1975.
102. Dods, L. *Pediatrics* (Springfield), vol. 10, 1952, p. 364.
103. Wood, B. et al. *Lancet,* vol. 2, 1972, p. 645.
104. Galton, L. *Patient's Guide to Surgery.* Avon, NY, 1977.
105. Registrar General. *Statistical Review,* 1954.
106. Cochrane, A. L. *Effectiveness and Efficiency.* Nuffield Provincial Hospitals Trust, 1972.
107. Bolande, R. P., *NEJM,* vol. 280, 1969, p. 591.
108. Harper, P. *Preventive Pediatrics,* Appleton Century Crofts, NY, 1962.
109. Said, G. *J. of Epidemiology and Comm. Health,* vol. 32, 1978, pp. 97-101.
110. *See* reference 96 above.
111. Rachman, C. and Philips, C. *Psychology and Medicine.* Pelican, 1978.
112. Mawson, S. R. Quotation. *Daily Mail*, 10 Apr. 1972.
113. Dronfield, M. *Lancet,* vol. 1, 1978, p. 1126.
114. Editorial. *Lancet*, no. 8151, 17 Nov. 1979.
115. Lock, S. and Smith, T. *The Medical Risks of Life*, Penguin, 1976.
116. Editorial. *BMJ,* 1 March 1980, p. 590.
117. Huntingford, P. Quotation. *Guardian,* 9 March 1981, p. 8.
118. Editorial. *BMJ,* 12 April 1980, p. 1037.
119. Editorial. *BMJ,* 10 May 1980.
120. Wolfers, David and Helen. *Vasectomy and Vasectomania,* Mayflower, 1974.

Part Four: Birth
 1. *Social Science and Medicine,* 6th International Conference, vol. 31A, no. 5, 1979.
 2. Haire, Doris. *The Cultural Warping of Childbirth.* International Childbirth Education Association, Seattle, USA, 1972.
 3. Morris, Norman, Chairman, National Childbirth Trust symposium, Royal Society of Medicine, 10 Feb. 1981.
 4. Tew, M. *Lancet,* vol. 1, 30 June 1978, p. 1388.
 5. Editorial. *BMJ,* vol. 282, 23 May 1981, pp. 1648–9.
 6. Marsh, G. N. *BMJ,* vol. 2, 15 Oct, 1977, pp. 1004–6.
 7. Bunker, J., Barnes, B. and Mosteller, F. (eds.) *Costs, Risks and Benefits of Surgery.* OUP, NY, 1978.
 8. Haire, Doris. *See* reference 2 above.
 9. Richards, M. *New Scientist,* no. 1121, 21 Sept. 1978, pp. 847–9.
10. O'Driscoll, Prof. Keiran. Quotation: Kitzinger, Sheila. *The Experience of Childbirth.* Pelican, 1978, p. 178.
11. O'Driscoll, K. *British J. of Anaesthetics,* vol. 47, 1975, p. 1053.
12. Hoult, I. *BMJ,* vol. 1, 1 Jan. 1977, pp. 14–16.
13. Rosefsky, J. *NEJM,* vol. 278, 1968, pp. 530–3.
14. Lewis, M. *Amer. J. of Dis. Child.,* vol. 113, 1967, pp. 462–5.
15. Doering, et al. *Amer. J. of Orthopsychiatry,* vol. 45, 1975, pp. 825–37.
16. Brown W. et al. *Psychosomatic Medicine,* vol. 34, 1972, pp. 119–27.
17. Ginzler, A. *Science,* vol. 210, 1980, p. 193.
18. Blankfield, A. *Med. J. of Australia,* vol. 2, 1965, pp. 666–8.
19. Haire, Doris. *See* reference 2 above.
20. Campbell, N. *BMJ,* vol. 2, 1975, pp. 548–54.
21. Chalmers, I. *BMJ,* vol. 2, 1975, pp. 116–18.
22. D'Souza, S. *Brit. J. of Obstetrics and Gyn.,* vol. 86, 1979, p.
23. Haire, Doris. *See* reference 2 above.
24. Butler, N. *A national long term study of perinatal hazards –* British births survey. 6th Working Congress of the Fed. Intnl Gyn. and Obstet., 1970.
25. FDA. *Drug Bulletin,* Oct. 1978.
26. Beard, R *Lancet,* no. 8152, 24 Nov. 1979, pp. 1117-19.
27. Banta, H. and Thacker, S. B. *Costs and Benefits of Electronic Foetal Monitoring,* US Department of Health Publications No. PMS 79–3245, 1979.
28. Stratmeyer, M. E., *Birth and Family Journal* (USA), Summer 1980, pp. 92–100.
29. *Diagnostic Ultrasound Equipment Federal Register,* Part III, 2 Feb. 1979.
30. Starkman, M. N. *Psychosomatic Medicine,* vol. 38, 1976, pp. 269–77.
31. Kantor, H. et al. *Obstet. and Gynaec.,* vol. 25, 1965, pp. 509–12.
32. Burchell, R. *Obstet. and Gynaec.,* vol. 24., 1964, pp. 272–3.
33. Romney, M. L., *Obstet and Gynaec.* vol. 1, 1980, pp. 33–5.
34. Romney, M. L. and Gordon, H., *BMJ,* vol. 282, 18 April 1981, pp. 1269-71.
35. Butler, N. *See* reference 24 above.
36. Haire, Doris, *see* reference 2 above.

37. Flynn, A. et al. *BMJ,* no. 6137, 26 Aug. 1978, pp. 591–3.
38. Kitzinger, S. *see* reference 10 above.
39. Haire, Doris, *see* reference 2 above.
40. *Drug and Therapeutics Bulletin,* 'Psychoprophylaxis', vol. 16, no. 14, 1978, pp. 53–5.
41. Sosa, R. et al. *NEJM,* vol. 303, no. 11, 11 Sept. 1980, p. 597.
42. Klopfer, P. M. et al. *Proc. Nat Acad. of Sciences (USA),* vol. 52, 1964, pp. 911–14.
43. Scott, J. P. *Genetics and Social Behaviour of Dogs.* University of Chicago Press, 1965.
44. Klaus, M. H. *NEJM,* vol. 286, 2 Mar. 1972, pp. 460–8.
45. Doering, S. et al. *Am. J. of Orthopsychiatry,* vol. 45, 1975, pp. 825–37.
46. Doll, R. *Nature,* vol. 265, 17 Feb. 1977, p. 589.
47. Lock, S. and Smith T. *The Medical Risks of Life,* Penguin, 1976.
48. Carmichael, J. *Lancet,* vol. 1, 14 Feb. 1976, p. 351.
49. Fletcher, E. W. *Lancet,* vol. 1, 18 Mar. 1978, p. 600.
50. Science Report. *Times,* 16 Nov. 1979, p. p. 14.
51. *Developmental Medicine and Child Neurology,* vol. 21, 1979, p. 582.
52. Tucker, Anthony. *Guardian,* 19 Nov. 1976, p. 5.

ive: Tests

th, G. T. *The Health Care Dilemma.* OHE, London, 1975.
ell, A. R. *Lancet,* vol. 2, 1974, p. 1071.
ence 1 above.
V. et al. *Int. J. of Epidemiology,* vol. 6, no. 4, OUP,

ng brochure for patients, 1979.
ation and Health: Everybody's business.* HMSO,

Drug Bulletin, Apr. 1975, pp. 7–8.
FDA. *Drug Bulletin,* Oct. 1976, p. 32.
9. DHSS. *Prevention and Health: Everybody's business.* HMSO, 1976.
10. Cochrane, A. L. *Effectiveness and Efficiency,* NPHT, 1972.
11. Editorial. *Lancet,* 11 Nov. 1978. pp. 1029–30.
12. Editorial *BMJ,* vol. 281, 6 Sept. 1980, p. 629.
13. Wynn, M. *New Society,* 22 Nov. 1979, pp. 433–4.
14. Editorial. *Lancet,* 16 Dec. 1978, p. 1287.
15. DHSS. *see* reference 9 above.
16. MRC Working Party on Amniocentesis Report. *Brit. J. of Obstet. and Gynaec.,* vol. 85, suppl. 2, 1978.
17. Editorial. *Lancet,* 16 Dec. 1978, p. 1287.
18. Kennedy, I. 'The defect.' BBC Radio 3, 25 Oct. 1978.
19. Cochrane, A. L. *Medicines for Year 2000.* OHE., London, 1979.
20. Editorial. *BMJ,* no. 6153, 16 Dec. 1978, pp. 1661–2.
21. *New Scientist,* 8 Mar. 1979, p. 747.
22. 'Cash cuts raise the risks of cancer.' *Guardian,* 22 Feb. 1977.
23. Department of Health (DHEW), USA Press release. Sept. 1979.
24. Department of Health (DHEW), USA Population exp. to X-rays. 1970.

25. NRPB. *Three Surveys of X-Ray Exposure in Britain.* Oct. 1980.
26. *New Scientist,* no. 1221, 2 Oct. 1980, p. 3.
27. Tucker, A., 'Exposure to X-rays causing concern', *Guardian,* 1 Oct. 1980.
28. Morgan, Karl. *New Scientist,* vol. 82, no. 1149, 5 Apr. 1979, p. 18.
29. FDA *Consumer,* Feb. 1977.
30. FDA *Drug Bulletin,* Nov. 1978, pp. 30–1.
31. Modan, B. *Lancet,* vol. 1. no. 7852, 23 Feb. 1974, pp. 277–9.
32. FDA *Drug Bulletin*, July 1974.
33. FDA *Consumer,* July 1976.
34. Wall, B. et al. *Brit. J. of Radiology,* vol. 52, 1979, p. 189.
35. 'Scanning for X-ray hazards.' *New Scientist,* vol. 81, no. 1147, 22 Mar. 1979.
36. Rippere, V. Personal communication, and *see* letter in *Journal of Human Nutrition,* vol. 35, 1981, p. 4.
37. *New Scientist,* no. 1183, 20 Nov. 1979, p. 675.

Part Six: Dentistry

1. Sheiham, A. *Lancet,* vol. 2, 27 Aug. 1977, p. 442.
2. Boggs, D. G. J. *Am. Dental Assoc.,* vol. 90, 1975, p. 644.
3. *Daily Telegraph,* 27 Aug. 1977.
4. 'New cavity in dental lore.' *Observer,* 4 Sept. 1977.
5. *Guardian,* 7 Mar. 1977.
6. Radical Health Statistics Group. *In Defence of the NHS.* 1977.
7. Morrison, J. and Barnett, M. *FDA Consumer,* Feb. 1977.
8. Laws, P. *Medical and Dental X-rays – A Consumer Guide to Avoiding Unnecessary Radiation Exposure.* Public Citizens' Health Research Group, 1974.
9. Galley, A. Quotation: Gillie, Oliver. 'Death at Dentists.' *Sunday Times,* 6 Oct. 1974.
10. Royal College of Physicians. *Fluoride, Teeth and Health.* Pitman. 1976.
11. Bourne, J. G. Letter. *Lancet,* vol. 1, 1970, p. 525.
12. Laws, I. *The Practitioner,* vol. 214, Mar. 1975, p. 365.
13. Inman, W. *BMJ,* vol. 1, 1974, p. 5.
14. *JAMA,* vol. 197, 1966, p 775.
15. *Drug and Therapeutics Bulletin,* vol. 14, no. 12, 1976, p. 47.
16. Royal College of Physicians. *Fluoride, Teeth and Health.* Pitman, 1976.
17. National Pure Water Association Indictment of the Royal College Report. July 1976.
18. Rapaport, I. *Revue de Stomatologie (Paris),* vol. 64, 1963, p. 207.
19. Iliffe. *New Scientist,* vol. 21, p. 766, and vol. 22, 1964, p. 306.
20 Krieger, M. *New Scientist,* vol. 44, 13 Nov. 1969, p. 371.
21. Voors. *Lancet,* vol. 2, 1969, p. 1337.

Part Seven: Contraception

1. FPA. Information Service, May 1979, London.
2. FDA. HEW Publication no. (FDA) 78–3069, 1978.
3. Editorial. *BMJ,* 22 July 1978, p. 233.

4. Snowden, R. et al. *The IUD – A Practical Guide*. Croom Helm, London 1977.
5. Westrom, L. *Am. J. of Obstet. and Gynaec.,* vol. 121, 1975, p. 707, and *Lancet,* vol. 2, 1976, p. 221.
6. Vessey, M. *Lancet,* vol. 12, no. 8141, 8 Sept. 1979, p. 501.
7. Booth, M. et al. *BMJ,* 12 July 1980, p. 114.
8. Department of Health (USA), HEW publication no. (FDA) 79–4012.
9. Family Planning Association. Information Service, May 1979, London.
10. *Martindale's Extra Pharmacopoeia*. Pharmaceutical Society, 22nd edn.
11. Schwallie, P. C. et al. *Contraception,* vol. 6, 1972, p. 315.
12. *Guardian*, 14 Aug. 1979.
13. Rebound, S. et al. *Nature,* vol. 241, 1973, p. 398.
14. MacKeith, Nancy (ed.). *New Women's Health Handbook*. Virago, 1978.
15. Shapiro, S. and Sloane, D. *Am. J. of Epidemiology* (in press).
16. *Drug and Therapeutics Bulletin,* vol. 18, no. 2, 18 Jan. 1980.
17. Grant, E. Speech delivered at conference for the Society of Clinical Ecology, at the Royal College of Physicians, London, 1 June 1979.
18. Vessey, M. and Doll, R. *Proc. Royal Society,* vol. 195, 1976, pp. 69–80.
19. Seaman, G. and B. *Women and the Crisis in Sex Hormones*. Rawson, NY, 1977.
20. FDA. *Drug Bulletin,* vol. 8, no. 2, Mar. 1978, p. 12.
21. Harlap, S. and Davies, M. *The Pill and Births: the Jerusalem study*. Nat. Inst. of Child Health and Development,USA, 1978.
22. Janerich, D. *JAMA,* vol. 238, 1977, p. 1808.
23. Janerich, D. *NEJM,* vol. 296, 1977, p. 67.
24. FDA. *Drug Bulletin,* July 1975.
25. Large, P. and Beral, V., 'RCGP Oral Contraception Study', *Lancet,* no. 8214, 7 Mar. 1981, pp. 541–6.
26. Lawrence, R. L. and Black, J. W. *The Medicine You Take,* Fontana, 1978.
27. Editorial. *BMJ,* 27 June 1981, pp. 2075–6.
28. Baum, J. *Lancet,* vol. 2, 1973, pp. 926–9.
29. Mays, E. T. *JAMA,* vol. 235, 1976, pp. 730–2.
30. Neuberger, J. *Lancet,* no. 8163, 9 Feb. 1980, pp. 273–6.
31. Silverberg, S. et al. *J. of Obstet and Gynaec.,* vol. 46, 1975, pp. 503–6.
32. Graedon, Joe. *The People's Pharmacy*. Avon Books, NY, 1976.
33. Schering Ltd. Data sheet.
34. FDA. HEW publication no. (FDA) 78–3069.
35. Bacon, J. et al. *BMJ,* vol. 2, no. 6210, 2 Feb. 1980, p. 293.
36. Editorial. *BMJ,* no. 6233, 12 July 1980, pp. 93–4.
37. Boston Collaborative Drug Surveillance Prog. *Lancet,* vol. 1, pp. 1399–1404.
38. Lewis and Hoghughi. *Brit. J. of Psych.* quotation: MacKeith, Nancy (ed.) *New Women's Health Handbook*. Virago, 1978.
39. Lewis, A. et al. *Brit. J. of Psychiatry,* vol. 115, pp. 697–701.

Part Eight: Drugs Prescribed by Doctors
1. Letter. *BMJ*, 5 July 1980.
2. Letter. *BMJ*, 19 July 1980.
3. Illingworth, R. N. and Prescott, L. F., *BMJ*, 14 June 1980, p. 1418.
4. Hemminki, E., *BMJ*, 22 Mar. 1980, pp. 833–6.
5. Herxheimer, A., 'How to make the most of your doctor', *Lancet*, 11 Dec. 1976, p. 1294.
6. Figures of drug sales used in *Health Shock* have been kindly provided to the author by Mr H. W. Tomski, FPS, of the Pharmaceutical Business Analysis Service (PBAS), Pinner, Middlesex. The figures are taken and derived from the PBAS 1978 survey of 200,000 prescriptions dispensed from 100 pharmacies all over the UK.
7. Coleman, Vernon. *The Medicine Men*. Arrow, 1977.
8. *Psychopharmacology*, vol. 62, p. 61, and *New Scientist*, no. 1154, 10 May 1979.
9. Wolfe, S. *A Government welfare programme for the drug industry: wasting money and promoting bad medicine through Medicaid*. Public Citizens' Health Research Group, May 1979.
10. FDA *Consumer*, Oct. 1978.
11. Clark, T. Quotation. *Boston Globe*, 11 Sept. 1979.
12. Rawlins, M. and Smith, A. *BMJ*, vol. 2, 13 Aug. 1977, p. 447.
13. Lynch, M. Letter. *BMJ*, vol. 1. 1975, p. 266.
14. Horrobin, D. Letter. *Lancet*, 5 May, 1979, p. 778.
15. Genest, J. Letter. *Lancet*, 16 Jun. 1979, p. 1306.
19. Milkovich, L. *NEJM*, vol. 291. 12 Dec. 1974, pp. 1268–71.
16. *New Scientist*, 26 Mar. 1981, p. 793.
17. Boyland, E. Letter. *Lancet*, 21 Feb. 1981.
18. Marchant, J. *New Scientist*, vol. 89, no. 1240, 12 Feb. 1981, p. 408.
19. Milkovich, L. *NEJM*, vol. 291, 12 Dec. 1974, pp. 1268–71.
20. Cree, J. *BMJ*, vol. 4, 1973, p. 251.
21. Hall, R. *Am. J. of Psychiatry*, vol. 129, 1972, p. 738.
22. Ryan, H. *JAMA*, vol. 203, 1968, p. 1137.
23. *Martindale's Extra Pharmacopoeia*. Pharmaceutical Society, 22nd edn.
24. FDA *Consumer*, Oct. 1978.
25. *New Scientist*, vol. 81, no. 1139, 25 Jan. 1979, p. 276.
26. Klass, A. *There's Gold in Them Thar Pills*. Penguin, 1975.
27. Committee on the Review of Medicines, *BMJ*, 29 Mar. 1980, pp. 910-12.
28. FDA, *Drug Bulletin*, Aug. 1979.
29. *New Scientist*, vol. 82, no. 1150, 12 Apr. 1979, p. 101.
30. *Drug and Therapeutics Bulletin*, vol. 16. no. 12, 1978, pp. 46–8.
31. *See* reference 7 above, p. 112.
32. National Academy of Sciences. *Sleeping Pills and Medical Practice*. 1979.
33. Kales, A. *JAMA*, vol. 227, 1974, p. 513.
34. Malpas, A. et al. *BMJ*, vol. 2, 1970, p.762.
35. Evans, J. G. *BMJ*, vol. 4, 1972, p. 487.
36. Evans, J. G. Letter. *BMJ*, vol. 1, 1973, p. 488.

37. MacDonald, J. B. and E. T. *BMJ*, Aug. 1977.
38. *Drug and Therapeutics Bulletin,* vol. 18, no. 3, 1980, pp. 9–11.
39. FDA. *Drug Bulletin,* Jan. 1978.
40. *The Medicine Show.* US Consumers' Union, Pantheon, 1976.
41. Communicable and tropical diseases, part 1, *Medicine,* vol. 3, Mar. 1978.
42. Shooter, R. *Lancet,* vol. 2, 1971, p. 390.
43. Wingate, Peter. *Penguin Medical Encyclopaedia.* Penguin, London, 1972.
44. Katz, S. E. *J. Assoc. of Anal. Chem.* vol. 56, 1973, p. 77.
45. *J. of Hygiene,* vol. 80, p. 229, and *New Scientist,* vol. 78, no. 1100, 27 Apr. 1978, p. 211.
46. Herter, F. *Am. J. of Surgery,* vol. 113, 1967, p. 165.
47. Day, T. K. *Lancet,* vol. 2, 1975, p. 1174.
48. Dentkos, M. C., *Am. J. of Hospital Pharm.,* vol. 23, 1966, p. 139.
49. Laurence, D. R. and Black, J. W. *The Medicine You Take.* Fontana, 1978, p. 47.
50. *British National Formulary*, no. 1, 1981.
51. 'Warning on antibiotic-induced colitis'. *Lancet,* 16 June 1979.
52. McCormack, W. 'Antimicrob. agents chemother', Nov. 1977. pp. 630–5.
53. Nicholas Peter. *New York State J. of Med.,* Nov. 1977, p. 2088.
54. Boston Collaborative Drug Surveillance Prog. *JAMA,* vol. 224, 1973, p. 515.
55. Stewart, D. J. *BMJ,* vol. 3, 1973, p. 320.
56. Renson, Dr R. E. Quotation. *London Evening Standard,* 30 Sept. 1977.
57. Pickard, T. *Guardian,* 24 Jan. 1977.
58. Roberts and Roberts, *BMJ,* vol. 2, 1979, p. 14.
59. Howie, J. and Brigg, A., *BMJ,* 22 Mar. 1980, pp. 836–8.
60. Houvinen, P. *BMJ,* no. 6207, 12 Jan. 1980, pp. 72–4.
61. Parrish, Peter. Medicines: *A Guide for Everybody.* Penguin, 1976.
62. *Drug and Therapeutics Bulletin,* vol. 17, no. 17, 1979, pp. 65–8.
63. *Drug and Therapeutics Bulletin,* vol. 14, no. 14, 2 July 1976.
64. *Medical Letter,* vol. 17, 1975, p. 53.
65. FDA. *Drug Bulletin,* vol. 6, no. 2, Apr. 1976, pp. 22–3.
66. Goldman, P., *NEJM,* vol. 303, no. 21, 20 Nov. 1980, pp. 1212–16.
67. Malleson, A. *Need your Doctor be so Useless.* W. H. Allen, London, 1973.
68. Wolfe, S. Evidence to US Department of Health, 31 May 1975.
69. Young, R. J. and Lawson, A. Letter. *BMJ,* 30 Aug., 1980.
70. Mosstrel, C. G. et al, *NEJM,* vol. 286, 1972, pp. 813–15.
71. Miller, R. *JAMA,* vol. 213, 1970, pp. 996–1006; Hopkinson, J. M. et al. *Curr. Ther. Research,* vol. 19, 1976, pp. 622-30.
72. Tennant, F. S. *Archives of Internal Surgery,* 132, 1973, p. 191.
73. *Curr. Ther. Research.* July 1961, p. 289; FDA. *Drug Bulletin*, March 1979.
74. Salguero, C. H. *JAMA,* vol. 210, 1969, p. 135.
75. Whittington, R. M. *BMJ,* vol. 2, 16 July 1977 pp. 172–3.

76. *Dawn Quarterly Report,* Jan./Mar. 1978.
77. FDA. *Drug Bulletin,* Jan. 1979, p. 34.
78. *See* reference 23 above.
79. *See* reference 7 above.
80. *See* reference 50 above.
81. Wilkinson, D. S. *Lancet,* 1980, p. 75.
82. Cotterill, J. A. Quoted in *Lancet.* Editorial vol. 1, 12 Jan, 1980, p. 75.
83. Editorial. *Lancet,* 21 Apr. 1973.
84. Klugman, A. *JAMA,* vol. 229, 1974, p. 60.
85. Sneddon, I. *B. J. Derm.,* vol. 87, 1972, p. 452.
86. Milne, J. A. *Practitioner,* vol. 205, 1970 p. 452.
87. Sparkes, C. G. *B. J. Derm.,* vol. 90, 1974, p. 197.
88. Burde, R. M. *JAMA,* vol. 213, 1970, p. 2075.
89. Wilkes, E. *Prescriber's Journal,* vol. 14, Oct. 1974, p. 98.
90. *See* reference 61 above.
91. FDA Register Part II. Over the counter drugs. Proposed rules, 9 Sept. 1976. p. 38341.
92. *See* reference 23 above.
93. Goodman, L. S. and Gillman, A. (eds.) *Pharmacological Basis of Therapeutics.* Macmillan, NY, 1955, pp. 1069–70.
94. *See* reference 91 above, p. 38357.
95. *See* reference 91 above, p. 38350.
96. *See* reference 40 above.
97. *See* reference 50 above.
98. Editorial, *BMJ,* vol. 2, no. 6203, 8 Dec. 1979, p. 1456.
99. Dixon, B. Editorial. *New Scientist,* vol. 77, no. 1091, 23 Feb. 1978, p. 482.
100. Peart and Miall. Letter. *Lancet,* 12 Jan. 1980, pp. 104–5.
101. FDA. *Drug Bulletin,* vol. 8, no. 2, Mar. 1978, p. 13.
102. Greenblatt, D. J. et al. *Drugs,* vol. 7, Basle, 1974, p. 118.
103. Editorial. *Lancet,* 30 Aug. 1980, pp. 459–61.
104. Campbell, D. M. *Brit. J. of Obstet. and Gynaec.,* vol. 82, 1975, p. 572.
105. Bauer, G. E. *Med. J. Australia,* vol. 1, 1973, p. 930.
106. Alexander, W. D. *BMJ,* vol. 2, 1975, p. 501.
107. Editorial, *Lancet,* 25 Nov. 1978, p. 1131–2.
108. Kark, J. D. et al. *J. Chron. Dis.,* vol. 33, 1980, pp. 311–12.
109. Editorial. *Lancet,* 2 Aug. 1980, pp. 243–4.
110. MacMichael, Sir J. Letter. *Lancet,* 1 Dec. 1979, p. 1183.
111. Smith, T. W. *Am. J. Med.,* vol. 58, 1975, p. 470.
112. Editorial. *BMJ,* no. 6200 p. 1246.
113. Editorial. *Lancet,* 16 Dec. 1978, pp. 1288–90.
114. Personal communication. Professor Michael Rawlins.
115. MacGregor, G. *Lancet,* 24 Feb. 1979, p. 397.
116. FDA. *Drug Bulletin,* vol. 7, no. 2, July 1977, p. 7.
117. Noble, I. M. *Practitioner,* vol. 212, 1974, p. 657.
118. Dargie, H. J., *BMJ,* vol. 4, 1974, p. 316–19.
119. *See* reference 50 above.
120. Letters, *BMJ,* vol. 3, 1975, p. 162 and p. 436.
121. Cochrane, A. L. *Effectiveness and Efficiency.* Nuffield Provincial Hospitals Trust, 1972.

122. University Group Diabetes Prog. (UGDP). *JAMA*, vol. 218, 1971, pp. 1400–10.
123. Shen, S. W. et al. *NEJM*, vol. 296, no. 14, 1977, pp. 787–93.
124. FDA. *Drug Bulletin*, vol. 8, no. 6, Jan. 1979, p. 34.
125. Hadden, D. R. *Lancet*, vol. 1, 1972, pp. 335–8.
126. Wissler, R. W. et al. *FDA*, no. 72–114, 15 Feb. 1975.
127. Wu, C. F., et al. *Clinical Res.*, vol. 22, no. 3. Apr. 1975, p. 215A.
128. Warner, R. et al. *Off Diabetes Pills,* Public Citizens' Health Research Group, Washington DC, USA, 1978.
129. *Isr. J. of Med. Science,* vol. 1, 1971, p. 1209.
130. Gale, E. and Tattersall, R. *BMJ*, vol. 2, 1976, pp. 972–5.
131. Editorial. *Lancet,* 9 Dec. 1978.
132. Picard, R. G. *BMJ*, vol. 1, 1979, p. 662.
133. Van Thiel, D. *NEJM*, vol. 300 (18), 3 May 1979, pp.1012–5.
134. Maurice, J., *Sunday Times,* 11 Jan. 1981.
135. Editorial. *BMJ*, vol. 282, 11 April 1981, pp. 1178–9.
136. Nelson, M. M. *BMJ,* 1971, p. 523.
137. Personal communication. Dr Tom Lind. *See also* Weitz, M., 'Why any old iron won't do if you're pregnant', *Guardian*, 10 June 1980.
138. Starfield, B. and Hemminki, E. *B. J. Obstet. & Gynaec.,* vol. 85, 1978, p. 404.
139 Editorial, *BMJ* no: 6148, 11 Nov. 1978, p. 1317.
140 Lind, T. *B. J. Obstet. & Gynaec.,* vol. 83, 1976, p. 760.
141. *See* reference 50 above.
142. Forfar, J. P. *Prescriber's Journal,* vol. 13, 1973, p. 130.
143. Inman, W. *Lancet,* vol. 2, 1969, p. 279.
144. PBAS. Drug sales analysis. *See* reference 6 above.
145. Marks, M. B. *Am. J. Dis. Child.,* vol. 128, 1974, p. 301.
146. Silverman, M. *Thorax*, vol. 28, p. 574.
147. *New Scientist,* vol. 83, no. 1171, 6 Sept. 1979, p. 707.
148. *Clinical Allergy,* vol. 9, 1979, pp. 237 and 241.
149. Dyson, A. *BMJ,* no. 6211, 9 Feb. 1980. p. 360.
150. Letter. Prowse, K., *BMJ,* 1 Mar, 1980, p. 646.
151. Mulley and Mitchell, *Lancet,* 26 Jun. 1976.
152. *Drug and Therapeutics Bulletin,* vol. 16, no. 4, 17 Feb. 1978.
153. Weitz, M. and Woolf, D. 'The happiness pill'. *World in Action,* Granada TV, June 1978.
154. Liebermann, Sharon, 'Majority report', New York, US, 1977.
155. Letter. Campbell, S. et al. *BMJ,* 5 Nov. 1977, pp. 1218-19.
156. Coope, J. et al. *BMJ,* vol. 4, 1975, p. 139.
157. Zeil, H. and Finkle, W. *NEJM,* vol. 293, 1975, p. 1167.
158. Paterson, M. E. L. et al. *BMJ,* 22 Mar. 1980, pp. 822-4.
159. Campbell and Whitehead, quoted by Evans, B., *World Medicine,* 8 Feb. 1978.
160. Editorial. *BMJ*, 30 Aug. 1980, pp. 572-3.
161. Silverberg, et al. *Obstet. Gynaec., NY,* vol. 46, 1975, p. 503.
162. Hoover, R. *NEJM*, vol. 295, 1976, p. 401.
163. Personal communication. Dr Malcolm Whitehead.
164. Editorial. *BMJ*, vol. 1, 27 Jan, 1979, p. 212.
165. P. M. S. O'Brien, Selby & Symons, *BMJ*, 10 May 1980, pp. 1161-3.

166. *Drug and Therapeutics Bulletin*, vol. 17, no. 26, 1979, pp. 101–3.
167. Taylor, R. W. *Current Medical Research and Opinion*, vol. 4, 1977.
168. FDA. *Bulletin,* Mar. 1978, p. 10.
169. FDA. *Bulletin,* Nov. 1978, p. 31.
170. Beral, V. and Colwell, L., *BMJ*, vol. 281, 25 Oct. 1980, pp. 1098-1101.
171. *See* reference 50 above.
172. DHSS. Circular, ECL. 106/69 S. No. 5/77 Sept. 1977.
173. FDA *Consumer.* Annabel Hecht, April 1978.
174. *See* reference 7 above.
175. Petrie, J. C. *Postgrad. M. J.,* supp. 1, vol. 51, 1975, p. 139.
176. Bacon, G. *Curr. Ther. Res.,* vol. 9, 1967, p. 626.
177. *BMJ*, vol. 2, 1973, p. 49.
178. Editorial, *BMJ*, 17 Mar. 1979, p. 705.
179. Graedon, Joe. *The People's Pharmacy*. Avon Books, NY, 1976.
180. Stewart, M. A. *JAMA,* vol. 232, 1975, pp. 281–3.
181. Schrag, P. and Divorky, D. *The Myth of the Hyperactive Child and other means of Child Control*. Pantheon, 1976.
182. *Drug and Therapeutics Bulletin*, vol. 15, no. 6, 18 Mar. 1977, pp. 22–4.
183. Sahakian, B. *New Scientist*, vol. 80, no. 1127, 2 Nov. 1978, pp. 350–2.
184. FDA. *Drug Bulletin,* July 1976, p. 28.
185. FDA. *Drug Bulletin,* vol. 9, no. 3, Aug., 1979.

Part Nine: Over-the-Counter Drugs, Vaccines, Eye Care

 1. Public Citizens' Health Research Group. Letter to the FDA dated 8 Dec. 1976.
 2. 'Advertising of proprietary medicines, part 3'. Hearings before the Senate Small Business Committee, 1972, p. 1012.
 3. Graedon, Joe. *The People's Pharmacy*. Avon Books, NY, 1976.
 4. Euromonitor. UK Health Markets, 1978.
 5. *Martindale's Extra Pharmacopoeia*. Pharmaceutical Society, 22nd edn.
 6. Public Citizens' Health Research Group. Letter to the FDA dated 8 Dec. 1976.
 7. Parrish, Peter. *Medicines: a Guide for Everybody*. Penguin, 1976.
 8. *The Medicine Show*. US Consumers' Union, Pantheon, 1976.
 9. *See* reference 8 above, p. 35.
10. Livingston, P. H. *JAMA*, vol. 196, 1966, p. 1159.
11. Gibson, G. J. *Lancet* ii, 1972, p. 492.
12. Cane, F. J. *Am. J. of Psychiatry,* vol. 123, 1966, p. 484.
13. *See* reference 8 above.
14. Lock, S. and Smith, T. *The Medical Risks of Life*. Penguin, 1976.
15. *See* reference 8 above.
16. *British National Formulary*. BMA and Pharmaceutical Society, no. 1, 1981.
17. *See* reference 4 above.
18. *Which?* The Consumers Association, Mar. 1976.
19. Editorial. *Lancet*, 13 Dec. 1975, pp. 1189-91.

20. James et al. *Lancet,* vol. 2, 1975, p. 579.
21. Personal communication. Dr Laurence Prescott, June 1981.
22. Cove-Smith, J. R. *Q. J. of Medicine,* new series, vol. 1, Jan. 1978.
23. Burry et al. *M. J. of Australia,* vol. 1, 1974, p. 31.
24. *See* reference 16 above.
25. Editorial. *BMJ,* 11 Oct. 1980.
26. *See* reference 8 above, p. 150.
27. FDA. *Drug Bulletin,* Sept. 1978, pp. 26–7.
28. *Pharmaceutical Journal* vol. 209, no. 5680, 1972, p. 227.
29. FDA. *Drug Bulletin,* Feb. 1972.
30. Light, I. and Sutherland, J. *Pediatrics,* vol. 51, Springfield, 1973, p. 345.
31. Noah, N., *New Scientist,* no. 1214, 14 Aug. 1980, pp. 518-19.
32. *See* reference 16 above.
33. *See* reference 7 above.
34. *See* reference 5 above.
35. *See* reference 4 above.
36. FDA. *Vitamin and mineral drugs for over the counter human use,* Federal Register, part II, 16 March 1979.
37. *Drug and Therapeutics Bulletin,* Vol. 13, 1975, p. 64.
38. FDA. *Drug Bulletin,* Sept. 1978, p. 26.
39. Yaffe, S. J. *Pediatrics,* vol. 48, 1971, p. 655.
40. Editorial. *Lancet,* 15 Mar. 1980, pp. 575–6.
41. Editorial. *BMJ,* vol. 281, no. 6246, 11 Oct. 1980, pp. 957–8.
42. Coronary Drug Project Research Group. *JAMA,* vol. 231, 1975, p . 360.
43. *See* reference 36 above.
44. Stokes, J. et al. *Lancet,* vol. 1, 1972, p. 1177.
45. Wynn, V. *Lancet,* vol. 1, 1975, p. 561.
46. Greentree, L. *NEJM,* vol. 300, no. 3, 1979, p. 142.
47. Cochrane, A. L. *Health Services in the Developed World,* in press, 1979.
48. Hunter, R. *Lancet,* letter, vol. 1, 1967, p. 47.
49. *Medical Letter,* vol. 20, no. 9, 9 May 1978, p. 44.
50. FDA, *Drug Bulletin,* vol. 8 (6), Jan. 1979, p. 38.
51. FDA. *Drug Bulletin,* vol. 7, no. 5, Dec. 1977.
52. *New England J. of Med.* Vol. 299, 1978, p. 550.
53. *New Scientist,* Vol. 28, Sept. 1978, p. 920.
54. FDA. 16 March, 1979. *See* reference 36 above.
55. Editorial. *BMJ,* vol. 1. 1976, p. 606.
56. *See* reference 3 above.
57. Pauling, L. *Vitamin C and the Common Cold,* W. H. Freeman, 1970 & 1977.
58. Walker, G. H. et al. *BMJ,* vol. 1, 1967, p. 603.
59. GP Research Group. Report no. 17, *Practitioner,* vol. 200, 1968, p. 442.
60. Anderson, T. W. et al. *J. Canadian Medical Association,* vol. 107, 1972,
    p. 503.
61. Ibid. Vol. 11, 1974, p. 31.
62. Canon, M. et al. *BMJ,* vol. 1, 1974, p. 577.

63. Briggs, M. H. *Lancet,* vol. 2, 1974, p. 1211.
64. Karlowski, T. R. *JAMA*, vol. 231, 1975, p. 1038.
65. Coulehan, J. L. *NEJM*, vol. 295, p. 973.
66. Nature–Times News Service. *The Times*, 9 Nov. 1976.
67. *See* reference 36 above.
68. Briggs, M. H. *Lancet,* vol. 2, 1973, p. 677.
69. *See* reference 3 above, p. 125.
70. Briggs, M. H. *M. J. of Australia,* 4 May 1974, p. 722.
71. Cameron, E. and Pauling, L. *Proc. of Nat. Acad. of Science USA,* vol. 75, 1978, pp. 4538–42.
72. *National Medical Bulletin* (USA). Sept. 1979, p. 5.
73. Creagan E. et al. *NEJM*, vol. 301, no. 13, 1979, p. 687.
74. *New Scientist.* Vol. 82, no. 1153, May 1979, p. 359.
75. International Symposium on vitamin C (sponsored by Roche), Warwick University, England, 1981. Report from Neustatter, P., *Medical News*, 23 April 1981.
76. *See* reference 5 above.
76. *See reference* 36 above.
78. Friedman, N. F. et al. *Pediatrics*, vol. 43, 1969, Springfield, p. 12.
79. *BMJ*. Vol. 4, 1971, p. 251.
80. Watt, T. *Lancet,* letter, vol. 2, 1974, p. 354.
81. Durie, B., *New Scientist*, no. 1214, 14 Aug. 1980, pp. 516–17.
82. Gardiner, P. A. and Peckham, C., *BMJ*, vol. 281, 20 Sept. 1980, p. 780.
83. Gardiner, P. A. and Peckham, C., *BMJ*, 1979, pp. 1111–13.
84. Editorial. *BMJ*, vol. 281, 13 Dec. 1980, pp. 1586–7.
85. *Which?* June 1974, pp. 172–6.
86. Salmi, T. T. *Lancet,* letter, vol. 2, 1975, p. 811.
87. Assili, W. B. and Stewart, G. *Lancet,* vol. 1, 1976, p. 471 and p. 750.
88. *Canadian Med. Assoc. J.* Vol. 112, 1975, p. 1049.
89. *Doctor.* Vol. 27, April 1978, p. 15.
90. *Sunday Times,* 9 Jan. 1977.
91. Editorial. *Lancet*, 23 May 1981, pp. 1138–9.
92. DHSS Reports from the Committee on Safety of Medicines and the Joint Committee on Vaccination and Immunisation. London, HMSO, 1981.
93. Editorial, *BMJ*, vol. 282, pp. 1563–4.
94. Ström, J. *BMJ*, vol. 4. 1967, p. 320.
95. Editorial. *Lancet*, 12 Jan. 1980.
96. *See* reference 5 above.
97. Sommer, A. *Lancet,* vol. 1, 1973, p. 1230.
98. *BMJ*. Vol. 2, 1972, p. 594.
99. Smith, J. *Lancet,* vol. 2, 1974, p. 330.
100. Reuben, F. *JAMA,* vol. 230, 1974, p. 863.
101. *The Guardian,* 7 June 1979.
102. Miller, J. E. *Practitioner*, vol. 203, 1969, p. 352.
103. Pollock, T. M. *Lancet*, vol. 1, 1969, p. 281.
104. Editorial. *Lancet,* 'Polio Vaccine for Parents', 11 Nov. 1978, p. 1031.
105. *BMJ*, Vol. 3, 1975, p. 153.

106. Halsall, Sheila. Personal communication.
107. Brown, H. *JAMA*, vol. 204, 1968, p. 614.
108. *See* reference 5 above.
109. Lever, Judy. *PMT: The Unrecognised Illness.* NEL/Times Mirror, 1980.

Post Script
1. Editorial. *BMJ*, vol. 1, 5 Jan. 1980, pp. 1–2.
2. Cochrane, A. *Medicines for the Year 2000,* OHE, London, 1979.
3. Hewitt, D. and Wood, P. *Rheumatology & Rehabilitation ,* vol. XIV, no. 3, 1975, pp. 191–9.
4. Mathers, D. et al. Letter. *BMJ*, vol. 1, 2 Feb. 1980.
5. Ebrahim, S. Letter. *BMJ*, vol. 1, 2 Feb. 1980.
6. Cassell, E. MD, *The Healer's Art,* Penguin, London, 1979.

Index

Abicol 217
abortion 31-4, 108, 109, 111, 112
  risks to woman 32-4
  types of 31-2
Acebutol 215
Achromycin syrup 190
acne 152
Actifed 208
Actinac 184
Adcortyl 205
  with Graneodin 187
adenoids 66-70
Albamycin 190
alcohol 268
Aldactide 224
Aldactone 224
Aldomet 218-20
  risks with 219
Aleudrin 243
Alka Seltzer 268
allergy 118, 141
Alphaderm 205
alternative medicine 305
Aludrox 238
aluminium hydroxide 238
amenorrhoea 41
Amfipen 176
amniocentesis 107-13
amphetamines 255-8, 260-3
Ampicillin 155, 176, 181
Ampiclox 176
anaesthesia, damage caused by 25-7
  dentists and 27
  effects on fertility 27
anaesthetic
  death in dentistry 123, 125-7
  epidural, hazards of, in
    childbirth 83-5
anaesthetics, hazards of, in
    childbirth 82
  liver damage from 126
Andrews Liver Salts 270
anencephaly 108
angina pectoris 12, 50
  placebo operation for 21
anklosing spondilitis 40

antibiotics 67, 176-98, 239
  in pregnancy, hazards of 181
  resistance of bacteria to 178
  side effects of 177
antihistamines 154, 265-7
Anxon 159
Apgar test 84, 94, 95
Apisate 255
appendix operation 35-6
Aprinox 224
Apsin VK 177
Asilone 238-9
Askits 273
aspiration, vacuum (Vabra) 31, 51
aspirin 204, 268, 273
asthma 12, 13, 176, 215
  drugs 243-7
Atarax 159
Atenolol 215
Atensine 159
Ativan 159
Atromid-S 220-22
Audicort 187
Aurcomycin syrup 190

baby-battering 163-4
backache 12
Bactrim 193
barbiturate poisoning 175
barbiturates 154, 175-6
  and the Pill 175-6
  addiction to 176
  effect on asthma and bronchitis
    176
  effectiveness of 176
Barcaron 224
BC 500 240
BCG vaccine 299
bedwetting 258-60
Benafed 208
Benylin 208-11
Benzoctamine hydrochloride 159
Berkmycin syrup 190
Berkozide 224
Beta Cardone 212
Betaloc 212

337

NON-FICTION

GENERAL
- ☐ **Truly Murderous** — John Dunning — 95p
- ☐ **Shocktrauma** — Jon Franklin & Alan Doelp — £1.25
- ☐ **The War Machine** — James Avery Joyce — £1.50
- ☐ **The Fugu Plan** — Tokayer & Swartz — £1.75

BIOGRAPHY/AUTOBIOGRAPHY
- ☐ **Go-Boy** — Roger Caron — £1.25
- ☐ **The Queen Mother Herself** — Helen Cathcart — £1.25
- ☐ **Clues to the Unknown** — Robert Cracknell — £1.50
- ☐ **George Stephenson** — Hunter Davies — £1.50
- ☐ **The Borgias** — Harry Edgington — £1.50
- ☐ **The Admiral's Daughter** — Victoria Fyodorova — £1.50
- ☐ **Rachman** — Shirley Green — £1.50
- ☐ **50 Years with Mountbatten** — Charles Smith — £1.25
- ☐ **Kiss** — John Swenson — 95p

HEALTH/SELF-HELP
- ☐ **The Hamlyn Family First Aid Book** — Dr Robert Andrew — £1.50
- ☐ **Girl!** — Brandenburger & Curry — £1.25
- ☐ **The Good Health Guide for Women** — Cooke & Dworkin — £2.95
- ☐ **The Babysitter Book** — Curry & Cunningham — £1.25
- ☐ **Pulling Your Own Strings** — Dr Wayne W. Dyer — 95p
- ☐ **The Pick of Woman's Own Diets** — Jo Foley — 95p
- ☐ **Woman X Two** — Mary Kenny — £1.10
- ☐ **Cystitis: A Complete Self-help Guide** — Angela Kilmartin — £1.00
- ☐ **Fit for Life** — Donald Norfolk — £1.35
- ☐ **The Stress Factor** — Donald Norfolk — £1.25
- ☐ **Fat is a Feminist Issue** — Susie Orbach — 95p
- ☐ **Living With Your New Baby** — Rakowitz & Rubin — £1.50
- ☐ **Related to Sex** — Claire Rayner — £1.25
- ☐ **The Working Woman's Body Book** — Rowen with Winkler — 95p
- ☐ **Natural Sex** — Mary Shivanandan — £1.25
- ☐ **Woman's Own Birth Control** — Dr Michael Smith — £1.25
- ☐ **Overcoming Depression** — Dr Andrew Stanway — £1.50

POCKET HEALTH GUIDES
- ☐ **Migraine** — Dr Finlay Campbell — 65p
- ☐ **Pre-menstrual Tension** — June Clark — 65p
- ☐ **Back Pain** — Dr Paul Dudley — 65p
- ☐ **Allergies** — Robert Eagle — 65p
- ☐ **Arthritis & Rheumatism** — Dr Luke Fernandes — 65p
- ☐ **Skin Troubles** — Deanna Wilson — 65p

TRAVEL
- ☐ **Guide to the Channel Islands** — Anderson & Swinglehurst — 90p
- ☐ **The Complete Traveller** — Joan Bakewell — £1.95
- ☐ **Time Out London Shopping Guide** — Lindsey Bareham — £1.50
- ☐ **A Walk Around the Lakes** — Hunter Davies — £1.50
- ☐ **England by Bus** — Elizabeth Gundrey — £1.25
- ☐ **Britain at Your Feet** — Wickers & Pedersen — £1.75

HUMOUR
- ☐ **Ireland Strikes Back!** — Seamus B. Gorrah — 85p
- ☐ **Pun Fun** — Paul Jennings — 95p
- ☐ **1001 Logical Laws** — John Peers — 95p
- ☐ **The Devil's Bedside Book** — Leonard Rossiter — 85p

REFERENCE

☐ The Sunday Times Guide to Movies on Television	Angela & Elkan Allan	£1.50
☐ The Cheiro Book of Fate and Fortune		£1.50
☐ Hunter Davies's Book of British Lists		£1.25
☐ What's Wrong With Your Pet?	Hugo Kerr	95p
☐ Caring for Cats and Kittens	John Montgomery	95p
☐ The Drinker's Companion	Derek Nimmo	£1.25
☐ The Complete Book of Cleaning	Barty Phillips	£1.50
☐ The Oscar Movies from A-Z	Roy Pickard	£1.25
☐ Collecting For Profit	Sam Richards	£1.25
☐ Questions of Motoring Law	John Spencer	£1.25
☐ Questions of Law	Bill Thomas	£1.25
☐ It's A Fact 1, 2, 3, 4		85p

GAMES AND PASTIMES

☐ The Hamlyn Book of Brainteasers and Mindbenders	Ben Hamilton	85p
☐ The Hamlyn Book of Crosswords 2		60p
☐ The Hamlyn Book of Crosswords 3		60p
☐ The Hamlyn Book of Wordways 1		75p
☐ The Hamlyn Family Quiz Book		85p

WAR

☐ World War 3	Edited by Shelford Bidwell	£1.50
☐ The Black Angels	Rupert Butler	£1.35
☐ Gestapo	Rupert Butler	£1.50
☐ Hand of Steel	Rupert Butler	£1.35
☐ The Flight of the Mew Gull	Alex Henshaw	£1.75
☐ Sigh for a Merlin	Alex Henshaw	£1.50
☐ Hitler's Secret Life	Glenn B. Infield	£1.25
☐ Wing Leader	'Johnnie' Johnson	£1.25

GARDENING/HOBBIES

☐ 'Jock' Davidson's House Plant Book		£1.25
☐ A Vegetable Plot for Two — or More	D. B. Clay Jones	£1.00
☐ Salads the Year Round	Joy Larkcom	£1.25
☐ Sunday Telegraph Patio Gardening	Robert Pearson	£1.00
☐ Greenhouse Gardening	Sue Phillips	£1.25

COOKERY

☐ A-Z of Health Foods	Carol Bowen	£1.50
☐ The Giant Sandwich Book	Carol Bowen	£1.50
☐ Vegetarian Cookbook	Dave Dutton	£1.50
☐ Know Your Onions	Kate Hastrop	95p
☐ Indian Cooking	Attia Hosain and Sita Pasricha	£1.50
☐ Home Preserving and Bottling	Gladys Mann	80p
☐ Home Baked Breads & Cakes	Mary Norwak	75p

NAME ....

ADDRESS ....

....

Write to Hamlyn Paperbacks Cash Sales, PO Box 11, Falmouth, Cornwall TR10 9EN.

Please indicate order and enclose remittance to the value of the cover price plus:

U.K.: Please allow 40p for the first book 18p for the second book and 13p for each additional book ordered, to a maximum charge of £1.49.

B.F.P.O. & EIRE: Please allow 40p for the first book, 18p for the second book plus 13p per copy for the next 7 books, thereafter 7p per book.

OVERSEAS: Please allow 60p for the first book plus 18p per copy for each additional book.

Whilst every effort is made to keep prices low it is sometimes necessary to increase cover prices and also postage and packing rates at short notice. Hamlyn Paperbacks reserve the right to show new retail prices on covers which may differ from those previously advertised in the text or elsewhere.